Share the Joy of Good Home Cooking with *Taste of Home!*

Savor 500+ Delicious Recipes from Real Home Cooks.

Scrumptious dishes from real home cooks are what have made *Taste of Home* the No. 1 food and entertaining magazine in the world. In this brand-new collection, you'll discover a year's worth of wonderful recipes—dishes shared by family cooks from coast to coast. Now you can keep them all in one handy place: *Taste of Home Annual Recipes.*

This cookbook features the delicious dishes and heartwarming stories that make these recipes special to the cooks who share them. As you flip through the pages, you'll be inspired by ideas for entertaining, kitchen tips and the beautiful photographs and narratives that bring these recipes to life. Just consider these chapters:

- **Field Editor Favorites**
  Peek inside the recipe boxes of some of the magazine's top home cooks...and discover their favorite dishes!

- **Holiday & Seasonal Celebrations**
  Turn here for spring brunch favorites, frosty summertime treats, and the best Christmas cookies.

- **Main Dishes**
  Choose from more than 40 satisfying entrees, perfect for weeknights, family gatherings and even special occasions.

Five icons help you easily locate these dishes:

FAST FIX = Finished in 30 minutes or less

EAT SMART = Lower in calories, fat and sodium

SLOW COOKER = Made in a slow cooker

(5) INGREDIENTS = Made with 5 or fewer ingredients (excluding water, salt, pepper and canola/olive oil)

FREEZE IT = Freezing and reheating instructions are included

With *Taste of Home Annual Recipes,* it's simple to find the perfect dish for any occasion. Happy cooking!

BEST-LOVED RECIPES

Hearty breakfasts, crave-worthy snacks, tempting sweets...they're all here in *Taste of Home Annual Recipes.* Looking to expand your grill skills? Give Marinated Pork Chops (top) a try. To really wow your family at breakfast time, don't miss Apple-Cheddar Pancakes with Bacon (center). And for a heartwarming holiday open house, you won't want to miss Slow Cooker Christmas Punch (bottom).

Taste of Home
Annual Recipes 2017

48

130

90

245

EDITORIAL

Editor-in-Chief **Catherine Cassidy**
Vice President, Content Operations **Kerri Balliet**
Creative Director **Howard Greenberg**

Managing Editor/Print & Digital Books **Mark Hagen**
Associate Creative Director **Edwin Robles Jr.**

Editors **Christine Rukavena, Amy Glander, Hazel Wheaton**
Associate Editors **Molly Jasinski, Julie Kuczynski**
Art Director **Maggie Conners**
Layout Designers **Nancy Novak, Catherine Fletcher**
Editorial Production Manager **Dena Ahlers**
Editorial Production Coordinator **Jill Banks**
Copy Chief **Deb Warlaumont Mulvey**
Copy Editors **Dulcie Shoener, Ellie Piper, Chris McLaughlin**
Contributing Copy Editors **Kristin Sutter, Michael Juley**
Field Editor & Community Moderator **Susan Stetzel**
Editorial Intern **Maddie Rashid**

Content Director **Julie Blume Benedict**
Food Editors **Gina Nistico; James Schend; Peggy Woodward, RDN**
Recipe Editors **Sue Ryon (lead); Irene Yeh**
Editorial Services Administrator **Marie Brannon**

Test Kitchen & Food Styling Manager **Sarah Thompson**
Test Cooks **Nicholas Iverson (lead), Matthew Hass**
Food Stylists **Kathryn Conrad (lead), Lauren Knoelke, Shannon Roum**
Prep Cooks **Bethany Van Jacobson (lead), Melissa Hansen, Aria C. Thornton**
Culinary Team Assistant **Maria Petrella**

Photography Director **Stephanie Marchese**
Photographers **Dan Roberts, Jim Wieland**
Photographer/Set Stylist **Grace Natoli Sheldon**
Set Stylists **Melissa Franco (lead), Stacey Genaw, Dee Dee Jacq**
Set Stylist Assistant **Stephanie Chojnacki**

Business Architect, Publishing Technologies **Amanda Harmatys**
Solutions Architect, Publishing Technologies **John Mosey**
Business Analyst, Publishing Technologies **Kate Unger**
Junior Business Analyst, Publishing Technologies **Shannon Stroud**

Editorial Business Manager **Kristy Martin**
Rights & Permissions Associate **Samantha Lea Stoeger**
Editorial Business Associate **Andrea Heeg Polzin**

Editor, *Taste of Home* **Emily Betz Tyra**
Art Director, *Taste of Home* **Kristin Bowker**

BUSINESS

Vice President, Group Publisher **Kirsten Marchioli**
Publisher, *Taste of Home* **Donna Lindskog**
Business Development Director, Taste of Home Live **Laurel Osman**
Promotional Partnerships Manager, Taste of Home Live **Jamie Piette Andrzejewski**

TRUSTED MEDIA BRANDS, INC.

President & Chief Executive Officer **Bonnie Kintzer**
Chief Financial Officer **Dean Durbin**
Chief Marketing Officer **C. Alec Casey**
Chief Revenue Officer **Richard Sutton**
Chief Digital Officer **Vince Errico**
Senior Vice President, Global HR & Communications **Phyllis E. Gebhardt, SPHR; SHRM-SCP**
General Counsel **Mark Sirota**
Vice President, Magazine Marketing **Christopher Gaydos**
Vice President, Operations **Michael Garzone**
Vice President, Consumer Marketing Planning **Jim Woods**
Vice President, Digital Product & Technology **Nick Contardo**
Vice President, Digital Content & Audience Development **Diane Dragan**
Vice President, Financial Planning & Analysis **William Houston**
Publishing Director, Books **Debra Polansky**

COVER PHOTOGRAPHY

Photographer **Grace Natoli Sheldon**
Food Stylist **Kathryn Conrad**
Set Stylist **Stephanie Marchese**

Contents

PICTURED ON THE COVER
Cranberry Cheese Crumb Pie (p. 125),
Rich & Creamy Parmesan Mashed Potatoes (p. 60),
Roasted Sage Turkey with Vegetable Gravy (p. 296),
Roasted Acorn Squash & Brussels Sprouts (p. 55).

FOR OTHER INCREDIBLE TASTE OF HOME BOOKS AND PRODUCTS, VISIT
ShopTasteofHome.com

**CATHERINE CASSIDY'S
GUACAMOLE**
PAGE 13

Appetizers & Beverages

Whether you're looking for a yummy **after-school snack** for the kids or a **special beverage** to serve guests at a dinner party, this chapter has you covered. It's packed full of **delicious** options to help you dish out the **perfect refreshments.**

TAMARA BEARDSLEY CHOAT'S TACO MEATBALLS WITH DIPPING SAUCE *PAGE 9*

DANA HINCK'S PEACH-BASIL LEMONADE SLUSH *PAGE 7*

KRISTEN HEIGL'S TOMATO AND CORN CHEESY PASTRY BITES *PAGE 15*

Antipasto Bake

Stuffed with savory meats and cheeses, this hearty bake would satisfy an entire offensive line! It comes together quickly and bakes in under an hour, making it the perfect potluck bring-along. Introducing the all-stars in this ooey-gooey appetizer: salami, Swiss, pepperoni, Colby-Monterey Jack, prosciutto and provolone. A crisp topping finishes it off.

—**BREA BARCLAY** GREEN BAY, WI

PREP: 20 MIN. • **BAKE:** 45 MIN. + STANDING
MAKES: 20 SERVINGS

- 2 **tubes (8 ounces each) refrigerated crescent rolls**
- ¼ **pound thinly sliced hard salami**
- ¼ **pound thinly sliced Swiss cheese**
- ¼ **pound thinly sliced pepperoni**
- ¼ **pound thinly sliced Colby-Monterey Jack cheese**
- ¼ **pound thinly sliced prosciutto**
- ¼ **pound thinly sliced provolone cheese**
- 2 **large eggs**
- ½ **teaspoon garlic powder**
- ½ **teaspoon pepper**
- 1 **jar (12 ounces) roasted sweet red peppers, drained**
- 1 **large egg yolk, beaten**

1. Preheat oven to 350°. Unroll one tube of crescent dough into one long rectangle; press perforations to seal. Press onto bottom and up sides of an ungreased 11x7-in. baking dish.
2. Layer meats and cheeses on dough in the order listed. Whisk eggs and seasonings until well blended; pour into dish. Top with roasted pepper.
3. Unroll the remaining tube of dough into a long rectangle; press perforations to seal. Place over filling; pinch seams tight. Brush with the beaten egg yolk; cover with foil. Bake 30 minutes; remove foil. Bake until golden brown, about 15-20 minutes. Let stand 20 minutes.

PER SERVING *1 piece equals 229 cal., 15 g fat (7 g sat. fat), 58 mg chol., 662 mg sodium, 10 g carb. (2 g sugars, 0 fiber), 11 g pro.*

QUENTIN'S PEACH-BOURBON WINGS

Quentin's Peach-Bourbon Wings

My father and husband love bourbon flavor, so I add it to tangy wings baked in peach preserves. Stand back and watch these wings fly.

—**CHRISTINE WINSTON** RICHMOND, VA

PREP: 35 MIN. • **BAKE:** 35 MIN.
MAKES: 1½ DOZEN

- 1 **cup peach preserves**
- 2 **tablespoons brown sugar**
- 2 **garlic cloves, minced**
- ½ **teaspoon salt**
- ¼ **cup white vinegar**
- ¼ **cup bourbon**
- 2 **teaspoons cornstarch**
- 1 **tablespoon water**
- 4 **pounds chicken wings**

1. Preheat oven to 450°. Place peach preserves, brown sugar, garlic cloves and salt in a food processor; process until blended. Transfer to a small saucepan. Add vinegar and bourbon; bring to a boil. Reduce heat; simmer, uncovered, for 4-6 minutes or until slightly thickened.
2. In a small bowl, mix cornstarch and water until smooth; stir into preserve mixture. Return to a boil, stirring constantly; cook and stir 1-2 minutes or until thickened. Reserve ½ cup sauce for serving.
3. Using a sharp knife, cut through the two wing joints; discard the wing tips. Place the remaining wing pieces in a foil-lined 15x10x1-in. baking pan. Bake 30-35 minutes or until juices run clear, turning every 10 minutes and brushing with remaining sauce. Increase oven setting to broil.
4. Broil 4-6 in. from heat 2-3 minutes on each side or until golden brown. Serve with reserved sauce.

NOTE *Uncooked chicken wing sections (wingettes) may be substituted for whole chicken wings.*

PER SERVING *1 chicken wing with about 1 teaspoon sauce equals 165 cal., 7 g fat (2 g sat. fat), 32 mg chol., 97 mg sodium, 13 g carb., trace fiber, 10 g pro.*

> This chilly slush with peaches, lemon juice and garden-fresh basil is hands down the best lemonade ever. It tastes just like summer.
> —DANA HINCK PENSACOLA, FL

(5) INGREDIENTS
Peach-Basil Lemonade Slush

PREP: 15 MIN. • **COOK:** 10 MIN. + CHILLING
MAKES: 12 SERVINGS

- 2 cups sugar
- 3 cups chopped peeled fresh peaches (about 3 medium) or 1 pound frozen unsweetened sliced peaches
- 1 package (¾ ounce) fresh basil leaves or 20 large leaves
- 4 cups water
- 1½ cups fresh lemon juice
- 5 to 8 cups ice cubes
  Peach slices and fresh basil leaves

1. In a large saucepan, combine the sugar, peaches, basil and water; bring to a boil. Reduce heat; simmer 5 minutes. Remove from the heat; let stand for 30 minutes. Discard basil; stir in lemon juice. Refrigerate until cooled completely.
2. Process half of peach mixture and 2½ cups ice in a blender until blended, adding more ice if desired. Repeat with remaining peach mixture and ice. Pour into chilled glasses; serve with peach slices and basil.
PER SERVING *1 cup equals 152 cal., 0 fat (0 sat. fat), 0 chol., 1 mg sodium, 39 g carb., 1 g fiber, 1 g pro.*

EAT SMART
Fresh from the Garden Wraps

We moved into a house with a garden that needed tending. Using the herbs we found, we made these freshtastic wraps for our first dinner there.
—**CHRIS BUGHER** ASHEVILLE, NC

PREP: 20 MIN. + STANDING
MAKES: 8 SERVINGS

- 1 medium ear sweet corn
- 1 medium cucumber, chopped
- 1 cup shredded cabbage
- 1 medium tomato, chopped
- 1 small red onion, chopped
- 1 jalapeno pepper, seeded and minced
- 1 tablespoon minced fresh basil
- 1 tablespoon minced fresh cilantro
- 1 tablespoon minced fresh mint
- ⅓ cup Thai chili sauce
- 3 tablespoons rice vinegar
- 2 teaspoons reduced-sodium soy sauce
- 2 teaspoons creamy peanut butter
- 8 Bibb or Boston lettuce leaves

1. Cut corn from cob and place in a large bowl. Add cucumber, cabbage, tomato, onion, jalapeno and herbs.
2. Whisk together chili sauce, vinegar, soy sauce and peanut butter. Pour over vegetable mixture; toss to coat. Let stand 20 minutes.
3. Using a slotted spoon, place ½ cup salad in each lettuce leaf. Fold lettuce over filling.
NOTE *Wear disposable gloves when cutting hot peppers; the oils can burn skin. Avoid touching your face.*
PER SERVING *1 filled lettuce wrap equals 64 cal., 1 g fat (trace sat. fat), 0 chol., 319 mg sodium, 13 g carb., 2 g fiber, 2 g pro.* **Diabetic Exchanges:** *1 vegetable, ½ starch.*

FRESH FROM THE GARDEN WRAPS

Heirloom Tomato Galette with Pecorino

PREP: 10 MIN. + CHILLING
BAKE: 25 MIN. + COOLING
MAKES: 6 SERVINGS

- 1 **cup all-purpose flour**
- 1 **teaspoon baking powder**
- ¾ **teaspoon kosher salt, divided**
- ½ **cup cold unsalted butter, cubed**
- ½ **cup sour cream**
- 2 **cups cherry tomatoes, halved**
- 3 **ounces Pecorino Romano cheese, thinly sliced**

1. Whisk flour, baking powder and ½ teaspoon salt; cut in butter until mixture resembles coarse crumbs. Stir in sour cream until dough forms a ball. Shape into a disk; wrap in plastic wrap. Refrigerate until firm enough to roll, about 2 hours.

2. Meanwhile, place tomatoes in a colander; toss with remaining salt. Let stand 15 minutes.

3. Preheat oven to 425°. On a floured sheet of parchment paper, roll the dough into a 12-in. circle. Transfer to a baking sheet.

4. Place cheese slices over pastry to within 2 in. of edge; arrange tomatoes over cheese. Fold pastry edges over filling, pleating as you go and leaving center uncovered. Bake until crust is golden brown and cheese is bubbly, about 25 minutes. Cool 10 minutes before slicing.

PER SERVING *1 piece equals 317 cal., 23 g fat (15 g sat. fat), 68 mg chol., 559 mg sodium, 19 g carb., 1 g fiber, 9 g pro.*

I found beautiful heirloom tomatoes and had to show them off. In this easy galette, the tomatoes are tangy and the crust is beyond buttery.
—**JESSICA CHANG** PLAYA VISTA, CA

HEIRLOOM TOMATO GALETTE WITH PECORINO

Dilled Mushroom Turnovers

My bite-size mushroom pastries are hard to resist. For parties, I prep and freeze them before, then pop them in the oven.
—**ISABELLA MICHEL-CLARK** SPARKS, NV

PREP: 1 HOUR + CHILLING
BAKE: 15 MIN./BATCH
MAKES: ABOUT 5 DOZEN

- 1 **cup butter, softened**
- 2 **packages (8 ounces each) cream cheese, softened**
- 3 **cups all-purpose flour**

FILLING

- 3 **tablespoons butter**
- ½ **pound fresh mushrooms, finely chopped**
- 1 **large onion, finely chopped**
- ¼ **cup sour cream**
- 2 **tablespoons all-purpose flour**
- 1 **teaspoon salt**
- 1 **teaspoon snipped fresh dill**
- 1 **large egg, beaten**

1. In a large bowl, cream butter and cream cheese until smooth. Gradually beat the flour into creamed mixture. Divide dough in half. Shape each half into a disk; wrap in plastic wrap. Chill 1 hour or until firm enough to handle.

2. In a large skillet, heat butter over medium heat. Add mushrooms and onion; cook and stir 6-8 minutes or until tender. Remove from heat; stir in sour cream, flour, salt and dill. Cool.

3. Preheat the oven to 400°. On a floured surface, roll dough to ⅛-in. thickness. Cut circles with a floured 2½-in. round cookie cutter. Place about 1 teaspoon filling on one side of each. Brush edges with egg; fold dough over filling. Press edges with a fork to seal. Place on ungreased baking sheets; brush egg over tops. Bake until edges are golden brown, 12-14 minutes.

FREEZE OPTION *Cover and freeze unbaked turnovers on waxed paper-lined baking sheets until firm. Transfer to resealable plastic freezer bags. Bake frozen turnovers as directed, increasing time by 2-3 minutes.*

PER SERVING *1 turnover equals 87 cal., 7 g fat (4 g sat. fat), 22 mg chol., 98 mg sodium, 6 g carb., trace fiber, 1 g pro.*

TACO MEATBALLS WITH DIPPING SAUCE

Tasty Tomato Pizza

I'm known for bringing this party-style pizza everywhere I go. It's an easy bite when you use refrigerated dough and a big baking pan.

—**KIM EVARTS** BROCKPORT, NY

PREP: 20 MIN. • **BAKE:** 20 MIN.
MAKES: 24 PIECES

- 1 tube (13.8 ounces) refrigerated pizza crust
- ⅔ cup mayonnaise
- ⅓ cup grated Parmesan cheese
- 1 tablespoon minced fresh basil or 1 teaspoon dried basil
- ½ teaspoon garlic powder
- ½ teaspoon garlic salt
- 2 cups (8 ounces) shredded part-skim mozzarella cheese, divided
- 5 plum tomatoes (about 1½ pounds), cut into ¼-inch slices
- 1 can (2¼ ounces) sliced ripe olives, drained
- ¼ cup chopped green pepper, optional

1. Preheat oven to 375°. Unroll and press the dough onto bottom and ½ in. up sides of a greased 15x10x1-in. baking pan.
2. In a small bowl, combine the mayonnaise, Parmesan cheese, basil, garlic powder and garlic salt. Stir in 1½ cups mozzarella cheese. Spread over crust. Top with tomato slices, olives and, if desired, green pepper. Sprinkle with remaining cheese.
3. Bake 20-25 minutes or until crust is golden brown and cheese is melted.
PER SERVING *1 piece equals 123 cal., 8 g fat (2 g sat. fat), 9 mg chol., 276 mg sodium, 9 g carb., 1 g fiber, 4 g pro.*

TOP TIP

For meatballs to cook evenly, it's important for them to be the same size. The easiest way to do this is by using a 1- or 1½-inch cookie scoop. Scoop the meat mixture and level off the top. Gently roll into a ball or shape as the recipe directs.

Taco Meatballs with Dipping Sauce

My family likes food with a sense of fun. Here I combined Mexican and Italian cooking in these meatballs made with nacho-flavored tortilla chips.

—**TAMARA BEARDSLEY CHOAT** SHERIDAN, IN

PREP: 25 MIN. • **BAKE:** 15 MIN.
MAKES: 16 APPETIZERS

- 1 can (4 ounces) chopped green chilies
- 2 tablespoons taco seasoning
- 1 pound lean ground beef (90% lean)
- 3 ounces Colby-Monterey Jack cheese, cut into 16 cubes
- 1 large egg white
- 1 tablespoon water
- 1⅔ cups crushed nacho-flavored tortilla chips

SAUCE
- ⅓ cup taco sauce
- 3 tablespoons honey

1. Preheat oven to 400°. In a large bowl, combine the chilies and taco seasoning. Add beef; mix lightly but thoroughly. Divide into 16 portions. Shape each portion around a cheese cube to cover completely.
2. In a shallow bowl, whisk egg white and water. Place crushed chips in a separate bowl. Dip meatballs in the egg mixture, then in crushed chips, patting to help coating adhere. Place on a greased rack in a 15x10x1-in. baking pan. Bake 15-20 minutes or until cooked through.
3. Meanwhile, in a small microwave-safe bowl, mix the taco sauce and honey. Microwave, covered, on high for 30-45 seconds or until heated through. Serve with meatballs.
PER SERVING *1 meatball with 1½ teaspoons sauce equals 112 cal., 5 g fat (2 g sat. fat), 23 mg chol., 248 mg sodium, 8 g carb., trace fiber, 7 g pro.*

BAKED POT STICKERS WITH DIPPING SAUCE

Garden Fresh Seafood Cocktail

For something cool on a hot day, we mix shrimp and crabmeat with crunchy veggies straight from the garden. Look for adobo seasoning in your grocery's international section.

—**TERI RASEY** CADILLAC, MI

PREP: 15 MIN. + CHILLING
MAKES: 6 CUPS

- ¾ **pound peeled and deveined cooked shrimp (31-40 per pound), thawed**
- 1 **container (8 ounces) refrigerated jumbo lump crabmeat, drained**
- 3 **celery ribs, chopped**
- 1 **medium cucumber, peeled, seeded and chopped**
- 1 **medium sweet orange pepper, chopped**
- 2 **plum tomatoes, seeded and chopped**
- ½ **cup red onion, finely chopped**
- 1 **to 2 jalapeno peppers, seeded and finely chopped**
- ¼ **cup minced fresh cilantro**
- 3 **tablespoons lime juice**
- 1 **tablespoon olive oil**
- 2¼ **teaspoons adobo seasoning**

Combine first nine ingredients. Whisk together the lime juice, oil and adobo seasoning; drizzle over the shrimp mixture and toss gently to coat. Refrigerate at least 1 hour, tossing gently every 20 minutes. Place shrimp mixture in cocktail glasses.

PER SERVING *¾ cup equals 103 cal., 3 g fat (0 sat. fat), 92 mg chol., 619 mg sodium, 5 g carb., 1 g fiber, 15 g pro.*

Baked Pot Stickers with Dipping Sauce

Twisting these wonton wrappers like little candies makes them fuss-free, and the dipping sauce is packed with sweet heat.

—**TAYLOR MARSH** ALGONA, IA

PREP: 30 MIN. • **BAKE:** 15 MIN./BATCH
MAKES: 4 DOZEN (¾ CUP SAUCE)

- 2 **cups finely chopped cooked chicken breast**
- 1 **can (8 ounces) water chestnuts, drained and chopped**
- 4 **green onions, thinly sliced**
- ¼ **cup shredded carrots**
- ¼ **cup reduced-fat mayonnaise**
- 1 **large egg white**
- 1 **tablespoon reduced-sodium soy sauce**
- 1 **garlic clove, minced**
- 1 **teaspoon grated fresh gingerroot**
- 48 **wonton wrappers**
  Cooking spray

SAUCE
- ½ **cup jalapeno pepper jelly**
- ¼ **cup rice vinegar**
- 2 **tablespoons reduced-sodium soy sauce**

1. Preheat oven to 425°. In a large bowl, combine first nine ingredients. Place 2 teaspoons of filling in center of each wonton wrapper. (Cover the wrappers with a damp paper towel until ready to use.)
2. Moisten wrapper edges with water. Fold edge over filling and roll to form a log; twist ends to seal. Repeat with remaining wrappers and filling.
3. Place the pot stickers on a baking sheet coated with cooking spray; spritz each one with cooking spray. Bake for 12-15 minutes or until edges are golden brown.
4. Meanwhile, place jelly in a small microwave-safe bowl; microwave, covered, on high until melted. Stir in vinegar and soy sauce. Serve sauce with pot stickers.

PER SERVING *1 pot sticker with ¾ teaspoon sauce equals 52 cal., 1 g fat (trace sat. fat), 6 mg chol., 101 mg sodium, 8 g carb., trace fiber, 3 g pro.* **Diabetic Exchange:** *½ starch.*

GARDEN FRESH SEAFOOD COCKTAIL

Rainbow Spritzer

This drink gets its bubbly goodness from ginger ale and puckery lemonade.

—OLIVIA THOMPSON MILWAUKEE, WI

START TO FINISH: 20 MIN.
MAKES: 4 SERVINGS

- ½ **cup fresh blueberries**
- ½ **cup chopped peeled kiwifruit**
- ½ **cup chopped fresh pineapple**
- ½ **cup sliced fresh strawberries or fresh raspberries**
- 1 **cup chilled ginger ale**
- ½ **cup chilled unsweetened pineapple juice**
- ½ **cup chilled lemonade**

In four tall glasses, layer blueberries, kiwi, pineapple and strawberries. In a 2-cup glass measure or small pitcher, mix remaining ingredients; pour over fruit. Serve immediately.
PER SERVING *91 cal., trace fat (trace sat. fat), 0 chol., 8 mg sodium, 23 g carb., 2 g fiber, 1 g pro.*

Slow Cooker Crab & Green Onion Dip

This creamy dip reminds me of my dad, who took us crabbing as kids. Our fingers were tired after those excursions, but eating the fresh crab was worth it.

—NANCY ZIMMERMAN

CAPE MAY COURT HOUSE, NJ

PREP: 10 MIN. • **COOK:** 3 HOURS
MAKES: 16 SERVINGS (¼ CUP EACH)

- 3 **packages (8 ounces each) cream cheese, cubed**
- 2 **cans (6 ounces each) lump crabmeat, drained**
- 4 **green onions, chopped**
- ¼ **cup 2% milk**
- 2 **teaspoons prepared horseradish**
- 2 **teaspoons Worcestershire sauce**
- ¼ **teaspoon salt**
  Assorted fresh vegetables

In a greased 3-qt. slow cooker, combine the first seven ingredients. Cook, covered, on low for 3-4 hours or until heated through, stirring occasionally. Serve with vegetables.
PER SERVING *¼ cup (calculated without chips) equals 167 cal., 15 g fat (8 g sat. fat), 68 mg chol., 324 mg sodium, 2 g carb., trace fiber, 7 g pro.*

Lime Avocado Hummus

My mash-up of guacamole and hummus is light and bright, but also rich and satisfying. Serve with chips and veggies or as a cool sandwich spread.

—ANDREANN GEISE MYRTLE BEACH, SC

START TO FINISH: 15 MIN.
MAKES: 2½ CUPS

- 1 **teaspoon whole peppercorns**
- 1 **can (15 ounces) garbanzo beans or chickpeas, rinsed and drained**
- 1 **medium ripe avocado, peeled and pitted**
- ½ **cup fresh parsley sprigs**
- ½ **cup olive oil**
- ¼ **cup grated Romano cheese**
- ¼ **cup fresh cilantro leaves**
- ¼ **cup lime juice**
- 1 **garlic clove**
- ½ **teaspoon sugar**
- ¼ **teaspoon salt**
  Tortilla chips

Place the whole peppercorns in a food processor; process until ground. Add remaining ingredients except chips; process for 2-3 minutes longer or until smooth. Serve with chips.
PER SERVING *¼ cup (calculated without chips) equals 174 cal., 15 g fat (2 g sat. fat), 3 mg chol., 168 mg sodium, 9 g carb., 3 g fiber, 3 g pro.*

Our local deli makes terrific roast beef sandwiches. This pinwheel appetizer re-creates the taste. My family says the pinwheels have so many flavors for such a little treat.

—PAMELA SHANK
PARKERSBURG, WV

Smoked Gouda & Roast Beef Pinwheels

PREP: 20 MIN. • **BAKE:** 15 MIN./BATCH
MAKES: 4 DOZEN

- ¾ **pound sliced deli roast beef, finely chopped**
- 1 **package (10 ounces) frozen chopped spinach, thawed and squeezed dry**
- 1 **package (6½ ounces) garlic-herb spreadable cheese**
- 1 **cup (4 ounces) shredded smoked Gouda cheese**
- ¼ **cup finely chopped red onion**
- 2 **tubes (8 ounces each) refrigerated crescent rolls**

1. Preheat oven to 375°. In a small bowl, mix first five ingredients until blended. On a lightly floured surface, unroll one crescent tube into a long rectangle; press perforations to seal.
2. Spread half of roast beef mixture over dough. Roll up jelly-roll style, starting with a long side; pinch seam to seal. Using a serrated knife, cut roll crosswise into twenty-four ½-inch slices. Place on parchment paper-lined baking sheets, cut side down. Repeat with remaining crescent dough and roast beef mixture.
3. Bake 12-14 minutes or until golden brown. Refrigerate leftovers.
PER SERVING *1 appetizer equals 71 cal., 5 g fat (2 g sat. fat), 11 mg chol., 160 mg sodium, 4 g carb., trace fiber, 3 g pro.*

Bourbon Ham Balls

Grandma Nette created ham balls. I make them salty-sweet with a bourbon and vinegar kick. Serve them alone, in a sandwich or over pasta or rice.

—KIMLA CARSTEN GRAND JUNCTION, CO

PREP: 70 MIN. + FREEZING • **BAKE:** 15 MIN.
MAKES: ABOUT 3½ DOZEN

- 2 **pounds fully cooked boneless ham**
- 1 **thick boneless pork loin chop (8 ounces)**
- ½ **pound bacon strips**
- 1 **cup panko (Japanese) bread crumbs**
- 1 **cup 2% milk**
- 2 **large eggs, lightly beaten**
  Oil for frying

SAUCE
- 1½ **cups packed brown sugar**
- ½ **cup white vinegar**
- ½ **cup bourbon**
- 2 **teaspoons spicy brown mustard**

1. Cut ham, pork chop and bacon into 1-in. pieces; arrange in a single layer in a foil-lined 15x10x1-in. pan. Freeze 30 minutes or until partially frozen.
2. Preheat oven to 350°. Transfer meat to a food processor in batches; pulse until coarsely ground, about 20-24 pulses. In a large bowl, combine bread crumbs, milk and eggs. Add pork mixture; mix lightly but thoroughly. Shape into 1½-in. balls.
3. In a large skillet, heat ¼ in. of oil over medium heat. Add the ham balls in batches; cook for 3-4 minutes or until cooked through, turning occasionally. Remove from the pan; drain on paper towels.
4. In a large bowl, whisk sauce ingredients; reserve 1 cup for serving. Add ham balls to remaining sauce, a few at a time, allowing ham balls to soak 1-2 minutes. Transfer ham balls to a foil-lined 15x10x1-in. baking pan. Bake 15-20 minutes or until heated through, brushing occasionally with remaining sauce from soaking. Serve with reserved sauce.
PER SERVING *1 ham ball with 1 teaspoon sauce equals 138 cal., 8 g fat (2 g sat. fat), 27 mg chol., 276 mg sodium, 9 g carb., trace fiber, 6 g pro.*

BOURBON HAM BALLS

LEFTOVER
TURKEY TURNOVERS

Leftover Turkey Turnovers

I came up with this dish in 1993 while putting together a booklet called "Totally Turkey" for leftover turkey recipes. My children devour them in no time.
—**RENEE MURBY** JOHNSTON, RI

PREP: 40 MIN. + CHILLING
COOK: 5 MIN./BATCH
MAKES: 1 DOZEN

- 1¼ cups all-purpose flour
- ¼ teaspoon salt
- ½ cup shortening
- 1 large egg
- 2 tablespoons ice water, divided

FILLING

- 2 tablespoons canola oil
- ⅓ cup finely chopped onion
- ¼ teaspoon ground turmeric
- ¼ teaspoon ground cinnamon
- 1 garlic clove, minced
- 1 cup finely chopped cooked turkey
- ¼ cup raisins
- ¼ teaspoon salt
- ⅛ teaspoon pepper
  Oil for frying

1. In a large bowl, mix flour and salt; cut in the shortening until crumbly. Whisk egg and 1 tablespoon ice water; gradually add to flour with remaining water as needed, tossing with a fork until dough holds together when pressed. Turn onto a lightly floured surface; knead gently 6-8 times. Shape into a disk; wrap in plastic wrap. Refrigerate 1 hour or overnight.
2. In a large skillet, heat oil over medium-high heat. Add onion, turmeric and cinnamon; cook and stir 1-2 minutes or until tender. Add garlic; cook 30 seconds longer. Stir in turkey, raisins, salt and pepper.
3. On a lightly floured surface, roll dough to ⅛-in. thickness. Cut with a floured 4-in. round cookie cutter. Place a heaping tablespoon of filling in the center of each circle. Moisten edges with water; fold in half and press edges with a fork to seal. Repeat with remaining dough and filling.
4. In a deep skillet or electric skillet, heat ½ in. of oil to 375°. Fry turnovers, a few at a time, 2-3 minutes on each side or until golden brown. Drain on paper towels.
PER SERVING *1 turnover equals 212 cal., 15 g fat (3 g sat. fat), 27 mg chol., 117 mg sodium, 13 g carb., 1 g fiber, 5 g pro.*

EAT SMART

Catherine's Guacamole

Get the scoop on making a standout guacamole. A handful of chopped celery adds some fun crunch in this avocado dip—everyone's favorite fiesta starter.
—**CATHERINE CASSIDY** MILWAUKEE, WI

PREP: 15 MIN. + CHILLING
MAKES: 2½ CUPS

- 3 medium ripe avocados, peeled and pitted
- ⅓ cup chopped sweet onion
- 1 small tomato, seeded and chopped
- 1 celery rib, finely chopped
- 2 garlic cloves, minced
- 2 tablespoons lemon or lime juice
- 2 teaspoons Worcestershire sauce
- ½ teaspoon salt
- ¼ teaspoon pepper
- ¼ to ⅓ cup chopped fresh cilantro, optional
  Tortilla chips

In a small bowl, mash avocados. Stir in onion, tomato, celery, garlic, lemon juice, Worcestershire, salt, pepper and, if desired, cilantro. Chill 1 hour before serving. Serve with chips.
PER SERVING *¼ cup (calculated without chips) equals 75 cal., 6 g fat (1 g sat. fat), 0 chol., 136 mg sodium, 5 g carb., 3 g fiber, 1 g pro.* **Diabetic Exchange:** *1 fat.*

DID YOU KNOW?

Avocado is high in monounsaturated fat, a so-called "good fat" that can lower blood cholesterol along with the risk of stroke and heart disease.

Cheese Crispies

For years I've brought these crispy, crunchy snacks to work. They get high marks from everybody in the teachers lounge.
—**EILEEN BALL** CORNELIUS, NC

PREP: 15 MIN. + CHILLING
BAKE: 15 MIN./BATCH
MAKES: ABOUT 4½ DOZEN

- 1 **cup unsalted butter, softened**
- 2½ **cups (10 ounces) shredded extra-sharp cheddar cheese**
- 2 **cups all-purpose flour**
- ¾ **teaspoon salt**
- ½ **teaspoon cayenne pepper**
- 2½ **cups Rice Krispies**
  Pecan halves, optional

1. Beat the butter and cheese until blended. Whisk the flour, salt and cayenne; gradually beat into cheese mixture. Stir in the Rice Krispies. If necessary, turn onto a lightly floured surface and knead 4-6 times, forming a stiff dough.
2. Divide dough in half; shape each into a 7-in.-long roll. Wrap in plastic wrap; refrigerate 1 hour or overnight.
3. Preheat oven to 350°. Unwrap and cut dough crosswise into ¼-in. slices. Place 1 in. apart on parchment paper-lined baking sheets. If desired, top each slice with a pecan half. Bake 14-16 minutes or until edges are golden brown. Remove from pans to wire racks to cool.
FREEZE OPTION *Freeze wrapped logs in a resealable plastic freezer bag. To use, unwrap frozen logs and cut into slices. Bake as directed.*
PER SERVING *1 cracker (calculated without pecans) equals 73 cal., 5 g fat (3 g sat. fat), 15 mg chol., 73 mg sodium, 5 g carb., trace fiber, 2 g pro.*

TOP TIP

It's usually cheaper to buy cheese in blocks rather than already shredded. I purchase large quantities, then use my food processor to shred it myself. I store the shredded cheese in the freezer, so I have it when I need it.
—**EVELYN O.**, PARMA, OH

PICKLED SHRIMP WITH BASIL

Red wine vinegar plus the freshness of citrus and basil perk up marinated shrimp with hardly any prep. Serve over greens if you'd like a salad.
—**JAMES SCHEND** PLEASANT PRAIRIE, WI

Pickled Shrimp with Basil

PREP: 15 MIN. + MARINATING
MAKES: 20 SERVINGS (½ CUP EACH)

- ½ **cup red wine vinegar**
- ½ **cup olive oil**
- 2 **teaspoons seafood seasoning**
- 2 **teaspoons stone-ground mustard**
- 1 **garlic clove, minced**
- 2 **pounds peeled and deveined cooked shrimp (31-40 per pound)**
- 1 **medium lemon, thinly sliced**
- 1 **medium lime, thinly sliced**
- ½ **medium red onion, thinly sliced**
- ¼ **cup thinly sliced fresh basil**
- 2 **tablespoons capers, drained**
- ¼ **cup minced fresh basil**
- ½ **teaspoon kosher salt**
- ¼ **teaspoon coarsely ground pepper**

1. In a large bowl, whisk the first five ingredients. Add shrimp, lemon, lime, onion, sliced basil and capers; toss gently to coat. Refrigerate, covered, up to 8 hours, stirring occasionally.
2. Just before serving, stir minced basil, salt and pepper into shrimp mixture. Serve with a slotted spoon.
PER SERVING *½ cup equals 64 cal., 2 g fat (trace sat. fat), 69 mg chol., 111 mg sodium, 1 g carb., trace fiber, 9 g pro.* **Diabetic Exchanges:** *1 lean meat, ½ fat.*

Toasted Ravioli Puffs

I call toasted ravioli a fan favorite because it disappears faster than I can make it.
—**KATHY MORGAN** TEMECULA, CA

START TO FINISH: 30 MIN.
MAKES: 2 DOZEN

- 24 refrigerated cheese ravioli
- 1 tablespoon reduced-fat Italian salad dressing
- 1 tablespoon Italian-style panko (Japanese) bread crumbs
- 1 tablespoon grated Parmesan cheese
  Warm marinara sauce

1. Preheat oven to 400°. Cook ravioli according to package directions; drain. Transfer to greased baking sheet. Brush with salad dressing. In a small bowl, mix bread crumbs and cheese; sprinkle over ravioli.
2. Bake 12-15 minutes or until golden brown. Serve with marinara sauce.
PER SERVING *1 ravioli (calculated without marinara sauce) equals 21 cal., 1 g fat (trace sat. fat), 3 mg chol., 43 mg sodium, 3 g carb., trace fiber, 1 g pro.*

BBQ Chicken Bites

Chicken bites wrapped in bacon get a kick from Montreal seasoning and sweetness from barbecue sauce.
—**KATHRYN DAMPIER** QUAIL VALLEY, CA

START TO FINISH: 25 MIN.
MAKES: 1½ DOZEN

- 6 bacon strips
- ¾ pound boneless skinless chicken breasts, cut into 1-inch cubes (about 18)
- 3 teaspoons Montreal steak seasoning
- 1 teaspoon prepared horseradish, optional
- ½ cup barbecue sauce

1. Preheat oven to 400°. Cut bacon crosswise into thirds. Place bacon on a microwave-safe plate lined with paper towels. Cover with paper towels; microwave on high 3-4 minutes or until partially cooked but not crisp.
2. Place chicken in a small bowl; sprinkle with steak seasoning and toss

to coat. Wrap bacon piece around each chicken cube; secure with a toothpick. Place on a parchment paper-lined baking sheet.
3. Bake 10 minutes. If desired, add horseradish to the barbecue sauce; brush over the wrapped chicken. Bake for 5-10 minutes longer or until chicken is no longer pink and bacon is crisp.
PER SERVING *1 appetizer equals 47 cal., 2 g fat (trace sat. fat), 13 mg chol., 249 mg sodium, 3 g carb., trace fiber, 5 g pro.*

Tomato and Corn Cheesy Pastry Bites

Local veggies and herbs have a magical knack for inspiring me to cook. After my CSA box arrived, I used the fresh ingredients to create this adorable appetizer.
—**KRISTEN HEIGL** STATEN ISLAND, NY

PREP: 25 MIN. • **BAKE:** 20 MIN.
MAKES: 8 PASTRIES

- 1 tablespoon olive oil
- ½ cup finely chopped onion
- 1 cup fresh corn
- 1 teaspoon garlic powder
- ½ teaspoon minced fresh parsley
- ¼ teaspoon salt
- ⅛ teaspoon pepper
- 1 package (17.3 ounces) frozen puff pastry, thawed
- 1 large egg
- 1 tablespoon water
- ¾ cup quartered cherry tomatoes
- ½ cup crumbled goat cheese
- ½ cup shredded provolone cheese
- 2 tablespoons minced fresh basil

1. Preheat oven to 375°. In a large skillet, heat oil over medium heat. Add onion; cook and stir until tender, about 5 minutes. Stir in corn, garlic powder, parsley, salt and pepper; cook until corn is tender, about 2 minutes. Remove from heat.
2. Unfold puff pastry sheets. Using a floured 4-in. round cookie cutter, cut four circles in each sheet; place on parchment paper-lined baking sheets. Whisk together egg and water; brush over pastries. Spoon 2 tablespoons corn mixture onto each circle. Top with tomatoes and cheeses.

3. Bake until golden brown and cheese is melted, about 20 minutes. Sprinkle with basil.
PER SERVING *1 pastry equals 236 cal., 14 g fat (5 g sat. fat), 37 mg chol., 279 mg sodium, 22 g carb., 3 g fiber, 7 g pro.*

Slow Cooker Christmas Punch

Wind down with a warm pineapple punch made in the slow cooker. We like to use cinnamon and Red Hots to give it that cozy spiced flavor and welcome-home aroma.
—**ANGIE GOINS** TAZEWELL, TN

PREP: 5 MIN. • **COOK:** 3 HOURS
MAKES: 10 SERVINGS (¾ CUP EACH)

- 4 cups unsweetened pineapple juice
- 4 cups cranberry juice
- ⅓ cup Red Hots
- 2 cinnamon sticks (3 inches)
  Fresh cranberries and additional cinnamon sticks

In a 3- or 4-qt. slow cooker, combine all ingredients. Cook, covered, on low 3-4 hours or until heated through. Garnish with fresh cranberries and additional cinnamon sticks.
PER SERVING *¾ cup equals 129 cal., trace fat (trace sat. fat), 0 chol., 4 mg sodium, 33 g carb., trace fiber, 1 g pro.*

SLOW COOKER CHRISTMAS PUNCH

Broccoli-Cheddar Tassies

My family adores broccoli casserole. I wanted to try it as an appetizer, so I used a pecan tassie recipe for the crust. The result? We're talking scrumptious.

—GAIL GAISER EWING, NJ

PREP: 45 MIN. + CHILLING
BAKE: 20 MIN./BATCH
MAKES: ABOUT 4 DOZEN

- 1 **cup butter, softened**
- 6 **ounces cream cheese, softened**
- 2 **cups all-purpose flour**

FILLING

- 1 **package (16 ounces) frozen chopped broccoli**
- 1 **large egg, lightly beaten**
- 1 **can (10¾ ounces) condensed cream of celery soup, undiluted**
- ¼ **cup 2% milk**
- ¼ **cup mayonnaise**
- ½ **cup shredded sharp cheddar cheese**

TOPPING

- ¼ **cup dry bread crumbs**
- 1 **tablespoon butter, melted**

1. In a small bowl, cream butter and cream cheese until smooth. Gradually beat the flour into creamed mixture. Divide dough in half. Shape each into a disk; wrap in plastic wrap. Refrigerate 1 hour or until firm enough to handle.

2. Preheat oven to 350°. Shape the dough into 1-in. balls; place balls in greased mini-muffin cups. Using floured fingers, press evenly onto bottoms and up sides of cups.

3. Cook broccoli according to package directions; drain. In a large bowl, combine the egg, condensed soup, milk and mayonnaise; stir in the cheese and cooked broccoli. Spoon about 1 tablespoon filling into each cup. For topping, mix the dry bread crumbs and melted butter; sprinkle over filling.

4. Bake 18-22 minutes or until edges are golden brown. Cool in pans for 2 minutes before removing to wire racks. Serve warm.

FREEZE OPTION *Freeze the cooled pastries on waxed paper-lined baking sheets until firm. Transfer pastries to resealable plastic freezer bags. To use, reheat on ungreased baking sheets in a preheated 350° oven for 14-16 minutes or until lightly browned and heated through.*

PER SERVING *1 tassie equals 92 cal., 7 g fat (4 g sat. fat), 21 mg chol., 101 mg sodium, 6 g carb., 1 g fiber, 2 g pro.*

EAT SMART **5 INGREDIENTS** FAST FIX

Crabbie Phyllo Cups

I always like a little extra chili sauce on top of these easy snacks. If you're out of crab, try them with water-packed tuna.

—JOHNNA JOHNSON SCOTTSDALE, AZ

START TO FINISH: 20 MIN.
MAKES: 2½ DOZEN

- ½ **cup reduced-fat spreadable garden vegetable cream cheese**
- ½ **teaspoon seafood seasoning**
- ¾ **cup lump crabmeat, drained**
- 2 **packages (1.9 ounces each) frozen miniature phyllo tart shells**
- 5 **tablespoons chili sauce**

In a small bowl, mix cream cheese and seafood seasoning; gently stir in crab. Spoon 2 teaspoons crab mixture into each tart shell; top with chili sauce.

PER SERVING *1 filled phyllo cup equals 34 cal., 2 g fat (trace sat. fat), 5 mg chol., 103 mg sodium, 3 g carb., 0 fiber, 1 g pro.*

BROCCOLI-CHEDDAR TASSIES

Green & Gold Salsa

Edamame and corn give this unique salsa its unmistakable Green Bay Packers colors. A healthy alternative to creamy dips, it's good for the extra point. You can add a little salt if you like, too.

—**MAGGIE LOVAT** GREEN BAY, WI

PREP: 10 MIN. • **MAKES:** 3 CUPS

- 1 **cup frozen shelled edamame, thawed**
- 1 **cup (about 5 ounces) frozen corn, thawed**
- 1 **cup cubed avocado**
- 1 **cup pico de gallo**
  Sliced cucumber and tortilla chips

Combine edamame, corn, avocado and pico de gallo until well blended. Serve with cucumber slices and tortilla chips for scooping.

PER SERVING *1/4 cup 48 cal., 3 g fat (0 sat. fat), 0 chol., 4 mg sodium, 5 g carb. (1 g sugars, 2 g fiber), 2 g pro.*

⑤ INGREDIENTS

Cranberry Limeade

When cranberry and lime juice get together, the result is thirst-quenching. Add ice, and you've got a party in a glass.

—**MICHAEL PASSOW** POUGHKEEPSIE, NY

PREP: 15 MIN. + CHILLING
MAKES: 7 SERVINGS

- 2½ **to 3½ cups water, divided**
- 1¼ **cups sugar**
- 2 **to 3 cups cranberry juice**
- 1½ **cups lime juice (10 to 12 medium limes)**
- 1 **tablespoon grated lime peel (2 medium limes)**
  Ice cubes
  Lime slices, optional

Bring 1½ cups water and sugar to a boil. Remove from heat; stir in juices, lime peel and remaining water. Cover; refrigerate at least 1 hour. Serve over ice and, if desired, with lime slices.

PER SERVING *1 cup equals 186 cal., 0 fat (0 sat. fat), 0 chol., 3 mg sodium, 49 g carb. (46 g sugars, 0 fiber), 1 g pro.*

SLOW COOKER
SPINACH &
ARTICHOKE DIP

With this creamy dip, I can get my daughters to eat spinach and artichokes. We serve it with chips, toasted pita bread or fresh veggies.

—**JENNIFER STOWELL** SMITHVILLE, MO

SLOW COOKER 🍲
Slow Cooker Spinach & Artichoke Dip

PREP: 10 MIN. • **COOK:** 2 HOURS
MAKES: 8 CUPS (¼ CUP EACH)

- 2 **cans (14 ounces each) water-packed artichoke hearts, drained and chopped**
- 2 **packages (10 ounces each) frozen chopped spinach, thawed and squeezed dry**
- 1 **jar (15 ounces) Alfredo sauce**
- 1 **package (8 ounces) cream cheese, cubed**
- 2 **cups (8 ounces) shredded Italian cheese blend**
- 1 **cup (4 ounces) shredded part-skim mozzarella cheese**
- 1 **cup shredded Parmesan cheese**
- 1 **cup 2% milk**
- 2 **garlic cloves, minced**
  Assorted crackers and/or cucumber slices

In a greased 4-qt. slow cooker, combine the first nine ingredients. Cook, covered, on low 2-3 hours or until heated through. Serve with crackers and/or cucumber slices.

PER SERVING *1/4 cup (calculated without chips) equals 105 cal., 7 g fat (4 g sat. fat), 21 mg chol., 276 mg sodium, 5 g carb., 1 g fiber, 6 g pro.*

**TIFFANY MARTINEZ'S
VEGGIE STEAK SALAD**
PAGE 27

Salads & Dressings

How refreshing—**salad bowls** brimming with garden **veggies, herbs, fruits** and more. Whether you're craving a crisp, cool side or a light main course, look here for the **freshest selections!**

NANCY FOUST'S CRANBERRY EGGNOG SALAD
PAGE 29

LINDSAY TANNER'S CHICKEN & BRUSSELS SPROUTS SALAD PAGE 31

KALISKA RUSSELL'S SUMMER BUZZ FRUIT SALAD
PAGE 25

Minty Watermelon-Cucumber Salad

Capturing the fantastic flavors of summer, this refreshing, beautiful watermelon-cucumber salad will be the talk of any picnic or potluck.

—ROBLYNN HUNNISETT GUELPH, ON

START TO FINISH: 20 MIN.
MAKES: 16 SERVINGS (¾ CUP EACH)

- 8 **cups cubed seedless watermelon**
- 2 **English cucumbers, halved lengthwise and sliced**
- 6 **green onions, chopped**
- ¼ **cup minced fresh mint**
- ¼ **cup balsamic vinegar**
- ¼ **cup olive oil**
- ½ **teaspoon salt**
- ½ **teaspoon pepper**

In a large bowl, combine watermelon, cucumbers, green onions and mint. In a small bowl, whisk remaining ingredients. Pour over salad and toss to coat. Serve immediately or refrigerate, covered, for up to 2 hours before serving.

PER SERVING *¾ cup equals 60 cal., 3 g fat (trace sat. fat), 0 chol., 78 mg sodium, 9 g carb., 1 g fiber, 1 g pro.* **Diabetic Exchanges:** *½ fruit, ½ fat.*

MINTY WATERMELON-CUCUMBER SALAD

GARDEN BOUNTY PANZANELLA SALAD

My sister gave me fresh tomatoes and basil, so I made a bread salad known as panzanella. The longer it sits, the more the bread soaks up the seasonings.
—JANNINE FISK MALDEN, MA

Garden Bounty Panzanella Salad

PREP: 15 MIN. • **COOK:** 20 MIN.
MAKES: 16 SERVINGS (1 CUP EACH)

- ¼ **cup olive oil**
- 12 **ounces French or ciabatta bread, cut into 1-inch cubes (about 12 cups)**
- 4 **large tomatoes, coarsely chopped**
- 1 **large English cucumber, coarsely chopped**
- 1 **medium green pepper, cut into 1-inch pieces**
- 1 **medium sweet yellow pepper, cut into 1-inch pieces**
- 1 **small red onion, halved and thinly sliced**
- ½ **cup coarsely chopped fresh basil**
- ¼ **cup grated Parmesan cheese**
- ¾ **teaspoon kosher salt**
- ¼ **teaspoon coarsely ground pepper**
- ½ **cup Italian salad dressing**

1. In a large skillet, heat 2 tablespoons oil over medium heat. Add half of the bread cubes; cook and stir until toasted, about 8 minutes. Remove from pan. Repeat with the remaining oil and bread cubes.

2. Combine bread cubes, tomatoes, cucumber, peppers, onion, basil, cheese, salt and pepper. Drizzle with salad dressing; toss.

PER SERVING *1 cup equals 131 cal., 6 g fat (1 g sat. fat), 1 mg chol., 310 mg sodium, 18 g carb., 2 g fiber, 3 g pro.* **Diabetic Exchanges:** *1 starch, 1 vegetable, 1 fat.*

Grilled Jerk Shrimp Orzo Salad

It doesn't matter what the temperature is outside—you'll feel as if you're in the Caribbean when you take your first bite of this salad!

—**EILEEN BUDNYK** PALM BEACH GARDENS, FL

PREP: 25 MIN. • **GRILL:** 25 MIN.
MAKES: 2 SERVINGS

- 1 **large ear sweet corn in husk**
- 1 **teaspoon olive oil**
- ⅓ **cup uncooked whole wheat orzo pasta**
- 6 **fresh asparagus spears, trimmed**
- ½ **pound uncooked medium shrimp, peeled and deveined**
- 1 **tablespoon Caribbean jerk seasoning**
- 1 **small sweet red pepper, chopped**

DRESSING

- 2 **tablespoons white vinegar**
- 1 **tablespoon water**
- 1 **tablespoon lime juice**
- 1 **tablespoon olive oil**
- ⅛ **teaspoon salt**
- ⅛ **teaspoon pepper**

1. Carefully peel back corn husk to within 1 in. of bottom; remove silk. Brush corn with oil. Rewrap corn in husk and secure with kitchen string. Grill corn, covered, over medium heat for 25-30 minutes or until tender, turning often.

2. Meanwhile, cook orzo according to package directions. Drain and rinse in cold water; set aside.

3. Thread asparagus spears onto two parallel metal or soaked wooden skewers. Rub shrimp with the jerk seasoning; thread onto two skewers. Grill asparagus and shrimp, covered, over medium heat for 5-8 minutes or until asparagus is crisp-tender and shrimp turn pink, turning once.

4. Cut corn from cob; place in a large bowl. Cut asparagus into 1-in. pieces; add to bowl. Add the shrimp, orzo and red pepper. In a small bowl, whisk the dressing ingredients. Pour over salad; toss to coat.

PER SERVING *2 cups equals 352 cal., 12 g fat (2 g sat. fat), 138 mg chol., 719 mg sodium, 38 g carb., 8 g fiber, 26 g pro.* **Diabetic Exchanges:** *3 lean meat, 2 starch, 1 vegetable, 1 fat.*

Caesar Salad with Grilled Steak and Potatoes

We get our grill on for this sizzling steak and potatoes dinner. It's a quick and easy dish ideal for cooking outdoors.

—**EDIE DESPAIN** LOGAN, UT

PREP: 20 MIN. • **GRILL:** 25 MIN.
MAKES: 8 SERVINGS

- 2 **packages (20 ounces each) refrigerated red potato wedges**
- ¾ **teaspoon salt, divided**
- 1 **beef top sirloin steak (1½ inches thick and 2 pounds)**
- 2 **tablespoons plus ⅔ cup creamy Caesar salad dressing, divided**
- ¼ **teaspoon pepper**
- ⅔ **cup shredded Parmesan cheese**
- 8 **cups torn romaine**
- 4 **green onions, chopped**

1. Sprinkle potatoes with ½ teaspoon salt; divide between two double thicknesses of heavy-duty foil (about 18 in. square). Fold foil around the potatoes; seal tightly. Grill, covered, over medium heat for 20-25 minutes or until tender, turning once.

2. Brush steak with 2 tablespoons dressing; sprinkle with pepper and remaining salt. Grill, covered, over medium heat for 22-26 minutes or until meat reaches desired doneness (for medium-rare, a thermometer should read 145°; medium, 160°; well-done, 170°), turning once.

3. Open foil carefully to allow steam to escape; transfer potatoes to a large bowl. Add cheese and the remaining dressing. Thinly slice steak. Toss the romaine, green onions and steak with the potato mixture.

PER SERVING *359 cal., 15 g fat (5 g sat. fat), 59 mg chol., 1,058 mg sodium, 21 g carb., 5 g fiber, 32 g pro.*

CAESAR SALAD WITH GRILLED STEAK AND POTATOES

CHICKEN & ONION CAESAR SALAD

Summer Chicken Macaroni Salad

For lazy summertime dinners, I make a loaded macaroni salad. The blend of fresh vegetables, juicy peaches and rich, crunchy pistachios is a surprisingly delicious combo.

—**NANCY HEISHMAN** LAS VEGAS, NV

PREP: 25 MIN. + CHILLING
MAKES: 16 SERVINGS

- 1½ cups uncooked elbow macaroni
- 1 rotisserie chicken, skin removed, shredded
- ¾ cup fresh or frozen peas
- 5 green onions, finely chopped
- 2 celery ribs, thinly sliced
- ⅓ cup loosely packed basil leaves, thinly sliced
- ¼ cup lemon juice, divided
- 1 teaspoon kosher salt
- ¾ teaspoon coarsely ground pepper
- ¾ cup (6 ounces) plain yogurt
- ¾ cup reduced-fat mayonnaise
- 3 medium peaches, peeled and sliced
- 1 cup (4 ounces) sharp cheddar cheese, shredded
- ½ cup crumbled Gorgonzola cheese
- ¾ cup pistachios

1. Cook macaroni according to package directions. Meanwhile, mix chicken, peas, onions, celery, basil, 2 tablespoons lemon juice, salt and pepper. Drain macaroni; rinse with cold water, then drain again. Add to chicken mixture.

2. Mix yogurt, mayonnaise and the remaining lemon juice. Add to salad and mix well. Add peaches and the cheeses; toss gently. Refrigerate at least 2 hours. Sprinkle with pistachios before serving.

PER SERVING *¾ cup equals 312 cal., 16 g fat (5 g sat. fat), 85 mg chol., 379 mg sodium, 13 g carb., 2 g fiber, 29 g pro.*

FAST FIX
Chicken & Onion Caesar Salad

My Caesar with grilled chicken is a healthier alternative to gravy-laden meat and potatoes dishes. After grilling kabobs, we toss them in with the greens.
—**MELISSA ADAMS** TOOELE, UT

START TO FINISH: 30 MIN.
MAKES: 2 SERVINGS

- ½ pound boneless skinless chicken breasts, cut into 1-inch pieces
- 1 large sweet onion, cut into 2-inch pieces
- 6 tablespoons creamy Caesar salad dressing, divided
- 4 small red potatoes, halved
- ½ teaspoon lemon juice
- ⅛ teaspoon coarsely ground pepper
- 1 small bunch romaine, torn
- 2 tablespoons shredded Parmesan cheese

1. In a large bowl, combine chicken, onion and 2 tablespoons dressing; toss to coat. In a small bowl, combine potatoes with 2 tablespoons dressing.

2. Alternately thread chicken and onion onto metal or soaked wooden skewers, leaving space between each piece. Thread potatoes onto separate metal or soaked wooden skewers.

3. On a greased grill rack, grill the potatoes, covered, over medium heat 5 minutes. Add chicken kabobs; grill 10-15 minutes or until chicken is no longer pink and potatoes are tender, turning skewers occasionally.

4. In a large bowl, whisk lemon juice, pepper and remaining salad dressing. Add romaine, chicken, potatoes, onion and cheese; toss to coat.

PER SERVING *441 cal., 21 g fat (5 g sat. fat), 81 mg chol., 601 mg sodium, 31 g carb., 5 g fiber, 31 g pro.*

COLOR IT RUBY SALAD

Apple Maple Pecan Salad

A well-made salad has good taste and pleasing crunch. This one with cabbage, apples and pecans gets high marks in both, with extra points for color.

—EMILY TYRA MILWAUKEE, WI

PREP: 15 MIN. + STANDING
MAKES: 12 SERVINGS

- ¼ **cup lemon juice**
- ¼ **cup canola oil**
- ¼ **cup maple syrup**
- 1½ **teaspoons Dijon mustard**
- ½ **teaspoon coarsely ground pepper**
- 4 **cups shredded cabbage**
- 3 **large Granny Smith apples, julienned**
- ½ **cup crumbled Gorgonzola cheese**
- 1 **cup chopped pecans, toasted**

Whisk the first five ingredients until blended. Combine cabbage, apples and Gorgonzola; toss with dressing to coat. Let stand 30 minutes before serving. Sprinkle with pecans.

NOTE *To toast nuts, bake in a shallow pan in a 350° oven for 5-10 minutes or cook in a skillet over low heat until lightly browned, stirring occasionally.*

PER SERVING *¾ cup equals 169 cal., 13 g fat (2 g sat. fat), 4 mg chol., 84 mg sodium, 14 g carb. (9 g sugars, 3 g fiber), 2 g pro.* **Diabetic Exchanges:** *2½ fat, 1 starch.*

EAT SMART **FAST FIX**

Color It Ruby Salad

Just looking at this bright red salad cheers me up—and then I get to taste it! For garnish, sprinkle on fresh chives and mild white cheese.

—LORRAINE CALAND SHUNIAH, ON

START TO FINISH: 30 MIN.
MAKES: 12 SERVINGS

- 2 **tablespoons red wine vinegar**
- 1 **tablespoon Dijon mustard**
- ½ **teaspoon kosher salt**
- ¼ **teaspoon pepper**
- ⅓ **cup extra virgin olive oil**
- 1 **pound small tomatoes, quartered**
- ¾ **pound cherry tomatoes, halved**
- ¾ **pound fresh strawberries, hulled and sliced**
- 2 **cans (15 ounces each) beets, drained and chopped**

Mix vinegar, mustard, salt and pepper; gradually whisk in oil until blended. Toss with tomatoes, strawberries and beets. Serve immediately.

PER SERVING *1 cup equals 98 cal., 6 g fat (1 g sat. fat), 0 chol., 251 mg sodium, 10 g carb. (7 g sugars, 3 g fiber), 1 g pro.* **Diabetic Exchanges:** *1 fat, ½ starch.*

TOP TIP

Virgin or extra-virgin olive oils have a more delicate, complex flavor than the lower grades, making them ideal for salads and other cold foods.

APPLE MAPLE PECAN SALAD

Grapefruit & Fennel Salad with Mint Vinaigrette

My dad has a red grapefruit tree and shares his crop with me. I toss the grapefruit with onion, fennel and mint for a fresh, fabulous salad.

—CATHERINE WILKINSON DEWEY, AZ

START TO FINISH: 15 MIN. • **MAKES:** 4 SERVINGS

- 1 medium red grapefruit
- 1 medium fennel bulb, halved and thinly sliced
- ¼ cup thinly sliced red onion

VINAIGRETTE

- 3 tablespoons fresh mint leaves
- 2 tablespoons sherry vinegar
- 1½ teaspoons honey
- ⅛ teaspoon salt
- ⅛ teaspoon coarsely ground pepper
- 2 tablespoons olive oil

1. Cut a thin slice from the top and bottom of the grapefruit; stand grapefruit upright on a cutting board. With a knife, cut off peel and outer membrane from grapefruit. Cut along the membrane of each segment to remove fruit. Arrange fennel, grapefruit and onion on a serving platter.

2. Place mint, vinegar, honey, salt and pepper in a small food processor; cover and process until mint is finely chopped. While processing, gradually add oil in a steady stream. Drizzle over salad.

PER SERVING *114 cal., 7 g fat (1 g sat. fat), 0 chol., 107 mg sodium, 13 g carb., 3 g fiber, 1 g pro.* **Diabetic Exchanges:** *1½ fat, 1 vegetable, ½ fruit.*

SWEET-TART CUCUMBER SALAD

GRAPEFRUIT & FENNEL SALAD WITH MINT VINAIGRETTE

Sweet-Tart Cucumber Salad

A dear friend showed me how to use up cucumbers in a tangy salad. The longer it chills, the deeper the flavor. Look for lemon or pickling cucumbers.

—DIAN JORGENSEN SANTA ROSA, CA

PREP: 20 MIN. + CHILLING • **MAKES:** 8 SERVINGS

- 10 pickling cucumbers or 3 medium cucumbers, thinly sliced
- 1 tablespoon plus 1 teaspoon salt, divided
- 2 cups white vinegar
- 1 cup sugar
- ½ cup lemon juice
- 3 teaspoons celery seed
- 1 teaspoon pepper
- 2 medium onions, halved and thinly sliced

1. Place cucumbers in a colander over a plate; sprinkle with 1 tablespoon salt and toss. Let stand 30 minutes. Drain.

2. In a small bowl, whisk vinegar, sugar, lemon juice, celery seed, pepper and remaining salt until blended. In a large bowl, combine cucumbers and onions. Pour dressing over cucumber mixture; toss to coat. Refrigerate, covered, at least 2 hours before serving.

PER SERVING *¾ cup equals 139 cal., 1 g fat (trace sat. fat), 0 chol., 744 mg sodium, 34 g carb., 2 g fiber, 2 g pro.*

Baby Kale Salad with Avocado-Lime Dressing

We pull a bunch of ingredients from our garden when we make this salad of greens, zucchini and sweet onion. The yogurt dressing layers on big lime flavor.

—**SUZANNA ESTHER** STATE COLLEGE, PA

START TO FINISH: 20 MIN. • **MAKES:** 4 SERVINGS (¾ CUP DRESSING)

- 6 cups baby kale salad blend
- 1 cup julienned zucchini
- ½ cup thinly sliced sweet onion
- ½ medium ripe avocado, peeled
- ½ cup fat-free plain yogurt
- 3 green onions, chopped
- 2 tablespoons minced fresh parsley
- 2 tablespoons lime juice
- 1 garlic clove, minced
- ¼ teaspoon salt
- ⅛ teaspoon pepper

In a large bowl, combine salad blend, zucchini and sweet onion. Place remaining ingredients in blender; cover and process until smooth. Divide salad mixture among four plates; drizzle with dressing.

PER SERVING *1½ cups salad with 3 tablespoons dressing equals 74 cal., 3 g fat (1 g sat. fat), 1 mg chol., 197 mg sodium, 10 g carb., 4 g fiber, 4 g pro.* **Diabetic Exchanges:** *2 vegetable, ½ fat.*

SUMMER BUZZ FRUIT SALAD

BABY KALE SALAD WITH AVOCADO-LIME DRESSING

Summer Buzz Fruit Salad

For picnics, cookouts and showers, we adore this sweet salad of watermelon, cherries, blueberries and microgreens. No matter where I take it, it always delivers on wow factor.

—**KALISKA RUSSELL** TALKEETNA, AK

START TO FINISH: 15 MIN. • **MAKES:** 6 SERVINGS

- 2 cups watermelon balls
- 2 cups fresh sweet cherries, pitted and halved
- 1 cup fresh blueberries
- ½ cup cubed English cucumber
- ½ cup microgreens or torn mixed salad greens
- ½ cup crumbled feta cheese
- 3 fresh mint leaves, thinly sliced
- ¼ cup honey
- 1 tablespoon lemon juice
- 1 teaspoon grated lemon peel

Combine the first seven ingredients. In a small bowl, whisk together the remaining ingredients. Drizzle over salad; toss.

PER SERVING *¾ cup equals 131 cal., 2 g fat (1 g sat. fat), 5 mg chol., 94 mg sodium, 28 g carb., 2 g fiber, 3 g pro.* **Diabetic Exchanges:** *1 starch, 1 fruit.*

Blue Cheese & Grape Coleslaw

Dishes like coleslaw beg for a fresh approach. I update mine with almonds, grapes, blue cheese and bacon for a grand bowl of color and crunch.

—**JEANNINE BUNGE** HARTLEY, IA

PREP: 10 MIN. + CHILLING
MAKES: 8 SERVINGS

- 1 package (14 ounces) coleslaw mix
- ¾ cup sliced almonds, toasted
- ¾ cup quartered green grapes
- ¾ cup quartered seedless red grapes
- ½ cup crumbled blue cheese
- 3 bacon strips, cooked and crumbled
- ¼ teaspoon pepper
- ¾ cup coleslaw salad dressing

Combine the first seven ingredients. Pour dressing over salad; toss to coat. Refrigerate 1 hour.

NOTE *To toast nuts, bake in a shallow pan in a 350° oven for 5-10 minutes or cook in a skillet over low heat until lightly browned, stirring occasionally.*

PER SERVING *¾ cup equals 212 cal., 15 g fat (3 g sat. fat), 17 mg chol., 339 mg sodium, 16 g carb., 3 g fiber, 5 g pro.*

ORANGE POMEGRANATE
SALAD WITH HONEY

BLUE CHEESE & GRAPE COLESLAW

EAT SMART (5)INGREDIENTS FAST FIX

Orange Pomegranate Salad with Honey

I discovered this fragrant salad in a cooking class. If you can, try to find orange flower water (also called orange blossom water), which really perks up the orange segments. But orange juice will add a nice zip, too!

—**CAROL RICHARDSON MARTY**
LYNWOOD, WA

START TO FINISH: 15 MIN.
MAKES: 6 SERVINGS

- 5 medium oranges or 10 clementines
- ½ cup pomegranate seeds
- 2 tablespoons honey
- 1 to 2 teaspoons orange flower water or orange juice

1. Cut a thin slice from the top and bottom of each orange; stand orange upright on a cutting board. With a knife, cut off peel and outer membrane from oranges. Cut crosswise into ½-in. slices.

2. Arrange orange slices on a serving platter; sprinkle with pomegranate seeds. In a small bowl, mix honey and orange flower water; drizzle over fruit.

PER SERVING *⅔ cup equals 62 cal., trace fat (trace sat. fat), 0 chol., 2 mg sodium, 15 g carb., trace fiber, 1 g pro.* **Diabetic Exchange:** *1 fruit.*

Veggie Steak Salad

This salad just explodes with flavors. Easy and quick to prepare, it's a delicious, healthy dinner all on one plate.
—**TIFFANY MARTINEZ** ALISO VIEJO, CA

START TO FINISH: 30 MIN.
MAKES: 5 SERVINGS

- 2 medium ears sweet corn, husked
- 1 beef flank steak (1 pound)
- ¼ teaspoon salt
- ¼ teaspoon pepper
- 2 tablespoons olive oil

DRESSING

- 2 tablespoons olive oil
- 2 tablespoons balsamic vinegar
- 1 teaspoon garlic powder
- 1 teaspoon capers, drained
- 1 teaspoon Dijon mustard

SALAD

- 1 package (5 ounces) spring mix salad greens
- 1 large tomato, chopped
- 4 slices red onion, separated into rings
- ¼ cup minced fresh parsley
- ¼ cup shredded Parmesan cheese

1. In a 6-qt. stockpot, bring 8 cups of water to a boil. Add the corn and cook, uncovered, 3-5 minutes or until tender. Drain corn; immediately place in ice water. Cool about 10 minutes. Drain and pat dry. Cut corn from cobs.
2. Meanwhile, sprinkle steak with salt and pepper. In a large skillet, heat 2 tablespoons oil over medium heat. Add steak; cook 6-8 minutes on each side or until a thermometer reads 145° for medium rare. Remove from heat; let stand 5 minutes.
3. In a small bowl, whisk dressing ingredients until blended. Thinly slice steak across the grain. Place greens, tomato, onion, parsley, corn and steak in a large bowl; toss with dressing. Sprinkle with cheese.
PER SERVING *2 cups equals 301 cal., 19 g fat (5 g sat. fat), 46 mg chol., 301 mg sodium, 12 g carb. (5 g sugars, 2 g fiber), 21 g pro.* **Diabetic Exchanges:** *3 lean meat, 2½ fat, 2 vegetable.*

Michigan Cherry Salad

This recipe reminds me what I love so much about my home state: apple picking with my children, buying greens at the farmers market and tasting cherries on vacations.
—**JENNIFER GILBERT** BRIGHTON, MI

START TO FINISH: 15 MIN.
MAKES: 8 SERVINGS

- 7 ounces fresh baby spinach (about 9 cups)
- 3 ounces spring mix salad greens (about 5 cups)
- 1 large apple, chopped
- ½ cup coarsely chopped pecans, toasted
- ½ cup dried cherries
- ¼ cup crumbled Gorgonzola cheese

DRESSING

- ¼ cup fresh raspberries
- ¼ cup red wine vinegar
- 3 tablespoons cider vinegar
- 3 tablespoons cherry preserves
- 1 tablespoon sugar
- 2 tablespoons olive oil

1. In a large bowl, combine the first six ingredients.
2. Place the raspberries, vinegars, preserves and sugar in a blender. While processing, gradually add oil in a steady stream. Drizzle over salad; toss to coat.
NOTE *To toast nuts, bake in a shallow pan in a 350° oven for 5-10 minutes or cook in a skillet over low heat until lightly browned, stirring occasionally.*
PER SERVING *1½ cups equals 172 cal., 10 g fat (2 g sat. fat), 3 mg chol., 78 mg sodium, 21 g carb., 3 g fiber, 3 g pro.* **Diabetic Exchanges:** *2 vegetable, 2 fat, 1 starch.*

MICHIGAN CHERRY SALAD

Berry Chicken Salad

Bright berries and creamy goat cheese make this salad a winner! It's ideal for a luncheon or summer wedding shower. Also try it with feta instead of goat cheese.

—**WENDY BALL** BATTLE CREEK, MI

START TO FINISH: 20 MIN.
MAKES: 4 SERVINGS

- 4 **boneless skinless chicken breast halves (4 ounces each)**
- ¼ **teaspoon salt**
- ¼ **teaspoon pepper**
- 1 **package (6 ounces) fresh baby spinach**
- 1 **cup fresh raspberries**
- 1 **cup halved fresh strawberries**
- ⅔ **cup crumbled goat cheese**
- 3 **tablespoons chopped pecans, toasted**
- ¼ **cup prepared fat-free raspberry vinaigrette**

1. Sprinkle chicken with salt and pepper. On a greased grill rack, grill chicken, covered, over medium heat or broil 4 in. from heat 4-7 minutes on each side or until a thermometer reads 165°.

2. In a large bowl, combine spinach, berries, cheese and pecans. Cut chicken into slices; add to salad. Drizzle with vinaigrette and toss lightly to coat. Serve immediately.

PER SERVING *1½ cups salad with 1 chicken breast half and 1 tablespoon dressing equals 268 cal., 12 g fat (4 g sat. fat), 86 mg chol., 391 mg sodium, 15 g carb., 5 g fiber, 28 g pro.* **Diabetic Exchanges:** *4 lean meat, 1 vegetable, 1 fat, ½ fruit.*

Southwest Shredded Pork Salad

This knockout shredded pork makes a healthy, delicious and hearty salad with black beans, corn, cheese and greens.

—**MARY SHIVERS** ADA, OK

PREP: 20 MIN. • **COOK:** 6 HOURS
MAKES: 12 SERVINGS

- 1 **boneless pork loin roast (3 to 4 pounds)**
- 1½ **cups apple cider or juice**
- 1 **can (4 ounces) chopped green chilies, drained**
- 3 **garlic cloves, minced**
- 1½ **teaspoons salt**
- 1½ **teaspoons hot pepper sauce**
- 1 **teaspoon chili powder**
- 1 **teaspoon pepper**
- ½ **teaspoon ground cumin**
- ½ **teaspoon dried oregano**
- 12 **cups torn mixed salad greens**
- 1 **can (15 ounces) black beans, rinsed and drained**
- 2 **medium tomatoes, chopped**
- 1 **small red onion, chopped**
- 1 **cup fresh or frozen corn**
- 1 **cup (4 ounces) crumbled cotija or shredded part-skim mozzarella cheese**
  Salad dressing of your choice

1. Place pork in a 5- or 6-qt. slow cooker. In a small bowl, mix cider, green chilies, garlic, salt, pepper sauce, chili powder, pepper, cumin and oregano; pour over pork. Cook, covered, on low 6-8 hours or until meat is tender.

2. Remove roast from slow cooker; discard cooking juices. Shred pork with two forks. Arrange salad greens on a serving platter. Top with pork, black beans, tomatoes, onion, corn and cheese. Serve with salad dressing.

FREEZE OPTION *Place the shredded pork in a freezer container and top with cooking juices. Cool and freeze. Partially thaw in the refrigerator overnight. Heat through in a saucepan, stirring occasionally.*

PER SERVING *233 cal., 8 g fat (4 g sat. fat), 67 mg chol., 321 mg sodium, 12 g carb., 3 g fiber, 28 g pro.* **Diabetic Exchanges:** *4 lean meat, 1 vegetable, ½ starch.*

BERRY CHICKEN SALAD

NECTARINE ARUGULA SALAD

Cranberry Eggnog Salad

For a bright salad with a vintage holiday feel, I stack a layer of raspberry gelatin and cranberry sauce over pineapple and eggnog.

—**NANCY FOUST** STONEBORO, PA

PREP: 15 MIN. + CHILLING
MAKES: 12 SERVINGS

2½ cups boiling water
2 packages (3 ounces each) cranberry or raspberry gelatin
1 can (14 ounces) whole-berry cranberry sauce
1 can (20 ounces) crushed pineapple, undrained
2 envelopes unflavored gelatin
1½ cups eggnog
2 tablespoons lime juice

1. In a large bowl, add boiling water to cranberry gelatin; stir 2 minutes to completely dissolve. Refrigerate 40-50 minutes or until slightly thickened.
2. Place cranberry sauce in a small bowl; stir to break up. Fold into gelatin mixture. Pour into an 8-cup ring mold coated with cooking spray; refrigerate 15-20 minutes longer or until set but not firm.
3. Meanwhile, drain the crushed pineapple well, reserving juice in a small saucepan. Sprinkle unflavored gelatin over pineapple juice; let stand 1 minute. Heat and stir over low heat until gelatin is completely dissolved. Stir in the eggnog and lime juice. Refrigerate 12-15 minutes or until slightly thickened.
4. Fold pineapple into eggnog mixture. Carefully pour over gelatin in mold. Refrigerate until firm. Unmold onto a platter.
PER SERVING *1 slice equals 180 cal., 1 g fat (1 g sat. fat), 19 mg chol., 66 mg sodium, 37 g carb., 1 g fiber, 7 g pro.*

Nectarine Arugula Salad

Here's a summer salad that brightens any supper. The homemade dressing with a hint of berries is perfect with arugula, nectarines and blue cheese.

—**CHRISTINE LABA** ARLINGTON, VA

START TO FINISH: 20 MIN.
MAKES: 8 SERVINGS

4 cups fresh arugula or baby spinach
4 cups torn Bibb or Boston lettuce
3 medium nectarines, sliced
2 tablespoons pine nuts, toasted
2 tablespoons crumbled blue cheese

DRESSING
2 tablespoons raspberry vinegar
2 teaspoons sugar
1 teaspoon Dijon mustard
⅛ teaspoon salt
Dash pepper
3 tablespoons olive oil

In a large bowl, combine the first five ingredients. In a small bowl, whisk vinegar, sugar, mustard, salt and pepper. Gradually whisk in oil until blended. Drizzle over salad; toss to coat.
NOTE *To toast nuts, bake in a shallow pan in a 350° oven for 5-10 minutes or cook in a skillet over low heat until lightly browned, stirring occasionally.*
PER SERVING *1 cup equals 101 cal., 7 g fat (1 g sat. fat), 2 mg chol., 86 mg sodium, 9 g carb., 1 g fiber, 2 g pro. Diabetic Exchanges: 1½ fat, ½ starch.*

GRILLED VEGETABLE SALAD
WITH POPPY SEED DRESSING

German Apple Salad

In culinary school, I had to make a salad with Granny Smith apples. I remembered my mother's German potato salad and swapped out the potatoes.

—**SHARYN HILL** LAS CRUCES, NM

PREP: 10 MIN. • **COOK:** 25 MIN.
MAKES: 6 SERVINGS

- 6 **bacon strips, cut crosswise into ½-inch slices**
- ½ **cup chopped onion**
- 2 **tablespoons all-purpose flour**
- 1 **teaspoon salt**
- ½ **teaspoon pepper**
- 1 **cup water**
- ½ **cup cider vinegar**
- ¼ **cup sugar**
- 5½ **cups Granny Smith apples (about 4 large), cut into ½-inch slices**

1. In a large skillet, cook bacon over medium heat until crisp; drain on paper towels. Discard all but 2 tablespoons drippings. Add onion; cook until tender, 2-3 minutes. Stir in flour, salt and pepper until blended. Add water and vinegar; cook and stir until slightly thickened, about 1 minute. Stir in sugar until dissolved.
2. Return bacon to pan; gently add apple slices. Cook, stirring constantly, until apples are wilted and slightly caramelized, about 10-12 minutes. Remove from heat; serve warm.
PER SERVING *¾ cup equals 232 cal., 11 g fat (4 g sat. fat), 18 mg chol., 582 mg sodium, 29 g carb. (22 g sugars, 3 g fiber), 4 g pro.*

Grilled Vegetable Salad with Poppy Seed Dressing

My Italian-style grilled veggies have a wonderful sweet and sour dressing. Best of all, I pick the fresh veggies and herbs from my garden.

—**LAURA MAST** DEFIANCE, OH

START TO FINISH: 25 MIN.
MAKES: 2 SERVINGS

- 2 **tablespoons canola oil**
- 1 **tablespoon cider vinegar**
- 2 **teaspoons sugar**
- ½ **teaspoon grated onion**
- ½ **teaspoon poppy seeds**
- ¼ **teaspoon ground mustard**
  Dash salt

SALAD

- 1 **small zucchini, cut into ¾-inch pieces**
- 1 **small sweet yellow pepper, cut into 1-inch pieces**
- ⅔ **cup cherry tomatoes**
- 2 **teaspoons olive oil**
- ¼ **teaspoon salt**
- ⅛ **teaspoon freshly ground pepper**
- 2 **teaspoons minced fresh basil**
- 2 **teaspoons minced fresh parsley**
- 1 **teaspoon minced fresh thyme**

1. In a small bowl, whisk the first seven ingredients until blended. Refrigerate until serving.
2. In a large bowl, combine zucchini, yellow pepper and tomatoes. Add oil, salt and pepper; toss to coat. Transfer to a grill wok or an open grill basket; place on grill rack. Grill, covered, over medium-high heat for 10-12 minutes or until vegetables are crisp-tender, stirring occasionally.
3. Transfer vegetables to a serving bowl; sprinkle with herbs. Serve with dressing.
NOTE *If you do not have a grill wok or basket, use a disposable foil pan. Poke holes in the bottom of the pan with a meat fork to allow liquid to drain.*
PER SERVING *1 cup equals 219 cal., 19 g fat (2 g sat. fat), 0 chol., 378 mg sodium, 11 g carb., 2 g fiber, 2 g pro.*

GERMAN APPLE SALAD

Fresh Basil Salad Dressing

My sour cream and basil dressing has irresistible bistro flavor. We serve it with a green salad, but it's also a tasty addition to baked potatoes or fresh vegetable trays.

—**DEBORAH COMEAUX** POCOMOKE CITY, MD

START TO FINISH: 15 MIN.
MAKES: 2½ CUPS

- 1   cup packed fresh basil leaves
- 1   green onion, cut into large pieces
- 1   garlic clove, peeled and halved
- 1   cup mayonnaise
- 1   cup (8 ounces) sour cream
- ¼   cup lemon juice
- 1   teaspoon salt
- ½   teaspoon coarsely ground pepper

Place basil, onion and garlic in a food processor. Cover and process until finely chopped. Add the remaining ingredients; cover and process until blended. Cover and refrigerate until serving.

PER SERVING *2 tablespoons equals 104 cal., 11 g fat (3 g sat. fat), 12 mg chol., 182 mg sodium, 1 g carb., trace fiber, trace pro.*

EAT SMART | **FAST FIX**
Chicken & Brussels Sprouts Salad

My mom made the best salads; that's where my love for them started. I've turned her side salads into awesome meals with protein, veggies, nuts and cranberries.

—**LINDSAY TANNER** CATHEDRAL CITY, CA

START TO FINISH: 30 MIN.
MAKES: 6 SERVINGS

- 3   tablespoons olive oil
- 20 fresh Brussels sprouts, trimmed and halved
- 2   shallots, sliced
- ½   teaspoon salt
- ½   cup balsamic vinegar
- 1   skinned rotisserie chicken, shredded
- 3   cups torn romaine
- ⅔   cup chopped roasted sweet red peppers
- ½   cup chopped sun-dried tomatoes (not oil-packed)
- ½   cup balsamic vinaigrette
- ¾   cup pistachios, toasted
- ¾   cup dried cranberries
     Fresh goat cheese, optional

1. In a large skillet, heat oil over medium heat. Add Brussels sprouts and shallots; cook and stir until browned and tender, 10-12 minutes. Sprinkle with salt; drizzle with the balsamic vinegar. Cook 2-3 minutes, reducing liquid and stirring to loosen browned bits from pan.
2. Combine chicken, romaine, red pepper and sun-dried tomatoes. Toss with Brussels sprouts mixture and balsamic vinaigrette. Top with pistachios and dried cranberries; serve with goat cheese if desired.
NOTE *To toast nuts, bake in a shallow pan in a 350° oven for 5-10 minutes or cook in a skillet over low heat until lightly browned, stirring occasionally.*
PER SERVING *1⅓ cups equals 500 cal., 25 g fat (4 g sat. fat), 73 mg chol., 657 mg sodium, 39 g carb. (24 g sugars, 7 g fiber), 30 g pro.*

FRESH BASIL SALAD DRESSING

**DENISE MILLER'S BARBECUED
BASIL TURKEY BURGERS**
PAGE 49

Soups & Sandwiches

It's hard to beat **classic comfort food** like hot **chicken noodle soup,** toasty **grilled cheese,** piled-high **burgers** and veggie-packed **minestrone.** Turn here for **fresh takes** on all the favorites.

JEAN GLACKEN'S ITALIAN MEATBALL SUBS
PAGE 36

ANDREA EARLY'S ZIPPY CHICKEN & CORN CHOWDER
PAGE 47

ANGELA MCCLURE'S SPICY SHRIMP-SLAW PITAS
PAGE 42

SLOW COOKER

Slow Cooker Pork Pozole

When the snow begins falling, I make a heartwarming stew with pork ribs and hominy. This is a fill-you-up recipe of lightly spiced comfort.

—GENIE GUNN ASHEVILLE, NC

PREP: 10 MIN. • **COOK:** 3 HOURS
MAKES: 6 SERVINGS

- 1 can (15½ ounces) hominy, rinsed and drained
- 1 can (14½ ounces) diced tomatoes, undrained
- 1 can (14½ ounces) diced tomatoes with mild green chilies, undrained
- 1 can (10 ounces) green enchilada sauce
- 2 medium carrots, finely chopped
- 1 medium onion, finely chopped
- 3 garlic cloves, minced
- 2 teaspoons ground cumin
- ¼ teaspoon salt
- 1 pound boneless country-style pork ribs
  Lime wedges and minced fresh cilantro
  Corn tortillas, optional

1. In a 3- or 4-qt. slow cooker, combine the first nine ingredients; add pork. Cook, covered, on low 3-4 hours or until pork is tender.
2. Remove pork from slow cooker; cut into bite-size pieces and return to slow cooker. Serve with lime wedges and cilantro and, if desired, corn tortillas.
PER SERVING *1⅓ cups equals 223 cal., 8 g fat (3 g sat. fat), 44 mg chol., 991 mg sodium, 22 g carb., 5 g fiber, 15 g pro.*

SLOW COOKER
PORK POZOLE

PORK BURGERS WITH GRILLED PINEAPPLE & PEPPERS

FAST FIX

Pork Burgers with Grilled Pineapple & Peppers

I had ground pork and fresh pineapple, so I made them into burgers. In grilling season, we serve them with slaw and roasted potato wedges. My hubby loves them.

—HOPE WASYLENKI GAHANNA, OH

START TO FINISH: 30 MIN.
MAKES: 4 SERVINGS

- 3 tablespoons Dijon mustard
- 2 tablespoons honey
- 1 tablespoon reduced-sodium teriyaki sauce
- ½ pound ground pork
- 2 green onions, finely chopped
- ½ teaspoon grated fresh gingerroot
  Dash ground allspice
  Dash pepper
- 2 fresh pineapple slices (about ¼ inch thick)
- 4 green pepper rings, thinly sliced
- 4 Hawaiian sweet rolls, split
- 2 Bibb or Boston lettuce leaves, halved

1. In a small bowl, mix mustard, honey and teriyaki sauce.
2. In a large bowl, combine pork, onions, ginger, allspice and pepper, mixing lightly but thoroughly. Shape into four ¼-in.-thick patties.
3. Grill the burgers, covered, over medium heat 2-3 minutes on each side or until a thermometer reads 160°.
4. Meanwhile, brush pineapple slices with 1 tablespoon mustard mixture. Grill 2-3 minutes on each side or until lightly browned. Grill the pepper rings for 1-2 minutes on each side or until crisp-tender. Cut pineapple and pepper slices in half. Grill the buns, cut side down, for 30-60 seconds or until toasted.
5. Serve burgers on buns with lettuce, pineapple slices, pepper rings and remaining mustard mixture.
PER SERVING *1 burger equals 515 cal., 20 g fat (8 g sat. fat), 101 mg chol., 899 mg sodium, 56 g carb., 3 g fiber, 26 g pro.*

Weeknight Chicken Mozzarella Sandwiches

My husband is a big garlic fan, so I use garlic bread crumbs and garlic sauce for these baked chicken sandwiches. They're so comforting on a chilly day.

—BRIDGET SNYDER SYRACUSE, NY

START TO FINISH: 30 MIN.
MAKES: 4 SERVINGS

- 4 **boneless skinless chicken breast halves (6 ounces each)**
- 1 **cup garlic bread crumbs**
- 1 **cup garlic and herb pasta sauce**
- 1 **cup (4 ounces) shredded part-skim mozzarella cheese**
  Grated Parmesan cheese, optional
- 4 **kaiser rolls, split**

1. Preheat oven to 400°. Pound chicken with a meat mallet to ½-in. thickness. Place bread crumbs in a large resealable plastic bag. Add chicken, a few pieces at a time; close bag and shake to coat. Transfer to a greased 15x10x1-in. baking pan.
2. Bake, uncovered, 15-20 minutes or until no longer pink. Spoon pasta sauce over the chicken. Top with the mozzarella and, if desired, Parmesan cheese. Bake 2-3 minutes longer or until cheese is melted. Serve on rolls.
PER SERVING *1 sandwich (calculated without Parmesan cheese) equals 509 cal., 13 g fat (5 g sat. fat), 112 mg chol., 1,125 mg sodium, 46 g carb., 3 g fiber, 50 g pro.*

WEEKNIGHT CHICKEN
MOZZARELLA SANDWICHES

Italian Sausage & Kale Soup

The first time I made this colorful soup, our home smelled wonderful. I knew it would be a keeper to see us through cold winter days.

—SARAH STOMBAUGH CHICAGO, IL

PREP: 20 MIN. • **COOK:** 8 HOURS
MAKES: 8 SERVINGS (3½ QUARTS)

- 1 **pound bulk hot Italian sausage**
- 6 **cups chopped fresh kale**
- 2 **cans (15½ ounces each) great northern beans, rinsed and drained**
- 1 **can (28 ounces) crushed tomatoes**
- 4 **large carrots, finely chopped (about 3 cups)**
- 1 **medium onion, chopped**
- 3 **garlic cloves, minced**
- 1 **teaspoon dried oregano**
- ¼ **teaspoon salt**
- ⅛ **teaspoon pepper**
- 5 **cups chicken stock**
  Grated Parmesan cheese

1. In a large skillet, cook sausage over medium heat 6-8 minutes or until no longer pink, breaking into crumbles; drain. Transfer to a 5-qt. slow cooker.
2. Add kale, beans, tomatoes, carrots, onion, garlic, seasonings and stock to slow cooker. Cook, covered, on low 8-10 hours or until vegetables are tender. Top each serving with cheese.
PER SERVING *1¾ cups (calculated without cheese) equals 297 cal., 13 g fat (4 g sat. fat), 31 mg chol., 1,105 mg sodium, 31 g carb., 9 g fiber, 16 g pro.*

DID YOU KNOW?

Kale is a member of the cabbage family. The nutritious greens require long cooking to become tender. You can substitute collards, the leaves from Swiss chard or mustard greens.

SLOW COOKER
Italian Meatball Subs

This is one of those recipes you always come back to. A flavorful tomato sauce and mildly spiced meatballs make a hearty sandwich filling, or they can be served over pasta. I broil the meatballs first to quickly brown them.

—**JEAN GLACKEN** ELKTON, MD

PREP: 25 MIN. • **COOK:** 4 HOURS
MAKES: 6-7 SERVINGS

- 2 **large eggs, lightly beaten**
- ¼ **cup milk**
- ½ **cup dry bread crumbs**
- 2 **tablespoons grated Parmesan cheese**
- 1 **teaspoon salt**
- ¼ **teaspoon pepper**
- ⅛ **teaspoon garlic powder**
- 1 **pound ground beef**
- ½ **pound bulk Italian sausage**

SAUCE

- 1 **can (15 ounces) tomato sauce**
- 1 **can (6 ounces) tomato paste**
- 1 **small onion, chopped**
- ½ **cup chopped green pepper**
- ½ **cup dry red wine or beef broth**
- ⅓ **cup water**
- 2 **garlic cloves, minced**
- 1 **teaspoon dried oregano**
- 1 **teaspoon salt**
- ½ **teaspoon sugar**
- ½ **teaspoon pepper**
- 6 **to 7 Italian rolls, split**
  Shredded Parmesan cheese, optional

1. In a large bowl, combine eggs and milk; add the bread crumbs, cheese, salt, pepper and garlic powder. Add beef and sausage; mix well. Shape into 1-in. balls. Preheat broiler. Place meatballs in a 15x10x1-in. baking pan. Broil 4 in. from the heat for 4 minutes; turn and broil 3 minutes longer.
2. Transfer to a 5-qt. slow cooker. Combine the tomato sauce and paste, onion, green pepper, wine, water and seasonings; pour over the meatballs. Cover and cook on low for 4-5 hours. Serve on rolls. Sprinkle with shredded cheese if desired.
PER SERVING *1 sandwich equals 482 cal., 21 g fat (8 g sat. fat), 131 mg chol., 1,545 mg sodium, 40 g carb., 4 g fiber, 27 g pro.*

Creamy Butternut Squash & Sage Soup

I recently started experimenting with new soup recipes. I finally created a rich squash version that omits heavy cream altogether, making it a healthier way to curb my creamy-tooth.

—**NITHYA KUMAR** DAVIS, CA

PREP: 20 MIN. • **COOK:** 50 MIN.
MAKES: 4 SERVINGS

- 4 **cups cubed peeled butternut squash**
- 1 **tablespoon olive oil**
- 2 **tablespoons minced fresh sage**
- ¼ **teaspoon salt**
- ¼ **teaspoon pepper**

SOUP

- 1 **tablespoon olive oil**
- 2 **tablespoons butter, divided**
- 1 **medium onion, chopped**
- 1 **garlic clove, minced**
- ¾ **teaspoon salt**
- ¼ **to ½ teaspoon crushed red pepper flakes**
- ⅛ **teaspoon pepper**
- 4 **cups water**
- 1 **medium sweet potato, chopped**
- 1 **medium carrot, chopped**

1. Preheat oven to 400°. Place squash in a foil-lined 15x10x1-in. baking pan. Drizzle with oil; sprinkle with sage, salt and pepper. Toss to coat. Roast for 30-35 minutes or until tender, stirring occasionally.
2. Meanwhile, in a large saucepan, heat oil and 1 tablespoon butter over medium heat. Add onion and garlic; cook and stir 3-4 minutes or until softened. Reduce heat to medium-low; cook 30-40 minutes or until deep golden brown, stirring occasionally. Stir in salt, pepper flakes and pepper.
3. Add the water, sweet potato and carrot to the saucepan. Bring to a boil. Reduce the heat; cook, uncovered, for 10-15 minutes or until the vegetables are tender. Add squash mixture and remaining butter to soup. Puree the soup using an immersion blender. Or, cool soup slightly and puree in batches in a blender; return to pan and heat through.
PER SERVING *1½ cups equals 255 cal., 13 g fat (5 g sat. fat), 15 mg chol., 659 mg sodium, 36 g carb., 6 g fiber, 3 g pro.*

CREAMY BUTTERNUT SQUASH & SAGE SOUP

DEEP-DIVER TUNA SALAD SANDWICHES

Deep-Diver Tuna Salad Sandwiches

This bright and slightly spicy sandwich is one of our cafe's best-sellers. And it's a personal favorite of mine, too.
—GREG BAUTISTA MILWAUKEE, WI

PREP: 20 MIN. + CHILLING
MAKES: 6 SERVINGS

- 3 pouches (6½ ounces each) albacore white tuna in water
- ½ medium sweet red pepper, finely chopped
- 1 celery rib, finely chopped
- ½ cup mayonnaise
- ½ cup reduced-fat chipotle mayonnaise
- 3 tablespoons dried minced onion
- 1½ teaspoons sweet pickle relish
- 1 teaspoon dried parsley flakes
- 1 teaspoon curry powder
- ¾ teaspoon dill weed
- ½ teaspoon garlic powder
- ⅛ teaspoon salt
- 6 brioche buns, split and toasted

Mix the first 12 ingredients in a large bowl. Refrigerate 1 hour or until onion softens. Serve on buns.

PER SERVING *1 sandwich equals 438 cal., 24 g fat (4 g sat. fat), 52 mg chol., 884 mg sodium, 28 g carb., 2 g fiber, 26 g pro.*

Garden Minestrone

In Italian restaurants, I always order the minestrone. After doing many trial-and-error batches, I developed a hearty veggie soup my whole family craves—kids and all.
—HILLERY MARTIN FORT LEAVENWORTH, KS

PREP: 20 MIN. • **COOK:** 30 MIN.
MAKES: 10 SERVINGS (ABOUT 4 QUARTS)

- 2 tablespoons olive oil
- 7 medium carrots, chopped
- 7 celery ribs, chopped
- 1 medium onion, chopped
- 3 medium zucchini, chopped
- 2 yellow summer squash (about 3 cups), chopped
- 2 bay leaves
- ½ teaspoon salt
- ¼ teaspoon pepper
- ¼ teaspoon dried thyme
- ¼ teaspoon dried sage leaves
- ⅛ teaspoon crushed red pepper flakes, optional
- 3 garlic cloves, finely chopped
- 2 cans (15½ ounces each) great northern beans, rinsed and drained, divided
- 1 can (15 ounces) crushed tomatoes
- 2 cartons (32 ounces each) reduced-sodium chicken broth
- 1 cup uncooked ditalini or other small pasta
- 12 cups chopped fresh spinach (12 ounces)

1. In a 6-qt. stockpot, heat oil over medium heat. Add carrots, celery and onion; cook until tender, 6-8 minutes. Add zucchini, yellow squash and seasonings; cook and stir until squashes are crisp-tender, 4-6 minutes. Add garlic; cook for 1 minute longer.

2. Mash ½ cup beans with a fork. Stir mashed beans and tomatoes into vegetables. Add broth; bring to a boil. Reduce heat and simmer, covered, 10-12 minutes.

3. Stir in pasta and remaining beans; return to a boil. Cook, uncovered, 7-9 minutes or just until pasta is tender. Discard bay leaves. Stir in spinach; cook until spinach is wilted.

PER SERVING *1½ cups equals 209 cal., 4 g fat (1 g sat. fat), 0 chol., 929 mg sodium, 35 g carb., 9 g fiber, 12 g pro.*

GARDEN MINESTRONE

My Favorite Chili Dogs

The very thought of a hot dog dressed in chili makes me giddy. To get that straight-from-the-ballpark taste, I combine ketchup, mustard, chili and pepper sauce.

—PATRICIA PAULING ADAMS, NY

PREP: 20 MIN. • **COOK:** 1 HOUR
MAKES: 8 SERVINGS

- 1 **pound ground beef**
- 1 **finely chopped small onion**
- 1 **can (15 ounces) tomato puree**
- ½ **cup ketchup**
- 2 **tablespoons chili powder**
- 1 **tablespoon finely chopped green pepper**
- 1 **tablespoon white vinegar**
- 2 **teaspoons ground mustard**
- 1 **teaspoon hot pepper sauce**
- 1 **teaspoon onion salt**
- ½ **teaspoon garlic powder**
- 8 **hot dogs**
- 1 **package (12 ounces) hot dog buns, split**
  Finely chopped red onion
  Yellow mustard

1. In a large saucepan, cook and crumble beef over medium heat until no longer pink, 8-10 minutes; drain. Add the next 10 ingredients; simmer until thickened, about 45 minutes, stirring frequently.

2. Cook hot dogs according to package directions. Place in buns and top with chili, red onion and yellow mustard.
PER SERVING *1 hot dog equals 427 cal., 22 g fat (9 g sat. fat), 60 mg chol., 1,195 mg sodium, 33 g carb., 3 g fiber, 21 g pro.*

EAT SMART   FAST FIX

Quick Mushroom Barley Soup

I surprised my mother with a visit some years ago, and she was preparing this soup when I walked in. It was so wonderful that I asked for the recipe, and I've been fixing it ever since.

—EDIE IRWIN CORNWALL, NY

START TO FINISH: 30 MIN.
MAKES: 6 SERVINGS

- 1 **tablespoon olive oil**
- 1 **cup sliced fresh mushrooms**
- ½ **cup chopped carrot**
- ⅓ **cup chopped onion**
- 2 **cups water**
- ¾ **cup quick-cooking barley**
- 2 **tablespoons all-purpose flour**
- 3 **cups whole milk**
- 1½ **teaspoons salt**
- ½ **teaspoon pepper**

1. In a large saucepan, heat oil over medium heat. Add mushrooms, carrot and onion; cook and stir 5-6 minutes or until tender. Add water and barley. Bring to a boil. Reduce heat; simmer, uncovered, 12-15 minutes or until barley is tender.

2. In a small bowl, mix flour, milk, salt and pepper until smooth; stir into soup. Return to a boil, stirring constantly; cook and stir 1-2 minutes or until thickened.
PER SERVING *1 cup equals 196 cal., 7 g fat (3 g sat. fat), 12 mg chol., 654 mg sodium, 27 g carb., 5 g fiber, 8 g pro.* **Diabetic Exchanges:** *1½ starch, ½ whole milk, ½ fat.*

FAST FIX

Pepperoni Quesadillas

When my husband and I needed a quick meal, I made quesadillas using leftover ingredients. Unlike traditional quesadillas, mine call for Italian meats, cheeses and seasoning.

—BARBARA RUPERT EDGEFIELD, SC

START TO FINISH: 10 MIN.
MAKES: 4 SERVINGS

- 1 **cup meatless spaghetti sauce**
- 2 **teaspoons butter, softened**
- 4 **flour tortillas (10 inches)**
- 1 **cup (4 ounces) shredded part-skim mozzarella cheese**
- 8 **thin slices hard salami**
- 12 **slices pepperoni**
- ¼ **cup shredded Parmesan cheese**
- ½ **teaspoon dried oregano**

1. In a small saucepan, cook spaghetti sauce over medium-low heat for 3-4 minutes or until heated through.

2. Meanwhile, spread butter over one side of each tortilla. Sprinkle the unbuttered sides of two tortillas with mozzarella cheese; top with salami and pepperoni. Sprinkle with shredded Parmesan cheese and oregano. Top with the remaining tortillas, buttered side up.

3. Cook on a griddle over medium heat for 2-3 minutes on each side or until cheese is melted. Cut quesadillas into wedges; serve with warmed spaghetti sauce.
PER SERVING *½ quesadilla equals 444 cal., 20 g fat (9 g sat. fat), 48 mg chol., 1,366 mg sodium, 38 g carb., 7 g fiber, 22 g pro.*

MY FAVORITE CHILI DOGS

Southwest-Style Wedding Soup

One day, I turned leftover Mexican chicken burgers into meatballs and dreamed up this cozy soup. Now my Italian family asks for it over traditional wedding soup.
—**TEENA PETRUS** JOHNSTOWN, PA

START TO FINISH: 30 MIN.
MAKES: 6 SERVINGS

- 1 tablespoon canola oil
- 2 medium carrots, chopped
- 2 medium celery ribs, chopped
- ½ cup frozen corn, thawed
- 2 quarts chicken stock
- 1 cup soft bread crumbs
- 1 envelope reduced-sodium taco seasoning
- 1 large egg
- 1 pound ground chicken
- 1½ cups acini di pepe pasta
- 2 tablespoons minced fresh cilantro
- ¼ teaspoon salt
  Cubed avocado and sour cream

1. In a Dutch oven, heat oil over medium heat. Add carrots, celery and corn; cook until tender. Stir in stock. Increase heat to high; bring to a boil.
2. Meanwhile, combine the bread crumbs, taco seasoning, egg and chicken; mix lightly. With wet hands, shape into 1½-in. balls. Reduce heat to a simmer; gently drop meatballs into stock. Cook, covered, until meatballs are no longer pink, 8-10 minutes. Add pasta. Simmer, covered, until pasta is tender, 6-8 minutes. Sprinkle with cilantro and salt. Serve with avocado and sour cream.
NOTE *To make soft bread crumbs, tear bread into pieces and place in a food processor or blender. Cover and pulse until crumbs form. One slice of bread yields 1/2 to 3/4 cup crumbs.*
PER SERVING *1½ cups equals 455 cal., 10 g fat (2g sat. fat), 81 mg chol., 1,219 mg sodium, 63 g carb. (8 g sugars, 3 g fiber), 29 g pro.*

Papa Burger

When whipping up something for Father's Day or the Fourth of July, I go big and tall with this fully loaded, juicy yumburger.
—**CHASE BAILEY** COSTA MESA, CA

START TO FINISH: 30 MIN.
MAKES: 4 SERVINGS

- 1 pound ground beef or ground buffalo
- ⅓ cup finely chopped onion
- 1 slice whole wheat or white bread, broken into small pieces
- 2 tablespoons red wine vinegar
- 1 tablespoon liquid smoke
- 2 teaspoons Worcestershire sauce
- 1 teaspoon hamburger or steak seasoning
- ¼ to ½ teaspoon garlic salt
- ¼ to ½ teaspoon pepper
- ¼ cup all-purpose flour
- 4 onion hamburger buns, split
- 4 Bibb or Boston lettuce leaves
- ⅓ cup prepared Thousand Island salad dressing
- 4 slices red onion
- 1 large heirloom tomato, sliced

1. Combine first nine ingredients; mix lightly. Shape mixture into four ¾-in.-thick patties. Press patties into flour to lightly coat both sides.
2. In a large nonstick skillet, cook burgers over medium heat until a thermometer reads 160°, about 4-5 minutes per side. Layer bun bottoms with lettuce, burgers, salad dressing, and onion and tomato slices. Replace bun tops.
PER SERVING *1 burger equals 464 cal., 22 g fat (6 g sat. fat), 77 mg chol., 713 mg sodium, 37 g carb., 3 g fiber, 26 g pro.*

PAPA BURGER

OVER THE TOP

When it comes to soup, there are crackers—and then there are cheesy croutons, roasty pumpkin seeds and dashes of spice. These **Facebook friends sprinkle on the fun.**

1 Top tomato soup with **mini grilled cheese sandwiches.** I cut the sammies into pieces and throw them on.
—**JENNY MINNICK-STATES** PENROSE, CO

2 I never understood **shoestring potatoes** until a stroke of genius inspired me to top my soup with them.
—**KERRY ROBERTS KEUVELAAR** FOWLERVILLE, MI

3 For squash soups, I scatter on **roasted pumpkin seeds** and some fresh sage leaves quickly fried in a little olive oil.
—**KERI LARSON** MINNEAPOLIS, MN

4 Posole, a homey Mexican soup, is even better topped with a **crunchy and cool mix** of chopped radishes, green onions, diced avocado and shredded Monterey Jack, then splashed with taco sauce and fresh lime juice.
—**CAT CODIGA CAMPBELL** NORTH FORK, CA

5 Take leftover **corn bread crumbles** and saute in butter. Toss them onto cowboy soup (homemade hamburger stew) and you're ready.
—**DONNA MCANALLY HERRINGTON** LUMBERTON, TX

6 Down here in Cajun country we love our gumbo...topped with **homemade potato salad!** Creamy salad with rich gumbo—it's cold and hot balancing perfectly together in one amazing bowl. *Laissez les bons temps rouler!*
—**FAYE HOFFPAUER** CROWLEY, LA

7 I like **pesto** on my chicken noodle; for beef stew, I want fresh herbs and a dollop of Greek yogurt.
—**ANNA A. SIMS** DOYLESTOWN, PA

8 **Freeze-dried corn** from the Savory Spice Shop (savoryspiceshop.com).
—**LYNNE HUSKEY** LITTLETON, CO

9 Make **sourdough croutons.** Drizzle olive oil over pieces of sourdough bread; sprinkle them with Parmesan, basil and thyme. Toast under the broiler. Pile them onto just about any soup.
—**VALLERI GLASGOW** SURPRISE, AZ

10 I love throwing on some **cooked shrimp, thinly sliced basil** and, if I'm feeling daring, a little spicy horseradish.
—**SHARON MANSOUR** ORLANDO, FL

THE ULTIMATE CHICKEN NOODLE SOUP

The Ultimate Chicken Noodle Soup

My first Wisconsin winter was so cold, all I wanted to eat was soup. This recipe is in heavy rotation from November to April and has some devoted fans.

—**GINA NISTICO** MILWAUKEE, WI

PREP: 15 MIN. • **COOK:** 45 MIN. + STANDING
MAKES: 10 SERVINGS (3½ QUARTS)

- 2½ pounds bone-in chicken thighs
- 1¼ teaspoons pepper, divided
- ½ teaspoon salt
- 1 tablespoon canola oil
- 1 large onion, chopped (about 2 cups)
- 1 garlic clove, minced
- 10 cups chicken broth
- 4 celery ribs, chopped (about 2 cups)
- 4 medium carrots, chopped (about 2 cups)
- 2 bay leaves
- 1 teaspoon minced fresh thyme or ¼ teaspoon dried thyme
- 3 cups uncooked kluski or other egg noodles (about 8 ounces)
- 1 tablespoon chopped fresh parsley
- 1 tablespoon lemon juice

1. Pat chicken dry with paper towels; sprinkle with ½ teaspoon pepper and salt. In a 6-qt. stockpot, heat oil over medium-high heat. Add the chicken in batches, skin side down; cook for 3-4 minutes or until dark golden brown. Remove chicken from pan; remove and discard skin. Discard drippings, reserving 2 tablespoons.
2. Add onion to drippings; cook and stir over medium-high heat for 4-5 minutes or until tender. Add the garlic; cook 1 minute longer. Add broth, stirring to loosen browned bits from pan. Bring to a boil. Return chicken to pan. Add the celery, carrots, bay leaves and thyme. Reduce heat; simmer, covered, 25-30 minutes or until chicken is tender.
3. Transfer chicken to a plate. Remove soup from heat. Add noodles; let stand, covered, for 20-22 minutes or until noodles are tender.
4. When chicken is cool enough to handle, remove meat from bones; discard bones. Shred meat into bite-size pieces; return to soup. Add parsley and lemon juice. Season with salt and remaining ¾ teaspoon pepper. Discard bay leaves.
PER SERVING *1⅓ cups equals 239 cal., 12 g fat (3 g sat. fat), 68 mg chol., 1,176 mg sodium, 14 g carb., 2 g fiber, 18 g pro.*

Sesame Pulled Pork Sandwiches

I wanted to build a better pork sandwich, and this Asian-style filling was a huge hit with my husband and co-workers. Bring on the wasabi mayo.

—**JENNIFER BERRY** LEXINGTON, OH

PREP: 15 MIN. • **COOK:** 4½ HOURS
MAKES: 12 SERVINGS

- 3 pork tenderloins (1 pound each)
- 1¾ cups reduced-fat sesame ginger salad dressing, divided
- ¼ cup packed brown sugar

SLAW
- 1 package (14 ounces) coleslaw mix
- 4 green onions, chopped
- ¼ cup minced fresh cilantro
- 2 tablespoons reduced-fat sesame ginger salad dressing
- 2 teaspoons sesame oil
- 1 teaspoon sugar
- 1 teaspoon reduced-sodium soy sauce

TO SERVE
- 12 multigrain hamburger buns, split Wasabi mayonnaise, optional

1. Place tenderloins in a 5-qt. slow cooker coated with cooking spray; pour ¾ cup salad dressing over pork, turning to coat. Cook, covered, on low 4-5 hours or until meat is tender.
2. Remove pork; cool slightly. Shred meat into bite-size pieces; return to slow cooker. Stir in brown sugar and the remaining salad dressing. Cook, covered, for 30-45 minutes longer or until heated through.
3. Combine the slaw ingredients. Serve pork on buns with slaw and, if desired, mayonnaise.
NOTE *This recipe was tested with Newman's Own Sesame Ginger Dressing.*
PER SERVING *1 sandwich (calculated without mayonnaise) equals 324 cal., 9 g fat (2 g sat. fat), 64 mg chol., 756 mg sodium, 33 g carb., 3 g fiber, 27 g pro.* **Diabetic Exchanges:** *3 lean meat, 2 starch.*

SESAME PULLED PORK SANDWICHES

LOADED POTATO-LEEK SOUP

2. In a small skillet, heat oil over medium-high heat. Add reserved leek greens; cook 3-5 minutes or until light golden. Puree soup using an immersion blender, or cool soup slightly and puree in batches in a blender. Stir in lemon juice. Top with leek greens and, if desired, sour cream.

PER SERVING *1 cup (calculated without sour cream) equals 108 cal., 2 g fat (trace sat. fat), 0 chol., 593 mg sodium, 20 g carb., 2 g fiber, 4 g pro.* **Diabetic Exchanges:** *1 starch, ½ fat.*

EAT SMART

Spicy Shrimp-Slaw Pitas

My mother brought me peach salsa from Georgia, inspiring this recipe for shrimp pitas. Get awesome texture with edamame, or swap in baby lima beans.
—ANGELA McCLURE CARY, NC

PREP: 30 MIN. • **BROIL:** 5 MIN.
MAKES: 6 SERVINGS

- 1½ pounds uncooked shrimp (31-40 per pound), peeled, deveined and coarsely chopped
- 1 tablespoon olive oil
- 1 teaspoon paprika

SLAW

- ⅓ cup reduced-fat plain Greek yogurt
- ⅓ cup peach salsa or salsa of your choice
- 1 tablespoon honey
- ½ teaspoon salt
- ½ teaspoon pepper
- 1 package (12 ounces) broccoli coleslaw mix
- 2 cups fresh baby spinach
- ¼ cup shredded carrots
- ¼ cup frozen shelled edamame, thawed
- 12 whole wheat pita pocket halves

1. Preheat broiler. In a small bowl, toss shrimp with oil and paprika. Transfer to a foil-lined 15x10x1-in. baking pan. Broil 4-5 in. from heat 3-4 minutes or until shrimp turn pink, stirring once.

2. In a small bowl, whisk yogurt, salsa, honey, salt and pepper. Add coleslaw mix, spinach, carrots, edamame and shrimp; toss to coat.

3. Place pita pockets on a baking sheet. Broil 4-5 in. from heat for 1-2 minutes on each side or until lightly toasted. Fill each pita half with ½ cup shrimp mixture.

PER SERVING *2 filled pita halves equals 322 cal., 6 g fat (1 g sat. fat), 139 mg chol., 641 mg sodium, 41 g carb., 7 g fiber, 28 g pro.* **Diabetic Exchanges:** *3 lean meat, 2 starch, 1 vegetable, ½ fat.*

SPICY SHRIMP-SLAW PITAS

EAT SMART **SLOW COOKER**

Loaded Potato-Leek Soup

When I was growing up, my mother made potato and onion soup because it was fast and affordable. I've trimmed the calories, and it's still a deliciously comforting family favorite.
—COURTNEY STULTZ WEIR, KS

PREP: 20 MIN. • **COOK:** 6 HOURS
MAKES: 6 SERVINGS (ABOUT 1½ QUARTS)

- 1 medium leek
- 1½ pounds potatoes (about 2 large), peeled and finely chopped
- 2 cups fresh cauliflowerets
- ¾ teaspoon rubbed sage
- ½ teaspoon salt
- ¼ teaspoon pepper
- 4 cups reduced-sodium chicken or vegetable broth
- 2 teaspoons olive oil
- 2 teaspoons lemon juice
  Sour cream, optional

1. Finely chop white portion of leek. Cut leek greens into thin strips; reserve for topping. In a 3- or 4-qt. slow cooker, combine potatoes, cauliflower, seasonings, broth and chopped leek. Cook, covered, on low 6-8 hours or until vegetables are tender.

CURRIED PUMPKIN APPLE SOUP

FRENCH MARKET SANDWICHES

Curried Pumpkin Apple Soup

Sweet apples and spicy curry make a tasty pair in rich soup—it's everything you want on a chilly fall evening.

—JANE SHAPTON IRVINE, CA

PREP: 15 MIN. • **COOK:** 25 MIN.
MAKES: 8 SERVINGS (2 QUARTS)

- 2 **medium Golden Delicious apples, peeled and coarsely chopped**
- 1 **medium onion, chopped**
- 1 **medium leek (white portion only), sliced**
- 2 **tablespoons butter**
- 3 **garlic cloves, minced**
- 2 **to 3 teaspoons curry powder**
- 1 **can (15 ounces) solid-pack pumpkin**
- 4 **cups chicken broth**
- 1 **cup heavy whipping cream**
  Salt to taste

1. In a large saucepan, saute the apples, onion and leek in butter until tender. Add garlic and curry; cook 1 minute longer. Add pumpkin and broth; bring to a boil. Reduce heat; cover and simmer for 20 minutes. Stir in cream; heat through (do not boil).
2. Remove from the heat; cool slightly. In a blender, process soup in batches until smooth. Season with salt.
PER SERVING *1 cup equals 187 cal., 15 g fat (9 g sat. fat), 48 mg chol., 511 mg sodium, 13 g carb., 4 g fiber, 3 g pro.*

FAST FIX

French Market Sandwiches

I first tasted this warm ham and cheese sandwich at a luncheon, and it quickly became a favorite in our house. I keep some in the freezer for fast meals. My bridge club enjoys them with soup and fresh fruit.

—FLORENCE MCNULTY MONTEBELLO, CA

START TO FINISH: 25 MIN.
MAKES: 10 SERVINGS

- ½ **cup butter, softened**
- ½ **cup Dijon mustard**
- 2 **tablespoons chopped green onions**
- ½ **teaspoon poppy seeds**
- ¼ **teaspoon curry powder**
- 10 **croissants, split**
- 1¼ **pounds thinly sliced deli ham**
- 10 **slices Swiss cheese**

1. Preheat oven to 325°. In a small bowl, combine butter, mustard, onions, poppy seeds and curry powder. Spread over cut sides of croissants. Place ham and cheese on croissants; replace tops. Wrap individually in foil.
2. Bake 15-20 minutes or until heated through. Serve immediately.
PER SERVING *1 sandwich equals 476 cal., 30 g fat (18 g sat. fat), 108 mg chol., 1,303 mg sodium, 31 g carb., 2 g fiber, 21 g pro.*

FAST FIX

Dad's Cola Burgers

Before you hand out the drinks, save a little soda to make these delectable burgers. Cola really sparks the flavor—used in the meat mixture and brushed on during cooking, it takes this favorite to a whole new level.

—EMILY NELSON GREEN BAY, WI

START TO FINISH: 25 MIN.
MAKES: 6 SERVINGS

- ½ **cup crushed saltines (about 15 crackers)**
- ½ **cup (nondiet) cola, divided**
- 6 **tablespoons French salad dressing, divided**
- 1 **large egg**
- 2 **tablespoons grated Parmesan cheese**
- ½ **teaspoon salt, divided**
- 1½ **pounds lean ground beef (90% lean)**
- 6 **hamburger buns, split**
  Lettuce leaves and tomato and red onion slices, optional

1. Combine saltine crumbs, ¼ cup cola, 3 tablespoons salad dressing, egg, Parmesan and ¼ teaspoon salt. Add beef; mix well. Shape into six ¾-in.-thick patties (mixture will be moist); sprinkle with remaining salt. Combine remaining cola and salad dressing.
2. Grill patties, covered, over medium heat 3 minutes per side. Brush with cola mixture. Grill, brushing and turning occasionally, until a thermometer reads 160°, 3-4 minutes longer. Serve burgers on buns; if desired, top with lettuce, tomato and onion.
PER SERVING *1 burger equals 419 cal., 20 g fat (6 g sat. fat), 103 mg chol., 698 mg sodium, 30 g carb. (7 g sugars, 1 g fiber), 28 g pro.*

DAD'S COLA BURGERS

Snappy Tuna Melts

I lightened up a tuna melt by switching mayo to low-fat balsamic vinaigrette. Kids and adults both go for this quick meal hero.

—CHRISTINE SCHENHER EXETER, CA

START TO FINISH: 15 MIN.
MAKES: 4 SERVINGS

- 1 pouch (11 ounces) light tuna in water
- 1 hard-cooked large egg, chopped
- 2 tablespoons reduced-fat creamy balsamic vinaigrette
- 1 tablespoon stone-ground mustard, optional
- 4 whole wheat hamburger buns, split
- 8 slices tomato
- 8 slices reduced-fat Swiss cheese

1. In a small bowl, mix tuna, egg, vinaigrette and, if desired, mustard. Place buns on an ungreased baking sheet, cut side up. Broil 4-6 in. from heat 1-2 minutes or until golden brown.

2. Spread tuna mixture over buns; top with tomato and cheese. Broil 2-3 minutes longer or until cheese is melted.

PER SERVING *2 open-faced sandwiches equals 341 cal., 13 g fat (5 g sat. fat), 105 mg chol., 557 mg sodium, 27 g carb., 4 g fiber, 35 g pro. **Diabetic Exchanges:** 4 lean meat, 2 starch, 1 fat.*

SNAPPY TUNA MELTS

VEGGIE THAI CURRY SOUP

Veggie Thai Curry Soup

My go-to Thai restaurant inspired this curry soup. Shiitake mushrooms are my favorite, but any fresh mushroom will work. Fresh basil and lime add a burst of bright flavors.

—TRE BALCHOWSKY SAUSALITO, CA

START TO FINISH: 30 MIN.
MAKES: 6 SERVINGS

- 1 package (8.8 ounces) thin rice noodles or uncooked angel hair pasta
- 1 tablespoon sesame oil
- 2 tablespoons red curry paste
- 1 cup light coconut milk
- 1 carton (32 ounces) reduced-sodium vegetable or chicken broth
- 1 tablespoon reduced-sodium soy sauce or fish sauce
- 1 package (14 ounces) firm tofu, drained and cubed
- 1 can (8¾ ounces) whole baby corn, drained and cut in half
- 1 can (5 ounces) bamboo shoots, drained
- 1½ cups sliced fresh shiitake mushrooms
- ½ medium sweet red pepper, cut into thin strips
  Torn fresh basil leaves and lime wedges

1. Prepare noodles according to package directions.

2. Meanwhile, in a 6-qt. stockpot, heat oil over medium heat. Add the curry paste; cook 30 seconds or until aromatic. Gradually whisk in coconut milk until blended. Stir in broth and soy sauce; bring to a boil.

3. Add tofu and vegetables to the stockpot; cook 3-5 minutes or until vegetables are crisp-tender. Drain noodles; add to soup. Top each bowl with basil; serve with lime wedges.

PER SERVING *1⅔ cups equals 289 cal., 9 g fat (3 g sat. fat), 0 chol., 772 mg sodium, 41 g carb., 2 g fiber, 11 g pro. **Diabetic Exchanges:** 2½ starch, 1 medium-fat meat, ½ fat.*

Ham Barbecue

We have used this recipe for family gatherings and birthday parties many times. The sandwiches are so easy to make, and they taste great. I usually double the recipe so I have leftovers for lunches later in the week.

—JENNIFER MIDDLEKAUFF NEW HOLLAND, PA

PREP: 10 MIN. • **COOK:** 4 HOURS
MAKES: 12 SERVINGS

- 2 **pounds thinly sliced deli ham**
- 1 **cup water**
- 1 **cup ketchup**
- ¼ **cup packed brown sugar**
- ¼ **cup Worcestershire sauce**
- 2 **tablespoons white vinegar**
- 2 **teaspoons prepared mustard**
- 12 **hamburger buns, split and toasted**

Place the ham in a greased 3-qt. slow cooker. In a large bowl, combine water, ketchup, brown sugar, Worcestershire sauce, vinegar and mustard; pour over ham and stir well. Cover and cook on low 4-5 hours or until heated through. Serve on buns.

PER SERVING *1 sandwich equals 241 cal., 4 g fat (1 g sat. fat), 34 mg chol., 1,250 mg sodium, 34 g carb., 1 g fiber, 17 g pro.*

CHICKEN BAGEL MELTS

CLASSIC CREAM OF ASPARAGUS SOUP

FAST FIX

Chicken Bagel Melts

I love experimenting with sandwiches, and my wonderful husband is often my guinea pig when I try something new. Here's a great way to use up leftover chicken. It's a little on the spicy side, but we love it.

—SHANNON BROWN OMAHA, NE

START TO FINISH: 15 MIN.
MAKES: 4 SERVINGS

- ½ **cup mayonnaise**
- 4 **Asiago cheese bagels, split**
- ½ **pound sliced rotisserie chicken**
- 8 **strips ready-to-serve fully cooked bacon**
- ½ **medium sweet red pepper, sliced**
- 4 **slices cheddar cheese**
- ¼ **cup chipotle mustard**

1. Spread mayonnaise over bagel bottoms; layer with chicken, bacon, red pepper and cheese. Place on an ungreased baking sheet.

2. Broil 2-4 in. from the heat for 2-3 minutes or until cheese is melted. Spread mustard over bagel tops; place over cheese. Serve immediately.

PER SERVING *1 sandwich equals 838 cal., 45 g fat (15 g sat. fat), 100 mg chol., 1,332 mg sodium, 61 g carb., 2 g fiber, 43 g pro.*

FAST FIX

Classic Cream of Asparagus Soup

I created this recipe by substituting asparagus for broccoli in cream of broccoli soup. It's a big favorite at our house.

—WESTELLE GRISWA MONROE, CT

START TO FINISH: 30 MIN.
MAKES: 6 SERVINGS

- 4 **cups cut fresh asparagus (½-inch pieces)**
- 2 **cups water, divided**
- ¼ **cup finely chopped green onions or 1 teaspoon onion powder**
- 5 **tablespoons butter**
- 5 **tablespoons all-purpose flour**
- ½ **to 1 teaspoon salt**
- ¼ **teaspoon white pepper**
- 4 **cups milk**
- 1 **tablespoon chicken bouillon granules**

1. Place asparagus in a large saucepan and cover with 1 cup water. Bring to a boil, cover and cook for 3-5 minutes or until crisp-tender. Drain, reserving liquid.

2. In a another saucepan, saute onions in butter until tender. Stir in the flour, salt and pepper until blended. Gradually stir in the milk, bouillon, reserved cooking liquid and remaining water. Bring to a boil. Cook and stir for 2 minutes or until thickened and bubbly. Stir in the asparagus; heat through.

PER SERVING *1 cup equals 232 cal., 15 g fat (9 g sat. fat), 48 mg chol., 795 mg sodium, 17 g carb., 2 g fiber, 8 g pro.*

Pizza Soup

Dedicate just a few minutes of work to produce a tasty Italian soup unlike any you've had before. Sometimes I use bacon or salami instead of pepperoni.
—**JANET BELDMAN** LONDON, ON

PREP: 15 MIN. • **COOK:** 20 MIN.
MAKES: 6 SERVINGS

- 1 **pound ground beef**
- 1 **small onion, chopped**
- 1 **cup sliced fresh mushrooms**
- 1 **medium green pepper, cut into strips**
- 1 **can (28 ounces) diced tomatoes, undrained**
- 1 **cup beef broth**
- 1 **cup sliced pepperoni**
- 1 **teaspoon dried basil**
  Shredded mozzarella cheese

1. In a large saucepan, cook the beef, onion, mushrooms and green pepper over medium heat until the meat is no longer pink and vegetables are almost tender; drain. Stir in the tomatoes, broth, pepperoni and basil. Cook until heated through.
2. Ladle into ovenproof bowls; top with cheese. Broil or microwave until cheese melts and is bubbly.
PER SERVING *1 cup equals 245 cal., 15 g fat (6 g sat. fat), 59 mg chol., 621 mg sodium, 9 g carb., 3 g fiber, 18 g pro.*

WHERE'S THE BEEF

PIZZA SOUP

SLOW COOKER
Where's The Beef

This is particularly irresistible during winter months while cozying up for sporting events, game nights or movies.
—**CATHERINE CASSIDY** MILWAUKEE, WI

PREP: 30 MIN. • **COOK:** 7 HOURS
MAKES: 18 SERVINGS

- 1 **boneless beef chuck roast (4 to 5 pounds)**
- 4 **teaspoons Montreal steak seasoning**
- 3 **tablespoons butter**
- 1 **medium onion, chopped**
- 2 **celery ribs, chopped**
- 1 **small carrot, finely chopped**
- ½ **cup seeded and chopped pepperoncini**
- ½ **cup fresh basil leaves, thinly sliced**
- 4 **garlic cloves, minced**
- 2 **cups beef broth**
- 1½ **cups chili sauce**
- 1 **bottle (12 ounces) beer**
- 3 **tablespoons reduced-sodium soy sauce**
- 1 **tablespoon dried rosemary, crushed**
- 1 **bay leaf**
- ¼ **teaspoon salt**
- ¼ **teaspoon pepper**
ASSEMBLY
- 18 **mini buns, split**
  Additional chopped pepperoncini, sliced red onion, dill pickle slices and stone-ground mustard, optional

1. Trim roast; sprinkle with steak seasoning. Cut roast in half. In a large skillet, heat butter over medium heat; brown meat in batches. Transfer meat and drippings to a 6-qt. slow cooker. Add remaining ingredients. Cook, covered, on low 7-8 hours or until meat is tender.
2. Remove roast; cool slightly. Strain cooking juices, discarding vegetables and bay leaf; skim fat. Shred meat with two forks. Return meat and cooking juices to slow cooker; heat through. Using tongs, place meat on mini bun bottoms. Serve with cooking juices for dipping and toppings as desired.
PER SERVING *1 slider equals 305 cal., 13 g fat (5 g sat. fat), 72 mg chol., 973 mg sodium, 21 g carb., 1 g fiber, 23 g pro.*

Tomato Bisque

This rich and satisfying bisque is perfect for the cool weather. I love to serve it with a slice of homemade bread.

—**B.B. MALLORY** IRVING, TX

PREP: 25 MIN. • **COOK:** 35 MIN.
MAKES: 8 SERVINGS (2 QUARTS)

- 2 cans (14½ ounces each) diced tomatoes, undrained
- 2 teaspoons beef bouillon granules
- 1 tablespoon sugar
- 1 to 2 teaspoons salt
- 1 teaspoon onion powder
- 1 bay leaf
- ¼ teaspoon dried basil
- ¼ teaspoon white pepper
- ½ cup butter, cubed
- ⅓ cup all-purpose flour
- 4 cups milk

1. In a saucepan, combine the first eight ingredients; bring to a boil. Reduce heat; simmer, uncovered, for 30 minutes.

2. Discard bay leaf; press mixture through sieve and set aside. In a large saucepan, melt butter; stir in flour until smooth. Gradually stir in milk. Bring to a boil over medium heat, stirring constantly; cook and stir for 2 minutes. Reduce heat. Gradually stir in tomato mixture until smooth; heat through.

PER SERVING *1 cup equals 171 cal., 12 g fat (8 g sat. fat), 38 mg chol., 624 mg sodium, 11 g carb., trace fiber, 4 g pro.*

⑤ INGREDIENTS FAST FIX ▶

Portobello-Gouda Grilled Cheese

Take a simple grilled cheese sandwich to the next level with portobello mushrooms and Gouda cheese. Whip up a side of tomato soup, and lunch is done!

—**SHERYL BERGMAN** SHADY SIDE, MD

START TO FINISH: 20 MIN.
MAKES: 2 SERVINGS

- 1 cup sliced baby portobello mushrooms
- 1 tablespoon plus 4 teaspoons butter, divided
- 4 ounces smoked Gouda cheese, sliced
- 4 slices rye bread
- 1 plum tomato, sliced

TOMATO BISQUE

PORTOBELLO-GOUDA GRILLED CHEESE

1. In a large skillet, saute mushrooms in 1 tablespoon butter until tender. Place the cheese on two bread slices; top with mushrooms, tomato and remaining bread. Spread outsides of sandwiches with remaining butter.

2. In a small skillet over medium heat, toast sandwiches for 2-3 minutes on each side or until cheese is melted.

PER SERVING *1 sandwich equals 498 cal., 31 g fat (19 g sat. fat), 100 mg chol., 984 mg sodium, 35 g carb., 5 g fiber, 21 g pro.*

Zippy Chicken & Corn Chowder

Gently spiced corn chowder is always good for kids, but feel free to rev yours up with hot pepper sauce. This chowder is a lifesaver on busy weeknights.

—**ANDREA EARLY** HARRISONBURG, VA

PREP: 15 MIN. • **COOK:** 25 MIN.
MAKES: 8 SERVINGS (3 QUARTS)

- ¼ cup butter
- 1 large onion, chopped
- 1 medium green pepper, chopped
- ¼ cup all-purpose flour
- 1 tablespoon paprika
- 2 medium potatoes, peeled and chopped
- 1 carton (32 ounces) chicken broth
- 1 skinned rotisserie chicken, shredded
- 6 cups fresh or frozen corn
- 1 tablespoon Worcestershire sauce
- ½ to 1 teaspoon hot pepper sauce
- 1 teaspoon salt
- 1 cup 2% milk

1. In a stockpot, heat butter over medium-high heat. Add onion and pepper; cook, stirring, until vegetables are crisp-tender, 3-4 minutes. Stir in flour and paprika until blended.

2. Add potatoes; stir in broth. Bring to a boil; reduce heat and simmer, covered, until tender, 12-15 minutes.

3. Stir in chicken, corn, sauces and salt; bring to a boil. Reduce heat and cook, uncovered, until corn is tender, 4-6 minutes. Add milk; heat through (do not boil).

PER SERVING *1½ cups equals 351 cal., 12 g fat (5 g sat. fat), 75 mg chol., 920 mg sodium, 39 g carb. (7 g sugars, 4 g fiber), 25 g pro.*

Sloppy Ottos

My version of sloppy joes comes from an old family recipe. Give these sandwiches even more of a German flair by stacking the ingredients on a hearty pretzel bun.

—**JASON KOREN** MILWAUKEE, WI

START TO FINISH: 25 MIN.
MAKES: 8 SERVINGS

- 1 pound bulk spicy pork sausage
- 1½ cups sauerkraut, rinsed and well drained
- 2 medium green and/or sweet yellow peppers, chopped
- 1 medium onion, chopped
- 8 pretzel or regular hamburger buns, split
- 8 slices provolone cheese

1. Preheat oven to 350°. In a large skillet, cook sausage over medium heat 4-6 minutes or until no longer pink, breaking into crumbles; drain. Add sauerkraut, peppers and onion; cook and stir 8-10 minutes longer or until vegetables are tender.

2. Spoon meat mixture onto bun bottoms; place cheese over meat. Replace tops. Place on a baking sheet. Bake 4-6 minutes or until the cheese is melted.

PER SERVING *1 sandwich equals 494 cal., 24 g fat (7 g sat. fat), 46 mg chol., 1,042 mg sodium, 52 g carb., 3 g fiber, 20 g pro.*

SLOPPY OTTOS

BACON-POTATO CORN CHOWDER

Bacon-Potato Corn Chowder

I was raised on a farm, so a warm soup with homey ingredients, like this one, was always a treat after a chilly day outside. My hearty chowder nourishes the family.

—**KATIE LILLO** BIG LAKE, MN

START TO FINISH: 30 MIN.
MAKES: 6 SERVINGS

- ½ pound bacon strips, chopped
- ¼ cup chopped onion
- 1½ pounds Yukon Gold potatoes (about 5 medium), peeled and cubed
- 1 can (14¾ ounces) cream-style corn
- 1 can (12 ounces) evaporated milk
- ¼ teaspoon salt
- ¼ teaspoon pepper

1. In a large skillet, cook bacon over medium heat until crisp, stirring occasionally. Remove with a slotted spoon; drain on paper towels. Discard drippings, reserving 1½ teaspoons in pan. Add onion to drippings; cook and stir over medium-high heat until tender.

2. Meanwhile, place potatoes in a large saucepan; add water to cover. Bring to a boil over high heat. Reduce heat to medium; cook, uncovered, 10-15 minutes or until tender. Drain, reserving 1 cup potato water.

3. Add corn, milk, salt, pepper and reserved potato water to saucepan; heat through. Stir in bacon and onion.

PER SERVING *1 cup equals 271 cal., 11 g fat (5 g sat. fat), 30 mg chol., 555 mg sodium, 34 g carb., 2 g fiber, 10 g pro.*

TOP TIP

I buy several pounds of bacon when it's on sale. I put the strips in a single layer on jelly roll pans and pop them into the oven to bake at 350° until crisp. I then place the strips on paper towels to drain before storing them in single layers in a freezer container. It's easy to remove only the number of strips I need for a quick breakfast, sandwich or salad.

—**DALE H.** HOLLAND, MI

Grilled Seasoned Beer Bratwurst

For a savory take on an outdoor classic, this brat recipe is sure to please. Great summer eating for two can't get much easier.

—**MATTHEW HASS** FRANKLIN, WI

START TO FINISH: 25 MIN.
MAKES: 2 SERVINGS

- 2 uncooked turkey bratwurst links
- 1 can (12 ounces) beer or nonalcoholic beer
- 1 small onion, halved and sliced
- 1½ teaspoons fennel seed
- 2 brat buns, split and toasted

1. Place bratwurst in a large saucepan; add the beer, onion and fennel. Bring to a boil. Reduce heat; cover and simmer for 8-10 minutes or until the meat is no longer pink. Drain and discard beer mixture.
2. Grill the bratwurst, covered, over indirect medium heat for 7-8 minutes or until browned, turning occasionally. Serve bratwurst on buns with toppings of your choice.
PER SERVING *1 bratwurst with bun equals 440 cal., 21 g fat (5 g sat. fat), 75 mg chol., 1,052 mg sodium, 44 g carb., 2 g fiber, 23 g pro.*

BARBECUED BASIL TURKEY BURGERS

Barbecued Basil Turkey Burgers

My husband built me a patio planter for herbs, so I developed a turkey burger featuring fresh basil. We like to add toppings such as red onion, provolone and tomatoes.

—**DENISE MILLER** GREELEY, CO

START TO FINISH: 30 MIN.
MAKES: 4 SERVINGS

- ¼ cup chopped fresh basil
- 3 tablespoons mesquite smoke-flavored barbecue sauce
- 2 tablespoons quick-cooking oats or oat bran
- 1 garlic clove, minced
- ¼ teaspoon garlic salt
- ⅛ teaspoon pepper
- 1 pound lean ground turkey
- 4 whole wheat or multigrain hamburger buns, split
  Optional toppings: sliced provolone cheese, red onion slices, sliced tomato, fresh basil leaves and additional barbecue sauce

1. In a large bowl, combine basil, barbecue sauce, oats, garlic, garlic salt and pepper. Add turkey; mix lightly but thoroughly. Shape into four ½-in.-thick patties.
2. On a lightly greased grill rack, grill burgers, covered, over medium heat 5-7 minutes on each side or until a thermometer reads 165°. Grill buns over medium heat, cut side down, for 30-60 seconds or until toasted. Serve burgers on buns with toppings of your choice.
PER SERVING *1 burger (calculated without optional toppings) equals 315 cal., 11 g fat (3 g sat. fat), 78 mg chol., 482 mg sodium, 29 g carb., 4 g fiber, 27 g pro.* **Diabetic Exchanges:** *3 lean meat, 2 starch.*

Zippy Egg Salad

Egg salad is a refreshing, tasty change from lunch meat or peanut butter sandwiches. Everyone raves about this version with its touch of mustard and lemon juice.

—**ANNEMARIE PIETILA** FARMINGTON HILLS, MI

START TO FINISH: 10 MIN.
MAKES: 2 SERVINGS

- 3 tablespoons mayonnaise
- 1½ teaspoons prepared mustard
- ⅛ teaspoon salt
- ⅛ teaspoon pepper
- ⅛ teaspoon lemon juice
- 3 hard-cooked large eggs, coarsely chopped
- 1 tablespoon minced green onion
  Bread or crackers
  Sliced tomato, optional

In a small bowl, combine the mayonnaise, mustard, salt, pepper and lemon juice. Stir in eggs and onion. Serve on bread or crackers; top with tomato if desired.
PER SERVING *¼ cup equals 270 cal., 25 g fat (5 g sat. fat), 326 mg chol., 396 mg sodium, 1 g carb., trace fiber, 10 g pro.*

**WENDY BALL'S
MAKE-AHEAD CREAMY POTATOES**
PAGE 63

Side Dishes & Condiments

For summertime **cookouts,** Christmas **dinners** and everything in between, look here for the homey and **special sides** that make for **memorable meals.** Savor from-scratch pickles and relishes, too.

DANYELLE CRUM'S GRILLED VEGGIES WITH CAPER BUTTER *PAGE 63*

ANGELA LEMOINE'S ROASTED ACORN SQUASH & BRUSSELS SPROUTS *PAGE 55*

MELISSA PELKEY HASS' SLOW COOKER CREAMED CORN WITH BACON *PAGE 54*

Easy Strawberry Butter

After strawberry picking for the first time, I came up with this fruity butter. You can make other fruit variations using fresh raspberries or blackberries, or even seedless jams—like apricot, my favorite jam version.

—JULIE HERRERA-LEMLER ROCHESTER, MN

START TO FINISH: 5 MIN.
MAKES: 2¼ CUPS

- 6 **large fresh strawberries, stems removed and room temperature**
- 1 **cup butter, softened**
- ¾ **to 1 cup confectioners' sugar**

Pulse strawberries in a food processor until chopped. Add butter and ½ cup confectioners' sugar; process until blended. Add enough remaining confectioners' sugar to reach a spreading consistency and your desired level of sweetness. Store in the refrigerator.

PER SERVING *1 tablespoon equals 56 cal., 5 g fat (3 g sat. fat), 14 mg chol., 41 mg sodium, 3 g carb., 0 fiber, 0 pro.*

Roasted Grapes

Roasting these little sweeties transforms them into something really special. Sprinkle grapes onto salads or serve with grilled meats.

—TASTE OF HOME TEST KITCHEN

START TO FINISH: 20 MIN.
MAKES: 2 CUPS

- 3 **cups seedless red grapes**
- 2 **teaspoons canola oil**
- 2 **fresh thyme or rosemary sprigs**
- ½ **teaspoon sea salt**

Toss all ingredients together and roast at 450° just until grape skins start to split, about 15 minutes.

QUINOA TABBOULEH

Quinoa Tabbouleh

When my mom and sister developed several food allergies, we had to modify many recipes. I substituted quinoa for couscous in this tabbouleh, and now we make it all the time.

—JENNIFER KLANN CORBETT, OR

PREP: 35 MIN. + CHILLING
MAKES: 8 SERVINGS

- 2 **cups water**
- 1 **cup quinoa, rinsed**
- 1 **can (15 ounces) black beans, rinsed and drained**
- 1 **small cucumber, peeled and chopped**
- 1 **small sweet red pepper, chopped**
- ⅓ **cup minced fresh parsley**
- ¼ **cup lemon juice**
- 2 **tablespoons olive oil**
- ½ **teaspoon salt**
- ½ **teaspoon pepper**

1. In a large saucepan, bring water to a boil. Add quinoa. Reduce heat; cover and simmer for 12-15 minutes or until liquid is absorbed. Remove from the heat; fluff with a fork. Transfer to a bowl; cool completely.

2. Add the beans, cucumber, red pepper and parsley. In a small bowl, whisk the remaining ingredients; drizzle over salad and toss to coat. Refrigerate until chilled.

NOTE *Look for quinoa in the cereal, rice or organic food aisle.*

PER SERVING *¾ cup equals 159 cal., 5 g fat (1 g sat. fat), 0 chol., 255 mg sodium, 24 g carb., 4 g fiber, 6 g pro.*
Diabetic Exchanges: 1½ starch, 1 fat.

End of Garden Relish

We dollop this tangy relish on burgers, hot dogs and salads. It's a cool way to use up garden produce, and people love it at picnics and potlucks.

—**KAREN STUCKY** FREEMAN, SD

PREP: 45 MIN. + STANDING
PROCESS: 20 MIN.
MAKES: 6 PINTS

- 7 **large cucumbers, shredded**
- 3 **large onions, finely chopped**
- 3 **cups shredded carrots**
- 2 **medium sweet red peppers, finely chopped**
- 5 **tablespoons salt**
- 5 **cups sugar**
- 3 **cups white vinegar**
- 1 **tablespoon celery seed**
- 1 **tablespoon mustard seed**

1. Toss first five ingredients; let stand 3 hours. Drain; squeeze and blot dry with paper towels.

2. In a Dutch oven, mix sugar, vinegar, celery seed and mustard seed; bring to a boil. Reduce the heat; simmer, uncovered, 5 minutes. Add vegetables; bring to a boil. Reduce heat; simmer, uncovered, 20 minutes.

3. Ladle hot mixture into hot 1-pint jars, leaving ½-in. headspace. Remove air bubbles and adjust headspace, if necessary, by adding hot mixture. Wipe rims. Center lids on jars; screw on bands until fingertip tight.

4. Place the jars into a canner with simmering water, ensuring that they are completely covered with water. Bring to a boil; process for 20 minutes. Remove jars and cool.

NOTE *The processing time listed is for altitudes of 1,000 feet or less. For altitudes up to 3,000 feet, add 5 minutes; 6,000 feet, add 10 minutes; 8,000 feet, add 15 minutes; 10,000 feet, add 20 minutes.*

PER SERVING *2 tablespoons equals 8 cal., 0 fat (0 sat. fat), 0 chol., 7 mg sodium, 2 g carb., 0 fiber, 0 pro.*
Diabetic Exchange: *Free food.*

Orange-Glazed Carrots, Onions & Radishes

PREP: 15 MIN. • **COOK:** 20 MIN.
MAKES: 8 SERVINGS

- 1 **pound fresh pearl onions**
- ¼ **cup butter, cubed**
- 2 **pounds medium carrots, thinly sliced**
- 12 **radishes, thinly sliced**
- ½ **cup dark brown sugar**
- 4 **teaspoons grated orange peel**
- ½ **cup orange juice**
- 1 **cup chopped walnuts, toasted**

1. In a large saucepan, bring 4 cups water to a boil. Add pearl onions; boil 3 minutes. Drain and rinse with cold water. Peel.

2. In a large skillet, heat butter over medium heat. Add the carrots, pearl onions, radishes, brown sugar, orange peel and orange juice; cook, covered, for 10-15 minutes or until vegetables are tender, stirring occasionally. Cook, uncovered, 5-7 minutes longer or until slightly thickened. Sprinkle with walnuts.

NOTE *To toast nuts, bake in a shallow pan in a 350° oven for 5-10 minutes or cook in a skillet over low heat until lightly browned, stirring occasionally.*
PER SERVING *¾ cup equals 277 cal., 16 g fat (5 g sat. fat), 15 mg chol., 141 mg sodium, 34 g carb., 5 g fiber, 4 g pro.*

> Carrots and radishes give crunch to this sweet and spicy side. We never have leftovers. If you make it ahead, reheat it and add walnuts before serving.
> —**THOMAS FAGLON** SOMERSET, NJ

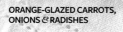

ORANGE-GLAZED CARROTS, ONIONS & RADISHES

Slow Cooker Creamed Corn with Bacon

Every time we take this rich corn to a get-together, we leave with an empty slow cooker. It's decadent, homey and so worth the splurge.

—MELISSA PELKEY HASS WALESKA, GA

PREP: 10 MIN. • **COOK:** 4 HOURS
MAKES: 20 SERVINGS (½ CUP EACH)

- 10 cups frozen corn (about 50 ounces), thawed
- 3 packages (8 ounces each) cream cheese, cubed
- ½ cup 2% milk
- ½ cup heavy whipping cream
- ½ cup butter, melted
- ¼ cup sugar
- 2 teaspoons salt
- ¼ teaspoon pepper
- 4 bacon strips, cooked and crumbled
  Chopped green onions

In a 5-qt. slow cooker, combine the first eight ingredients. Cook, covered, on low for 4-5 hours or until heated through. Stir just before serving. Sprinkle with bacon and green onions.
PER SERVING *1/2 cup equals 259 cal., 20 g fat (11 g sat. fat), 60 mg chol., 433 mg sodium, 18 g carb., 1 g fiber, 5 g pro.*

EAT SMART FAST FIX

Green Beans in Red Pepper Sauce

For easy veggies, I make a simple sauce of sweet red peppers, almonds and parsley. We also like the sauce with zucchini or roasted cauliflower.

—ELISABETH LARSEN PLEASANT GROVE, UT

START TO FINISH: 30 MIN.
MAKES: 6 SERVINGS

- 1 pound fresh green beans, trimmed
- ½ cup roasted sweet red peppers
- ¼ cup sliced almonds
- 2 tablespoons olive oil
- 2 tablespoons minced fresh parsley
- 2 tablespoons lemon juice
- 2 garlic cloves, halved
- ½ teaspoon salt

Place beans in a large saucepan; add water to cover. Bring to a boil. Cook, covered, until crisp-tender, about 2-4 minutes. Drain. Pulse remaining ingredients in a food processor until smooth. Toss with beans.
PER SERVING *3/4 cup equals 95 cal., 7 g fat (1g sat. fat), 0 chol., 276 mg sodium, 8 g carb. (3 g sugars, 3 g fiber), 2 g pro. Diabetic Exchanges: 1 vegetable, 1 fat.*

Grandma's Corn Bread Dressing

This dish was inspired by my grandma's recipe, which we had at every holiday dinner. Although she prepared hers with chicken that was cut into individual pieces and baked in with the dressing, my recipe bakes the dressing with no chicken in the pan.

—SUZANNE MOHME BASTROP, TX

PREP: 40 MIN. + COOLING • **BAKE:** 45 MIN.
MAKES: 12 SERVINGS (2/3 CUP EACH)

- 1 cup all-purpose flour
- 1 cup cornmeal
- 2 teaspoons baking powder
- 1 teaspoon salt
- 2 large eggs
- 1 cup buttermilk
- ¼ cup canola oil

DRESSING

- 1 tablespoon canola oil
- 1 medium onion, chopped
- 2 celery ribs, chopped
- 3 large eggs
- 2 cans (10¾ ounces each) condensed cream of chicken soup, undiluted
- 3 teaspoons poultry seasoning
- 1 teaspoon pepper
- ½ teaspoon salt
- 2 cups chicken broth

1. Preheat oven to 400°. In a large bowl, whisk flour, cornmeal, baking powder and salt. In another bowl, whisk eggs and buttermilk. Pour oil into an 8-in. ovenproof skillet; place skillet in oven 4 minutes.

2. Meanwhile, add buttermilk mixture to flour mixture; stir just until moistened.

3. Carefully tilt and rotate skillet to coat bottom with oil; add batter. Bake 20-25 minutes or until a toothpick inserted in center comes out clean. Cool completely in pan on a wire rack.

4. Reduce oven setting to 350°. For the dressing, in a large skillet, heat oil over medium-high heat. Add the onion and celery; cook and stir for 4-6 minutes or until tender. Remove from heat. Coarsely crumble corn bread into skillet; toss to combine. In a small bowl, whisk eggs, condensed soup and seasonings; stir into bread mixture. Stir in broth.

5. Transfer to a greased 13x9-in. baking dish. Bake 45-55 minutes or until lightly browned.
PER SERVING *2/3 cup equals 236 cal., 12 g fat (2 g sat. fat), 83 mg chol., 969 mg sodium, 25 g carb., 2 g fiber, 7 g pro.*

GRANDMA'S CORN BREAD DRESSING

**PATRIOTIC POTATOES
WITH MUSTARD SAUCE**

¼ teaspoon pepper
1¾ cups pecan halves
¼ cup maple syrup
3 tablespoons butter

1. Preheat oven to 375°. Cut squash lengthwise into quarters; remove and discard seeds. Cut each quarter crosswise into ½-in. slices; discard ends. Trim and halve Brussels sprouts.
2. Place squash and Brussels sprouts in a large bowl. Drizzle with olive oil; sprinkle with salt and pepper and toss to coat. Transfer to two foil-lined 15x10x1-in. baking pans. Roast for 30-35 minutes or until vegetables are tender, stirring occasionally.
3. Meanwhile, in a dry large skillet, toast pecans over medium-low heat 6-8 minutes or until lightly browned, stirring frequently. Stir in syrup and butter; cook until butter is melted.
4. Sprinkle vegetables with pecan mixture; gently toss to combine.
PER SERVING *¾ cup equals 300 cal., 24 g fat (5 g sat. fat), 11 mg chol., 198 mg sodium, 23 g carb., 5 g fiber, 4 g pro.*

Patriotic Potatoes with Mustard Sauce

Show your true spirit with a bowl of red, white and blue potatoes dressed with bacon and sour cream. They're tops in my hit parade of patriotic dishes.
—**JULIE MURPHY** PEACHTREE CITY, GA

PREP: 10 MIN. • **BAKE:** 30 MIN.
MAKES: 8 SERVINGS

8 small red potatoes
8 small white potatoes
8 small blue potatoes
3 tablespoons canola oil
1 garlic clove, minced
¼ teaspoon salt
¼ teaspoon dried basil
⅛ teaspoon pepper
SAUCE
6 bacon strips, cooked and crumbled
⅔ cup sour cream
⅓ cup mayonnaise
¼ cup stone-ground mustard
1 tablespoon brown sugar
2 teaspoons minced fresh chives
¼ teaspoon paprika

1. Preheat oven to 425°. Toss together the first eight ingredients. Transfer to a shallow roasting pan. Roast until tender, about 30-35 minutes, stirring occasionally.
2. Mix sauce ingredients. Serve with potatoes.
PER SERVING *3 potatoes with about 2 tablespoons sauce equals 300 cal., 19 g fat (4 g sat. fat), 23 mg chol., 402 mg sodium, 26 g carb., 3 g fiber, 6 g pro.*

⑤INGREDIENTS

Roasted Acorn Squash & Brussels Sprouts

I love creating dishes with few ingredients and easy steps, like squash with Brussels sprouts. Maple syrup adds a slight sweetness, and pecans give it a toasty crunch.
—**ANGELA LEMOINE** HOWELL, NJ

PREP: 15 MIN. • **BAKE:** 30 MIN.
MAKES: 8 SERVINGS

1 medium acorn squash
1 pound fresh Brussels sprouts
2 tablespoons olive oil
½ teaspoon salt

⑤INGREDIENTS FAST FIX ▶

Parmesan Asparagus

Nothing could be more simple than this tasty side dish. With just four ingredients, it's assembled in no time. Then I pop it into the oven, and it turns out perfect every time.
—**MARY ANN MARINO** WEST PITTSBURGH, PA

START TO FINISH: 20 MIN.
MAKES: 10-12 SERVINGS

4 pounds fresh asparagus, trimmed
¼ pound butter, melted
2 cups shredded Parmesan cheese
½ teaspoon pepper

1. In a large saucepan, bring ½ in. of water to a boil. Add asparagus; cover and boil for 3 minutes or until crisp-tender. Drain.
2. Arrange the asparagus in a greased 13x9-in. baking dish. Drizzle with the butter; sprinkle with Parmesan cheese and pepper. Bake, uncovered, at 350° for 10-15 minutes or until cheese is melted.
PER SERVING *107 cal., 8 g fat (5 g sat. fat), 20 mg chol., 273 mg sodium, 4 g carb., 1 g fiber, 7 g pro.*

EAT SMART
Smoky Quinoa with Mushrooms

Add quinoa cooked with smoked paprika to your list of top sides. Instead of leaving the spinach uncooked, you can quickly saute the leaves if desired.

—**ELLEN KANNER** MIAMI, FL

PREP: 15 MIN. • **COOK:** 35 MIN.
MAKES: 4 SERVINGS

- 4 teaspoons olive oil
- 1 pound sliced fresh mushrooms
- 3 garlic cloves, minced
- 3 tablespoons tomato paste
- 2 tablespoons smoked paprika
- 2 tablespoons lemon juice
- 1 teaspoon ground cumin
- ½ teaspoon salt
- 1 cup water or vegetable broth
- ¾ cup quinoa, rinsed
- 4 cups fresh baby spinach
  Minced fresh cilantro and lemon wedges

1. In a large saucepan, heat oil over medium-high heat. Add mushrooms; cook and stir for 6-8 minutes or until tender. Add the garlic; cook 1 minute longer. Reduce heat to medium-low; cook, covered, 10 minutes.

2. Stir in the tomato paste, paprika, lemon juice, cumin and salt until blended. Add water; bring to a boil. Add quinoa. Reduce heat; simmer, covered, for 15-18 minutes or until liquid is absorbed. Remove from the heat; fluff with a fork.

3. Arrange spinach on a serving plate; top with quinoa. Sprinkle with cilantro; serve with lemon wedges.

PER SERVING *217 cal., 8 g fat (1 g sat. fat), 0 chol., 337 mg sodium, 31 g carb., 6 g fiber, 10 g pro.* **Diabetic Exchanges:** *2 vegetable, 1½ starch, 1 fat.*

TOP TIP

Smoked paprika's rich, smoky flavor adds complexity to dishes. The spice is especially good in vegetable and bean recipes, where it lends a robust, meaty taste. You can also use it in recipes that call for ground chipotle pepper. Add cayenne or chili powder to boost the heat if desired.

ROASTED CARROTS & FENNEL

SMOKY QUINOA WITH MUSHROOMS

EAT SMART
Roasted Carrots & Fennel

This addictive combo is a fresh take on one of my mother's standard wintertime dishes. I usually add even more carrots—as many as the baking pans will hold.

—**LILY JULOW** LAWRENCEVILLE, GA

PREP: 15 MIN. • **BAKE:** 40 MIN.
MAKES: 8 SERVINGS

- 2½ pounds medium carrots, cut in half lengthwise
- 1 large fennel bulb, cut into ½-inch wedges
- 1 large red onion, cut into ½-inch wedges
- 1 medium lemon, thinly sliced
- ¼ cup olive oil
- 2 teaspoons ground coriander
- 1 teaspoon ground cumin
- ½ teaspoon salt
- ¼ teaspoon pepper
  Thinly sliced fresh basil leaves

1. Preheat oven to 375°. In a large bowl, combine carrots, fennel, onion and lemon. Mix oil, coriander, cumin, salt and pepper; drizzle over carrot mixture and toss to coat. Transfer to two foil-lined 15x10x1-in. baking pans.

2. Roast for 40-50 minutes or until the vegetables are tender, stirring occasionally. Sprinkle with basil.

PER SERVING *139 cal., 7 g fat (1 g sat. fat), 0 chol., 262 mg sodium, 18 g carb., 6 g fiber, 2 g pro.* **Diabetic Exchanges:** *2 vegetable, 1½ fat.*

Curried Sweet Potato Wedges

Sweet potatoes roasted with curry powder and smoked paprika delight everybody at our table. The mango chutney makes a tangy dip.

—**MAITREYI JOIS** STREAMWOOD, IL

START TO FINISH: 25 MIN.
MAKES: 4 SERVINGS

- 2 **medium sweet potatoes (about 1 pound), cut into ½-inch wedges**
- 2 **tablespoons olive oil**
- 1 **teaspoon curry powder**
- ½ **teaspoon salt**
- ½ **teaspoon smoked paprika**
- ⅛ **teaspoon coarsely ground pepper**
  Minced fresh cilantro
  Mango chutney, optional

1. Preheat oven to 425°. Place sweet potatoes in a large bowl. Mix oil and seasonings; drizzle over the sweet potatoes and toss to coat. Transfer to an ungreased 15x10x1-in. baking pan.
2. Roast 15-20 minutes or until tender, turning occasionally. Sprinkle with cilantro. If desired, serve with chutney.
PER SERVING (calculated without chutney) 159 cal., 7 g fat (1 g sat. fat), 0 chol., 305 mg sodium, 23 g carb., 3 g fiber, 2 g pro. **Diabetic Exchanges:** 1½ starch, 1½ fat.

Microwave Pickles

You can enjoy a small batch of sweet, crunchy pickles anytime without the work of traditional canning methods. They're loaded with flavor and so easy to make.

—**MARIE WLADYKA** LAND O'LAKES, FL

PREP: 10 MIN. + CHILLING
MAKES: 4-6 SERVINGS

- 1 **medium cucumber, thinly sliced**
- 2 **small onions, thinly sliced**
- ¾ **cup sugar**
- ½ **cup vinegar**
- 1 **teaspoon salt**
- ½ **teaspoon celery seed**
- ½ **teaspoon mustard seed**

In a large microwave-safe bowl, combine all of the ingredients. Microwave, uncovered, on high for 3 minutes; stir. Cook 2-3 minutes longer or until mixture is bubbly and cucumbers and onions are crisp-tender. Cover and refrigerate for at least 4 hours. Serve with a slotted spoon.
PER SERVING 115 cal., trace fat (trace sat. fat), 0 chol., 395 mg sodium, 29 g carb., 1 g fiber, 1 g pro.

Simple Vegetarian Slow-Cooked Beans

When I have a hungry family to feed, these tasty beans with spinach, tomatoes and carrots are a go-to dish. This veggie delight is frequently on the menu.

—**JENNIFER REID** FARMINGTON, ME

PREP: 15 MIN. • **COOK:** 4 HOURS
MAKES: 8 SERVINGS

- 4 **cans (15½ ounces each) great northern beans, rinsed and drained**
- 4 **medium carrots, finely chopped (about 2 cups)**
- 1 **cup vegetable stock**
- 6 **garlic cloves, minced**
- 2 **teaspoons ground cumin**
- ¾ **teaspoon salt**
- ⅛ **teaspoon chili powder**
- 4 **cups fresh baby spinach, coarsely chopped**
- 1 **cup oil-packed sun-dried tomatoes, patted dry and chopped**
- ⅓ **cup minced fresh cilantro**
- ⅓ **cup minced fresh parsley**

In a 3-qt. slow cooker, combine the first seven ingredients. Cook, covered, on low 4-5 hours or until carrots are tender, adding spinach and tomatoes during the last 10 minutes of cooking. Stir in cilantro and parsley.
PER SERVING ¾ cup equals 229 cal., 3 g fat (trace sat. fat), 0 chol., 672 mg sodium, 40 g carb., 13 g fiber, 12 g pro.

SIMPLE VEGETARIAN
SLOW-COOKED BEANS

EAT SMART **FAST FIX**
Rice Pilaf with Apples & Raisins

I've been adding apricots to my rice pilaf for a long time. So glad I swapped in dried apples and golden raisins one day.
—**ELIZABETH DUMONT** MADISON, MS

START TO FINISH: 25 MIN.
MAKES: 4 SERVINGS

- 2 tablespoons olive oil
- 1 small onion, finely chopped
- 1 cup uncooked jasmine rice
- 1½ cups water
- ¼ cup chopped dried apples
- ¼ cup golden raisins
- 1 teaspoon salt
- ¼ teaspoon dried thyme
- ¼ teaspoon ground allspice
- ¼ teaspoon ground cinnamon
- ⅛ teaspoon cayenne pepper

1. In a large saucepan, heat oil over medium heat. Add onion; cook and stir 4-6 minutes or until tender. Add rice; cook and stir 4-6 minutes or until rice is lightly browned.
2. Add remaining ingredients; bring to a boil. Reduce heat; simmer, covered, 15-20 minutes or until liquid is absorbed and rice is tender. Fluff with a fork.
PER SERVING ¾ cup equals 277 cal., 7 g fat (1 g sat. fat), 0 chol., 599 mg sodium, 50 g carb., 2 g fiber, 4 g pro.

EAT SMART **FAST FIX**
Rainbow Hash

To get my family to eat outside their comfort zone, I use lots of color. This tasty hash combines sweet potato, carrot, purple potato and kale.
—**COURTNEY STULTZ** WEIR, KS

START TO FINISH: 30 MIN.
MAKES: 2 SERVINGS

- 2 tablespoons olive or coconut oil
- 1 medium sweet potato, peeled and cubed
- 1 medium purple potato, peeled and cubed
- 1 large carrot, peeled and cubed
- ½ teaspoon dried oregano
- ½ teaspoon dried basil
- ½ teaspoon sea salt
- ½ teaspoon pepper
- 2 cups fresh kale or spinach, coarsely chopped
- 1 small garlic clove, minced

In a large skillet, heat oil over medium heat. Cook and stir potatoes, carrot and seasonings until vegetables are tender, about 10-12 minutes. Add kale and garlic; continue cooking until vegetables are lightly browned and kale is tender, 2-4 minutes.
PER SERVING 1 cup equals 304 cal., 14 g fat (2 g sat. fat), 0 chol., 523 mg sodium, 43 g carb. (12 g sugars, 5 g fiber), 4 g pro.

EAT SMART **FAST FIX**
Green Beans & Radishes with Tarragon Pesto

Whichever way my garden grows, I usually build my salad with green beans, radishes and a pesto made with tarragon. That adds a hint of licorice.
—**LILY JULOW** LAWRENCEVILLE, GA

START TO FINISH: 25 MIN.
MAKES: 10 SERVINGS

- 1½ pounds fresh green beans, trimmed
- 2 cups thinly sliced radishes
- ½ cup pecan or walnut pieces, toasted
- ¼ cup tarragon leaves
- 3 tablespoons grated Parmesan cheese
- ½ garlic clove
- ¼ teaspoon coarse sea salt or kosher salt
- ⅛ teaspoon crushed red pepper flakes
- 1½ teaspoons white wine vinegar
- ¼ cup olive oil

1. In a 6-qt. stockpot, bring 8 cups water to a boil. Add beans in batches; cook, uncovered, 2-3 minutes or just until crisp-tender. Remove beans and immediately drop into ice water. Drain and pat dry. Toss together beans and radishes.
2. Place pecans, tarragon, cheese, garlic, salt and pepper flakes in a small food processor; pulse until chopped. Add vinegar; process until blended. Continue processing while gradually adding oil in a steady stream. Toss with bean mixture.
PER SERVING 1 cup equals 115 cal., 10 g fat (1 g sat. fat), 1 mg chol., 89 mg sodium, 7 g carb., 3 g fiber, 2 g pro.
Diabetic Exchanges: 2 fat, 1 vegetable.

GREEN BEANS & RADISHES WITH TARRAGON PESTO

Belarus Pickled Carrots

My mom's holiday buffet always included pickled carrots. I kept the tradition going and passed the recipe to my daughter. A buffet isn't complete without them.

—LILY JULOW LAWRENCEVILLE, GA

PREP: 15 MIN. + CHILLING
MAKES: 10 SERVINGS

- 2 pounds medium carrots, cut diagonally into ⅛-inch slices
- 3 bay leaves
- 2 teaspoons caraway seeds
- 2 cups water
- 1 cup sugar
- 1 cup cider vinegar
- 2 tablespoons kosher salt

1. Place carrots and bay leaves in a large bowl. In a dry small saucepan, toast caraway seeds over medium heat 1-2 minutes or until aromatic, stirring frequently. Stir in water, sugar, vinegar and salt. Bring to a boil. Pour over carrots. Refrigerate, covered, overnight to allow flavors to blend.
2. Transfer mixture to covered jars. Refrigerate up to 1 month.
PER SERVING ¼ *cup equals 38 cal., trace fat (trace sat. fat), 0 chol., 74 mg sodium, 9 g carb., 3 g fiber, 1 g pro.*

Yellow Summer Squash Relish

My friends can barely wait for the growing season to arrive so I can make this incredible relish. The color really dresses up a hot dog.

—RUTH HAWKINS JACKSON, MS

PREP: 1 HOUR + MARINATING
PROCESS: 15 MIN.
MAKES: 6 PINTS

- 10 cups shredded yellow summer squash (about 4 pounds)
- 2 large onions, chopped
- 1 large green pepper, chopped
- 6 tablespoons canning salt
- 4 cups sugar
- 3 cups cider vinegar
- 1 tablespoon each celery seed, ground mustard and ground turmeric
- ½ teaspoon ground nutmeg
- ½ teaspoon pepper

ROASTED SWEET POTATOES
WITH DIJON & ROSEMARY

1. In a large container, combine squash, onions, green pepper and salt. Cover and refrigerate overnight. Drain; rinse and drain again.
2. In a Dutch oven, combine sugar, vinegar and seasonings; bring to a boil. Add squash mixture; return to a boil. Reduce heat; simmer 15 minutes. Remove from heat.
3. Carefully ladle hot mixture into six hot 1-pint jars, leaving ½-in. headspace. Remove air bubbles and adjust headspace, if necessary, by adding hot mixture. Wipe rims. Center lids on jars; screw on bands until fingertip tight.
4. Place jars into canner with simmering water, ensuring that they are completely covered with water. Bring to a boil; process for 15 minutes. Remove jars and cool. Refrigerate remaining relish for up to 1 week.
NOTE *The processing time listed is for altitudes of 1,000 feet or less. For altitudes up to 3,000 feet, add 5 minutes; 6,000 feet, add 10 minutes; 8,000 feet, add 15 minutes; 10,000 feet, add 20 minutes.*
PER SERVING ¼ *cup equals 36 cal., trace fat (trace sat. fat), 0 chol., 197 mg sodium, 8 g carb., 2 g fiber, 1 g pro.*

Roasted Sweet Potatoes with Dijon & Rosemary

After moving to Alabama, I learned that my friends and co-workers love sweet potatoes. I roast the potatoes with Dijon, fresh rosemary and a touch of honey.

—TAMARA HURON NEW MARKET, AL

PREP: 10 MIN. • **BAKE:** 25 MIN.
MAKES: 4 SERVINGS

- 2 medium sweet potatoes (about 1½ pounds)
- 2 tablespoons olive oil
- 2 teaspoons Dijon mustard
- 2 teaspoons honey
- 1 teaspoon minced fresh rosemary or ¼ teaspoon dried rosemary, crushed
- ¼ teaspoon salt
- ¼ teaspoon pepper

Preheat oven to 400°. Peel and cut each sweet potato lengthwise into ½-in.-thick wedges; place in a large bowl. Mix remaining ingredients; drizzle over potatoes and toss to coat. Transfer to a greased 15x10x1-in. baking pan. Roast 25-30 minutes or until tender, stirring occasionally.
PER SERVING *170 cal., 7 g fat (1 g sat. fat), 0 chol., 217 mg sodium, 26 g carb., 3 g fiber, 2 g pro.* **Diabetic Exchanges:** *2 starch, 1½ fat.*

RICH & CREAMY PARMESAN
MASHED POTATOES

Parmesan cheese and salt; heat through. If desired, serve with butter and additional Parmesan cheese.

PER SERVING ⅔ cup (calculated without butter and additional Parmesan cheese) equals 199 cal., 7 g fat (4 g sat. fat), 24 mg chol., 612 mg sodium, 26 g carb., 3 g fiber, 8 g pro. **Diabetic Exchanges:** 2 starch, 1½ fat.

I've made many types of scalloped potatoes, but I always come back to this rich, creamy and fail-proof recipe. This is a dish where the bottom gets scraped clean.

KALLEE KRONG-MCCREERY
ESCONDIDO, CA

EAT SMART ⑤INGREDIENTS FAST FIX

Super Simple Scalloped Potatoes

PREP: 20 MIN. • **BAKE:** 45 MIN. + STANDING
MAKES: 10 SERVINGS

- 3 cups heavy whipping cream
- 1½ teaspoons salt
- ½ teaspoon pepper
- 1 teaspoon minced fresh thyme, optional
- 3 pounds russet potatoes, thinly sliced (about 10 cups)

1. Preheat oven to 350°. In a large bowl, combine cream, salt, pepper and, if desired, thyme. Arrange potatoes in a greased 13x9-in. baking dish. Pour cream mixture over top.
2. Bake, uncovered, 45-55 minutes or until potatoes are tender and top is lightly browned. Let stand 10 minutes before serving.

PER SERVING ¾ cup equals 353 cal., 27 g fat (17 g sat. fat), 99 mg chol., 390 mg sodium, 26 g carb., 3 g fiber, 4 g pro.

SUPER SIMPLE
SCALLOPED POTATOES

EAT SMART ⑤INGREDIENTS

Rich & Creamy Parmesan Mashed Potatoes

For special occasions (like my husband's birthday dinners), I mash my potatoes with cream cheese, sour cream and Parmesan. It's divine comfort food.
—**JO ANN BURRINGTON** OSCEOLA, IN

PREP: 15 MIN. • **COOK:** 25 MIN.
MAKES: 6 SERVINGS

- 2 pounds red potatoes, cut into ½-inch cubes (about 6 cups)
- 1 cup chicken broth
- 4 ounces reduced-fat cream cheese
- ½ cup reduced-fat sour cream
- ¼ cup grated Parmesan cheese
- ¾ teaspoon salt
  Butter and additional grated Parmesan cheese, optional

1. Place potatoes in a large saucepan; add broth. Bring to a boil. Reduce heat; simmer, covered, 15-20 minutes or until potatoes are tender. Uncover; cook 4-6 minutes longer or until the broth is almost evaporated, stirring occasionally.
2. Reduce heat to low; stir in cream cheese until melted. Mash potatoes slightly, gradually adding sour cream,

Tangy Baked Seven Beans

Everyone needs a go-to side dish for school events, picnics and potlucks. Here's mine. Freeze leftovers for future outings.

—ROD LUNDWALL TOOELE, UT

PREP: 30 MIN. • **BAKE:** 1 HOUR
MAKES: 18 SERVINGS (¾ CUP EACH)

- 1 **pound bacon strips, chopped**
- 1 **large onion, chopped**
- 1 **large sweet yellow pepper, chopped**
- 1 **large sweet red pepper, chopped**
- 6 **garlic cloves, minced**
- 1 **teaspoon ground chipotle pepper**
- ½ **teaspoon pepper**
- 2 **cans (15 ounces each) pork and beans**
- 1 **can (16 ounces) butter beans, rinsed and drained**
- 1 **can (16 ounces) kidney beans, rinsed and drained**
- 1 **can (15½ ounces) black-eyed peas, rinsed and drained**
- 1 **can (15 ounces) garbanzo beans or chickpeas, rinsed and drained**
- 1 **can (15 ounces) pinto beans, rinsed and drained**
- 1 **can (15 ounces) black beans, rinsed and drained**
- 2 **bottles (18 ounces each) barbecue sauce**
- ⅓ **cup cider vinegar**
- 1 **tablespoon liquid smoke, optional**

1. Preheat oven to 350°. In an ovenproof Dutch oven, cook bacon over medium heat until crisp, stirring occasionally. Remove with a slotted spoon; drain on paper towels. Cook and stir onion, yellow pepper, red pepper, garlic, chipotle pepper and pepper in bacon drippings until vegetables are tender. Remove from heat.
2. Add beans and cooked bacon to Dutch oven; stir in barbecue sauce, vinegar and, if desired, liquid smoke.
3. Bake, covered, 1-1¼ hours or until heated through.

FREEZE OPTION *Freeze cooled beans in freezer containers. To use, partially thaw in refrigerator overnight. Heat through in a saucepan, stirring occasionally and adding a little water if necessary.*

PER SERVING *¾ cup equals 369 cal., 11 g fat (3 g sat. fat), 17 mg chol., 1,126 mg sodium, 56 g carb., 9 g fiber, 13 g pro.*

Shredded Gingered Brussels Sprouts

Even people who normally don't care for Brussels sprouts will ask for a second helping of these. I like to use a wok, but a skillet works fine.

—JAMES SCHEND PLEASANT PRAIRIE, WI

START TO FINISH: 25 MIN.
MAKES: 6 SERVINGS

- 1 **pound fresh Brussels sprouts (about 5½ cups)**
- 1 **tablespoon olive oil**
- 1 **small onion, finely chopped**
- 1 **tablespoon minced fresh gingerroot**
- 1 **garlic clove, minced**
- ½ **teaspoon salt**
- 2 **tablespoons water**
- ¼ **teaspoon pepper**

1. Trim Brussels sprouts. Cut sprouts lengthwise in half; cut crosswise into thin slices.
2. Place a large skillet over medium-high heat. Add Brussels sprouts; cook and stir 2-3 minutes or until sprouts begin to brown lightly. Add oil and toss to coat. Stir in onion, ginger, garlic and salt. Add water; reduce heat to medium and cook, covered, 1-2 minutes or until vegetables are tender. Stir in pepper.

PER SERVING *¾ cup equals 56 cal., 2 g fat (trace sat. fat), 0 chol., 214 mg sodium, 8 g carb., 3 g fiber, 2 g pro. Diabetic Exchanges: 1 vegetable, ½ fat.*

SHREDDED GINGERED BRUSSELS SPROUTS

TANGY BAKED SEVEN BEANS

BERRY BBQ SAUCE

EAT SMART ⑤**INGREDIENTS FAST FIX**

Berry BBQ Sauce

On weekends, I jazz up our favorite BBQ sauce with blackberries and blueberries. They make a marvelous spread for basting and saucing grilled baby back ribs.

—**JANET HIX** AUSTIN, TX

START TO FINISH: 30 MIN.
MAKES: 4 CUPS

- 2 cups fresh or frozen blackberries
- 2 cups fresh or frozen blueberries
- ½ cup sugar
- ¼ cup water
- 1 to 2 cups barbecue sauce

1. In a large saucepan, combine berries, sugar and water. Bring to a boil. Reduce heat; simmer, uncovered, 15-20 minutes or until thickened, stirring occasionally.

2. Stir in desired amount of barbecue sauce; cook 10-15 minutes longer or until thickened. Store in an airtight container in the refrigerator for up to 3 days.

PER SERVING *2 tablespoons equals 36 cal., trace fat (trace sat. fat), 0 chol., 88 mg sodium, 9 g carb., 1 g fiber, trace pro.* **Diabetic Exchange:** *½ starch.*

Butternut Squash Oven Risotto

Squash and beer make my risotto taste different and delicious. Plus, cooking it in the oven cuts down on the hands-on time typically spent preparing risotto.

—**KATIE FERRIER** HOUSTON, TX

PREP: 20 MIN. • **BAKE:** 30 MIN.
MAKES: 10 SERVINGS

- 6 cups cubed peeled butternut squash (1 inch)
- 4 tablespoons olive oil, divided
- ½ teaspoon salt
- ¼ teaspoon pepper
- 1 carton (32 ounces) chicken broth
- 1 cup water
- 1 small onion, chopped
- 2 cups uncooked arborio rice
- 2 garlic cloves, minced
- 1 cup beer
- 2 tablespoons butter
- ½ teaspoon chili powder
- ¼ teaspoon ground nutmeg
- 1 cup grated Parmesan cheese

1. Preheat oven to 375°. Place squash in a greased 15x10x1-in. baking pan.

Drizzle with 2 tablespoons of olive oil; sprinkle with salt and pepper. Toss to coat. Roast on a lower oven rack for 30-35 minutes or until tender, stirring occasionally.

2. Meanwhile, in a large saucepan, bring broth and water to a simmer; keep hot. In an ovenproof Dutch oven, heat remaining oil over medium heat. Add onion; cook and stir 4-6 minutes or until tender. Add rice and garlic; cook and stir 1-2 minutes longer or until rice is coated.

3. Stir in beer. Reduce the heat to maintain a simmer; cook and stir until the beer is absorbed. Stir in 4 cups hot broth mixture. Place Dutch oven on an oven rack above squash; bake, covered, 20-25 minutes or until rice is tender but firm to the bite, risotto is creamy and liquid is almost absorbed.

4. Remove Dutch oven from oven. Add butter, chili powder, nutmeg and the remaining broth mixture. Stir vigorously until blended and liquid is almost absorbed. Stir in roasted squash and cheese. Serve immediately.

PER SERVING *¾ cup equals 311 cal., 11 g fat (4 g sat. fat), 15 mg chol., 662 mg sodium, 46 g carb., 3 g fiber, 7 g pro.*

BUTTERNUT SQUASH OVEN RISOTTO

Grilled Veggies with Caper Butter

No one likes a bland veggie, and caper butter helps peppers, squash and zucchini shine. We love the tart, peppery taste of capers.

—DANYELLE CRUM INDIAN TRAIL, NC

PREP: 25 MIN. • **GRILL:** 10 MIN.
MAKES: 8 SERVINGS

- ¼ **cup butter, cubed**
- 2 **garlic cloves, minced**
- 1 **tablespoon lemon juice**
- 2 **teaspoons capers, drained and chopped**
- 1 **tablespoon minced fresh parsley**
- 2 **medium zucchini, cut in half lengthwise**
- 2 **medium crookneck or yellow summer squash, cut in half lengthwise**
- 1 **medium sweet yellow or orange pepper, quartered**
- 1 **medium sweet red pepper, quartered**
- 2 **large portobello mushrooms, stems removed**
- 3 **green onions, trimmed**
- 2 **tablespoons olive oil**
- ½ **teaspoon salt**
- ¼ **teaspoon pepper**

1. In a small saucepan, melt butter over medium-low heat. Add garlic; cook 2 minutes. Add lemon juice and capers; cook 2 minutes. Stir in parsley.
2. Brush vegetables with oil; sprinkle with salt and pepper.
3. Grill the zucchini, squash and peppers, covered, over medium heat 4-5 minutes on each side or until crisp-tender, basting occasionally with butter mixture. Grill mushrooms and onions, covered, 1-2 minutes on each side or until tender, basting occasionally with butter mixture.
4. Cut vegetables as desired; transfer to a serving platter. Drizzle with the remaining butter mixture.
PER SERVING *117 cal., 10 g fat (4 g sat. fat), 15 mg chol., 219 mg sodium, 7 g carb., 2 g fiber, 2 g pro.*

MAKE-AHEAD CREAMY POTATOES

Make-Ahead Creamy Potatoes

For the holidays, I usually serve the traditional foods plus a new spin or two on family favorites. I put together these creamy potatoes the night before and simply bake the day of to save precious holiday time.

—WENDY BALL BATTLE CREEK, MI

PREP: 1 HOUR + CHILLING • **BAKE:** 55 MIN.
MAKES: 16 SERVINGS (¾ CUP EACH)

- 5 **pounds potatoes (about 6 large)**
- ½ **cup butter, divided**
- ½ **cup chopped fresh mushrooms**
- 2 **tablespoons all-purpose flour**
- 1 **cup 2% milk or half-and-half cream**
- 1 **teaspoon salt**
- ½ **teaspoon pepper**
- ½ **teaspoon dried thyme**
- 2 **cups (8 ounces) shredded sharp cheddar cheese**
- 2 **cups (16 ounces) sour cream**
- 1 **medium onion, chopped**
- ½ **cup dry bread crumbs**
- ¼ **cup grated Parmesan cheese**

1. Place whole potatoes in a large stockpot; add water to cover. Bring to a boil. Reduce heat; cook, uncovered, 20-25 minutes or until tender. Drain.
2. Meanwhile, in a large saucepan, heat ¼ cup butter over medium-high heat. Add mushrooms; cook and stir 2-4 minutes or until tender. Stir in flour until blended; gradually whisk in milk, salt, pepper and thyme. Bring to a boil, stirring constantly; cook and stir 1-2 minutes or until thickened.
3. Peel and cube potatoes when cool enough to handle. Press through a potato ricer or strainer into a large bowl; stir in the cheddar cheese, sour cream, mushroom mixture, onion and remaining butter. Transfer potato mixture to a greased 13x9-in. baking dish. Refrigerate, covered, overnight.
4. Preheat the oven to 375°. Remove potatoes from refrigerator; uncover and let stand while the oven heats. Sprinkle with the bread crumbs and Parmesan cheese. Bake, uncovered, 55-65 minutes or until heated through.
PER SERVING *¾ cup equals 283 cal., 16 g fat (11 g sat. fat), 52 mg chol., 345 mg sodium, 25 g carb., 2 g fiber, 8 g pro.*

TERRI KEENAN'S TACO LASAGNA *PAGE 66*

Main Dishes

When cooking up **delicious dinners,** these main courses are ready to play the starring role. You'll find quick **weeknight fare,** sizzling **grilled specialties** and perfect **company's-coming dinners.**

PAUL WARGASKI'S SHRIMP & SWEET POTATO SKEWERS *PAGE 71*

JAN VALDEZ'S LEMON & SAGE ROASTED CHICKEN *PAGE 84*

DEVON DELANEY'S PISTACHIO-CRUSTED SALMON WITH RAINBOW VEGETABLE CREAM *PAGE 78*

Taco Lasagna

If you like foods with Southwestern flair, this recipe just might become a new favorite. The leftovers would be a treat for lunch, but I rarely have any to spare.
—**TERRI KEENAN** TUSCALOOSA, AL

PREP: 20 MIN. • **BAKE:** 25 MIN.
MAKES: 9 SERVINGS

- 1 **pound ground beef**
- ½ **cup chopped green pepper**
- ½ **cup chopped onion**
- ⅔ **cup water**
- 1 **envelope taco seasoning**
- 1 **can (15 ounces) black beans, rinsed and drained**
- 1 **can (14½ ounces) Mexican diced tomatoes, undrained**
- 6 **flour tortillas (8 inches)**
- 1 **can (16 ounces) refried beans**
- 3 **cups (12 ounces) shredded Mexican cheese blend**

1. In a large skillet, cook the beef, green pepper and onion over medium heat until the meat is no longer pink; drain. Add water and taco seasoning; simmer, uncovered, for 2 minutes. Stir in black beans and tomatoes. Simmer, uncovered, for 10 minutes.

2. Place two tortillas in a greased 13x9-in. baking dish. Spread with half of the refried beans and half of the beef mixture; sprinkle with 1 cup cheese. Repeat layers. Top with remaining tortillas and cheese. Cover and bake at 350° for 25-30 minutes or until heated through and cheese is melted.

PER SERVING *1 piece equals 448 cal., 21 g fat (11 g sat. fat), 69 mg chol., 1,152 mg sodium, 39 g carb., 5 g fiber, 25 g pro.*

READER RAVE

This is delicious! I did add extra cheese—I love cheese! I added chopped roma tomatoes, sliced black olives and sour cream to the top when serving. I think I'll add chopped green onions the next time. Love this, and my husband loved it, too! Will definitely make again.

—**BBOHANNON**
TASTEOFHOME.COM

MARINATED PORK CHOPS

FREEZE IT
Marinated Pork Chops

I make these tasty grilled loin chops all the time, and my family never tires of them. The secret to the tender pork is overnight marinating.
—**JEAN NEITZEL** BELOIT, WI

PREP: 5 MIN. + MARINATING • **GRILL:** 20 MIN.
MAKES: 6 SERVINGS

- ¾ **cup canola oil**
- ⅓ **cup reduced-sodium soy sauce**
- ¼ **cup white vinegar**
- 2 **tablespoons Worcestershire sauce**
- 1 **tablespoon lemon juice**
- 1 **tablespoon prepared mustard**
- 1 **teaspoon salt**
- 1 **teaspoon pepper**
- 1 **teaspoon dried parsley flakes**
- 1 **garlic clove, minced**
- 6 **bone-in pork loin chops (1 inch thick and 8 ounces each)**

1. In a large resealable plastic bag, combine the first 10 ingredients; add the pork chops. Seal bag and turn to coat; refrigerate overnight.

2. Drain pork, discarding marinade. Grill, covered, over medium heat, for 4-5 minutes on each side or until a thermometer reads 145°. Let meat stand for 5 minutes before serving.

FREEZE OPTION *Freeze uncooked pork in bag with marinade. To use, completely thaw in refrigerator. Grill as directed.*

PER SERVING *1 pork chop equals 452 cal., 32 g fat (8 g sat. fat), 111 mg chol., 569 mg sodium, 1 g carb., 0 fiber, 37 g pro.*

Baja Fish Tacos

Crisp mahi mahi pans out beautifully when dressed up with fresh cilantro, lime and smoky adobo. One bite, and you'll be hooked!

—BROOKE KELLER LEXINGTON, KY

PREP: 30 MIN. • **COOK:** 5 MIN./BATCH
MAKES: 8 SERVINGS

- 1 cup reduced-fat ranch salad dressing
- 3 tablespoons adobo sauce
- 2 tablespoons minced fresh cilantro
- 2 tablespoons lime juice
- 2 pounds mahi mahi, cut into 1-inch strips
- ¼ teaspoon salt
- ¼ teaspoon pepper
- ⅔ cup all-purpose flour
- 3 large eggs, beaten
- 2 cups panko (Japanese) bread crumbs
- 1 cup canola oil
- 16 corn tortillas (6 inches), warmed
- 3 cups shredded cabbage
  Additional minced fresh cilantro and lime wedges

1. In a small bowl, combine the salad dressing, adobo sauce, cilantro and lime juice. Chill until serving.

2. Sprinkle mahi mahi with salt and pepper. Place the flour, eggs and bread crumbs in separate shallow bowls. Coat mahi mahi with flour, then dip in eggs and coat with bread crumbs. In a large skillet, heat oil over medium heat; cook fish in batches 2-3 minutes on each side or until golden brown. Drain on paper towels.

3. Place fish in tortillas; top with cabbage, sauce mixture and additional cilantro. Serve with lime wedges.

PER SERVING *2 tacos equals 544 cal., 29 g fat (3 g sat. fat), 151 mg chol., 727 mg sodium, 43 g carb., 4 g fiber, 29 g pro.*

Grilled Flank Steak with Summer Relish

My garden produces a nice harvest of tomatoes, scallions, corn, garlic and poblanos, so that's what I use to make relish for this tasty steak.

—BRENDA WASHNOCK NEGAUNEE, MI

PREP: 25 MIN. + STANDING • **GRILL:** 20 MIN.
MAKES: 4 SERVINGS

- 3 garlic cloves, minced
- 1 teaspoon sea salt
- 1 teaspoon dried rosemary, crushed
- 1 tablespoon olive oil
- 1 beef flank steak (1½ pounds)

RELISH

- 4 large ears sweet corn, husks removed
- 4 green onions
- 2 medium tomatoes
- 1 poblano pepper
- 2 tablespoons olive oil, divided
- 1 medium ripe avocado, peeled and cubed
- 1 teaspoon balsamic vinegar
- ½ teaspoon salt

1. Mix garlic, salt, rosemary and oil; rub over both sides of steak. Let stand at least 30 minutes. Meanwhile, brush corn, onions, tomatoes and poblano with 1 tablespoon oil. Grill, covered, over medium-high heat 5-10 minutes or until vegetables are charred and tender, turning occasionally.

2. Grill steak, covered, over medium heat 5-8 minutes on each side or until meat reaches desired doneness (for medium-rare, a thermometer should read 145°; medium, 160°; well-done, 170°). Let stand 5 minutes.

3. When corn is cool enough to handle, cut kernels from cobs; place in a large bowl. Remove skin and seeds from tomatoes and poblano. Chop onions, tomatoes and poblano; add to bowl. Gently stir in avocado, vinegar, salt and the remaining oil. Thinly slice steak across the grain. Serve with relish.

PER SERVING *5 ounces cooked beef and 1 cup relish equals 547 cal., 30 g fat (8 g sat. fat), 81 mg chol., 907 mg sodium, 36 g carb., 7 g fiber, 39 g pro.*

GRILLED FLANK STEAK WITH SUMMER RELISH

We once owned an organic greenhouse and produce business. Weekends were hectic, so I made no-fuss meals like yummy beef tips to fortify us at day's end. —SUE GRONHOLZ BEAVER DAM, WI

FESTIVE SLOW-COOKED BEEF TIPS

SLOW COOKER
Festive Slow-Cooked Beef Tips

PREP: 45 MIN. • **COOK:** 6 HOURS
MAKES: 8 SERVINGS

- 1 boneless beef chuck roast (about 2 pounds), cut into 2-inch pieces
- 1 teaspoon salt
- ¼ teaspoon pepper
- 2 tablespoons canola oil
- 1 medium onion, coarsely chopped
- 1 celery rib, coarsely chopped
- 6 garlic cloves, halved
- 2 cups beef broth
- 1½ cups dry red wine
- 1 fresh rosemary sprig
- 1 bay leaf
- 2 cans (4 ounces each) sliced mushrooms
- 2 tablespoons cornstarch
- ½ cup water
- 1 tablespoon balsamic vinegar
  Hot cooked egg noodles

1. Sprinkle beef with salt and pepper. In a large skillet, heat oil over medium-high heat. Brown beef in batches. Remove with a slotted spoon to a 3- or 4-qt. slow cooker.
2. In same pan, add onion and celery; cook and stir 6-8 minutes or until tender. Add garlic; cook 1 minute longer. Add broth, wine, rosemary and bay leaf. Bring to a boil; cook 8-10 minutes or until liquid is reduced to about 2 cups.
3. Pour over beef in slow cooker; stir in mushrooms. Cook, covered, on low 6-8 hours or until meat is tender. Remove rosemary and bay leaf.
4. In a small bowl, mix cornstarch, water and vinegar until smooth; gradually stir into beef mixture. Serve with noodles.
PER SERVING *1 cup (calculated without noodles) equals 290 cal., 15 g fat (4 g sat. fat), 74 mg chol., 691 mg sodium, 7 g carb., 1 g fiber, 24 g pro.*

Creamy Macaroni and Cheese

This is the ultimate mac and cheese. It's creamy, thick and very rich, and it has a wonderful cheddar cheese flavor. Sour cream is the secret ingredient.
—**CINDY HARTLEY** CHESAPEAKE, VA

PREP: 20 MIN. • **BAKE:** 35 MIN.
MAKES: 6 SERVINGS

- 2 cups uncooked elbow macaroni
- ½ cup butter, cubed
- ½ cup all-purpose flour
- 1½ to 2 cups 2% milk
- 1 cup (8 ounces) sour cream
- 8 ounces process cheese (Velveeta), cubed
- ¼ cup grated Parmesan cheese
- ½ teaspoon salt
- ½ teaspoon ground mustard
- ½ teaspoon pepper
- 2 cups (8 ounces) shredded cheddar cheese

1. Cook macaroni according to the package directions.
2. Meanwhile, preheat oven to 350°. In a large saucepan, melt butter. Stir in flour until smooth. Gradually add milk. Bring to a boil; cook and stir 2 minutes or until thickened. Reduce the heat; stir in sour cream, cubed process cheese, Parmesan cheese, salt, mustard and pepper until smooth and cheese is melted.
3. Drain macaroni; toss with cheddar cheese. Transfer to a greased 3-qt. baking dish. Stir in cream sauce.
4. Bake, uncovered, 35-40 minutes or until golden brown and bubbly.
PER SERVING *1 cup equals 653 cal., 46 g fat (30 g sat. fat), 143 mg chol., 1,141 mg sodium, 35 g carb., 1 g fiber, 25 g pro.*

DID YOU KNOW?

Cheddar gets its name from a village in England that is known for the delicious cheese.

Crazy Delicious Baby Back Ribs

My husband craves baby back ribs, so we cook them multiple ways. This low and slow method with a tangy sauce is the best we've found.

—JAN WHITWORTH ROEBUCK, SC

PREP: 15 MIN. • **COOK:** 5¼ HOURS
MAKES: 8 SERVINGS

- 2 tablespoons smoked paprika
- 2 teaspoons chili powder
- 2 teaspoons garlic salt
- 1 teaspoon onion powder
- 1 teaspoon pepper
- ½ teaspoon cayenne pepper
- 4 pounds pork baby back ribs

SAUCE
- ½ cup Worcestershire sauce
- ½ cup mayonnaise
- ½ cup yellow mustard
- ¼ cup reduced-sodium soy sauce
- 3 tablespoons hot pepper sauce

1. In a small bowl, combine the first six ingredients. Cut ribs into serving-size pieces; rub with seasoning mixture. Place ribs in a 6-qt. slow cooker. Cook, covered, on low for 5-6 hours or until meat is tender.
2. Preheat oven to 375°. In a small bowl, whisk the sauce ingredients. Transfer ribs to a foil-lined 15x10x1-in. baking pan; brush with some of the sauce. Bake 15-20 minutes or until browned, turning once and brushing occasionally with sauce. Serve with remaining sauce.
PER SERVING *420 cal., 33 g fat (9 g sat. fat), 86 mg chol., 1,082 mg sodium, 6 g carb., 2 g fiber, 24 g pro.*

Coconut Curry Chicken

My husband and I love this yummy dish! It's a breeze to prepare in the slow cooker, and it tastes just like a meal you'd have at your favorite Indian or Thai restaurant.

—ANDI KAUFFMAN BEAVERCREEK, OR

PREP: 20 MIN. • **COOK:** 5 HOURS
MAKES: 4 SERVINGS

- 2 medium potatoes, peeled and cubed
- 1 small onion, chopped
- 4 boneless skinless chicken breast halves (4 ounces each)
- 1 cup light coconut milk
- 4 teaspoons curry powder
- 1 garlic clove, minced
- 1 teaspoon reduced-sodium chicken bouillon granules
- ¼ teaspoon salt
- ¼ teaspoon pepper
- 2 cups hot cooked rice
- ¼ cup thinly sliced green onions
  Raisins, flaked coconut and chopped unsalted peanuts, optional

1. Place potatoes and onion in a 3- or 4-qt. slow cooker. In a large nonstick skillet coated with cooking spray, brown chicken on both sides.
2. Transfer to slow cooker. In a small bowl, combine the coconut milk, curry, garlic, bouillon, salt and pepper; pour over chicken. Cover and cook on low for 5-6 hours or until meat is tender.
3. Serve the chicken and sauce with rice; sprinkle with green onions. Garnish with raisins, coconut and peanuts if desired.
PER SERVING *(calculated without optional ingredients) 396 cal., 11 g fat (7 g sat. fat), 63 mg chol., 309 mg sodium, 43 g carb., 3 g fiber, 27 g pro.* **Diabetic Exchanges:** *3 lean meat, 2½ starch, 2 fat.*

CRAZY DELICIOUS BABY BACK RIBS

Soda Pop Chops with Smashed Potatoes

Root beer gives this family-friendly recipe a tangy taste that kids will love. Served alongside smashed potatoes, the chops make a scrumptious meal any weeknight.

—*TASTE OF HOME* TEST KITCHEN

PREP: 25 MIN. • **COOK:** 15 MIN.
MAKES: 4 SERVINGS

- 1½ **pounds small red potatoes, halved**
- 1 **cup root beer**
- 1 **cup ketchup**
- 1 **tablespoon brown sugar**
- 2 **teaspoons chili powder**
- 2 **teaspoons Worcestershire sauce**
- ½ **teaspoon garlic powder, divided**
- 2 **tablespoons all-purpose flour**
- ¾ **teaspoon pepper, divided**
- ½ **teaspoon salt, divided**
- 4 **bone-in pork loin chops (7 ounces each)**
- 2 **tablespoons olive oil**
- 2 **tablespoons butter**

1. Place potatoes in a large saucepan and cover with water. Bring to a boil. Reduce the heat; cover and cook for 15-20 minutes or until tender.
2. Meanwhile, in a small bowl, combine the root beer, ketchup, brown sugar, chili powder, Worcestershire sauce and ¼ teaspoon garlic powder; set aside. In a large resealable plastic bag, combine the flour, ½ teaspoon pepper and ¼ teaspoon salt. Add pork chops, one at a time, and shake to coat.
3. In a large skillet, cook chops in oil over medium heat for 2-3 minutes on each side or until chops are lightly browned; drain. Add the root beer mixture. Bring to a boil. Reduce heat; cover and simmer for 6-8 minutes or until a thermometer reads 145°. Remove pork and keep warm. Let stand for 5 minutes before serving.
4. Bring sauce to a boil; cook until liquid is reduced by half. Meanwhile, drain potatoes; mash with butter, remaining garlic powder and the remaining salt and pepper. Serve with pork chops and sauce.

PER SERVING *1 pork chop with ½ cup potatoes and ⅓ cup sauce equals 637 cal., 29 g fat (11 g sat. fat), 112 mg chol., 1,222 mg sodium, 59 g carb., 4 g fiber, 36 g pro.*

EAT SMART

Chickpea & Chipotle Tostadas

I often take a not-so-healthy dish and create something good for my family. My young twins love colorful meals they can eat with their hands, and this dinner is perfect.

—**AMBER MASSEY** ARGYLE, TX

PREP: 20 MIN. • **COOK:** 25 MIN.
MAKES: 6 SERVINGS

- 1 **medium sweet red pepper, chopped**
- 1 **medium onion, chopped**
- 2 **garlic cloves, minced**
- 2 **cans (15 ounces each) chickpeas, rinsed**
- 1 **cup vegetable broth**
- 2 **minced chipotle peppers plus 2 teaspoons adobo sauce**
- 1 **teaspoon ground cumin**
- ½ **teaspoon salt**
- ½ **cup minced fresh cilantro**
- 2 **tablespoons lime juice**
- 12 **corn tortillas (6 inches)**
  Cooking spray
- ½ **medium head iceberg lettuce, shredded**
- 3 **plum tomatoes, chopped**
- 1 **medium ripe avocado, peeled and cubed**
- ¾ **cup fat-free sour cream**
- ½ **cup salsa verde**
  Shredded reduced-fat cheddar cheese

1. In a large skillet coated with cooking spray, cook and stir chopped red pepper and onion until tender, about 6-8 minutes. Add garlic; cook 1 minute longer. Stir in the next five ingredients. Bring to a boil; reduce heat. Cover and simmer 5 minutes.
2. Coarsely mash with a potato masher. Stir in the cilantro and lime juice. Cook until thickened, about 2-3 minutes.
3. Meanwhile, spritz both sides of tortillas with cooking spray. Place in a single layer on baking sheets; broil 4 in. from heat until crisp, about 2 minutes per side.
4. Spread chickpea mixture over the tortillas. Top with lettuce, tomatoes and avocado. Stir together sour cream and salsa; drizzle over tortillas. Sprinkle with cheese. Serve immediately.

PER SERVING *2 tostadas equals 337 cal., 8 g fat (1 g sat. fat), 5 mg chol., 737 mg sodium, 57 g carb. (10 g sugars, 12 g fiber), 11 g pro.*

CHICKPEA & CHIPOTLE TOSTADAS

Shrimp & Sweet Potato Skewers

These skewers make romantic picnic food. I perfected them for a date with my wife. We like them with couscous and a glass of chilled wine.

—PAUL WARGASKI CHICAGO, IL

PREP: 35 MIN. • **GRILL:** 5 MIN.
MAKES: 2 SERVINGS

- ¾ **pound sweet potatoes (about 2 small), cut into 1-inch pieces**
- 3 **tablespoons olive oil, divided**
- 1 **teaspoon minced fresh rosemary**
- ¾ **teaspoon paprika, divided**
- 12 **uncooked shrimp (26-30 per pound), peeled and deveined**
- ¼ **teaspoon salt**
- ⅛ **teaspoon pepper**
- 4½ **teaspoons lemon juice**
   Hot cooked couscous

1. Preheat oven to 450°. Place sweet potatoes in a greased 15x10x1-in. baking pan. Mix 1 tablespoon oil, rosemary and ½ teaspoon paprika; drizzle over potatoes. Toss to coat. Roast 25-35 minutes or just until just tender, stirring occasionally.

2. On six metal or soaked wooden skewers, alternately thread shrimp and sweet potatoes; sprinkle with the salt and pepper. Grill, covered, over medium heat 5-7 minutes or until shrimp turn pink, turning once.

3. Meanwhile, in a small bowl, whisk lemon juice and the remaining oil and paprika until blended. Serve skewers with couscous and drizzle with the lemon mixture.

PER SERVING *(calculated without couscous) 443 cal., 22 g fat (3 g sat. fat), 119 mg chol., 429 mg sodium, 43 g carb., 6 g fiber, 19 g pro.*

MEDITERRANEAN CHICKEN ORZO

Mediterranean Chicken Orzo

Orzo pasta with chicken, olives and herbes de Provence has the bright flavors of Mediterranean cuisine. Here's a bonus: Leftovers reheat well.

—THOMAS FAGLON SOMERSET, NJ

PREP: 15 MIN. • **COOK:** 4 HOURS
MAKES: 6 SERVINGS

- 1½ **pounds boneless skinless chicken thighs, cut into 1-inch pieces**
- 2 **cups reduced-sodium chicken broth**
- 2 **medium tomatoes, finely chopped**
- 1 **cup sliced pitted green olives**
- 1 **cup sliced pitted ripe olives**
- 1 **large carrot, finely chopped**
- 1 **small red onion, finely chopped**
- 1 **tablespoon grated lemon peel**
- 3 **tablespoons lemon juice**
- 2 **tablespoons butter**
- 1 **tablespoon herbes de Provence**
- 1 **cup uncooked orzo pasta**

In a 3- or 4-qt. slow cooker, combine the first 11 ingredients. Cook, covered, on low for 4-5 hours or until the chicken, vegetables and orzo are tender, adding orzo during the last 30 minutes of cooking.

PER SERVING *1⅓ cups equals 415 cal., 19 g fat (5 g sat. fat), 86 mg chol., 941 mg sodium, 33 g carb., 3 g fiber, 27 g pro.*

SLOW COOKER
Green Chili Ribs

I like my food with a spicy kick; my wife does not. These ribs with green chilies suit her taste. For more firepower, add cayenne or jalapenos.

—GUY NEWTON NEDERLAND, CO

PREP: 20 MIN. • **COOK:** 5 HOURS
MAKES: 8 SERVINGS

- 4 **pounds pork baby back ribs**
- 2 **tablespoons ground cumin, divided**
- 2 **tablespoons olive oil**
- 1 **small onion, finely chopped**
- 1 **jar (16 ounces) salsa verde**
- 3 **cans (4 ounces each) chopped green chilies**
- 2 **cups beef broth**
- ¼ **cup minced fresh cilantro**
- 1 **tablespoon all-purpose flour**
- 3 **garlic cloves, minced**
- ¼ **teaspoon cayenne pepper**
  Additional minced fresh cilantro

1. Cut ribs into serving-size pieces; rub with 1 tablespoon cumin. In a large skillet, heat the oil over medium-high heat. Brown ribs in batches. Place ribs in a 6-qt. slow cooker.

2. Add onion to same pan; cook and stir 2-3 minutes or until onions are tender. Add salsa verde, green chilies, broth, cilantro, flour, garlic, cayenne and remaining cumin to slow cooker. Cook, covered, on low 5-6 hours or until meat is tender. Sprinkle with additional cilantro.

PER SERVING *349 cal., 25 g fat (8 g sat. fat), 81 mg chol., 797 mg sodium, 8 g carb., 1 g fiber, 24 g pro.*

Barbecued Chicken Pizzas

Throw a pizza on the grill at your next backyard cookout and say goodbye to ordinary barbecued chicken. This super simple recipe is easy to customize, so have fun adding different toppings.

—ALICIA TREVITHICK TEMECULA, CA

PREP: 25 MIN. • **GRILL:** 10 MIN.
MAKES: 2 PIZZAS (4 PIECES EACH)

- 2 **boneless skinless chicken breast halves (6 ounces each)**
- ¼ **teaspoon salt**
- ¼ **teaspoon pepper**
- 1 **cup barbecue sauce, divided**
- 1 **tube (13.8 ounces) refrigerated pizza crust**
- 2 **teaspoons olive oil**
- 1 **medium red onion, thinly sliced**
- 2 **cups (8 ounces) shredded Gouda cheese**
- ¼ **cup minced fresh cilantro**

1. Sprinkle chicken with salt and pepper. On a greased grill rack, grill the chicken, covered, over medium heat or broil chicken 4 in. from heat for 5-7 minutes on each side or until a thermometer reads 170°, basting frequently with ½ cup of barbecue sauce. Set aside and keep warm.

2. Divide dough in half. On a lightly floured surface, roll each portion into a 12x10-in. rectangle. Lightly brush both sides of dough with oil; place on grill. Cover and grill over medium heat for 1-2 minutes or until bottoms are lightly browned.

3. Remove from grill. Cut the chicken into ½-in. cubes. Spread the grilled side of each crust with ¼ cup barbecue sauce, then layer with chicken, onion, cheese and cilantro. Return to grill; cover. Cook each pizza for 4-5 minutes or until the bottom is lightly browned and cheese is melted.

PER SERVING *1 piece equals 312 cal., 12 g fat (6 g sat. fat), 56 mg chol., 938 mg sodium, 28 g carb., 1 g fiber, 21 g pro.*

GREEN CHILI RIBS

IRISH-SPICED BEEF

NOTE *This is a fresh beef brisket, not corned beef.*
PER SERVING *4 ounces cooked beef (calculated without mustard and bread) equals 268 cal., 8 g fat (3 g sat. fat), 83 mg chol., 560 mg sodium, 6 g carb., trace fiber, 40 g pro.*

FREEZE IT
Spaghetti Casserole

Here's an easy dish to prepare ahead of time and bake just before dinnertime. Sour cream and canned mushroom soup make for a deliciously creamy casserole.
—**KIM ROCKER** LAGRANGE, GA

PREP: 20 MIN. • **BAKE:** 55 MIN.
MAKES: 2 CASSEROLES (6 SERVINGS EACH)

- 1 **package (16 ounces) spaghetti**
- 1½ **pounds ground beef**
- 1 **jar (26 ounces) spaghetti sauce**
- 2 **cans (8 ounces each) tomato sauce**
- 1 **can (10¾ ounces) condensed cream of mushroom soup, undiluted**
- 1 **cup (8 ounces) sour cream**
- 2 **cups (8 ounces) shredded Colby-Monterey Jack cheese**

1. Preheat the oven to 350°. Cook pasta according to package directions. Meanwhile, in a large skillet, cook the beef over medium heat until no longer pink; drain. Stir in spaghetti sauce and tomato sauce. Remove from the heat.
2. Drain pasta. Combine the soup and sour cream. In two 8-in. square baking dishes, layer half of the meat sauce, pasta, soup mixture and shredded cheese. Repeat layers.
3. Cover and bake 55-65 minutes or until cheese is melted.
FREEZE OPTION *Cover and freeze unbaked casseroles up to 3 months. To use, partially thaw in refrigerator overnight. Remove from refrigerator 30 minutes before baking. Preheat the oven to 350°. Bake the casseroles, increasing time as necessary to heat through and for a thermometer inserted in center to read 165°.*
PER SERVING *430 cal., 19 g fat (10 g sat. fat), 68 mg chol., 818 mg sodium, 39 g carb., 3 g fiber, 22 g pro.*

Irish-Spiced Beef

The story goes that my Irish ancestors brought this recipe along when they immigrated to the States. It takes nearly a week from start to finish, but that gives the meat time to become really tender and flavorful.
—**MARY SHENK** DEKALB, IL

PREP: 20 MIN. + CHILLING
BAKE: 4 HOURS + CHILLING
MAKES: 14 SERVINGS

- 1 **fresh beef brisket (6 pounds)**
- ⅓ **cup packed brown sugar**
- ¾ **cup coarse sea salt**
- ¼ **cup chopped onion**
- 4 **bay leaves, crushed**
- 3 **teaspoons pepper**
- 2 **teaspoons dried rosemary, crushed**
- 2 **teaspoons dried thyme**
- 1½ **teaspoons ground allspice**
- 1½ **teaspoons ground cloves**
- 4 **medium onions, sliced**
- 4 **medium carrots, sliced**
- 2 **celery ribs, sliced**
- 2 **cups stout or beef broth**
    Rye bread, Swiss cheese slices and Dijon mustard

1. Place the beef in a 15x10x1-in. baking pan; rub with brown sugar. Refrigerate, covered, 24 hours.
2. In a small bowl, mix salt, chopped onion, bay leaves and seasonings; rub over beef. Refrigerate, covered, 3 days, turning and rubbing salt mixture into beef once each day.
3. Preheat oven to 325°. Remove and discard the salt mixture. Place beef, onions, carrots, celery and stout in a roasting pan. Add water to halfway up sides of the brisket. Roast, covered, 4–4½ hours or until meat is tender. Cool meat in cooking juices for 1 hour.
4. Remove beef; discard vegetables and cooking juices. Transfer beef to a 13x9-in. baking dish and refrigerate, covered, overnight.
5. Cut diagonally across the grain into thin slices. Serve with rye bread, Swiss cheese and mustard.

Teriyaki Chicken Thighs

Asian-style chicken and rice is a slow cooker sensation. It always goes over big with my family.

—GIGI MILLER STOUGHTON, WI

PREP: 15 MIN. • **COOK:** 4 HOURS
MAKES: 8 SERVINGS

- 3 **pounds boneless skinless chicken thighs**
- ¾ **cup sugar**
- ¾ **cup reduced-sodium soy sauce**
- ⅓ **cup cider vinegar**
- 1 **garlic clove, minced**
- ¾ **teaspoon ground ginger**
- ¼ **teaspoon pepper**
- 4 **teaspoons cornstarch**
- 4 **teaspoons cold water**
  Hot cooked rice, optional

1. Place chicken in a 4- or 5-qt. slow cooker. In a small bowl, mix the sugar, soy sauce, vinegar, garlic, ginger and pepper; pour over the chicken. Cook, covered, on low for 4-5 hours or until chicken is tender.

2. Remove the chicken to a serving platter; keep warm. Transfer cooking juices to a small saucepan; skim fat, then bring cooking juices to a boil. In a small bowl, mix cornstarch and cold water until smooth; stir into cooking juices. Return to a boil; cook and stir 1-2 minutes or until thickened. Serve with chicken and, if desired, rice.

PER SERVING *5 ounces cooked chicken with ⅓ cup sauce equals 342 cal., 12 g fat (3 g sat. fat), 113 mg chol., 958 mg sodium, 22 g carb., 0 g fiber, 33 g pro.*

TERIYAKI CHICKEN THIGHS

LIME CHICKEN TACOS

Lime Chicken Tacos

Lime juice adds bright flavor to an easy and surprisingly healthy taco filling. This fun recipe is great for a casual dinner with friends and family.

—TRACY GUNTER BOISE, ID

PREP: 10 MIN. • **COOK:** 5½ HOURS
MAKES: 12 SERVINGS

- 1½ **pounds boneless skinless chicken breasts**
- 3 **tablespoons lime juice**
- 1 **tablespoon chili powder**
- 1 **cup frozen corn**
- 1 **cup chunky salsa**
- 12 **fat-free flour tortillas (6 inches), warmed**
  Sour cream, shredded cheddar cheese and shredded lettuce, optional

1. Place the chicken in a 3-qt. slow cooker. Combine lime juice and chili powder; pour over chicken. Cover and cook on low for 5-6 hours or until the chicken is tender.

2. Remove chicken; cool slightly. Shred the meat with two forks and return to the slow cooker. Stir in corn and salsa.

3. Cover and cook on low 30 minutes or until heated through. Place filling on tortillas; serve with sour cream, cheese and lettuce if desired.

PER SERVING *1 taco (calculated without sour cream and cheese) equals 148 cal., 2 g fat (trace sat. fat), 31 mg chol., 338 mg sodium, 18 g carb., 1 g fiber, 14 g pro.* **Diabetic Exchanges:** *2 lean meat, 1 starch.*

Reuben Casserole

This is an absolute favorite of ours. I recently served it at a Christmas gathering. People loved it, and many requested the recipe.

—JOY HAGEN WEBSTER, SD

PREP: 20 MIN. • **BAKE:** 40 MIN.
MAKES: 5 SERVINGS

- 5 cups uncooked egg noodles
- 2 cans (14 ounces each) sauerkraut, rinsed and well drained
- 2 cans (10¾ ounces each) condensed cream of chicken soup, undiluted
- ¾ cup milk
- ½ cup chopped onion
- 3 tablespoons prepared mustard
- ¾ pound sliced deli corned beef, chopped
- 2 cups (8 ounces) shredded Swiss cheese
- 2 slices day-old light rye bread
- 2 tablespoons butter, melted

1. Cook noodles according to package directions. Meanwhile, in a large bowl, combine the sauerkraut, soup, milk, onion and mustard.

2. Drain noodles; stir into sauerkraut mixture. Transfer to a greased 13x9-in. baking dish. Sprinkle with corned beef and Swiss cheese.

3. Place bread in a food processor; cover and process until the mixture resembles coarse crumbs. Toss the crumbs with butter; sprinkle mixture over casserole.

4. Bake, uncovered, at 350° for 40-45 minutes or until bubbly.

PER SERVING *1½ cups equals 621 cal., 30 g fat (15 g sat. fat), 141 mg chol., 3,130 mg sodium, 53 g carb., 7 g fiber, 35 g pro.*

READER RAVE

This casserole is delicious! I cut the recipe in half, baked it in a 9x9-inch pan and served Thousand Island dressing on the side. My husband and I really enjoyed it, and I will definitely make it again.

—SGRUNHOLZ
TASTEOFHOME.COM

Cheeseburger Mini Muffins

I developed these cute little muffins so I could enjoy the flavor of cheeseburgers without resorting to visiting a fast-food restaurant. I often freeze a batch and reheat however many I need.

—TERESA KRAUS CORTEZ, CO

PREP: 20 MIN. • **BAKE:** 15 MIN.
MAKES: 5 DOZEN

- ½ pound ground beef
- 1 small onion, finely chopped
- 2½ cups all-purpose flour
- 1 tablespoon sugar
- 2 teaspoons baking powder
- 1 teaspoon salt
- ¾ cup ketchup
- ¾ cup milk
- ½ cup butter, melted
- 2 large eggs
- 1 teaspoon prepared mustard
- 2 cups (8 ounces) shredded cheddar cheese

1. In a large skillet, cook beef and onion over medium heat until meat is no longer pink; drain.

2. In a small bowl, combine flour, sugar, baking powder and salt. In another bowl, combine the ketchup, milk, butter, eggs and mustard; stir into the dry ingredients just until moistened. Fold in the beef mixture and cheese.

3. Fill greased miniature muffin cups three-fourths full with muffin batter. Bake at 425° for 15-18 minutes or until a toothpick comes out clean. Cool for 5 minutes before removing from pans to wire racks. Serve warm. Refrigerate the leftovers.

NOTE *Muffin batter may be baked in regular-size muffin cups for 20-25 minutes; recipe makes 2 dozen.*

PER SERVING *4 muffins equal 242 cal., 16 g fat (8 g sat. fat), 70 mg chol., 534 mg sodium, 22 g carb., trace fiber, 10 g pro.*

CHEESEBURGER MINI MUFFINS

Zesty Horseradish Meat Loaf

You'll love the bit of heat in this tasty meat loaf. Make sandwiches out of the leftovers to get double duty from this classic comfort food.

—NANCY ZIMMERMAN

CAPE MAY COURT HOUSE, NJ

PREP: 15 MIN. • **BAKE:** 45 MIN. + STANDING
MAKES: 8 SERVINGS

- 4 slices whole wheat bread, crumbled
- ¼ cup fat-free milk
- ½ cup finely chopped celery
- ¼ cup finely chopped onion
- ¼ cup prepared horseradish
- 2 tablespoons Dijon mustard
- 2 tablespoons chili sauce
- 1 large egg, lightly beaten
- 1½ teaspoons Worcestershire sauce
- ½ teaspoon salt
- ¼ teaspoon pepper
- 1½ pounds lean ground beef (90% lean)
- ½ cup ketchup

1. Soak bread in milk for 5 minutes. Drain and discard milk. Stir in celery, onion, horseradish, mustard, chili sauce, egg, Worcestershire sauce, salt and pepper. Crumble beef over bread mixture and mix well.

2. Shape into a loaf in an 11x7-in. baking dish coated with cooking spray. Spread top with ketchup. Bake at 350° until a thermometer reads 160°, about 45-55 minutes. Let stand 10 minutes before cutting.

FREEZE OPTION *Omitting ketchup, bake as directed. Securely wrap cooled meat loaf in plastic wrap and foil, then freeze. To use, partially thaw in refrigerator overnight. Unwrap and spread top with ketchup. Reheat on a greased baking pan in a preheated 350° oven until a thermometer inserted in center reads 160°. Let stand 10 minutes before cutting.*

PER SERVING *1 slice equals 207 cal., 8 g fat (3 g sat. fat), 79 mg chol., 640 mg sodium, 14 g carb., 1 g fiber, 19 g pro.* **Diabetic Exchanges:** *2 lean meat, 1 starch.*

Golden Chicken Cordon Bleu

For an entree that's as elegant as it is easy, try this tender chicken classic. It's a simple recipe that's also really special.

—TASTE OF HOME TEST KITCHEN

PREP: 20 MIN. • **BAKE:** 20 MIN.
MAKES: 2 SERVINGS

- 2 boneless skinless chicken breast halves (6 ounces each)
- 2 slices deli ham (¾ ounce each)
- 2 slices Swiss cheese (¾ ounce each)
- ½ cup all-purpose flour
- ¼ teaspoon salt
- ⅛ teaspoon paprika
- ⅛ teaspoon pepper
- 1 large egg
- 2 tablespoons 2% milk
- ½ cup seasoned bread crumbs
- 1 tablespoon canola oil
- 1 tablespoon butter, melted

1. Flatten chicken to ¼-in. thickness; top with ham and cheese. Roll up and tuck in ends; secure with toothpicks.

2. In a shallow bowl, combine flour, salt, paprika and pepper. In another bowl, whisk egg and milk. Place bread crumbs in a third bowl. Dip chicken in flour mixture, then egg mixture; roll in bread crumbs.

3. In a small skillet, brown chicken in oil on all sides, then transfer to an 8-in. square baking dish coated with cooking spray.

4. Bake, uncovered, at 350° for 20-25 minutes or until a thermometer reads 170°. Discard toothpicks and drizzle with butter.

PER SERVING *501 cal., 23 g fat (9 g sat. fat), 172 mg chol., 728 mg sodium, 23 g carb., 1 g fiber, 49 g pro.*

GOLDEN CHICKEN CORDON BLEU

Key Lime Chicken Thighs

I love trying new recipes. The key lime juice in this one is a nice change from the lemon juice used in many chicken dishes.
—**IDELLA KOEN** METOLIUS, OR

PREP: 5 MIN. • **BAKE:** 30 MIN.
MAKES: 4 SERVINGS

- 8 bone-in chicken thighs, skin removed (6 ounces each)
- 3 tablespoons butter
- 2 to 3 tablespoons Key lime juice or lime juice
- 12 to 16 drops hot pepper sauce
- 1 teaspoon brown sugar
- 1 teaspoon chicken bouillon granules
- ½ teaspoon salt
- ½ teaspoon poultry seasoning
- ½ teaspoon dried rosemary, crushed
- ¼ to ½ teaspoon pepper
- ¼ teaspoon paprika

1. Place chicken in a greased 13x9-in. baking dish. Dot with butter; sprinkle with the lime juice and pepper sauce. Combine the remaining ingredients; sprinkle evenly over chicken.
2. In a 425° oven, bake, uncovered, for 30 minutes or until a thermometer reads 180°.
PER SERVING *460 cal., 27 g fat (11 g sat. fat), 196 mg chol., 712 mg sodium, 2 g carb. (2 g sugars, trace fiber), 48 g pro.*

FREEZE IT
Four-Cheese Sausage Rigatoni

To make this twist on traditional baked pasta, we start with creamy goat cheese and build from there.
—**TERESA RALSTON** NEW ALBANY, OH

PREP: 35 MIN. • **BAKE:** 30 MIN.
MAKES: 12 SERVINGS

- 1 package (16 ounces) rigatoni pasta
- 1 pound bulk Italian sausage
- 1 medium sweet red pepper, chopped
- 1 small onion, chopped
- 2 garlic cloves, minced
- ¾ cup heavy whipping cream
- 1 can (28 ounces) crushed tomatoes in puree
- 1 can (6 ounces) tomato paste

FOUR-CHEESE SAUSAGE RIGATONI

- 2 teaspoons Italian seasoning
- ½ teaspoon crushed red pepper flakes
- 1 carton (15 ounces) whole-milk ricotta cheese
- 1 cup shredded Parmesan cheese, divided
- 1 log (4 ounces) fresh goat cheese, softened
- 1 large egg, lightly beaten
- 1 teaspoon salt
- ½ teaspoon pepper
- 8 ounces fresh mozzarella cheese, cubed
  Torn fresh basil, optional

1. Preheat oven to 350°. In a 6-qt. stockpot, cook rigatoni according to package directions. Drain; transfer to a bowl.
2. In same stockpot, cook and crumble the sausage with red pepper and onion over medium heat until the meat is no longer pink. Add garlic; cook 1 minute longer. Drain. Add cream; cook 5 more minutes, stirring occasionally. Stir in the tomatoes, tomato paste, Italian seasoning and pepper flakes. Cook, uncovered, over medium-low heat until sauce thickens slightly, about

5 minutes. Meanwhile, combine the ricotta, ½ cup Parmesan, goat cheese, egg and seasonings.
3. Stir rigatoni into the meat sauce. Spread 3 cups into each of two greased 11x7-in. baking dishes. Top each with half of cheese mixture, then half of remaining pasta mixture.
4. Bake, covered, 25 minutes. Sprinkle with the mozzarella and remaining Parmesan. Bake, uncovered, until the cheeses are melted, about 5 minutes. If desired, sprinkle with basil.
FREEZE OPTION *Prepare casseroles without mozzarella or remaining ½ cup Parmesan cheese; freeze cheeses separately in resealable plastic freezer bags. Cover and freeze unbaked casseroles. To use, partially thaw in refrigerator overnight. Remove from refrigerator 30 minutes before baking. Preheat oven to 350°. Bake casseroles as directed, increasing time as necessary to heat through and for a thermometer inserted in center to read 165°. If desired, sprinkle with basil.*
PER SERVING *1¼ cups equals 474 cal., 26 g fat (13 g sat. fat), 97 mg chol., 793 mg sodium, 40 g carb. (9 g sugars, 3 g fiber), 23 g pro.*

GRANDMA'S CAJUN CHICKEN & SPAGHETTI

Pistachio-Crusted Salmon with Rainbow Vegetable Cream

I make salmon often, so I experiment with it. In this version I use pistachios for crunch and a sauce inspired by the cream cheese on my bagels.

—**DEVON DELANEY** WESTPORT, CT

PREP: 35 MIN. • **BAKE:** 10 MIN.
MAKES: 4 SERVINGS

- ½ cup onion and garlic salad croutons
- ½ cup pistachios
- 1 large egg white, beaten
- 2 tablespoons water
- 4 salmon fillets (6 ounces each), about 1 inch thick
- 4 ounces reduced-fat cream cheese
- 2 tablespoons lemon juice
- 2 tablespoons snipped fresh dill
- 1 tablespoon capers, drained
- 2 tablespoons olive oil, divided
- 1½ cups julienned fresh carrots
- 1½ cups julienned yellow summer squash
- 1½ cups julienned sweet red pepper
- ½ teaspoon salt
- ¼ cup radishes, halved and finely sliced

1. Pulse croutons and pistachios in a food processor until finely chopped. Whisk egg white with water. Pat the salmon fillets dry; dip in egg white, then roll in crouton-pistachio mixture. Refrigerate 30 minutes. Meanwhile, combine cream cheese, lemon juice, dill and capers until well blended.
2. Preheat oven to 350°. In a large ovenproof skillet, heat 1 tablespoon oil over medium-high heat. Add carrots, squash, peppers and salt; cook and stir until tender and lightly caramelized, 6-8 minutes. Remove.
3. In same skillet, heat remaining oil over medium heat. Add salmon; cook 1 minute on each side or until golden brown. Place skillet in oven; bake until fish just begins to flake easily with a fork, 8-10 minutes. Serve vegetables with salmon; top with sauce. Sprinkle with radishes.

PER SERVING *1 fillet with ¾ cup veggies and 3 tablespoons sauce equals 550 cal., 37 g fat (9 g sat. fat), 106 mg chol., 722 mg sodium, 18 g carb. (8 g sugars, 4 g fiber), 38 g pro.*

Grandma's Cajun Chicken & Spaghetti

I'm originally from Louisiana, where my grandma spoke Cajun French as she taught me her spicy chicken spaghetti, lovingly made on an old woodstove.

—**BRENDA MELANCON** MCCOMB, MS

PREP: 15 MIN. • **COOK:** 1¼ HOURS
MAKES: 10 SERVINGS

- 1 broiler/fryer chicken (3 to 4 pounds), cut up
- 1 to 1½ teaspoons cayenne pepper
- ¾ teaspoon salt
- 3 tablespoons canola oil
- 1 package (14 ounces) smoked sausage, sliced
- 1 large sweet onion, chopped
- 1 medium green pepper, chopped
- 1 celery rib, chopped
- 2 garlic cloves, minced
- 2 cans (14½ ounces each) diced tomatoes, undrained
- 1 can (14½ ounces) diced tomatoes with mild green chilies, undrained
- 1 package (16 ounces) spaghetti

1. Sprinkle chicken with cayenne and salt. In a Dutch oven, heat the oil over medium-high heat. Brown chicken in batches. Remove from pan.
2. Add sausage, onion, green pepper and celery to same pan; cook and stir over medium heat for 3 minutes. Add the garlic; cook 1 minute longer. Stir in tomatoes. Return chicken to pan; bring to a boil. Reduce heat; simmer, covered, for 1 hour or until chicken juices run clear.
3. Cook the spaghetti according to package directions. Remove chicken from the pan. When cool enough to handle, remove meat from bones; discard skin and bones. Shred meat with two forks; return to pan. Bring to a boil. Reduce the heat and simmer, uncovered, for 8-10 minutes or until slightly thickened. Skim fat. Drain the spaghetti; serve with chicken mixture.

PER SERVING *¾ cup chicken mixture with ¾ cup spaghetti equals 550 cal., 26 g fat (8 g sat. fat), 89 mg chol., 917 mg sodium, 45 g carb., 4 g fiber, 33 g pro.*

Teriyaki Pineapple Drumsticks

We have a large family and throw big parties, so I look for ways to free my husband from the grill. Roasted drumsticks keep everyone happy.
—**ERICA ALLEN** TUCKERTON, NJ

PREP: 35 MIN. • **BAKE:** 1½ HOURS
MAKES: 12 SERVINGS

- 1 tablespoon garlic salt
- 1 tablespoon minced chives
- 1½ teaspoons paprika
- 1½ teaspoons pepper
- ½ teaspoon salt
- 24 chicken drumsticks
- ½ cup canola oil
- 1 can (8 ounces) crushed pineapple
- ½ cup water
- ¼ cup packed brown sugar
- ¼ cup Worcestershire sauce
- ¼ cup yellow mustard
- 4 teaspoons cornstarch
- 2 tablespoons cold water

1. Preheat oven to 350°. In a small bowl, mix the first five ingredients; sprinkle over the chicken. In a large skillet, heat oil over medium-high heat. Brown drumsticks in batches. Transfer to a roasting pan.
2. Combine pineapple, ½ cup water, brown sugar, Worcestershire sauce and mustard; pour over chicken. Cover; bake until tender, 1½-2 hours, uncovering in last 20-30 minutes of baking to let skin crisp.
3. Remove drumsticks to a platter; keep warm. Transfer cooking juices to a small saucepan; skim fat. Bring cooking juices to a boil. In a small bowl, mix cornstarch and cold water until smooth; stir into cooking juices. Return to a boil; cook and stir sauce for 1-2 minutes or until thickened. Serve with drumsticks.

PER SERVING *2 chicken drumsticks equals 360 cal., 22 g fat (4 g sat. fat), 95 mg chol., 540 mg sodium, 11 g carb., 1 g fiber, 29 g pro.*

PIZZA PASTA CASSEROLE

Pizza Pasta Casserole

Kids will line up for this pizza-flavored dish. The recipe makes two casseroles, so you can serve one to your family right away and keep the other in the freezer for another night.
—**NANCY SCARLETT** GRAHAM, NC

PREP: 20 MIN. • **BAKE:** 25 MIN.
MAKES: 2 CASSEROLES (8-10 SERVINGS EACH)

- 2 pounds ground beef
- 1 large onion, chopped
- 3½ cups spaghetti sauce
- 1 package (16 ounces) spiral pasta, cooked and drained
- 4 cups (16 ounces) shredded part-skim mozzarella cheese
- 8 ounces sliced pepperoni

1. Preheat oven to 350°. In a large skillet, cook the beef and onion over medium heat until meat is no longer pink; drain. Stir in spaghetti sauce and pasta.
2. Transfer to two greased 13x9-in. baking dishes. Sprinkle with cheese. Arrange pepperoni over the top.
3. Bake, uncovered, 25-30 minutes or until heated through.

FREEZE OPTION *Cool the unbaked casseroles; cover and freeze for up to 3 months. To use, partially thaw in the refrigerator overnight. Remove from refrigerator 30 minutes before baking. Preheat oven to 350°. Bake as directed, increasing the time to 35-40 minutes or until heated through and a thermometer reads 165°.*

PER SERVING *301 cal., 15 g fat (6 g sat. fat), 46 mg chol., 545 mg sodium, 22 g carb., 1 g fiber, 19 g pro.*

TERIYAKI PINEAPPLE DRUMSTICKS

HONEY GRILLED SHRIMP

(5) INGREDIENTS

Honey Grilled Shrimp

My husband got this super simple recipe from a man who sold shrimp at the fish market. It's now become our family's absolute favorite shrimp recipe. We serve it to company often, with great success. Enjoy!

—LISA BLACKWELL HENDERSON, NC

PREP: 20 MIN. + MARINATING
GRILL: 10 MIN. • **MAKES:** 8 SERVINGS

- ¾ cup Italian salad dressing
- ¾ cup honey
- ¼ teaspoon minced garlic
- 2 pounds uncooked medium shrimp, peeled and deveined

1. In a small bowl, combine the salad dressing, honey and garlic; set aside ½ cup. Pour remaining marinade into a large resealable plastic bag; add the shrimp. Seal the bag and turn to coat; refrigerate for 30 minutes. Cover and refrigerate the reserved marinade for basting.
2. Drain shrimp, discarding marinade from bag. Thread shrimp onto eight metal or soaked wooden skewers.
3. On a greased grill rack, grill shrimp, uncovered, over medium heat or broil 4 in. from the heat for 1½-2 minutes on each side. Baste with the reserved marinade. Grill or broil 2-3 minutes longer or until shrimp are pink and firm, turning and basting frequently.
PER SERVING *175 cal., 5 g fat (1 g sat. fat), 168 mg chol., 383 mg sodium, 14 g carb., trace fiber, 18 g pro.* **Diabetic Exchanges:** *3 lean meat, 1 starch, 1 fat.*

Pina Colada Pork Chops with Tropical Fruit Salsa

PREP: 25 MIN. + MARINATING
GRILL: 15 MIN. • **MAKES:** 8 SERVINGS

- 1 can (10 ounces) frozen non-alcoholic pina colada mix, thawed and divided
- 4 bone-in pork loin chops (15 ounces each)
- ½ teaspoon salt
- ¼ teaspoon pepper
- 1 cup chicken broth
- 1 tablespoon lemon juice
- 1 tablespoon lime juice
- ⅛ teaspoon cayenne pepper
- 2 tablespoons cold butter

SALSA
- 2 medium kiwifruit, peeled and finely chopped
- ½ medium banana, finely chopped
- ½ medium ripe avocado, peeled and finely chopped
- 2 teaspoons lime juice
- 1 teaspoon minced fresh cilantro
- 1 teaspoon minced fresh basil

1. Place ¾ cup pina colada mix in a shallow dish. Add pork; turn to coat. Refrigerate at least 1 hour.
2. Drain pork, discarding marinade. Sprinkle with salt and pepper. Grill, covered, over medium-high heat, or broil 4 in. from the heat, or until a thermometer reads 145°, 6-8 minutes on each side. Let stand 5 minutes.
3. Meanwhile, in a small saucepan, combine the broth, remaining pina colada mix, lemon juice, lime juice and cayenne. Bring to a boil; cook, uncovered, until liquid is slightly thickened, 10-12 minutes. Remove sauce from heat. Whisk in the butter, 1 tablespoon at a time, until creamy. If needed, return pan briefly to very low heat to soften the butter. (Do not allow butter to melt completely or sauce may separate.)
4. Mix salsa ingredients. Slice pork chops; serve with salsa and sauce.
PER SERVING *½ pork chop with 1 tablespoon salsa and 1 tablespoon sauce equals 417 cal., 23 g fat (9 g sat. fat), 112 mg chol., 373 mg sodium, 17 g carb., 1 g fiber, 35 g pro.*

These zesty chops with kiwi, banana and avocado salsa are a one-way ticket to the tropics. The grilled pork and fruit make a perfect pair. —JENN TIDWELL FAIR OAKS, CA

PINA COLADA PORK CHOPS WITH TROPICAL FRUIT SALSA

Southwestern Shepherd's Pie

Everyone will eat this hearty classic right up! The recipe makes two pies, so you can freeze one of them for another day.

—SUZETTE JURY KEENE, CA

PREP: 35 MIN. • **BAKE:** 25 MIN.
MAKES: 2 CASSEROLES (7 SERVINGS EACH)

- 3 **pounds ground beef**
- 1 **cup chopped onion**
- 2 **cans (10 ounces each) enchilada sauce**
- 2 **tablespoons all-purpose flour**
- 2 **teaspoons chopped chipotle peppers in adobo sauce**
- 1 **teaspoon ground cumin**
- 1 **teaspoon dried oregano**
- 2½ **cups water**
- 2 **cups milk**
- ⅓ **cup butter, cubed**
- 1 **teaspoon salt**
- 4 **cups mashed potato flakes**
- 2 **cans (4 ounces each) chopped green chilies, undrained**
- 2 **cups (8 ounces) shredded Mexican cheese blend, divided**
- 2 **cans (11 ounces each) Mexicorn, drained**
- ⅔ **cup chopped green onions**
  Paprika

1. In a Dutch oven, cook beef and onion over medium heat until the meat is no longer pink; drain. Add the enchilada sauce, flour, chipotle peppers, cumin and oregano; bring to a boil. Reduce the heat; simmer, uncovered, for 5 minutes.
2. Meanwhile, in a large saucepan, combine the water, milk, butter and salt; bring to a boil. Remove from the heat. Stir in the potato flakes until combined. Add chilies and ½ cup cheese.
3. Transfer meat mixture to two greased 11x7-in. baking dishes. Layer with corn, mashed potato mixture and remaining cheese. Sprinkle with green onions. Cover and freeze one casserole for up to 3 months.
4. Cover and bake the remaining casserole at 375° for 20 minutes. Uncover and bake 5-10 minutes longer or until bubbly. Sprinkle with paprika.

SLOW COOKER CURRY CHICKEN

TO USE FROZEN CASSEROLE *Thaw in the refrigerator overnight. Remove from refrigerator 30 minutes before baking. Cover and bake at 375° for 20 minutes. Uncover and bake for 5-20 minutes longer or until bubbly. Sprinkle with paprika.*
PER SERVING *1 cup equals 399 cal., 20 g fat (11 g sat. fat), 77 mg chol., 973 mg sodium, 32 g carb., 3 g fiber, 26 g pro.*

Slow Cooker Curry Chicken

My husband travels for business and discovered that he likes Indian cuisine. This simple slow-cooked recipe has the flavors he really enjoys. Use parsley if you don't have cilantro.

—KATIE SCHULTZ TEMPLE, GA

PREP: 15 MIN. • **COOK:** 3 HOURS
MAKES: 4 SERVINGS

- 2 **medium onions, cut into wedges**
- 2 **medium sweet red peppers, cut into 1-inch strips**
- 4 **boneless skinless chicken breast halves (6 ounces each)**
- 2 **tablespoons curry powder, divided**
- 1 **teaspoon salt, divided**
- 1 **cup light coconut milk**
- ½ **cup chicken broth**
- 3 **garlic cloves, minced**
- ½ **teaspoon pepper**
- 1 **cup chopped dried apricots (about 6 ounces)**
  Hot cooked rice and lime wedges
  Chopped cashews and minced fresh cilantro, optional

1. Place onions and peppers in a 4-qt. slow cooker. Sprinkle chicken with 1 tablespoon curry powder and ½ teaspoon salt; place over vegetables.
2. In a small bowl, whisk coconut milk, broth, garlic, pepper and the remaining curry powder and salt. Pour into slow cooker. Cook, covered, on low 3–3½ hours or until chicken is tender (a thermometer should read at least 165°), adding apricots during the last 30 minutes of cooking.
3. Serve with rice and lime wedges. If desired, sprinkle with cashews and cilantro.
PER SERVING *1 chicken breast half with about 1 cup vegetable mixture (calculated without optional ingredients) equals 367 cal., 9 g fat (4 g sat. fat), 95 mg chol., 824 mg sodium, 34 g carb., 6 g fiber, 37 g pro.*

(5) INGREDIENTS FAST FIX

Jalapeno-Lime Chicken Drumsticks

Bottled hot sauce isn't my thing, so I developed a fresh pepper glaze for grilled chicken. These drumsticks practically fly off the plate.

—KRISTEEN DEVORSS FARMINGTON, NM

START TO FINISH: 25 MIN.
MAKES: 6 SERVINGS

- 1 jar (10 ounces) red jalapeno pepper jelly
- ¼ cup lime juice
- 12 chicken drumsticks (about 3 pounds)
- 1 teaspoon salt
- ½ teaspoon pepper

1. In a small saucepan, heat jelly and lime juice over medium heat until melted. Set aside ½ cup for serving.
2. Sprinkle chicken with salt and pepper. On a greased grill rack, grill chicken, covered, over medium heat 15-20 minutes or until a thermometer reads 170°-175°, turning occasionally and basting with the remaining jelly mixture during the last 5 minutes of cooking. Serve drumsticks with the reserved jelly mixture.

PER SERVING *2 chicken drumsticks equals 361 cal., 12 g fat (3 g sat. fat), 95 mg chol., 494 mg sodium, 34 g carb., 1 g fiber, 29 g pro.*

SAUCY BAKED CHICKEN

JALAPENO-LIME CHICKEN DRUMSTICKS

(5) INGREDIENTS

Saucy Baked Chicken

This irresistible chicken gets its wonderful flavor from bubbling in honey and soy sauce while baking. It's always a hit.

—CAROLINE CHAMPOUX
LONDONDERRY, NH

PREP: 25 MIN. • **BAKE:** 30 MIN.
MAKES: 6 SERVINGS

- 6 boneless skinless chicken breast halves (6 ounces each)
- 1 cup honey
- ½ cup reduced-sodium soy sauce
- 2 tablespoons olive oil
- 2 tablespoons ketchup
- 1 garlic clove, minced
- ¼ teaspoon salt
- ⅛ teaspoon pepper

1. Preheat oven to 375°. Place the chicken in a greased 13x9-in. baking dish. In a small bowl, mix remaining ingredients; pour over chicken.
2. Bake, uncovered, 30-35 minutes or until a thermometer reads 165°, basting occasionally. Remove chicken from the baking dish and keep warm.
3. Transfer sauce to a small saucepan. Bring to a boil; cook and stir for 12-15 minutes or until sauce is reduced to 1¼ cups.

PER SERVING *1 chicken breast half with about 3 tablespoons sauce equals 412 cal., 8 g fat (2 g sat. fat), 94 mg chol., 1,013 mg sodium, 49 g carb., trace fiber, 36 g pro.*

MAIN DISHES

Confetti Spaghetti

It's not uncommon for folks to go back for second helpings of this hearty main dish when I share it at church potluck suppers.
—**KATHERINE MOSS** GAFFNEY, SC

PREP: 20 MIN. • **BAKE:** 35 MIN.
MAKES: 12 SERVINGS

- 1 package (16 ounces) spaghetti
- 1½ pounds ground beef
- 1 medium green pepper, chopped
- 1 medium onion, chopped
- 1 can (14½ ounces) diced tomatoes, undrained
- 1 can (8 ounces) tomato sauce
- 1 tablespoon brown sugar
- 1 teaspoon salt
- 1 teaspoon chili powder
- ½ teaspoon pepper
- ¼ teaspoon garlic powder
- ⅛ teaspoon cayenne pepper
- ¾ cup shredded cheddar cheese

1. Preheat the oven to 350°. Cook the spaghetti according to package directions. Meanwhile, in a large skillet, cook beef, green pepper and onion over medium heat until meat is no longer pink; drain. Stir in next eight ingredients. Drain spaghetti; add to beef mixture.

2. Transfer to a greased 13x9-in. baking dish. Cover and bake for 30 minutes. Uncover; sprinkle with cheese. Bake until cheese is melted, about 5 minutes longer.

PER SERVING *1 cup equals 259 cal., 10 g fat (4 g sat. fat), 42 mg chol., 424 mg sodium, 27 g carb., 2 g fiber, 16 g pro.*

EAT SMART
Butternut & Portobello Lasagna

Lasagna gets fresh flavor and color when you make it with roasted butternut squash, portobello mushrooms, basil and spinach. We feast on this.
—**EDWARD AND DANIELLE WALKER**
TRAVERSE CITY, MI

PREP: 1 HOUR • **BAKE:** 45 MIN. + STANDING
MAKES: 12 SERVINGS

- 1 package (10 ounces) frozen cubed butternut squash, thawed
- 2 teaspoons olive oil
- 1 teaspoon brown sugar
- ¼ teaspoon salt
- ⅛ teaspoon pepper

MUSHROOMS
- 4 large portobello mushrooms, coarsely chopped
- 2 teaspoons balsamic vinegar
- 2 teaspoons olive oil
- ¼ teaspoon salt
- ⅛ teaspoon pepper

SAUCE
- 2 cans (28 ounces each) whole tomatoes, undrained
- 2 teaspoons olive oil
- 2 garlic cloves, minced
- 1 teaspoon crushed red pepper flakes
- ½ cup fresh basil leaves, thinly sliced
- ¼ teaspoon salt
- ⅛ teaspoon pepper

LASAGNA
- 4 ounces fresh baby spinach (about 5 cups)
- 9 no-cook lasagna noodles
- 3 cups part-skim ricotta cheese
- 1½ cups (6 ounces) shredded part-skim mozzarella cheese

1. Preheat the oven to 350°. In a large bowl, combine first five ingredients. In another bowl, combine the mushroom ingredients. Transfer the vegetables to separate foil-lined 15x10x1-in. baking pans. Roast for 14-16 minutes or until tender, stirring occasionally.

2. Meanwhile, for the sauce, drain tomatoes, reserving juices; coarsely chop tomatoes. In a large saucepan, heat oil over medium heat. Add garlic and pepper flakes; cook for 1 minute longer. Stir in the chopped tomatoes, reserved tomato juices, basil, salt and pepper; bring to a boil. Reduce heat; simmer, uncovered, 35-45 minutes or until thickened, stirring occasionally.

3. Spread 1 cup sauce into a greased 13x9-in. baking dish. Layer with three noodles, 1 cup of sauce, spinach and mushrooms. Continue layering with three noodles, 1 cup of sauce, ricotta cheese and roasted squash. Top with remaining noodles and sauce. Sprinkle with mozzarella cheese.

4. Bake, covered, 30 minutes. Bake, uncovered, 15-20 minutes longer or until bubbly. Let stand 15 minutes before serving.

PER SERVING *1 piece equals 252 cal., 10 g fat (5 g sat. fat), 27 mg chol., 508 mg sodium, 25 g carb., 4 g fiber, 15 g pro.* **Diabetic Exchanges:** *2 starch, 1 medium-fat meat, ½ fat.*

BUTTERNUT & PORTOBELLO LASAGNA

Chicken with Citrus Chimichurri Sauce

Chimichurri is a green sauce from South America that goes with grilled meats. My citrus version brightens up grilled chicken, which gets its juiciness from brining.

—**TYFFANIE PEREZ** SPRINGVILLE, UT

PREP: 20 MIN. + MARINATING
GRILL: 10 MIN. • **MAKES:** 4 SERVINGS

- 4 cups water
- ¼ cup kosher salt
- 1 tablespoon honey
- 1 teaspoon grated lemon peel
- 1 teaspoon grated orange peel
- 4 boneless skinless chicken breast halves (6 ounces each)

CHIMICHURRI SAUCE

- ½ cup olive oil
- ¼ cup packed fresh parsley sprigs
- 1 tablespoon minced fresh thyme
- 1 tablespoon lemon juice
- 1 tablespoon orange juice
- 1 garlic clove, peeled
- ¼ teaspoon salt
- ⅛ teaspoon pepper

1. In a large bowl, whisk water, salt, honey and peels until salt is dissolved. Add chicken, making sure that it is submerged. Refrigerate up to 2 hours.
2. Pulse sauce ingredients in a food processor until smooth. Reserve ½ cup sauce for serving.
3. Remove chicken; rinse and pat dry. Brush chicken with remaining sauce. Grill, covered, over medium-high heat or broil 4 in. from heat until a thermometer reads 165°, 4-6 minutes on each side. Serve with the reserved chimichurri sauce.

PER SERVING *1 chicken breast half with 2 tablespoons sauce equals 427 cal., 31 g fat (5 g sat. fat), 94 mg chol., 279 mg sodium, 1 g carb., 0 fiber, 35 g pro.*

Lemon & Sage Roasted Chicken

First soak the chicken in marinade, then bake it in the oven. This allows plenty of time to do other things in and around the kitchen.

—**JAN VALDEZ** CHICAGO, IL

PREP: 20 MIN. + MARINATING
BAKE: 2¼ HOURS + STANDING
MAKES: 8 SERVINGS

- ¼ cup lemon juice
- ¼ cup plus 3 tablespoons olive oil, divided
- 5 garlic cloves, minced
- 2 tablespoons minced fresh sage
- 1 roasting chicken (6 to 7 pounds)
- 2 tablespoons butter, softened
- 1 medium lemon, cut into wedges
- 8 medium potatoes, quartered
- 2 medium onions, quartered
- ½ teaspoon salt
- ¼ teaspoon pepper

1. Combine the lemon juice, ¼ cup oil, garlic and sage in a shallow dish. Add chicken; turn to coat. Cover and refrigerate for at least 4 hours. Drain and discard marinade.
2. Loosen chicken skin; rub butter underneath. Fill cavity with lemon wedges. Place chicken, breast side up, on a rack in a roasting pan.
3. Stir together potatoes, onions, salt, pepper and remaining oil. Arrange around chicken. Roast, uncovered, at 350° until a thermometer inserted in thickest part of thigh reads 170°-175°. If chicken browns too quickly, cover loosely with foil. Let stand 15 minutes before carving.

ROASTED LIME CHICKEN *Replace marinade ingredients with ½ cup Dijon mustard; ¼ cup each lime juice and soy sauce; 2 teaspoons each dried parsley flakes, rosemary, thyme and rubbed sage; and 1 teaspoon each white pepper and ground nutmeg. Omit the butter. Substitute lime for lemon.*

PER SERVING *6 ounces cooked chicken equals 674 cal., 35 g fat (10 g sat. fat), 142 mg chol., 314 mg sodium, 41 g carb. (3 g sugars, 5 g fiber), 47 g pro.*

CHICKEN WITH CITRUS
CHIMICHURRI SAUCE

SUNDAY POT ROAST

SLOW COOKER

Sunday Pot Roast

With the slow cooker's help, we make a homey roast for any day of the week. This savory pork loin with aromatic caraway is beyond tender.

—BRANDY SCHAEFER GLEN CARBON, IL

PREP: 10 MIN. + CHILLING • **COOK:** 8 HOURS
MAKES: 14 SERVINGS

- 1 teaspoon dried oregano
- ½ teaspoon onion salt
- ½ teaspoon caraway seeds
- ½ teaspoon pepper
- ¼ teaspoon garlic salt
- 1 boneless pork loin roast (3½-4 pounds), trimmed
- 6 medium carrots, peeled and cut into 1½-inch pieces
- 3 large potatoes, peeled and quartered
- 3 small onions, quartered
- 1½ cups beef broth
- ⅓ cup all-purpose flour
- ⅓ cup cold water
- ¼ teaspoon browning sauce, optional

1. Combine the first five ingredients; rub over the roast. Wrap in plastic and refrigerate overnight.
2. Place carrots, potatoes and onions in a 6-qt. slow cooker; add beef broth. Unwrap roast; place in slow cooker. Cook, covered, on low until meat and vegetables are tender, 8-10 hours.
3. Transfer roast and vegetables to a serving platter; tent with foil. Pour cooking juices into a small saucepan. Mix the flour and water until smooth; stir into pan. Bring to a boil; cook and stir until thickened, about 2 minutes. If desired, add browning sauce. Serve roast with gravy and vegetables.
PER SERVING *233 cal., 5 g fat (2 g sat. fat), 56 mg chol., 249 mg sodium, 21 g carb., 2 g fiber, 24 g pro.* **Diabetic Exchanges:** *3 lean meat, 1½ starch.*

Lemony Salmon Patties

These patties bake up golden brown in a muffin pan. They're impressive enough for company, but easy enough that I can prepare them any time.

—LORICE BRITT SEVERN, NC

PREP: 20 MIN. • **BAKE:** 45 MIN.
MAKES: 4 SERVINGS

- 1 can (14¾ ounces) pink salmon, drained, skin and bones removed
- ¾ cup milk
- 1 cup soft bread crumbs
- 1 large egg, lightly beaten
- 1 tablespoon minced fresh parsley
- 1 teaspoon finely chopped onion
- ½ teaspoon Worcestershire sauce
- ¼ teaspoon salt
- ⅛ teaspoon pepper

LEMON SAUCE
- 2 tablespoons butter
- 4 teaspoons all-purpose flour
- ¾ cup milk
- 2 tablespoons lemon juice
- ¼ teaspoon salt
- ⅛ to ¼ teaspoon cayenne pepper

1. Preheat the oven to 350°. In a large bowl, combine the first nine ingredients. Fill eight greased muffin cups with ¼ cup salmon mixture. Bake for 45 minutes or until patties are lightly browned.
2. Meanwhile, melt butter in a small saucepan; stir in flour until smooth. Gradually stir in milk; bring to a boil over medium heat. Cook and stir for 2 minutes or until thickened. Remove from heat; stir in lemon juice, salt and cayenne. Serve with patties.
SALMON BURGERS *Omit the sauce. Shape the salmon mixture into four patties. In a large nonstick skillet coated with cooking spray, cook patties over medium heat for 4-5 minutes on each side or until lightly browned. Serve on English muffin halves or hamburger buns with lettuce and tomato if desired.*
PER SERVING *328 cal., 18 g fat (8 g sat. fat), 127 mg chol., 1,044 mg sodium, 13 g carb., trace fiber, 27 g pro.*

LEMONY SALMON PATTIES

DONNA MARIE RYAN'S UPSIDE-DOWN BANANA MONKEY BREAD *PAGE 94*

Breads, Rolls & Muffins

Everybody loves **hot homemade bread,** and these **loaves,** muffins, rolls and **scones** will steal hearts while they **warm your home** with enchanting aromas. Your **fresh-baked** delights will disappear fast.

**GAYE O'DELL'S
HONEY SPICE BREAD**
PAGE 89

**NICHOLE JONES'
CHOCOLATE CHIP-CRANBERRY
SCONES** *PAGE 93*

**LINDA SCHEND'S
QUICK & EASY HERB
FOCACCIA ROLLS** *PAGE 90*

⑤ INGREDIENTS

Sour Cream Blueberry Muffins

When we were growing up, my mom made these delicious muffins on chilly mornings. I'm now in college and enjoy baking them for friends.

—TORY ROSS CINCINNATI, OH

PREP: 15 MIN. • **BAKE:** 20 MIN.
MAKES: 1 DOZEN

- 2 cups biscuit/baking mix
- ¾ cup plus 2 tablespoons sugar, divided
- 2 large eggs
- 1 cup (8 ounces) sour cream
- 1 cup fresh or frozen blueberries

1. Preheat oven to 375°. In a large bowl, combine biscuit mix and ¾ cup sugar. In a small bowl, combine the eggs and sour cream; stir into the dry ingredients just until combined. Fold in blueberries.

2. Fill greased muffin cups three-fourths full. Sprinkle with remaining sugar. Bake for 20-25 minutes or until a toothpick inserted in muffin comes out clean. Cool for 5 minutes before removing from pan to a wire rack.

NOTE *If using frozen blueberries, use berries without thawing to avoid discoloring the batter.*

PER SERVING *1 muffin equals 195 cal., 7 g fat (3 g sat. fat), 48 mg chol., 272 mg sodium, 29 g carb., 1 g fiber, 3 g pro.*

Cinnamon Raisin Bread

Here's my version of the time-honored cinnamon swirl bread. Confectioners' sugar icing makes it even more special. The recipe makes two loaves, perfect for sharing with the neighbors.

—DEANNA PATTERSON GREENVILLE, TX

PREP: 25 MIN. + RISING • **BAKE:** 30 MIN.
MAKES: 2 LOAVES (16 SLICES EACH)

- 1 package (¼ ounce) active dry yeast
- ¼ cup warm water (110° to 115°)
- 2 cups warm milk (110° to 115°)
- ⅓ cup plus ½ cup sugar, divided
- ¼ cup canola oil
- 2 teaspoons salt
- 5¾ to 6¼ cups all-purpose flour
- 2 cups raisins
- 1 tablespoon ground cinnamon
- 1 tablespoon water

GLAZE
- ½ cup confectioners' sugar
- 1 tablespoon milk

1. In a large bowl, dissolve yeast in warm water. Add milk, ⅓ cup sugar, oil, salt and 2 cups flour. Beat until smooth. Add the raisins and enough remaining flour to form a soft dough.

2. Turn onto a floured surface; knead until dough smooth and elastic, about 6-8 minutes. Place in a greased bowl, turning once to grease the top. Cover and let the dough rise in a warm place until doubled, about 1¼ hours.

3. Punch dough down. On a lightly floured surface, divide in half. Roll each portion into a 15x7-in. rectangle. Combine cinnamon and remaining sugar; sprinkle over dough. Sprinkle with water. Starting with a short side, roll up tightly, jelly-roll style. Pinch seams and ends to seal. Place, seam side down, in two greased 9x5-in. loaf pans. Cover pans and let rise until doubled, about 1 hour.

4. Preheat the oven to 350°. Bake for 30-35 minutes or until golden brown. Remove from pans to wire racks to cool completely. Combine the glaze ingredients; drizzle glaze over the warm loaves.

PER SERVING *1 slice equals 162 cal., 3 g fat (1 g sat. fat), 2 mg chol., 157 mg sodium, 32 g carb., 1 g fiber, 3 g pro.*

SOUR CREAM BLUEBERRY MUFFINS

Honey Spice Bread

The texture of this bread is almost like a cake, so I usually serve slices of it for dessert. Plus, the glaze drizzled on top makes the loaf looks so festive.

—GAYE O'DELL BINGHAMTON, NY

PREP: 20 MIN. • **BAKE:** 50 MIN. + COOLING
MAKES: 1 LOAF (12 SLICES)

- ⅔ **cup packed brown sugar**
- ⅓ **cup 2% milk**
- 2 **cups all-purpose flour**
- 1½ **teaspoons baking powder**
- ½ **teaspoon ground cinnamon**
- ½ **teaspoon ground nutmeg**
- ⅛ **teaspoon ground cloves**
- 2 **large eggs**
- ½ **cup honey**
- ⅓ **cup canola oil**

GLAZE
- ⅓ **cup confectioners' sugar**
- 2 **teaspoons 2% milk**

1. Preheat oven to 325°. In a small saucepan, combine brown sugar and milk. Cook and stir over low heat until sugar is dissolved. Remove from heat.
2. In a large bowl, whisk flour, baking powder, cinnamon, nutmeg and cloves. In another bowl, whisk eggs, honey, oil and brown sugar mixture until blended. Add to flour mixture; stir just until moistened.
3. Transfer to a greased 8x4-in. loaf pan. Bake 50-60 minutes or until a toothpick inserted in center comes out clean (cover top loosely with foil if needed to prevent overbrowning).
4. Cool bread in pan for 10 minutes before removing to a wire rack to cool completely. In a small bowl, stir glaze ingredients until smooth; drizzle over the bread.

FREEZE OPTION *Securely wrap and freeze cooled loaf in plastic wrap and foil. To use, thaw at room temperature. Glaze as directed.*

NOTE *To remove bread easily, use solid shortening to grease pan.*

PER SERVING *1 slice equals 187 cal., 6 g fat (1 g sat. fat), 27 mg chol., 53 mg sodium, 33 g carb., 1 g fiber, 3 g pro. Diabetic Exchanges: 2 starch, 1 fat.*

RUSTIC OATMEAL SCONES

EAT SMART
Rustic Oatmeal Scones

Surprise a loved one with these delightful treats! Great with coffee or tea, the classic bites promise to bring smiles to everyone at your brunch.

—GAIL D'URSO CARLISLE, PA

PREP: 20 MIN. • **BAKE:** 15 MIN.
MAKES: 16 SCONES

- 1½ **cups all-purpose flour**
- ½ **cup whole wheat flour**
- ½ **cup sugar**
- 2 **teaspoons baking powder**
- 1 **teaspoon baking soda**
- ¾ **teaspoon salt**
- ¼ **cup cold butter, cubed**
- 2 **cups quick-cooking oats**
- 1 **cup dried blueberries or raisins**
- 1 **cup (8 ounces) plain yogurt**
- 3 **tablespoons fat-free milk, divided**
  Coarse sugar

1. Preheat oven to 400°. In a large bowl, whisk the first six ingredients. Cut in butter until mixture resembles coarse crumbs. Stir in the oats and blueberries. In another bowl, whisk yogurt and 1 tablespoon milk until blended; stir into crumb mixture just until moistened.
2. Turn onto a lightly floured surface; knead gently 10 times. Divide dough in half; pat each into a 7-in. circle. Cut each into eight wedges. Place wedges on a baking sheet coated with cooking spray. Brush tops with remaining milk. Sprinkle with coarse sugar.
3. Bake 13-15 minutes or until golden brown. Serve warm.

PER SERVING *1 scone (calculated without coarse sugar) equals 186 cal., 4 g fat (2 g sat. fat), 11 mg chol., 273 mg sodium, 32 g carb., 3 g fiber, 4 g pro. Diabetic Exchanges: 2 starch, 1 fat.*

Quick & Easy Herb Focaccia Rolls

Yeast rolls speckled with fresh rosemary and thyme are a breeze to make, with no kneading and just one short time for rising. Break out the good butter for these adorable rolls.

—**LINDA SCHEND** KENOSHA, WI

PREP: 15 MIN. + RISING • **BAKE:** 20 MIN.
MAKES: 1½ DOZEN

- 3 **cups all-purpose flour**
- 1 **package (¼ ounce) quick-rise yeast**
- 2 **tablespoons minced fresh thyme, divided**
- 2 **tablespoons minced fresh rosemary, divided**
- 1 **tablespoon sugar**
- 1½ **teaspoons kosher salt, divided**
- 1½ **cups warm water (120° to 130°)**
- 6 **tablespoons extra-virgin olive oil, divided**

1. Combine flour, yeast, 1 tablespoon thyme, 1 tablespoon rosemary, sugar and 1 teaspoon salt. Add the water and 2 tablespoons of oil; beat for 1 minute (dough will be very sticky).

2. Divide dough among 18 greased muffin cups. Let rise in a warm place until doubled, about 30 minutes.

3. Preheat oven to 375°. In a small saucepan over medium-low heat, stir together remaining seasonings and oil just until herbs are fragrant and oil is hot, about 1½ minutes. Remove from heat; cool.

4. Gently spoon cooled herb mixture over each roll. Bake until the rolls are golden brown, 20-25 minutes.

NOTE *For standard focaccia, spread dough in a greased 13x9-in. pan. Let rise in a warm place until doubled, about 30 minutes. Top with the herb mixture; bake at 375° until golden brown, 25-30 minutes.*

PER SERVING *1 roll equals 120 cal., 5 g fat (1 g sat. fat), 0 chol., 161 mg sodium, 17 g carb., 1 g fiber, 2 g pro.*

GRILLED GARDEN VEGGIE FLATBREAD

EAT SMART **FAST FIX**

Grilled Garden Veggie Flatbread

Grilled flatbread is a tasty way to put fresh garden vegetables to use. It's so versatile: Simply change up the vegetables and cheese to suit your family's taste. The recipe also works well indoors, cooked on a grill pan with a lid.

—**CARLY CURTIN** ELLICOTT CITY, MD

START TO FINISH: 20 MIN.
MAKES: 8 SERVINGS

- 2 **whole grain naan flatbreads**
- 2 **teaspoons olive oil**
- 1 **medium yellow or red tomato, thinly sliced**
- ¼ **cup thinly sliced onion**
- ½ **cup shredded part-skim mozzarella cheese**
- 2 **tablespoons shredded Parmesan cheese**
- 1 **tablespoon minced fresh basil**
- ½ **teaspoon garlic powder**
- 1 **teaspoon balsamic vinegar**
- ½ **teaspoon coarse sea salt**

1. Grill the flatbreads, covered, over indirect medium heat 2-3 minutes or until bottoms are lightly browned.

2. Remove from grill. Brush grilled sides with oil; top with tomato and onion to within ½ in. of edges. In a small bowl, toss cheeses with basil and garlic powder; sprinkle over the vegetables. Drizzle with the vinegar; sprinkle with salt. Return to grill; cook, covered, 2-3 minutes longer or until cheese is melted. Cut naans into wedges.

PER SERVING *1 wedge equals 132 cal., 5 g fat (2 g sat. fat), 8 mg chol., 390 mg sodium, 16 g carb., 2 g fiber, 5 g pro.*
Diabetic Exchanges: 1 starch, 1 fat.

Spinach-Stuffed Bread

Appetizers are the highlight of parties at our home. And slices of this golden loaf swirled with spinach and cheese disappear in a hurry. They're a tasty accompaniment to most any meal, too.

—TERRY BYRNE WARWICK, NY

PREP: 15 MIN. + RISING • **BAKE:** 25 MIN.
MAKES: 6 SERVINGS

- 1 loaf (1 pound) frozen bread dough
- 1 medium onion, chopped
- 1 to 2 garlic cloves, minced
- 2 teaspoons olive oil
- 1 package (10 ounces) frozen chopped spinach, thawed and squeezed dry
- 2 cups (8 ounces) shredded reduced-fat cheddar or part-skim mozzarella

1. Thaw the bread dough according to package directions; let rise until doubled. Meanwhile, in a skillet, saute onion and garlic in oil until tender. Stir in spinach.

2. On a lightly floured surface, roll the dough into a 14x10-in. rectangle. Spread the spinach mixture to within ½ in. of edges; sprinkle with cheese. Roll up jelly-roll style, starting with a long side; pinch seam to seal. Place roll seam side down on a baking sheet coated with cooking spray; tuck the ends under.

3. Bake at 350° for 25-30 minutes or until golden brown. Remove from pan to a wire rack; let stand for 10 minutes before slicing. Serve warm.

PER SERVING *340 cal., 11 g fat (4 g sat. fat), 20 mg chol., 687 mg sodium, 45 g carb., 4 g fiber, 21 g pro.* **Diabetic Exchanges:** *2 starch, 2 lean meat, 1½ fat.*

💬 TOP TIP

To quickly peel fresh garlic, gently crush the clove with the flat side of a large knife blade to loosen the peel. If you don't have a large knife, you can crush the garlic with a small can.

EAT SMART

Herb & Olive Oil Corn Bread

PREP: 25 MIN. • **BAKE:** 15 MIN.
MAKES: 8 SERVINGS

- ¾ cup cornmeal
- ½ cup all-purpose flour
- 1 tablespoon sugar
- 1 tablespoon grated Parmesan cheese
- 1½ teaspoons baking powder
- 1 teaspoon minced fresh rosemary or ¼ teaspoon dried rosemary, crushed
- 1 teaspoon minced fresh thyme or ¼ teaspoon dried thyme
- ½ teaspoon salt
- 1 large egg
- ¾ cup buttermilk
- 3 tablespoons olive oil, divided
- ½ cup plus 2 tablespoons shredded Italian cheese blend, divided

1. Preheat oven to 425°. Place an 8-in. cast-iron skillet in oven; heat skillet 10 minutes.

2. Meanwhile, in a large bowl, whisk the first eight ingredients. In another bowl, whisk the egg, buttermilk and 2 tablespoons oil until blended. Add to cornmeal mixture; stir just until moistened. Stir in ½ cup cheese.

3. Carefully remove hot skillet from oven. Add remaining oil to skillet; tilt pan to coat the bottom and sides. Add the batter, spreading evenly. Sprinkle with remaining cheese.

4. Bake 12-15 minutes or until golden brown and a toothpick inserted in the center comes out clean. Cut bread into wedges; serve warm.

PER SERVING *1 wedge equals 183 cal., 8 g fat (2 g sat. fat), 31 mg chol., 352 mg sodium, 21 g carb., 1 g fiber, 6 g pro.* **Diabetic Exchanges:** *1½ starch, 1½ fat.*

Olive oil helps showcase the flavor of fresh herbs in this fragrant corn bread. It is always a huge hit with my family and friends! —LISA SPEER PALM BEACH, FL

HERB & OLIVE OIL CORN BREAD

Grapefruit Poppy Seed Bread

I had grapefruits lying around, so I used the zest and juice to make a lovely quick bread. It's got a nice little tang and a tender crumb.
—LISA MORIARTY WILTON, NH

PREP: 15 MIN. • **BAKE:** 55 MIN. + COOLING
MAKES: 1 LOAF (16 SLICES)

- 1 cup butter, softened
- 1⅔ cups sugar, divided
- 3 large eggs
- ¾ cup (6 ounces) vanilla yogurt
- 3 tablespoons poppy seeds
- 2 tablespoons grated grapefruit peel
- 1½ teaspoons vanilla extract
- 2 cups all-purpose flour
- ½ teaspoon baking soda
- ¼ teaspoon salt
- ¼ cup grapefruit juice

GLAZE

- 1 cup confectioners' sugar
- 2 tablespoons grapefruit juice

1. Preheat the oven to 350°. In a large bowl, cream butter and 1⅓ cups sugar until light and fluffy. Add eggs, one at a time, beating well after each addition. Beat in yogurt, poppy seeds, grapefruit peel and vanilla. In another bowl, whisk the flour, baking soda and salt; gradually beat into creamed mixture.

2. Transfer to a greased 9x5-in. loaf pan. Bake for 55-65 minutes or until a toothpick inserted in center comes out clean. Meanwhile, in a small bowl, mix grapefruit juice and remaining sugar.

3. Remove the bread from the oven. Immediately poke holes in bread with a fork; slowly pour juice mixture over bread. Cool in the pan for 10 minutes before removing bread to a wire rack to cool completely.

4. In a small bowl, mix the grapefruit glaze ingredients; drizzle over bread.

PER SERVING *1 slice equals 296 cal., 13 g fat (8 g sat. fat), 66 mg chol., 189 mg sodium, 43 g carb., 1 g fiber, 4 g pro.*

40-MINUTE HAMBURGER BUNS

(5) INGREDIENTS

40-Minute Hamburger Buns

Here on our ranch, I cook for three men who love hamburgers. These fluffy yet hearty buns are just right for their big appetites. I also serve the buns plain with a meal.
—JESSIE MCKENNEY TWO DOT, MT

PREP: 20 MIN. + RESTING • **BAKE:** 10 MIN.
MAKES: 1 DOZEN

- 2 tablespoons active dry yeast
- 1 cup plus 2 tablespoons warm water (110° to 115°)
- ⅓ cup canola oil
- ¼ cup sugar
- 1 large egg
- 1 teaspoon salt
- 3 to 3½ cups all-purpose flour

1. In a large bowl, dissolve the yeast in warm water. Add oil and sugar; let stand for 5 minutes. Add the egg, salt and enough flour to form a soft dough.

2. Turn onto a floured surface; knead until smooth and elastic, about 3-5 minutes. Do not let rise. Divide into 12 pieces; shape each into a ball. Place 3 in. apart on greased baking sheets.

3. Cover and let rest for 10 minutes. Bake at 425° for 8-12 minutes or until golden brown. Remove from pans to wire racks to cool.

PER SERVING *1 bun equals 195 cal., 7 g fat (1 g sat. fat), 18 mg chol., 204 mg sodium, 29 g carb., 1 g fiber, 5 g pro.*

GRAPEFRUIT POPPY SEED BREAD

Cranberry-Walnut Toasting Bread

Looking for a great bread to start your day? My multigrain loaf is fabulous toasted. It is also good for sandwiches or served warm with dinner.

—**TISH STEVENSON** WYOMING, MI

PREP: 30 MIN. + RISING • **BAKE:** 45 MIN.
MAKES: 2 LOAVES (12 SLICES EACH)

- 6 to 6½ cups all-purpose flour
- 1 cup old-fashioned oats
- ½ cup whole wheat flour
- ⅓ cup packed brown sugar
- 2 teaspoons salt
- 1 package (¼ ounce) active dry yeast
- 2½ cups water
- 2 tablespoons butter
- 1¼ cups dried cranberries or cherries
- ¾ cup chopped walnuts, toasted

1. In a large bowl, combine 3 cups of all-purpose flour, oats, whole wheat flour, brown sugar, salt and yeast. In a small saucepan, heat water and butter to 120°-130°. Add to dry ingredients; beat just until moistened. Stir in the cranberries, walnuts and enough remaining all-purpose flour to form a soft dough.

2. Turn onto a floured surface; knead dough until smooth and elastic, about 6-8 minutes. Place in a greased bowl, turning once to grease the top. Cover and let dough rise in a warm place until doubled, about 1 hour.

3. Punch dough down; divide in half. Shape into loaves; place in two greased 9x5-in. loaf pans. Cover and let rise until doubled, about 45 minutes. Bake at 350° for 45-50 minutes or until the loaves are golden brown. Remove from pans to wire racks to cool. To serve, cut into thick slices and toast.

PER SERVING *1 slice equals 198 cal., 4 g fat (1 g sat. fat), 3 mg chol., 206 mg sodium, 37 g carb., 2 g fiber, 5 g pro.*

Chocolate Chip-Cranberry Scones

My daughter started making scones as a healthier alternative to cookies, since we seem to like cookies of any kind. For a more citrusy flavor, use orange-flavored cranberries.

—**NICHOLE JONES** IDAHO FALLS, ID

START TO FINISH: 30 MIN.
MAKES: 1 DOZEN

- 2 cups all-purpose flour
- 3 tablespoons brown sugar
- 2 teaspoons baking powder
- 1 teaspoon grated orange peel
- ½ teaspoon salt
- ½ teaspoon baking soda
- ¼ cup cold butter
- 1 cup (8 ounces) plain yogurt
- 1 large egg yolk
- ½ cup dried cranberries
- ½ cup semisweet chocolate chips

1. Preheat oven to 400°. In a large bowl, whisk the first six ingredients. Cut in butter until mixture resembles coarse crumbs. In another bowl, whisk yogurt and egg yolk; stir into crumb mixture just until moistened. Stir cranberries and chocolate chips into the dough.

2. Turn onto a floured surface; knead gently 10 times. Pat the dough into an 8-in. circle. Cut into 12 wedges. Place wedges on a baking sheet coated with cooking spray. Bake 10-12 minutes or until golden brown. Serve warm.

FREEZE OPTION *Freeze the cooled scones in resealable plastic freezer bags. To use, thaw scones at room temperature or, if desired, microwave each scone on high for 20-30 seconds or until heated through.*

PER SERVING *1 scone equals 189 cal., 7 g fat (4 g sat. fat), 28 mg chol., 264 mg sodium, 29 g carb., 1 g fiber, 3 g pro.* **Diabetic Exchanges:** *2 starch, 1 fat.*

CHOCOLATE CHIP-CRANBERRY SCONES

Upside-Down Banana Monkey Bread

Everyone digs into monkey bread thanks to its pull-apart design. I add bananas and pecans to a scrumptious showpiece for a brunch or family gathering.

—DONNA MARIE RYAN TOPSFIELD, MA

PREP: 45 MIN. + RISING • **BAKE:** 25 MIN.
MAKES: 24 SERVINGS

- 2 **teaspoons active dry yeast**
- 1 **tablespoon plus ½ cup packed brown sugar, divided**
- 1 **cup warm 2% milk (110° to 115°)**
- 1 **cup mashed ripe bananas (about 2 large)**
- 1 **large egg**
- 2 **tablespoons butter, melted**
- 1 **teaspoon salt**
- 1 **teaspoon ground cinnamon**
- 5¼ to 5¾ **cups all-purpose flour**
- 2 **teaspoons banana extract, optional**

GLAZE
- ⅔ **cup packed brown sugar**
- ½ **cup half-and-half cream**
- 6 **tablespoons butter, cubed**

COATING
- ¾ **cup chopped pecans, toasted**
- 6 **tablespoons butter, melted**
- 1¼ **cups sugar**
- 2½ **teaspoons ground cinnamon**
- 1 **large banana, sliced**

1. In a small bowl, dissolve yeast and 1 tablespoon brown sugar in warm milk. In a large bowl, combine bananas, egg, butter, yeast mixture, salt, cinnamon, 1½ cups flour and remaining brown sugar; if desired, add extract. Beat on medium speed 2 minutes. Stir in the enough remaining flour to form a soft dough (dough will be sticky).

2. Turn dough onto a floured surface; knead until smooth and elastic, about 6-8 minutes. Place in a greased bowl, turning once to grease the top. Cover with plastic wrap and let rise in a warm place until doubled, about 1 hour.

3. In a small saucepan, combine glaze ingredients; bring just to a boil, stirring constantly. Reserve ¼ cup for topping. Pour remaining glaze into a greased 13x9-in. baking pan; sprinkle with the chopped pecans.

4. Pour melted butter into a shallow bowl. In another shallow bowl, mix sugar and cinnamon. Punch down dough. Turn onto a lightly floured surface; divide and shape into 48 balls.

5. Dip the balls in butter, roll in sugar mixture and place in the prepared pan. Cover with a kitchen towel; let rise in a warm place until the dough is almost doubled, about 30 minutes. Preheat oven to 375°.

6. Bake 25-30 minutes or until golden brown. Cool bread in pan 5 minutes before inverting onto a serving plate. Top with sliced banana; drizzle with reserved glaze. Serve warm.

NOTE *To toast nuts, bake in a shallow pan in a 350° oven for 5-10 minutes or cook in a skillet over low heat until lightly browned, stirring occasionally.*
PER SERVING *2 pieces equals 296 cal., 10 g fat (5 g sat. fat), 29 mg chol., 166 mg sodium, 47 g carb., 2 g fiber, 4 g pro.*

Pumpkin Chip Muffins

I started cooking at a young age, just as my sisters and brothers did. Our mother was a very good teacher, and she inspired us all to learn our way around the kitchen.

—CINDY MIDDLETON CHAMPION, AB

PREP: 20 MIN. • **BAKE:** 15 MIN. + COOLING
MAKES: ABOUT 2 DOZEN

- 4 **large eggs**
- 2 **cups sugar**
- 1 **can (15 ounces) solid-pack pumpkin**
- 1½ **cups canola oil**
- 3 **cups all-purpose flour**

PUMPKIN CHIP MUFFINS

- 2 **teaspoons baking soda**
- 1 **teaspoon baking powder**
- 1 **teaspoon ground cinnamon**
- 1 **teaspoon salt**
- 2 **cups (12 ounces) semisweet chocolate chips**

1. In a large bowl, beat eggs, sugar, pumpkin and oil until smooth. Combine the flour, baking soda, baking powder, cinnamon and salt; gradually add to pumpkin mixture and mix well. Fold in chocolate chips. Fill greased or paper-lined muffin cups three-fourths full.

2. Bake at 400° for 15-18 minutes or until a toothpick inserted in center comes out clean. Cool the muffins in pans for 10 minutes before removing to wire racks.

PER SERVING *1 muffin equals 328 cal., 19 g fat (4 g sat. fat), 35 mg chol., 250 mg sodium, 39 g carb., 2 g fiber, 4 g pro.*

READER RAVE

These are delicious. I omitted the chocolate chips because I'm not a fan, but I don't believe that hurt anything. A friend said she made them with white chocolate chips and LOVED them that way, too.
—ANGELA32 TASTEOFHOME.COM

Grilled Garlic Naan

Indian food is my all-time favorite, and no meal is complete without some naan. I like to top my grilled or baked naan with lots of butter, garlic and a little finely chopped fresh cilantro.

—JERRY GULLEY PLEASANT PRAIRIE, WI

START TO FINISH: 20 MIN.
MAKES: 4 SERVINGS

- 2 tablespoons butter, melted
- 3 garlic cloves, minced
- 2 naan flatbreads

1. Stir together butter and garlic. Place naan on grill rack; grill over medium-high heat until bottom is golden brown, about 2 minutes.
2. Flip naans and brush the tops with garlic butter. Grill until the bottoms are golden brown. Remove from grill; cut each naan in half.

PER SERVING *1 slice equals 134 cal., 8 g fat (4 g sat. fat), 18 mg chol., 286 mg sodium, 15 g carb., 1 g fiber, 2 g pro.*

Zucchini Muffins

These yummy zucchini, currant and walnut muffins are an excellent way to use your garden overload of zucchini.

—PEG GAUSZ WATCHUNG, NJ

PREP: 20 MIN. • **BAKE:** 25 MIN.
MAKES: 6 MUFFINS

- ¾ cup all-purpose flour
- ½ cup sugar
- ¼ teaspoon baking powder
- ¼ teaspoon baking soda
- ¼ teaspoon salt
- ¼ teaspoon ground cinnamon
- 1 large egg
- ¼ cup canola oil
- 1 cup finely shredded unpeeled zucchini
- ½ cup chopped walnuts
- ¼ cup dried currants or chopped raisins

1. In a bowl, combine the first six ingredients. Combine the egg and oil; stir into the dry ingredients just until moistened. Fold in zucchini, walnuts and currants.
2. Coat muffin cups with cooking spray or use paper liners; fill three-fourths full with batter. Bake at 350° for 22-25 minutes or until a toothpick comes out clean. Cool the muffins for 5 minutes before removing from pan to a wire rack.

PER SERVING *1 muffin equals 318 cal., 16 g fat (1 g sat. fat), 35 mg chol., 180 mg sodium, 40 g. carb., 2 g fiber, 6 g pro.*

Mom's Chocolate Bread

PREP: 10 MIN. • **BAKE:** 30 MIN. + COOLING
MAKES: 1 LOAF (12 SLICES)

- 4 tablespoons sugar, divided
- 3 tablespoons all-purpose flour
- 1 tablespoon cold butter
- 1 to 3 tablespoons ground cinnamon
- 1 tube (8 ounces) refrigerated crescent rolls
- ⅔ cup semisweet chocolate chips
- 1 tablespoon butter, melted

1. Preheat oven to 375°. For streusel, in a small bowl, mix 3 tablespoons sugar and flour; cut in butter until crumbly. Reserve half of streusel for topping. Stir cinnamon and remaining sugar into remaining streusel.
2. Unroll crescent dough into one long rectangle; press perforations to seal. Sprinkle with chocolate chips and cinnamon mixture. Roll dough up jelly-roll style, starting with a long side; pinch the seam to seal. Fold the roll in half lengthwise; transfer to a greased 8x4-in. loaf pan. Brush with butter; sprinkle with reserved streusel.
3. Bake 30-35 minutes or until golden brown. Cool bread in pan 10 minutes before removing loaf to a wire rack to cool completely.

PER SERVING *1 slice equals 164 cal., 9 g fat (4 g sat. fat), 5 mg chol., 165 mg sodium, 21 g carb., 2 g fiber, 2 g pro.*

My mom made this divine chocolaty bread only for holidays or special requests, but it makes any old morning even better. I always think of our family when I smell it baking.

—RACHEL RHODES BEDFORD, PA

MOM'S CHOCOLATE BREAD

Blackberry Muffins

No one can resist these buttery muffins bursting with juicy blackberries. They make a nice addition to any breakfast table.

—JULIE WALLBERG CARSON CITY, NV

PREP: 15 MIN. • **BAKE:** 20 MIN.
MAKES: 1½ DOZEN

- ½ **cup butter, softened**
- 1¼ **cups plus 1 tablespoon sugar, divided**
- 2 **large eggs**
- 2 **cups all-purpose flour**
- 2 **teaspoons baking powder**
- ½ **teaspoon salt**
- ½ **cup whole milk**
- 2 **cups fresh or frozen blackberries**

1. In a large bowl, cream butter and 1¼ cups sugar. Add the eggs, one at a time, beating well after each addition. Combine the flour, baking powder and salt; gradually stir into the creamed mixture alternately with milk. beating well after each addition. Gently fold in the blackberries.

2. Fill greased or paper-lined muffin cups two-thirds full. Sprinkle with remaining sugar. Bake at 375° for 20-25 minutes or until a toothpick inserted near the center comes out clean. Cool for muffins for 5 minutes before removing from pans to wire racks. Serve warm.

NOTE *If using frozen blackberries, do not thaw before adding to batter.*

PER SERVING *1 muffin equals 172 cal., 6 g fat (3 g sat. fat), 38 mg chol., 172 mg sodium, 28 g carb., 1 g fiber, 3 g pro.*

Triple Citrus Scones

PREP: 20 MIN. • **BAKE:** 15 MIN.
MAKES: 8 SCONES

- 2¼ **cups all-purpose flour**
- ¼ **cup plus 1 tablespoon sugar, divided**
- 4 **teaspoons grated orange peel**
- 2 **teaspoons grated lemon peel**
- 1½ **teaspoons grated lime peel**
- 3 **teaspoons baking powder**
- ½ **teaspoon salt**
- 6 **tablespoons cold butter, cubed**
- 1 **large egg**
- ¼ **cup orange juice**
- ¼ **cup buttermilk**
- 1 **tablespoon butter, melted**

GLAZE

- ¼ **cup confectioners' sugar**
- 1½ **teaspoons grated lime peel**
- 1 **tablespoon lime juice**
- 1 **tablespoon orange juice**

1. Preheat oven to 400°. Place flour, ¼ cup sugar, citrus peels, baking powder and salt in a food processor; pulse until blended. Add cold butter; pulse until butter is the size of peas. Transfer to a large bowl. In a small bowl, whisk egg, orange juice and buttermilk until blended; stir into the crumb mixture just until moistened.

2. Turn onto a lightly floured surface; knead gently 6-8 times. Pat dough into a 6-in. circle. Cut into eight wedges. Place wedges on a parchment paper-lined baking sheet. Brush with melted butter; sprinkle with remaining sugar.

3. Bake 14-18 minutes or until golden brown. Meanwhile, in a small bowl, mix the citrus glaze ingredients until smooth. Remove the scones from the oven; immediately brush with glaze. Serve warm.

PER SERVING *1 scone equals 281 cal., 11 g fat (7 g sat. fat), 50 mg chol., 403 mg sodium, 41 g carb., 1 g fiber, 5 g pro.*

I love the bright and buttery flavor of these tender scones. Serve them with a yummy jam, or try them as a base for strawberry shortcake.

—**ANGELA LEMOINE** HOWELL, NJ

TRIPLE CITRUS SCONES

BAKER'S DOZEN YEAST ROLLS

Pumpkin Bread

I keep my freezer stocked with homemade goodies like this spiced pumpkin bread. For add-ins, think about raisins, coconut, candied ginger—even cinnamon chips.

—**JOYCE JACKSON** BRIDGETOWN, NS

PREP: 15 MIN. • **BAKE:** 65 MIN. + COOLING
MAKES: 1 LOAF (16 SLICES)

- 1⅔ **cups all-purpose flour**
- 1½ **cups sugar**
- 1 **teaspoon baking soda**
- 1 **teaspoon ground cinnamon**
- ¾ **teaspoon salt**
- ½ **teaspoon baking powder**
- ½ **teaspoon ground nutmeg**
- ¼ **teaspoon ground cloves**
- 2 **large eggs**
- 1 **cup canned pumpkin**
- ½ **cup canola oil**
- ½ **cup water**
- ½ **cup chopped walnuts**
- ½ **cup raisins, optional**

1. Preheat oven to 350°. Combine first eight ingredients. Whisk together eggs, pumpkin, oil and water; stir into the dry ingredients just until moistened. Fold in walnuts and, if desired, raisins.
2. Pour into a greased 9x5-in. loaf pan. Bake until a toothpick inserted in the center of loaf comes out clean, about 65-70 minutes. Cool in pan 10 minutes before removing to a wire rack.
PER SERVING *1 slice equals 221 cal., 10 g fat (1 g sat. fat), 23 mg chol., 212 mg sodium, 31 g carb., 1 g fiber, 3 g pro.*

PUMPKIN BREAD

Baker's Dozen Yeast Rolls

A yummy honey-garlic topping turns these easy dinner rolls into something extra special. A batch goes great with a pot of chili or soup.

—*TASTE OF HOME* **TEST KITCHEN**

PREP: 25 MIN. + RISING
BAKE: 15 MIN. + COOLING
MAKES: 13 ROLLS

- 2 **to 2½ cups all-purpose flour**
- 2 **tablespoons sugar**
- 1 **package (¼ ounce) quick-rise yeast**
- ½ **teaspoon salt**
- ¾ **cup warm water (120° to 130°)**
- 2 **tablespoons plus 4 teaspoons butter, melted, divided**
- ¾ **cup shredded sharp cheddar cheese**
- 2 **teaspoons honey**
- ⅛ **teaspoon garlic salt**

1. In a large bowl, combine 1½ cups flour, sugar, yeast and salt. Add water and 2 tablespoons of butter; beat on medium speed for 3 minutes or until smooth. Stir in cheese and enough remaining flour to form a soft dough.
2. Turn onto a lightly floured surface; knead until smooth and elastic, about 4-6 minutes. Cover dough and let rest for 10 minutes. Divide into 13 pieces. Shape each into a ball. Place the rolls in a greased 9-in. round baking pan. Cover rolls and let rise in a warm place until doubled, about 30 minutes.
3. Preheat oven to 375°. Bake rolls 11-14 minutes or until lightly browned. Combine the honey, garlic salt and remaining butter; brush over rolls. Remove from pan to wire rack.
PER SERVING *1 roll equals 131 cal., 5 g fat (3 g sat. fat), 15 mg chol., 169 mg sodium, 18 g carb., 1 g fiber, 4 g pro. Diabetic Exchanges: 1 starch, 1 fat.*

**KIM SCURIO'S
CHOCOLATE PRETZEL RINGS**
PAGE 105

Cookies, Bars & Candies

Fingers will move fast at **parties and potlucks** when these mouthwatering **sweet treats** are sighted. **Who can resist** a batch of **yummy** blondies or **rich** fudge?

**TRISHA KRUSE'S
PECAN BUTTERSCOTCH
COOKIES** *PAGE 102*

**DIANE HEIER'S
SPEEDY BROWNIES**
PAGE 107

**JENNIFER FISHER'S
ROOT BEER FLOAT FUDGE**
PAGE 104

Strawberry Cream Cookies

These delicate cream cheese cookies look lovely on a tea tray or dessert platter. Feel free to experiment with other jam flavors such as raspberry, blueberry or apricot.

—**GLENNA ABERLE** SABETHA, KS

PREP: 25 MIN. + CHILLING
BAKE: 10 MIN./BATCH
MAKES: 5 DOZEN

- 1 cup butter, softened
- 1 package (3 ounces) cream cheese, softened
- 1 cup sugar
- 1 large egg yolk
- 3 teaspoons vanilla extract
- 2½ cups all-purpose flour
  Seedless strawberry jam

1. In a large bowl, cream the butter, cream cheese and sugar until light and fluffy. Beat in egg yolk and vanilla. Add flour and mix well. Cover and refrigerate for 1 hour or until easy to handle.

2. Shape dough into 1-in. balls. Place 2 in. apart on ungreased baking sheets. Using the end of a wooden spoon handle, make a ½-in.-deep indentation in the center of each ball; fill with about ¼ teaspoon jam. Bake at 350° for 10-12 minutes or until set. Remove to wire racks to cool.

PER SERVING 2 cookies equals 139 cal., 7 g fat (4 g sat. fat), 27 mg chol., 71 mg sodium, 17 g carb., trace fiber, 1 g pro.

BACON CHOCOLATE CHIP CHEESECAKE BLONDIES

STRAWBERRY CREAM COOKIES

Bacon Chocolate Chip Cheesecake Blondies

If you're a sweet and savory fan like me, you'll absolutely love these. I mean, really, nothing is much better than a cookie, a brownie and cheesecake all mixed up together with bacon to top it off.

—**KATIE O'KEEFFE** DERRY, NH

PREP: 30 MIN. • **BAKE:** 45 MIN. + CHILLING
MAKES: 16 SERVINGS

- 8 bacon strips, cooked and crumbled
- 1 cup butter, softened
- ¾ cup sugar
- ¾ cup packed brown sugar
- 2 large eggs
- 1 teaspoon vanilla extract
- 2¼ cups all-purpose flour
- 1 teaspoon salt
- 1 teaspoon baking soda
- 2 cups (12 ounces) semisweet chocolate chips

CHEESECAKE LAYER
- 2 packages (8 ounces each) cream cheese, softened
- 1 cup sugar
- 2 large eggs
- ¾ cup 2% milk
- 2 teaspoons vanilla extract

1. Preheat oven to 375°. Line a 9-in. square baking pan with foil, letting ends extend up sides; grease foil.

2. Reserve ¼ cup crumbled bacon for top. In a large bowl, cream butter and sugars until light and fluffy. Beat in eggs and vanilla. In another bowl, whisk flour, salt and baking soda; gradually beat into creamed mixture. Stir in chocolate chips and remaining bacon. Press half of the dough onto bottom of prepared pan.

3. For cheesecake layer, in a large bowl, beat cream cheese and sugar until smooth. Add eggs, milk and vanilla; beat on low speed just until blended. Pour over dough in prepared pan; drop the remaining dough by rounded tablespoons over cheesecake layer. Sprinkle with reserved bacon.

4. Bake 45-50 minutes or until golden brown. Cool in pan on a wire rack. Refrigerate at least 4 hours before cutting. Lifting with foil, remove from pan. Cut into bars.

PER SERVING 1 bar equals 534 cal., 31 g fat (18 g sat. fat), 113 mg chol., 523 mg sodium, 61 g carb., 2 g fiber, 8 g pro.

Lemon Poppy Seed Slices

My mom taught me to bake, and I use lots of recipes from her abundant collection, including this one.

—PAULINE PIRAINO BAY SHORE, NY

PREP: 10 MIN. + CHILLING
BAKE: 10 MIN./BATCH
MAKES: 5½ DOZEN

- ¾ cup butter, softened
- 1 cup sugar
- 1 large egg
- 1 tablespoon 2% milk
- 2 teaspoons finely grated lemon peel
- ½ teaspoon vanilla extract
- ½ teaspoon lemon extract, optional
- 2½ cups all-purpose flour
- ¼ cup poppy seeds

1. In a large bowl, cream butter and sugar until light and fluffy. Beat in egg, milk, lemon peel and extracts. Gradually add flour and mix well. Stir in poppy seeds. Shape into two 8-in. rolls; wrap each in plastic wrap. Refrigerate 3 hours or until firm.

2. Preheat oven to 350°. Unwrap and cut into ¼-in. slices. Place 2 in. apart on ungreased baking sheets. Bake 10-12 minutes or until edges are golden. Cool 2 minutes before removing to wire racks to cool completely.

PER SERVING *2 cookies equals 103 cal., 5 g fat (3 g sat. fat), 18 mg chol., 45 mg sodium, 14 g carb., trace fiber, 1 g pro.*

LEMON POPPY SEED SLICES

These coveted brownie bars are homey and chocolaty awesome. They've been a sought-after staple on Christmas cookie trays for years.
—MATT SHAW WARRENTON, OR

PISTACHIO BROWNIE TOFFEE BARS

Pistachio Brownie Toffee Bars

PREP: 20 MIN. • **BAKE:** 30 MIN. + COOLING
MAKES: 3 DOZEN

- ¾ cup butter, softened
- ¾ cup packed brown sugar
- 1 large egg yolk
- ¾ teaspoon vanilla extract
- 1½ cups all-purpose flour

FILLING

- 1 package fudge brownie mix (13x9-inch pan size)
- ⅓ cup water
- ⅓ cup canola oil
- 1 large egg

TOPPING

- 1 package (11½ ounces) milk chocolate chips, melted
- ¾ cup finely chopped salted roasted pistachios

1. Preheat oven to 350°. In a large bowl, cream butter and brown sugar until light and fluffy. Beat in egg yolk and vanilla; gradually add flour to creamed mixture, mixing well.

2. Press dough onto bottom of a greased 15x10x1-in. baking pan. Bake 12-14 minutes or until golden brown. Meanwhile, in a large bowl, combine brownie mix, water, oil and egg until blended.

3. Spread brownie batter over hot crust. Bake 14-16 minutes longer or until center is set. Cool completely in pan on a wire rack.

4. Spread melted chocolate over bars; sprinkle with pistachios. Let stand until set. Cut into bars.

PER SERVING *1 bar equals 219 cal., 12 g fat (5 g sat. fat), 23 mg chol., 112 mg sodium, 27 g carb., 1 g fiber, 3 g pro.*

⑤ INGREDIENTS FAST FIX ▶
Pecan Butterscotch Cookies

I come back to this recipe often. These are the quickest, tastiest cookies I've ever made. Change the pudding flavor or nuts for a twist.

—TRISHA KRUSE EAGLE, ID

START TO FINISH: 25 MIN.
MAKES: ABOUT 1½ DOZEN

- 1 **cup complete buttermilk pancake mix**
- 1 **package (3.4 ounces) instant butterscotch pudding mix**
- ⅓ **cup butter, melted**
- 1 **large egg**
- ½ **cup chopped pecans, toasted**

1. In a large bowl, beat the pancake mix, dry pudding mix, butter and egg until blended. Stir in pecans.
2. Roll into 1½-in. balls. Place 2 in. apart on greased baking sheets. Flatten with the bottom of a glass. Bake at 350° for 8-10 minutes or until the edges begin to brown. Remove to wire racks to cool.
NOTE *You may substitute regular biscuit/baking mix for the complete buttermilk pancake mix.*
PER SERVING *1 cookie equals 88 cal., 6 g fat (2 g sat. fat), 18 mg chol., 167 mg sodium, 8 g carb., trace fiber, 1 g pro.*
Diabetic Exchanges: 1 fat, ½ starch.

Amish Sugar Cookies

These easy-to-make cookies simply melt in your mouth! I've passed the recipe around to many friends. After I gave the recipe to my sister, she entered the cookies in a local fair and won the "best of show" prize!

—SYLVIA FORD KENNETT, MO

PREP: 10 MIN. • **BAKE:** 10 MIN./BATCH
MAKES: ABOUT 5 DOZEN

- 1 **cup butter, softened**
- 1 **cup vegetable oil**
- 1 **cup sugar**
- 1 **cup confectioners' sugar**
- 2 **large eggs**
- 1 **teaspoon vanilla extract**
- 4½ **cups all-purpose flour**
- 1 **teaspoon baking soda**
- 1 **teaspoon cream of tartar**

1. In a large bowl, beat the butter, oil and sugars. Beat in eggs until well blended. Beat in vanilla. Combine the flour, baking soda and cream of tartar; gradually add to creamed mixture.
2. Drop by small teaspoonfuls onto ungreased baking sheets. Bake at 375° for 8-10 minutes or until lightly browned. Remove to wire racks to cool.
PER SERVING *2 cookies equals 233 cal., 14 g fat (5 g sat. fat), 31 mg chol., 108 mg sodium, 25 g carb., 1 g fiber, 2 g pro.*

FREEZE IT
White Chocolate Macadamia Cookies

White baking chips and macadamia nuts are a fantastic duo in these buttery cookies that are a nice change from the classic chocolate chip ones.

—CATHY LENNON NEWPORT, TN

PREP: 15 MIN. • **BAKE:** 10 MIN./BATCH
MAKES: 4½ DOZEN

- ½ **cup butter, softened**
- ⅔ **cup sugar**
- 1 **large egg**
- 1 **teaspoon vanilla extract**
- 1 **cup plus 2 tablespoons all-purpose flour**
- ½ **teaspoon baking soda**
- 1 **cup macadamia nuts, chopped**
- 1 **cup white baking chips**

1. Preheat oven to 350°. In a large bowl, cream butter and sugar until light and fluffy. Beat in egg and vanilla. In another bowl, whisk flour and baking soda; gradually beat into creamed mixture. Stir in nuts and baking chips.
2. Drop by heaping teaspoonfuls 2 in. apart onto ungreased baking sheets. Bake 10-12 minutes or until golden brown. Cool on pans 1 minute. Remove to wire racks to cool.
FREEZE OPTION *Freeze cookies, layered between waxed paper, in freezer containers. To use, thaw before serving or, if desired, reheat on a baking sheet in a preheated 350° oven 3-4 minutes.*
PER SERVING *1 cookie equals 70 cal., 5 g fat (2 g sat. fat), 9 mg chol., 38 mg sodium, 7 g carb., 0 fiber, 1 g pro.*

WHITE CHOCOLATE MACADAMIA COOKIES

Rhubarb Custard Bars

Once I tried these rich, gooey bars, I just had to have the recipe so I could make them for my family and friends. The shortbread-like crust and the rhubarb and custard layers inspire people to track down rhubarb they can use to fix a batch for themselves.

—**SHARI ROACH** SOUTH MILWAUKEE, WI

PREP: 25 MIN. + CHILLING • **BAKE:** 50 MIN.
MAKES: 3 DOZEN

- 2 **cups all-purpose flour**
- ¼ **cup sugar**
- 1 **cup cold butter**

FILLING

- 2 **cups sugar**
- 7 **tablespoons all-purpose flour**
- 1 **cup heavy whipping cream**
- 3 **large eggs, beaten**
- 5 **cups finely chopped fresh or frozen rhubarb, thawed and drained**

TOPPING

- 6 **ounces cream cheese, softened**
- ½ **cup sugar**
- ½ **teaspoon vanilla extract**
- 1 **cup heavy whipping cream, whipped**

1. In a bowl, combine the flour and sugar; cut in butter until the mixture resembles coarse crumbs. Press into a greased 13x9-in. baking pan. Bake at 350° for 10 minutes.

2. Meanwhile, for filling, combine sugar and flour in a bowl. Whisk in cream and eggs. Stir in the rhubarb. Pour over crust. Bake at 350° for 40-45 minutes or until custard is set. Cool.

3. For topping, beat cream cheese, sugar and vanilla until smooth; fold in whipped cream. Spread over top. Cover and chill. Cut into bars. Store in the refrigerator.

PER SERVING *1 bar equals 198 cal., 11 g fat (7 g sat. fat), 52 mg chol., 70 mg sodium, 23 g carb., 1 g fiber, 2 g pro.*

CRANBERRY CLEMENTINE BARS

Cranberry Clementine Bars

I love a good lemon bar, but when the holidays roll around and clementines are everywhere, I make this holiday twist on a classic dessert.

—**LAURIE LUFKIN** ESSEX, MA

PREP: 25 MIN. • **BAKE:** 35 MIN. + COOLING
MAKES: 2 DOZEN

- 1½ **cups all-purpose flour**
- ½ **cup dried cranberries**
- ¼ **cup confectioners' sugar**
- ½ **teaspoon salt**
- 1 **cup cold butter, cubed**

FILLING

- 5 **large eggs**
- 1¾ **cups sugar**
- 3 **tablespoons cornstarch**
- 2 **tablespoons butter, melted**
- 1 **to 2 tablespoons grated clementine or orange peel**
- ⅓ **cup clementine or orange juice**
- 1 **teaspoon vanilla extract**
- ½ **teaspoon salt**
  Confectioners' sugar

1. Preheat oven to 350°. Line a 13x9-in. baking pan with foil, letting ends extend up sides; grease foil.

2. Place flour, cranberries, confectioners' sugar and salt in a food processor; pulse until blended. Add butter; pulse until butter is the size of peas. Press onto bottom of prepared pan. Bake 14-18 minutes or until edges are golden brown.

3. In a large bowl, whisk eggs, sugar, cornstarch, melted butter, clementine peel, juice, vanilla and salt until blended. Pour over warm crust. Bake 18-22 minutes longer or until filling is set. Cool completely in pan on a wire rack.

4. Dust with confectioners' sugar. Lifting with foil, remove from pan. Cut into bars. Refrigerate leftovers.

PER SERVING *1 bar equals 195 cal., 10 g fat (6 g sat. fat), 62 mg chol., 182 mg sodium, 25 g carb., trace fiber, 2 g pro.*

My children have always loved root beer floats, so I came up with this fudgy treat just for them. Sweet and creamy with that nostalgic root beer flavor, it's always a best-seller at bake sales.
—**JENNIFER FISHER** AUSTIN, TX

Root Beer Float Fudge

PREP: 15 MIN. • **COOK:** 15 MIN. + CHILLING
MAKES: ABOUT 3 POUNDS (81 PIECES)

- 1 teaspoon plus ¾ cup butter, divided
- 3 cups sugar
- 1 can (5 ounces) evaporated milk
- 1 package (10 to 12 ounces) white baking chips
- 1 jar (7 ounces) marshmallow creme
- ½ teaspoon vanilla extract
- 2 teaspoons root beer concentrate

1. Line a 9-in.-square baking pan with foil; grease foil with 1 teaspoon butter. In a large heavy saucepan, combine sugar, milk and remaining butter. Bring to a rapid boil over medium heat, stirring constantly. Cook and stir 4 minutes.
2. Remove from heat. Stir in baking chips and marshmallow creme until melted. Pour one-third of the mixture into a small bowl; stir in vanilla.
3. To remaining mixture, stir in the root beer concentrate; immediately spread into prepared pan. Spread vanilla mixture over top. Refrigerate for 1 hour or until firm.
4. Using foil, lift fudge out of the pan. Remove foil; cut fudge into 1-in. squares. Store between layers of waxed paper in an airtight container in the refrigerator.
NOTE *This recipe was tested with McCormick root beer concentrate.*
PER SERVING *1 piece equals 74 cal., 3 g fat (2 g sat. fat), 6 mg chol., 19 mg sodium, 12 g carb., 0 fiber, trace pro.*

BUTTERY COCONUT BARS

Buttery Coconut Bars

My coconut bars are an American version of a Filipino coconut cake called *bibingka*. These are a crispier, sweeter take on the Christmas tradition I grew up with.
—**DENISE NYLAND** PANAMA CITY, FL

PREP: 20 MIN. + COOLING
BAKE: 40 MIN. + COOLING
MAKES: 3 DOZEN

- 2 cups all-purpose flour
- 1 cup packed brown sugar
- ½ teaspoon salt
- 1 cup butter, melted

FILLING
- 3 large eggs
- 1 can (14 ounces) sweetened condensed milk
- ½ cup all-purpose flour
- ¼ cup packed brown sugar
- ¼ cup butter, melted
- 3 teaspoons vanilla extract
- ½ teaspoon salt
- 4 cups flaked coconut, divided

1. Preheat the oven to 350°. Line a 13x9-in. baking pan with parchment paper, letting ends extend up sides.
2. In a large bowl, mix flour, brown sugar and salt; stir in 1 cup melted butter. Press onto bottom of the prepared pan. Bake 12-15 minutes or until light brown. Cool 10 minutes on a wire rack. Reduce oven setting to 325°.
3. In a large bowl, whisk the first seven filling ingredients until blended; stir in 3 cups coconut. Pour mixture over crust; sprinkle with the remaining coconut. Bake for 25-30 minutes or until light golden brown. Cool in the pan on a wire rack. Lifting with parchment paper, remove from the pan. Cut into bars.
PER SERVING *1 bar equals 211 cal., 12 g fat (8 g sat. fat), 36 mg chol., 166 mg sodium, 25 g carb., 1 g fiber, 3 g pro.*

Chocolate Pretzel Rings

These easy snacks are positively delicious!
You can switch them up for any season by
choosing different colored M&M's.

—KIM SCURIO CAROL STREAM, IL

START TO FINISH: 30 MIN.
MAKES: ABOUT 4 DOZEN

- 48 to 50 pretzel rings or squares
- 48 to 50 milk chocolate or striped chocolate kisses
- ¼ cup milk chocolate M&M's

1. Place the pretzels on greased
baking sheets; place a chocolate kiss
in the center of each pretzel. Bake at
275° for 2-3 minutes or until chocolate
is softened. Remove from the oven.
2. Place an M&M's candy on each,
pressing down slightly so chocolate
fills the pretzel holes. Refrigerate for
5-10 minutes or until the chocolate
is firm. Store in an airtight container
at room temperature.

PER SERVING *2 pieces equals 69 cal.,
3 g fat (2 g sat. fat), 2 mg chol., 55 mg
sodium, 9 g carb., trace fiber, 1 g pro.*

SALTED PECAN
SHORTBREAD SQUARES

CHOCOLATE PRETZEL RINGS

Salted Pecan Shortbread Squares

My shortbread squares are the ultimate
go-to for cookie trays and gift giving. The
buttery caramel and toasted nuts make
it tough to eat just one.

—DIANA ASHCRAFT MONMOUTH, OR

PREP: 25 MIN. • **BAKE:** 25 MIN. + COOLING
MAKES: 4 DOZEN

- 1½ cups all-purpose flour
- 1 cup confectioners' sugar
- ½ cup cornstarch
- 1 teaspoon sea salt
- 1 cup cold unsalted butter, cubed

FILLING

- ¾ cup unsalted butter, cubed
- 1½ cups packed brown sugar
- ½ cup dark corn syrup
- ½ teaspoon sea salt
- ½ cup milk chocolate chips
- ¼ cup heavy whipping cream
- 1 teaspoon vanilla extract
- 4 cups coarsely chopped pecans, toasted

1. Preheat the oven to 350°. Line
two 13x9-in. baking pans with foil,
letting ends extend up sides of pan.
2. Place flour, confectioners' sugar,
cornstarch and salt in a food processor;
pulse until blended. Add butter; pulse
until butter is the size of peas. Divide
mixture between prepared pans;
press onto bottom of pans. Bake
10-12 minutes or until light brown.
Cool on a wire rack.
3. For filling, melt butter in a large
saucepan. Stir in brown sugar, corn
syrup and salt; bring to a boil. Reduce
heat to medium; cook and stir until
sugar is completely dissolved, about
3 minutes. Remove from heat; stir in
chocolate chips, cream and vanilla
until smooth. Stir in pecans. Spread
over crusts.
4. Bake 12-15 minutes or until filling
is bubbly. Cool completely in pans on
wire racks. Using foil, lift bars out of
pans. Gently peel off foil; cut into bars.
Store in an airtight container.

NOTE *To toast nuts, bake in a shallow
pan in a 350° oven for 5-10 minutes or
cook in a skillet over low heat until
lightly browned, stirring occasionally.*

PER SERVING *1 bar equals 201 cal.,
14 g fat (5 g sat. fat), 20 mg chol., 70 mg
sodium, 18 g carb., 1 g fiber, 1 g pro.*

Three-Chocolate Fudge

Each year I hand out this smooth and creamy fudge as gifts. My tradition started when I made more than my family could devour, and my friends and neighbors couldn't be happier.

—BETTY GRANTHAM HANCEVILLE, AL

PREP: 35 MIN. + CHILLING
MAKES: ABOUT 5½ POUNDS (150 PIECES)

- 1 tablespoon butter
- 3⅓ cups sugar
- 1 cup packed dark brown sugar
- 1 can (12 ounces) evaporated milk
- 1 cup butter, cubed
- 32 large marshmallows, halved
- 1 teaspoon vanilla extract
- 2 cups (12 ounces) semisweet chocolate chips
- 14 ounces milk chocolate, chopped
- 2 ounces semisweet chocolate, chopped
- 2 cups chopped pecans, toasted

1. Line a 15x10x1-in. pan with foil; grease foil with 1 tablespoon butter.
2. In a heavy large saucepan, combine the sugars, milk and cubed butter. Bring to a rapid boil over medium heat, stirring constantly; cook and stir for 5 minutes. Remove from heat. Stir in the marshmallows and vanilla until blended.
3. Gradually stir in chocolate chips and chopped chocolate until melted. Fold in pecans. Immediately spread into prepared pan. Refrigerate 1 hour or until firm. Using foil, lift fudge out of pan. Remove foil; cut fudge into 1-in. squares. Store between layers of waxed paper in an airtight container.

PER SERVING *1 piece equals 79 cal., 4 g fat (2 g sat. fat), 5 mg chol., 16 mg sodium, 11 g carb., trace fiber, 1 g pro.*

Pumpkin Delight Magic Bars

I improvised these bars the way my mother always did, throwing together ingredients with flavors of the holiday. With every bite, we honor Mom, the tradition of family and sharing special moments.

—LISA GLASSMAN BOYNTON BEACH, FL

PREP: 20 MIN. • **BAKE:** 45 MIN. + COOLING
MAKES: 2 DOZEN

- 1 package (11 ounces) vanilla wafers
- ½ cup butter, melted
- 3 ounces cream cheese, softened
- 1 can (14 ounces) sweetened condensed milk
- ½ teaspoon pumpkin pie spice
- 1 can (15 ounces) solid-pack pumpkin
- 1 cup dried cranberries
- 1½ cups flaked coconut
- 1 cup white baking chips
- 1 cup chopped pecans

1. Preheat oven to 350°. Place wafers in a food processor; pulse until coarse crumbs form. Drizzle with melted butter; pulse until blended. Press into bottom of a greased 13x9-in. baking pan.
2. In a large bowl, beat the cream cheese, milk and pie spice until smooth. Beat in pumpkin; stir in cranberries. Pour over crust. Layer with coconut, baking chips and pecans.
3. Bake 45-55 minutes or until golden brown. Cool in pan on a wire rack for 10 minutes.
4. Loosen sides from pan with a knife; cool completely. Cut into bars. Refrigerate leftovers.

PER SERVING *1 bar equals 299 cal., 17 g fat (8 g sat. fat), 25 mg chol., 144 mg sodium, 35 g carb., 2 g fiber, 4 g pro.*

PUMPKIN DELIGHT MAGIC BARS

THREE-CHOCOLATE FUDGE

Speedy Brownies

Since you "dump" all the ingredients together for these brownies, they take very little time to prepare. There's no mistaking the homemade goodness of a freshly baked batch—they are rich and fudgy!

—DIANE HEIER HARWOOD, ND

PREP: 15 MIN. • **BAKE:** 30 MIN.
MAKES: ABOUT 3 DOZEN

- 2 cups sugar
- 1¾ cups all-purpose flour
- ½ cup baking cocoa
- 1 teaspoon salt
- 5 large eggs
- 1 cup canola oil
- 1 teaspoon vanilla extract
- 1 cup (6 ounces) semisweet chocolate chips

1. In a large bowl, beat the first seven ingredients. Pour into a greased 13x9-in. baking pan. Sprinkle with chocolate chips.
2. Bake at 350° for 30 minutes or until a toothpick inserted near the center comes out clean. Cool in pan on a wire rack.
PER SERVING *1 brownie equals 155 cal., 8 g fat (2 g sat. fat), 30 mg chol., 75 mg sodium, 19 g carb., 1 g fiber, 2 g pro.*

(5) INGREDIENTS
Chocolaty Caramel Cookies

Kids will look forward to going back to school with one of these in a lunch box. Each scrumptious chocolate cookie has a fun caramel surprise in the middle.

—MELANIE STEELE PLANO, TX

PREP: 25 MIN. • **BAKE:** 10 MIN./BATCH
MAKES: ABOUT 2½ DOZEN

- 2 large eggs
- ⅓ cup canola oil
- 1 devil's food cake mix (regular size)
- 32 Rolo candies
- Chopped hazelnuts

1. Preheat oven to 350°. Beat together eggs and oil; gradually beat in cake mix. Roll tablespoonfuls of dough into balls. Press a candy into each; reshape balls. Dip tops in hazelnuts.
2. Place 2 in. apart on ungreased baking sheets. Bake until tops are cracked, 8-10 minutes. Cool on pans for 2 minutes. Remove to wire racks to cool. Store in an airtight container.
NOTE *If the dough is sticky, spray hands lightly with nonstick cooking spray before rolling into balls.*
PER SERVING *1 cookie equals 90 cal., 4 g fat (1 g sat. fat), 10 mg chol., 104 mg sodium, 12 g carb., 1 g fiber, 1 g pro.*

Sour Cream & Cranberry Bars

I turned sour cream raisin pie into a cookie bar with a crunchy oatmeal crust, custard-style filling and crisp topping.

—SHELLY L BEVINGTON HERMISTON, OR

PREP: 35 MIN. • **BAKE:** 35 MIN. + COOLING
MAKES: 2 DOZEN

- 3 large egg yolks
- 1½ cups (12 ounces) sour cream
- 1 cup sugar
- 3 tablespoons cornstarch
- ⅛ teaspoon salt
- 1 cup dried cranberries
- 1 teaspoon vanilla extract

CRUST
- 1 cup butter, softened
- 1 cup sugar
- 2 teaspoons vanilla extract
- 1¾ cups all-purpose flour
- 1⅓ cups quick-cooking oats
- 1 teaspoon salt
- 1 teaspoon baking soda
- 1 cup flaked coconut

1. Preheat oven to 350°. In top of a double boiler or a metal bowl over simmering water, whisk the first five ingredients until blended; stir in cranberries. Cook and stir 15-20 minutes until thickened. Remove from heat; stir in vanilla.
2. Meanwhile, in a large bowl, cream butter and sugar until light and fluffy. Beat in vanilla. In another bowl, whisk the flour, oats, salt and baking soda; gradually beat into the creamed mixture. Stir in coconut. Reserve half of the dough for topping. Press remaining onto the bottom of a greased 13x9-in. baking dish. Bake 8-10 minutes or until set.
3. Spread sour cream mixture over crust; crumble reserved dough over top. Bake 25-30 minutes or until filling is set and top is golden brown. Cool in pan on a wire rack. Cut into bars.
PER SERVING *1 bar equals 260 cal., 13 g fat (8 g sat. fat), 53 mg chol., 241 mg sodium, 34 g carb., 1 g fiber, 3 g pro.*

SOUR CREAM & CRANBERRY BARS

Licorice Caramels

Fans of black licorice won't be able to stop eating these gooey caramels. I appreciate the ease of preparation.
—**DONNA HIGBEE** RIVERTON, UT

PREP: 20 MIN. • **COOK:** 20 MIN. + STANDING
MAKES: ABOUT 12 DOZEN

- 1 teaspoon plus 1 cup butter, divided
- 2 cups sugar
- 1½ cups light corn syrup
- 1 can (14 ounces) sweetened condensed milk
- ½ teaspoon salt
- 2 teaspoons anise extract
- ¼ teaspoon black food coloring

1. Line an 8-in. square dish with foil; grease foil with 1 teaspoon butter.
2. In a large heavy saucepan, combine sugar, corn syrup, milk, salt and remaining butter; cook and stir over medium until a candy thermometer reads 244° (firm-ball stage).
3. Remove from the heat; stir in anise extract and food coloring. Immediately pour into prepared pan (do not scrape saucepan). Let stand until firm.
4. Using foil, lift candy out of pan; remove foil. Using a buttered knife, cut into ¼-in. strips. Cut each strip in half lengthwise; cut crosswise into three pieces. Wrap individually in waxed paper; twist ends.
NOTE *We recommend that you test your candy thermometer before each use by bringing water to a boil; the thermometer should read 212°. Adjust your recipe temperature up or down based on your test.*
PER SERVING *1 piece equals 92 cal., 3 g fat (2 g sat. fat), 10 mg chol., 65 mg sodium, 16 g carb., 0 fiber, 1 g pro.*

DID YOU KNOW?

While making caramels, you should pour the candy into the prepared pan without scraping the saucepan. This prevents the candy syrup from forming crystals or becoming grainy, because the crystallization of the mixture that's easily poured out of the pan differs from what's near the bottom of the pan.

PUMPKIN WHOOPIE PIES

Pumpkin Whoopie Pies

My kids start begging me for these cake-like sandwich cookies as soon as autumn arrives. I haven't met a person yet who doesn't like these fun treats.
—**DEB STUBER** CARLISLE, PA

PREP: 30 MIN. • **BAKE:** 10 MIN.
MAKES: ABOUT 2 DOZEN

- 1 cup shortening
- 2 cups packed brown sugar
- 2 large eggs
- 1 teaspoon vanilla extract
- 3½ cups all-purpose flour
- 1½ teaspoons baking powder
- 1½ teaspoons baking soda
- 1 teaspoon salt
- 1 teaspoon ground cinnamon
- 1 teaspoon ground ginger
- 1½ cups canned pumpkin

FILLING
- ¼ cup all-purpose flour
    Dash salt
- ¾ cup milk
- 1 cup shortening
- 2 cups confectioners' sugar
- 2 teaspoons vanilla extract

1. In a large bowl, cream shortening and brown sugar until light and fluffy. Add eggs, one at a time, beating well after each addition. Beat in vanilla. Combine the flour, baking powder, baking soda, salt, cinnamon and ginger; add to creamed mixture alternately with pumpkin.
2. Drop by rounded tablespoonfuls 2 in. apart onto greased baking pans; flatten slightly with the back of a spoon. Bake at 400° for 10-11 minutes. Remove to wire racks to cool.
3. For filling, in a small saucepan, combine flour and salt. Gradually whisk in milk until smooth; bring to a boil. Reduce heat; cook and stir over medium heat 2 minutes or until thickened. Cover and refrigerate until completely cooled.
4. In a small bowl, beat shortening, confectioners' sugar and vanilla until smooth. Add chilled milk mixture; beat for 7 minutes or until light and fluffy. Spread on the bottoms of half of the cookies; top with remaining cookies. Store in the refrigerator.
PER SERVING *1 whoopie pie equals 340 cal., 17 g fat (4 g sat. fat), 19 mg chol., 225 mg sodium, 44 g carb., 1 g fiber, 3 g pro.*

Oatmeal Surprise Cookies

Chocolate-covered raisins and the fall-like flavor of pumpkin pie spice turn these oatmeal cookies into prizewinning gourmet treats. Tuck one into your child's lunch for a special surprise.

—**REBECCA CLARK** WARRIOR, AL

PREP: 20 MIN. • **BAKE:** 15 MIN./BATCH
MAKES: 3 DOZEN

- 1 cup butter, softened
- ¾ cup packed brown sugar
- ½ cup sugar
- 2 large eggs
- 1½ cups all-purpose flour
- 1 teaspoon baking soda
- 1 teaspoon pumpkin pie spice
- 2¾ cups quick-cooking oats
- 1½ cups chocolate-covered raisins

1. Preheat the oven to 350°. In a large bowl, cream butter and sugars until light and fluffy. Beat in eggs. Combine the flour, baking soda and pie spice; gradually add to creamed mixture and mix well. Stir in oats and raisins.

2. Drop by tablespoonfuls 2 in. apart onto greased baking sheets. Flatten slightly. Bake 13-15 minutes or until golden brown. Cool 5 minutes before removing to wire racks. Store in an airtight container.

PER SERVING *1 cookie equals 149 cal., 7 g fat (4 g sat. fat), 25 mg chol., 80 mg sodium, 21 g carb., 1 g fiber, 2 g pro.*
***Diabetic Exchanges:** 1½ starch, 1 fat.*

HUMBLE BUMBLE CRUMBLE BARS

OATMEAL SURPRISE COOKIES

EAT SMART
Humble Bumble Crumble Bars

While developing a treat for my bingo group, I asked my husband for ideas. He suggested a fruity bar. This berry version is lightly sweet and so easy.

—**NANCY PHILLIPS** PORTLAND, ME

PREP: 30 MIN. • **BAKE:** 45 MIN. + COOLING
MAKES: 15 SERVINGS

- ½ cup butter, softened
- ¾ cup sugar
- 1 large egg
- 2½ cups all-purpose flour
- ½ teaspoon baking powder
- ¼ teaspoon salt
- ¼ cup packed brown sugar
- 1 teaspoon ground cinnamon

FILLING

- 2 cups chunky applesauce
- ½ teaspoon ground cinnamon
- ⅛ teaspoon ground nutmeg
- 2 cups fresh blackberries
- 2 cups fresh raspberries

1. Preheat oven to 350°. In a large bowl, cream butter and sugar until light and fluffy. Beat in the egg. In another bowl, whisk flour, baking powder and salt; gradually beat into creamed mixture. Reserve ½ cup crumb mixture for topping. Press the remaining mixture onto the bottom of a greased 13x9-in. baking pan. Bake for 12-15 minutes or until lightly browned. Cool in pan on a wire rack.

2. Stir brown sugar and cinnamon into reserved topping; set aside. In a large bowl, combine applesauce, cinnamon and nutmeg until blended. Spread over crust; top with berries and reserved topping. Bake for 30-35 minutes or until golden brown. Cool in pan on a wire rack. Cut into bars.

PER SERVING *1 piece equals 228 cal., 7 g fat (4 g sat. fat), 29 mg chol., 109 mg sodium, 39 g carb., 3 g fiber, 3 g pro.*

WINNIE'S MINI RHUBARB
& STRAWBERRY PIES FROM
SHAWN CARLETON PAGE 114

Cakes & Pies

Turn to these recipes when you want to whip up **oven-fresh, made-at-home bakery delights** just like Mom's. Here you'll find a luscious assortment of cakes, cupcakes and pies.

VIRGINIA LAPIERRE'S ZUCCHINI CUPCAKES
PAGE 113

SCARLETT ELROD'S CHERRY & CHOCOLATE ICE CREAM PIE *PAGE 121*

ASHLEY EAGON'S BAKLAVA TARTLETS
PAGE 118

Maple Pecan Tarts

I absolutely love pecans. I combine them with maple and vanilla to create the ultimate tart, made even richer with a dollop of whipped cream.
—**REDAWNA KALYNCHUK** BARRHEAD, AB

PREP: 25 MIN. + CHILLING
BAKE: 25 MIN. + COOLING
MAKES: 1 DOZEN

- 1 cup butter, softened
- 6 ounces cream cheese, softened
- 2 cups all-purpose flour

FILLING
- 4 large eggs
- 1 cup packed brown sugar
- ¾ cup maple syrup
- ⅔ cup butter, melted
- 2 teaspoons vanilla extract
  Dash salt
- 3 cups pecan halves
  Vanilla ice cream, optional

1. In a large bowl, cream butter and cream cheese until smooth. Gradually beat flour into creamed mixture. Shape into a disk; wrap in plastic wrap. Refrigerate 1 hour or until firm enough to handle.
2. Divide dough into 12 portions. Roll each portion into a 5-in. circle; transfer to 12 ungreased 4-in. fluted tart pans with removable bottoms. Trim pastry even with edges; place in 15x10x1-in. baking pans. Refrigerate 20 minutes. Preheat oven to 375°.
3. Meanwhile, in a large bowl, whisk the first six filling ingredients. Pour into tart shells; arrange pecans over tops. Bake 25-30 minutes or until centers are just set (mixture will jiggle). Cool on wire racks. If desired, serve with ice cream. Refrigerate any leftovers.
PER SERVING *1 tart (calculated without ice cream) equals 669 cal., 50 g fat (21 g sat. fat), 145 mg chol., 299 mg sodium, 52 g carb., 3 g fiber, 8 g pro.*

SOUR CREAM POUND CAKE

Sour Cream Pound Cake

I'm our town's postmaster, and my busy schedule doesn't leave much time for baking. But when I do find time, I enjoy making desserts like this one. It tastes great as is, or add a scoop of ice cream and a drizzle of chocolate syrup.
—**KAREN CONRAD** EAST TROY, WI

PREP: 15 MIN. • **BAKE:** 80 MIN. + COOLING
MAKES: 20 SERVINGS

- 1 cup butter, softened
- 3 cups sugar
- 6 large eggs
- 3 cups all-purpose flour
- ¼ teaspoon baking soda
- ¼ teaspoon salt
- 1 cup (8 ounces) sour cream
- 2 teaspoons vanilla extract
  Confectioners' sugar, optional

In a bowl, cream butter. Gradually beat in sugar until light and fluffy, about 5-7 minutes. Add eggs, one at a time, beating well after each addition. Combine flour, baking soda and salt; add to creamed mixture alternately with sour cream and vanilla. Beat on low just until blended. Pour into a greased and floured 10-in. tube pan. Bake at 325° for 1 hour and 25 minutes or until cake tests done. Cool in pan 15 minutes before removing to a wire rack to cool completely. Sprinkle with confectioners' sugar if desired.
PER SERVING *1 piece equals 311 cal., 13 g fat (7 g sat. fat), 96 mg chol., 163 mg sodium, 45 g carb., 1 g fiber, 4 g pro.*

Zucchini Cupcakes

I asked my grandmother for this recipe after trying these irresistible zucchini cupcakes at her home. I love the creamy caramel frosting on top. They are so scrumptious you may actually forget you're eating a vegetable, too! See photo on page 111.

—VIRGINIA LAPIERRE GREENSBORO BEND, VT

PREP: 20 MIN. • **BAKE:** 20 MIN. + COOLING
MAKES: ABOUT 1½ DOZEN

- 3 large eggs
- 1⅓ cups sugar
- ½ cup canola oil
- ½ cup orange juice
- 1 teaspoon almond extract
- 2½ cups all-purpose flour
- 2 teaspoons ground cinnamon
- 2 teaspoons baking powder
- 1 teaspoon baking soda
- 1 teaspoon salt
- ½ teaspoon ground cloves
- 1½ cups shredded zucchini

FROSTING
- 1 cup packed brown sugar
- ½ cup butter, cubed
- ¼ cup 2% milk
- 1 teaspoon vanilla extract
- 1½ to 2 cups confectioners' sugar

1. Preheat oven to 350°. Beat first five ingredients. Combine dry ingredients; gradually add to the egg mixture and blend well. Stir in zucchini.
2. Fill paper-lined muffin cups two-thirds full. Bake until a toothpick inserted in center comes out clean, 20-25 minutes. Cool for 10 minutes before removing to a wire rack.
3. For frosting, combine brown sugar, butter and milk in a large saucepan. Bring to a boil over medium heat; cook and stir until thickened, 1-2 minutes. Remove from heat; stir in the vanilla. Cool to lukewarm.
4. Gradually beat in confectioners' sugar until frosting reaches spreading consistency. Frost cupcakes.
PER SERVING *1 cupcake equals 327 cal., 12g fat (4g sat. fat), 45mg chol., 305mg sodium, 52g carb. (38g sugars, 1g fiber), 3g pro.*

Chocolate Silk Pie

Chocolate lovers, rejoice! This dreamy pie not only melts in your mouth, it also melts any and all resistance to dessert!

—MARY RELYEA CANASTOTA, NY

PREP: 30 MIN. + CHILLING
MAKES: 6-8 SERVINGS

- 1 unbaked pastry shell (9 inches)
- 1 jar (7 ounces) marshmallow creme
- 1 cup (6 ounces) semisweet chocolate chips
- ¼ cup butter, cubed
- 2 ounces unsweetened chocolate
- 2 tablespoons strong brewed coffee
- 1 cup heavy whipping cream, whipped

TOPPING
- 1 cup heavy whipping cream
- 2 tablespoons confectioners' sugar Chocolate curls, optional

1. Preheat oven to 450°. Line the unpricked pastry shell with a double thickness of heavy-duty foil. Bake for 8 minutes. Remove the foil; bake for 5 minutes. Cool on a wire rack.
2. Meanwhile, in a heavy saucepan, combine the marshmallow creme, chocolate chips, butter, unsweetened chocolate and coffee; cook and stir over low heat until chocolate is melted and mixture is smooth. Cool. Fold in whipped cream; pour into crust.
3. For topping, in a large bowl, beat cream until it begins to thicken. Add confectioners' sugar; beat until stiff peaks form. Spread over filling. Refrigerate at least 3 hours before serving. Garnish with chocolate curls if desired.

FOR QUICK CHOCOLATE CURLS
Use a vegetable peeler to "peel" curls from a solid block of chocolate. To keep the strips intact, allow them to fall gently onto a plate or a single layer of waxed paper. If you get only shavings, your chocolate may be too hard, so warm it slightly.

PER SERVING *1 piece equals 602 cal., 45g fat (26g sat. fat), 102 mg chol., 188 mg sodium, 53g carb., 2g fiber, 4g pro.*

CHOCOLATE SILK PIE

All-American Sheet Cake

My sweet and tangy sheet cake loaded with fresh-whipped cream and juicy fruit is the perfect summer dessert. But it's so good, you'll want to eat it all year long.

—JAMES SCHEND PLEASANT PRAIRIE, WI

PREP: 20 MIN. • **BAKE:** 25 MIN. + COOLING
MAKES: 15 SERVINGS

- 1 package white cake mix (regular size)
- 1 cup buttermilk
- ⅓ cup canola oil
- 3 large eggs
- 2 to 3 cups sweetened whipped cream
- 3 to 4 cups assorted fresh fruit

1. Preheat oven to 350°. Combine the cake mix, buttermilk, oil and eggs; beat on low speed for 30 seconds. Beat on medium for 2 minutes.

2. Pour into a 13x9-in. baking pan coated with cooking spray. Bake until a toothpick inserted near the center comes out clean, 25-30 minutes. Cool completely on a wire rack.

3. Spread whipped cream over cake; top with fruit. Refrigerate.

PER SERVING *1 piece equals 257 cal., 15 g fat (5 g sat. fat), 56 mg chol., 261 mg sodium, 29 g carb., trace fiber, 4 g pro.*

ALL-AMERICAN SHEET CAKE

Winnie's Mini Rhubarb & Strawberry Pies

Every spring, we had strawberries and rhubarb on our farm outside Seattle. These fruity hand pies remind me of those happy times and of my Grandma Winnie's baking. See photo on page 110.

—SHAWN CARLETON SAN DIEGO, CA

PREP: 25 MIN. + CHILLING
BAKE: 15 MIN. + COOLING
MAKES: 2 DOZEN

- 3 tablespoons quick-cooking tapioca
- 4 cups sliced fresh strawberries
- 2 cups sliced fresh rhubarb
- ¾ cup sugar
- 1 teaspoon grated orange peel
- 1 teaspoon vanilla extract
- ¼ teaspoon salt
- ¼ teaspoon ground cinnamon
- 3 drops red food coloring, optional
  Pastry for double-crust pie (9 inches)

1. Preheat oven to 425°. Place tapioca in a small food processor or spice grinder; process until finely ground.

2. In a large saucepan, combine the strawberries, rhubarb, sugar, orange peel, vanilla, salt, cinnamon, tapioca and, if desired, food coloring; bring to a boil. Reduce heat; simmer, covered, 15-20 minutes or until strawberries are tender, stirring occasionally. Transfer to a large bowl; cover and refrigerate overnight.

3. On a lightly floured surface, roll one half of dough to an 18-in. circle. Cut 12 circles with a 4-in. biscuit cutter, rerolling scraps as necessary; press dough onto bottom and up sides of ungreased muffin cups. Repeat with remaining dough. Spoon strawberry mixture into muffin cups.

4. Bake 12-15 minutes or until filling is bubbly and crust is golden brown. Cool in pan 5 minutes; remove to wire racks to cool.

PER SERVING *1 mini pie equals 155 cal., 8 g fat (5 g sat. fat), 20 mg chol., 129 mg sodium, 20 g carb., 1 g fiber, 2 g pro.*

3. Transfer half the batter to prepared pan; layer with cream cheese mixture, then remaining batter. Bake 50-60 minutes or until a toothpick inserted in cake portion comes out clean. Cool 10 minutes before removing to a wire rack to cool completely.

4. For icing, in a large saucepan, combine the brown sugar, butter and milk; bring to a boil. Cook and stir for 1 minute. Remove from heat; whisk in confectioners' sugar and vanilla until smooth. Drizzle over cake. Sprinkle with toasted pecans.

NOTE *To remove cakes easily, use solid shortening to grease plain and fluted tube pans. To toast nuts, bake in a shallow pan in a 350° oven for 5-10 minutes or cook in a skillet over low heat until lightly browned, stirring occasionally.*

PER SERVING *1 slice equals 614 cal., 36 g fat (9 g sat. fat), 102 mg chol., 407 mg sodium, 68 g carb., 2 g fiber, 7 g pro.*

(5)INGREDIENTS

Layered Lemon Pie

A bright citrus dessert is a fitting finale to almost any meal. The creamy lemon filling in this layered pie is always a hit with my dessert-loving husband.

—**ELIZABETH YODER** BELCOURT, ND

PREP: 20 MIN. + CHILLING
MAKES: 8 SERVINGS

- 8 **ounces cream cheese, softened**
- ½ **cup sugar**
- 1 **can (15¾ ounces) lemon pie filling, divided**
- 1 **carton (8 ounces) frozen whipped topping, thawed**
- 1 **graham cracker crust (9 inches)**

In a small bowl, beat the cream cheese and sugar until smooth. Beat in half of the pie filling. Fold in the whipped topping. Spoon into graham cracker crust. Spread the remaining pie filling over cream cheese layer. Refrigerate for at least 15 minutes before serving.

PER SERVING *1 piece equals 526 cal., 24 g fat (13 g sat. fat), 104 mg chol., 251 mg sodium, 72 g carb., 1 g fiber, 6 g pro.*

I bake my apple cake to usher in the fall season. It's a family favorite and tastes so good that eating one piece is nearly impossible!

—**JAMIE JONES** MADISON, GA

Never-Miss Apple Cake

PREP: 40 MIN. • **BAKE:** 50 MIN. + COOLING
MAKES: 12 SERVINGS

- 8 **ounces cream cheese, softened**
- ¼ **cup sugar**
- 1 **large egg**

CAKE

- 1¾ **cups sugar**
- 1 **cup canola oil**
- 3 **large eggs**
- 2 **cups all-purpose flour**
- 2 **teaspoons baking powder**
- 2 **teaspoons ground cinnamon**
- 1 **teaspoon salt**
- ¼ **teaspoon baking soda**
- 2 **cups chopped peeled tart apples**
- 1 **cup shredded carrots**
- ½ **cup chopped pecans, toasted**

PRALINE ICING

- ½ **cup packed brown sugar**
- ¼ **cup butter, cubed**
- 2 **tablespoons 2% milk**
- ½ **cup confectioners' sugar**
- ½ **teaspoon vanilla extract**
- ¼ **cup chopped pecans, toasted**

1. Preheat oven to 350°. Grease and flour a 10-in. fluted tube pan. In a small bowl, beat cream cheese and sugar until smooth; beat in egg.

2. For cake, in a large bowl, beat the sugar, oil and eggs until well blended. In another bowl, whisk flour, baking powder, cinnamon, salt and baking soda; gradually beat into the sugar mixture. Stir in apples, carrots and toasted pecans.

PUMPKIN SPICE CUPCAKES WITH CREAM CHEESE FROSTING

Pineapple Pudding Cake

My mother used to love making this easy dessert in the summertime. It's so cool and refreshing that it never lasts very long!

—**KATHLEEN WORDEN** NORTH ANDOVER, MA

PREP: 25 MIN. • **BAKE:** 15 MIN. + CHILLING
MAKES: 20 SERVINGS

- 1 package (9 ounces) yellow cake mix
- 1½ cups cold fat-free milk
- 1 package (1 ounce) sugar-free instant vanilla pudding mix
- 8 ounces fat-free cream cheese
- 1 can (20 ounces) unsweetened crushed pineapple, well drained
- 1 carton (8 ounces) frozen fat-free whipped topping, thawed
- ¼ cup chopped walnuts, toasted
- 20 maraschino cherries, well drained

1. Prepare the yellow cake mix batter according to package directions; pour into a 13x9-in. baking pan coated with cooking spray.
2. Bake at 350° for 15-20 minutes or until a toothpick inserted near the center comes out clean. Cool completely on a wire rack.
3. In a large bowl, whisk the milk and pudding mix for 2 minutes. Let stand for 2 minutes or until soft-set.
4. In a small bowl, beat cream cheese until smooth. Beat in pudding mixture until blended. Spread evenly over cake. Sprinkle with pineapple; spread with whipped topping. Sprinkle with walnuts and garnish with cherries. Refrigerate until serving.
PER SERVING *1 piece equals 131 cal., 2 g fat (1 g sat. fat), 1 mg chol., 217 mg sodium, 24 g carb., 1 g fiber, 3 g pro.* **Diabetic Exchange:** *1½ starch.*

READER RAVE

This was a huge hit with my co-workers. I increased the pudding to two boxes with 3 cups of milk. Crumbled the cake and layered in a trifle bowl with the pineapple and added strawberries. Very pretty and delicious!

—**JULESK** TASTEOFHOME.COM

Pumpkin Spice Cupcakes with Cream Cheese Frosting

I love the flavor of pumpkin, especially during fall. Generously spiced with cinnamon, the cream cheese frosting in this recipe adds an extra-special touch.

—**DEBBIE WIGGINS** LONGMONT, CO

PREP: 25 MIN. • **BAKE:** 20 MIN. + COOLING
MAKES: 2 DOZEN

- ¾ cup butter, softened
- 2½ cups sugar
- 3 large eggs
- 1 can (15 ounces) solid-pack pumpkin
- 2⅓ cups all-purpose flour
- 1 tablespoon pumpkin pie spice
- 1 teaspoon baking powder
- 1 teaspoon ground cinnamon
- ¾ teaspoon salt
- ½ teaspoon baking soda
- ½ teaspoon ground ginger
- 1 cup buttermilk

FROSTING

- 8 ounces cream cheese, softened
- ½ cup butter, softened
- 4 cups confectioners' sugar
- 1 teaspoon vanilla extract
- 2 teaspoons ground cinnamon

1. Preheat oven to 350°. In a large bowl, cream butter and sugar until light and fluffy. Add eggs, one at a time, beating well after each addition. Add pumpkin. Combine flour, pie spice, baking powder, cinnamon, salt, baking soda and ground ginger; add to the creamed mixture alternately with the buttermilk, beating well after each addition.
2. Fill paper-lined muffin cups three-fourths full. Bake 20-25 minutes or until a toothpick inserted in the center comes out clean. Cool 10 minutes before removing from pans to wire racks to cool completely.
3. For frosting, in a large bowl, beat cream cheese and butter until fluffy. Add confectioners' sugar, vanilla and cinnamon; beat until smooth. Frost cupcakes. Refrigerate leftovers.
PER SERVING *1 cupcake equals 340 cal., 14 g fat (8 g sat. fat), 62 mg chol., 233 mg sodium, 53 g carb., 1 g fiber, 4 g pro.*

Blueberry, Basil and Goat Cheese Pie

A good friend of mine was moving to Los Angeles, and I wanted to send her off with a farewell treat. This galette of blueberries, creamy goat cheese and fresh basil looks special and tastes delicious. Bake one, share it and create a precious memory.

—ASHLEY LECKER GREEN BAY, WI

PREP: 15 MIN. • **BAKE:** 40 MIN. + COOLING
MAKES: 6 SERVINGS

- Pastry for single-crust pie (9 inches)
- 2 cups fresh blueberries
- 2 tablespoons plus 2 teaspoons sugar, divided
- 1 tablespoon cornstarch
- 1 tablespoon minced fresh basil
- 1 large egg
- 1 teaspoon water
- ¼ cup crumbled goat cheese
  Fresh basil leaves, torn

1. Preheat oven to 375°. On a floured sheet of parchment paper, roll pastry into a 10-in. circle. Transfer to a baking sheet.

2. Mix blueberries, 2 tablespoons sugar, cornstarch and basil. Spoon blueberry mixture over pastry to within 2 in. of edge. Fold pastry edge over filling, pleating as you go and leaving the center uncovered.

3. Whisk egg and water; brush over pastry. Sprinkle with remaining sugar. Bake 30 minutes. Sprinkle with goat cheese; bake until crust is golden and filling bubbly, about 10 minutes. Transfer to a wire rack to cool. Top with torn basil leaves before serving.

PASTRY FOR SINGLE-CRUST PIE (9 INCHES) *Combine 1¼ cups all-purpose flour and ¼ tsp. salt; cut in ½ cup cold butter until crumbly. Gradually add 3-5 Tbsp. ice water, tossing with a fork until dough holds together when pressed. Wrap in plastic wrap and refrigerate 1 hour.*

PER SERVING *1 piece equals 308 cal., 18 g fat (11 g sat. fat), 77 mg chol., 241 mg sodium, 34 g carb., 2 g fiber, 5 g pro.*

Apricot-Blackberry Pie

Blackberries became my all-time favorite fruit after we harvested them from my grandfather's yard in Greece. I mix them with apricots to make the filling for the pie of my dreams.

—SIMONE BAZOS BALTIMORE, MD

PREP: 15 MIN. + CHILLING
BAKE: 65 MIN. + COOLING
MAKES: 8 SERVINGS

- ½ cup unblanched almonds, toasted
- 2½ cups all-purpose flour
- ¼ cup plus 2 tablespoons sugar
- ¼ teaspoon salt
- ½ cup cold butter, cubed
- 2 tablespoons cream cheese
- ¾ cup plus 2 tablespoons buttermilk

FILLING
- ¾ cup sugar
- 1 tablespoon cornstarch
- ¼ teaspoon salt
- 5 cups peeled and sliced fresh apricots
- 1½ cups fresh blackberries

EGG WASH
- 1 large egg
- 1 tablespoon water
  Coarse sugar

1. Place almonds in a food processor; pulse until finely ground. Add flour, sugar and salt; pulse until blended.

Add butter and cream cheese; pulse until butter is the size of peas. While pulsing, gradually add buttermilk until mixture starts to form a ball. Divide dough in half. Shape each into a disk; wrap in plastic wrap. Refrigerate 1 hour or overnight.

2. In a large bowl, whisk sugar, cornstarch and salt. Add apricots and berries; toss to coat. Let stand 10 minutes. Filling will be very juicy.

3. Preheat oven to 425°. On a lightly floured surface, roll one half of dough to a ⅛-in.-thick circle; transfer to a 9-in. pie plate. Trim pastry to ½ in. beyond rim of plate. Add filling. Roll remaining dough to a ⅛-in.-thick circle; cut into strips about ½ in. wide. Arrange over filling in a lattice pattern. Trim and seal strips to edge of bottom pastry; flute edge.

4. In a small bowl, whisk egg with water. Brush over lattice strips; sprinkle with sugar. Bake 20 minutes.

5. Reduce oven setting to 375°. Bake 45-50 minutes longer or until crust is golden brown and filling is bubbly. Cool on a wire rack.

PER SERVING *1 piece equals 506 cal., 19 g fat (9 g sat. fat), 59 mg chol., 316 mg sodium, 77 g carb., 5 g fiber, 10 g pro.*

APRICOT-BLACKBERRY PIE

Rich Rum Cake

PREP: 35 MIN. • **BAKE:** 25 MIN. + COOLING
MAKES: 12 SERVINGS

- 4 **large eggs, separated**
- 2½ **cups confectioners' sugar**
- ¾ **cup orange juice**
- ¼ **cup butter, cubed**
- ¾ **cup rum**
- 1 **cup all-purpose flour**
- 1 **teaspoon baking powder**
- ½ **teaspoon ground cinnamon**
- ¼ **teaspoon salt**
- ¼ **teaspoon ground nutmeg**
- ½ **cup packed brown sugar, divided**
- 1 **teaspoon vanilla extract**
- ¾ **cup butter, melted**
  **Whipped cream and finely
    chopped glazed pecans, optional**

1. Place egg whites in a large bowl; let stand at room temperature 30 minutes. For sauce, in a saucepan, combine confectioners' sugar, juice and ¼ cup butter; cook and stir over medium-low heat until sugar is dissolved. Remove from heat; stir in rum. Reserve ¾ cup for serving.

2. Preheat oven to 375°. Grease and flour a 10-in. tube pan. Sift flour, baking powder, cinnamon, salt and nutmeg together twice; set aside.

3. In a bowl, beat egg whites on medium until soft peaks form. Gradually add ¼ cup brown sugar, 1 tablespoon at a time, beating on high after each addition until sugar is dissolved. Continue beating until stiff peaks form.

4. In another bowl, beat egg yolks until slightly thickened. Gradually add ¼ cup brown sugar and vanilla, beating on high speed until thick. Fold a fourth of the egg whites into batter. Alternately fold in the flour mixture and remaining egg whites. Fold in the melted butter.

5. Transfer to prepared pan. Bake on lowest oven rack 25-30 minutes or until the top springs back when lightly touched. Immediately poke holes in cake with a fork; slowly pour remaining sauce over cake, allowing the sauce to absorb into cake. Cool completely in pan on a wire rack. Invert onto a serving plate. Serve with reserved sauce and, if desired, whipped cream and candied pecans.

NOTE *To remove cakes easily, use solid shortening to grease plain and fluted tube pans.*

PER SERVING *1 slice (calculated without whipped cream and pecans) equals 371 cal., 17 g fat (10 g sat. fat), 103 mg chol., 233 mg sodium, 44 g carb., trace fiber, 3 g pro.*

We like a touch of rum for the holidays, and this orange rum cake hits the spot. Try it on its own or with big swoops of whipped cream. It's decadent either way!
—**NANCY HEISHMAN** LAS VEGAS, NV

RICH RUM CAKE

FAST FIX
Baklava Tartlets

Want a quick treat that's delicious and easy to make? These tartlets will do the trick. Serve them right away or let them chill in the fridge for about an hour if you like them cold. See photo on page 111.
—**ASHLEY EAGON** KETTERING, OH

START TO FINISH: 25 MIN.
MAKES: 45 TARTLETS

- ¾ **cup honey**
- ½ **cup butter, melted**
- 1 **teaspoon ground cinnamon**
- 1 **teaspoon lemon juice**
- ¼ **teaspoon ground cloves**
- 2 **cups finely chopped walnuts**
- 3 **packages (1.9 ounces each) frozen miniature phyllo tart shells**

In a small bowl, mix the first five ingredients until blended; stir in the finely chopped walnuts. Spoon 2 teaspoons mixture into each tart shell. Refrigerate until serving.

PER SERVING *1 tartlet equals 76 cal., 5 g fat (1 g sat. fat), 5 mg chol., 24 mg sodium, 6 g carb., trace fiber, 2 g pro.*

Carrot Layer Cake

My sister gave me this recipe for what she calls "the ultimate carrot cake," and it really lives up to the name. When people taste it, they're bowled over by the tender cake and unexpected pecan filling.

—LINDA VAN HOLLAND INNISFAIL, AB

PREP: 55 MIN. • **BAKE:** 35 MIN. + COOLING
MAKES: 16-20 SERVINGS

FILLING
- 1 cup sugar
- 2 tablespoons all-purpose flour
- ¼ teaspoon salt
- 1 cup heavy whipping cream
- ½ cup butter
- 1 cup chopped pecans
- 1 teaspoon vanilla extract

CAKE
- 1¼ cups canola oil
- 2 cups sugar
- 2 cups all-purpose flour
- 2 teaspoons ground cinnamon
- 2 teaspoons baking powder
- 1 teaspoon baking soda
- 1 teaspoon salt
- 4 large eggs
- 4 cups finely shredded carrots
- 1 cup raisins
- 1 cup chopped pecans

FROSTING
- ¾ cup butter, softened
- 6 ounces cream cheese, softened
- 1 teaspoon vanilla extract
- 3 cups confectioners' sugar

1. In a large heavy saucepan, combine sugar, flour and salt. Stir in cream; add the butter. Cook and stir over medium heat until butter is melted; bring to a boil. Reduce heat. Simmer, uncovered, 30 minutes, stirring occasionally. Stir in pecans and vanilla. Cool; set aside.
2. In a large bowl, beat oil and sugar until well blended. Combine the flour, cinnamon, baking powder, baking soda and salt; add to the creamed mixture alternately with eggs, beating well after each addition. Stir in the carrots, raisins and nuts.
3. Pour into three greased and floured 9-in. round baking pans. Bake at 350° for 35-40 minutes or until a toothpick inserted near the center comes out clean. Coo cakes l in pans 10 minutes before removing to wire racks to cool completely.

4. For frosting, in a small bowl, beat the butter, cream cheese and vanilla until fluffy. Gradually beat in sugar until smooth. Spread the filling between the cake layers. Frost the top and sides of cake. Store cake in the refrigerator.
PER SERVING *1 piece equals 641 cal., 41 g fat (14 g sat. fat), 94 mg chol., 405 mg sodium, 68 g carb., 3 g fiber, 5 g pro.*

Buttermilk Lemon Meringue Pie

This lemon meringue pie with a hint of buttermilk may just start a revolution among lemon lovers everywhere. In my camp, it beats the traditional kind every time. The compliments roll when I serve it.

—ELLEN RILEY MURFREESBORO, TN

PREP: 30 MIN. • **BAKE:** 15 MIN. + CHILLING
MAKES: 8 SERVINGS

- 1½ cups graham cracker crumbs
- ¼ cup sugar
- ⅓ cup butter, melted

FILLING
- ¾ cup sugar
- 3 tablespoons cornstarch
- 1½ cups buttermilk
- 3 large egg yolks
- 2 tablespoons butter
- 2 tablespoons lemon juice
- 2 teaspoons grated lemon peel

MERINGUE
- 3 large egg whites
- ½ teaspoon vanilla extract
- ¼ teaspoon cream of tartar
- 6 tablespoons sugar

1. Combine the cracker crumbs, sugar and butter; press onto the bottom and up the sides of an ungreased 9-in. pie plate. Bake at 350° for 10-12 minutes or until crust is lightly browned. Cool on a wire rack.
2. For filling, in a large saucepan, combine sugar and cornstarch. Stir in the buttermilk until smooth. Cook and stir over medium-high heat until thickened and bubbly. Reduce heat to low; cook and stir for 2 minutes longer. Remove from the heat. Stir 1 cup of hot mixture into the egg yolks; return all to pan, stirring constantly. Bring to a gentle boil; cook and stir for 2 minutes longer. Remove from the heat. Stir in butter. Gently stir in lemon juice and peel. Pour hot filling into pastry shell.
3. For meringue, beat the egg whites, vanilla and cream of tartar on medium speed until soft peaks form. Gradually beat in sugar, 1 tablespoon at a time, on high until stiff peaks form. Spread over hot filling, sealing edges to crust.
4. Bake for 15-20 minutes or until golden brown. Cool on a wire rack for 1 hour; refrigerate for 1-2 hours before serving. Refrigerate leftovers.
PER SERVING *1 piece equals 350 cal., 14 g fat (8 g sat. fat), 106 mg chol., 242 mg sodium, 52 g carb., 1 g fiber, 5 g pro.*

BUTTERMILK LEMON MERINGUE PIE

Plum & Hazelnut Pie

My mom taught me about Italian prune plums and pie. I sprinkle the crust with ground hazelnuts for luscious flavor and to keep it from getting soggy.

—**TRISHA KRUSE** EAGLE, ID

PREP: 15 MIN. + CHILLING
BAKE: 45 MIN. + COOLING
MAKES: 8 SERVINGS

Pastry for single-crust deep-dish pie (9 inches)
4 cups sliced fresh plums (about 8)
2 tablespoons hazelnut liqueur, optional
½ cup sugar
¼ cup all-purpose flour
¼ teaspoon salt

TOPPING
½ cup packed brown sugar
⅓ cup all-purpose flour
¼ cup finely chopped hazelnuts, toasted
3 tablespoons cold butter, cubed

1. On a lightly floured surface, roll dough to a ⅛-in.-thick circle; transfer to a 9-in. deep-dish pie plate. Trim pastry to ½ in. beyond rim of plate; flute edge. Refrigerate 30 minutes.
2. Preheat oven to 375°. Toss plums with liqueur if desired. Mix sugar, flour and salt; add to plums and toss to coat. Transfer to pastry shell.
3. For topping, combine brown sugar, flour and hazelnuts; cut in butter until crumbly. Sprinkle over plum mixture.
4. Bake until crust is golden brown and filling is bubbly, 45-55 minutes. Cool on a wire rack.

PASTRY FOR SINGLE-CRUST DEEP-DISH PIE (9 INCHES) *Combine 1½ cups all-purpose flour and ¼ tsp. salt; cut in ⅔ cup cold butter until crumbly. Gradually add 3-6 Tbsp. ice water, tossing with a fork until dough holds together when pressed. Wrap in plastic wrap and refrigerate 1 hour.*
PER SERVING *1 piece equals 454 cal., 22 g fat (13 g sat. fat), 52 mg chol., 308 mg sodium, 61 g carb., 2 g fiber, 5 g pro.*

BOSTON CREAM CUPCAKES

Boston Cream Cupcakes

Boston cream doughnuts have been my favorite bakery treat since I was a child, so I created this easy-to-make cupcake version that is just as luscious.

—**JEANNE HOLT** MENDOTA HEIGHTS, MN

PREP: 25 MIN. • **BAKE:** 15 MIN. + COOLING
MAKES: ½ DOZEN

3 tablespoons shortening
⅓ cup sugar
1 large egg
½ teaspoon vanilla extract
½ cup all-purpose flour
½ teaspoon baking powder
¼ teaspoon salt
3 tablespoons 2% milk
⅔ cup prepared vanilla pudding
½ cup semisweet chocolate chips
¼ cup heavy whipping cream

1. In a small bowl, cream shortening and sugar until light and fluffy. Beat in egg. Beat in vanilla. Combine the flour, baking powder and salt; add to the creamed mixture alternately with milk, beating well after each addition.
2. Fill paper-lined muffin cups half full. Bake at 350° for 15-20 minutes or until a toothpick inserted near the center comes out clean. Cool for 10 minutes before removing from pan to a wire rack to cool completely.
3. Cut a small hole in the corner of a pastry or plastic bag; insert a small tip. Fill with pudding. Push the tip through the top to fill each cupcake.
4. Place chocolate chips in a small bowl. In a small saucepan, bring cream just to a boil. Pour over chocolate; whisk until smooth. Cool, stirring occasionally, to room temperature or until ganache thickens slightly, about 10 minutes. Spoon over cupcakes. Let stand until set. Store in an airtight container in the refrigerator.

PER SERVING *1 cupcake equals 288 cal., 16 g fat (7 g sat. fat), 53 mg chol., 198 mg sodium, 35 g carb., 1 g fiber, 4 g pro.*

Cherry & Chocolate Ice Cream Pie

We took cherry pie to a whole new level as a frozen treat. With a luscious layer of chocolate fudge inside, this is one impressive pie. See photo on page 111.

—SCARLETT ELROD NEWNAN, GA

PREP: 20 MIN. + FREEZING
MAKES: 8 SERVINGS

- 15 **Oreo cookies**
- ¼ **cup butter, melted**
- ¾ **cup hot fudge ice cream topping**
- 4 **cups vanilla ice cream, softened**
- 3 **cups fresh or frozen dark sweet cherries, pitted and quartered, divided**
- ½ **cup water**
- ¼ **cup sugar**
- 2 **tablespoons thawed cranberry juice concentrate**
- 1 **tablespoon cornstarch**
- 1 **tablespoon cherry liqueur, optional**

1. Pulse cookies in a food processor until fine crumbs form. Add butter; process until blended. Press mixture onto the bottom and up the sides of an ungreased 9-in. pie plate. Freeze until firm, about 15 minutes. Carefully spread hot fudge topping over bottom of the crust. Freeze until firm, about 30 minutes.

2. Combine the ice cream and 1 cup cherries; spread over hot fudge. Freeze until firm, about 8 hours.

3. Meanwhile, in a large saucepan, combine water, sugar, cranberry juice concentrate and cornstarch; bring to a boil over medium heat, stirring constantly. Stir in the remaining cherries. Reduce heat; simmer, uncovered, until thickened and cherries are soft, about 5 minutes. Remove from heat; if desired, stir in cherry liqueur. Cool completely.

4. Remove the pie from the freezer 10 minutes before cutting. Serve with sauce.

PER SERVING *1 piece equals 460 cal., 19 g fat (10 g sat. fat), 44 mg chol., 224 mg sodium, 69 g carb., 2 g fiber, 5 g pro.*

Contest-Winning Fresh Blueberry Pie

I've been making this dessert for years. Blueberries are readily available in my home state of Michigan, and nothing says summer like a piece of fresh berry pie!

—LINDA KERNAN MASON, MI

PREP: 15 MIN. + COOLING
MAKES: 8 SERVINGS

- ¾ **cup sugar**
- 3 **tablespoons cornstarch**
- ⅛ **teaspoon salt**
- ¼ **cup cold water**
- 5 **cups fresh blueberries, divided**
- 1 **tablespoon butter**
- 1 **tablespoon lemon juice**
- 1 **pastry shell (9 inches), baked**

1. In a saucepan over medium heat, combine the sugar, cornstarch, salt and water until smooth. Add 3 cups blueberries. Bring to a boil; cook and stir for 2 minutes or until thickened and bubbly.

2. Remove from the heat. Add butter, lemon juice and remaining berries; stir until butter is melted. Cool. Pour into pastry shell. Refrigerate until serving.

PER SERVING *1 piece equals 269 cal., 9 g fat (4 g sat. fat), 9 mg chol., 153 mg sodium, 48 g carb., 2 g fiber, 2 g pro.*

CONTEST-WINNING FRESH BLUEBERRY PIE

Potluck Banana Cake

I found this recipe many years ago and have been making it for potlucks and family gatherings ever since. The coffee-flavored frosting is a nice complement to the moist banana cake.

—**KATHY HOFFMAN** TOPTON, PA

PREP: 25 MIN. • **BAKE:** 35 MIN. + COOLING
MAKES: 12-15 SERVINGS

- ½ cup butter, softened
- 1 cup sugar
- 2 large eggs
- 1 teaspoon vanilla extract
- 2 cups all-purpose flour
- 2 teaspoons baking soda
- ½ teaspoon salt
- 1½ cups mashed ripe bananas (about 3 medium)
- 1 cup (8 ounces) sour cream

COFFEE FROSTING

- ⅓ cup butter, softened
- 2½ cups confectioners' sugar
- 2 teaspoons instant coffee granules
- 2 to 3 tablespoons milk

1. In a large bowl, cream butter and sugar until light and fluffy. Add eggs, one at a time, beating well after each addition. Stir in vanilla. Combine the flour, baking soda and salt; add to creamed mixture alternately with bananas and sour cream, beating well after each addition.

2. Pour batter into a greased 13x9-in. baking dish. Bake at 350° for 35-40 minutes or until a toothpick inserted near the center comes out clean. Cool completely on a wire rack.

3. For frosting, in a small bowl, beat butter and confectioners' sugar until smooth. Dissolve coffee granules in milk; add to butter mixture and beat until smooth. Spread over cake.

PER SERVING *1 piece equals 344 cal., 14 g fat (8 g sat. fat), 67 mg chol., 368 mg sodium, 52 g carb., 1 g fiber, 4 g pro.*

Buttermilk Chocolate Cupcakes

Cupcakes make a great get-up-and-go treat when you need something fast on a busy day. These are gone in a flash.

—**ELLEN MOORE** SPRINGFIELD, NH

PREP: 30 MIN. • **BAKE:** 15 MIN. + COOLING
MAKES: 2 DOZEN

- ½ cup butter, softened
- 1½ cups sugar
- 2 large eggs
- 1 teaspoon vanilla extract
- 1½ cups all-purpose flour
- ½ cup baking cocoa
- 1 teaspoon baking soda
- ¼ teaspoon salt
- ½ cup buttermilk
- ½ cup water

FROSTING

- ½ cup butter, softened
- 3¾ cups confectioners' sugar
- 2 ounces unsweetened chocolate, melted
- 2 tablespoons evaporated milk
- 1 teaspoon vanilla extract
- ¼ teaspoon salt
  Chocolate sprinkles

1. Preheat oven to 375°. In a large bowl, cream butter and sugar until light and fluffy. Add eggs, one at a time, beating well after each addition. Beat in vanilla. Combine flour, cocoa, baking soda and salt. Combine buttermilk and water. Add dry ingredients to creamed mixture alternately with buttermilk and water, beating well after each addition.

2. Fill paper-lined muffin cups two-thirds full. Bake 15-20 minutes or until a toothpick inserted in center comes out clean. Cool for 10 minutes before removing from pans to wire racks to cool completely.

3. For frosting, in a small bowl, beat butter and confectioners' sugar until smooth. Beat in melted chocolate, milk, vanilla and salt. Frost cupcakes; garnish with chocolate sprinkles.

PER SERVING *1 cupcake equals 239 cal., 9 g fat (5 g sat. fat), 39 mg chol., 191 mg sodium, 39 g carb., 1 g fiber, 2 g pro.*

POTLUCK BANANA CAKE

Lemonade Layer Cake

Lemonade concentrate gives both the tender cake and sweet frosting a fantastic flavor. I garnish this sunny dessert with lemon slices and mint leaves.

—JANA RANDICH PHOENIX, AZ

PREP: 40 MIN. • **BAKE:** 20 MIN. + CHILLING
MAKES: 16 SERVINGS

- 6 **tablespoons butter, softened**
- 1⅓ **cups sugar**
- 3 **tablespoons thawed lemonade concentrate**
- 2 **tablespoons grated lemon peel**
- 2 **teaspoons vanilla extract**
- 2 **large eggs**
- 2 **large egg whites**
- 2 **cups all-purpose flour**
- 1 **teaspoon baking powder**
- ½ **teaspoon baking soda**
- ¼ **teaspoon salt**
- 1¼ **cups buttermilk**

FROSTING

- 8 **ounces reduced-fat cream cheese**
- 2 **tablespoons butter, softened**
- 2 **tablespoons grated lemon peel**
- 2 **teaspoons thawed lemonade concentrate**
- 1 **teaspoon vanilla extract**
- 3½ **cups confectioners' sugar**

1. In a large bowl, beat butter and sugar until crumbly, about 2 minutes. Add the lemonade concentrate, lemon peel and vanilla; mix well. Add eggs and egg whites, one at a time, beating well after each addition. Combine the flour, baking powder, baking soda and salt. Add to butter mixture alternately with buttermilk, beating well after each addition.

2. Coat two 9-in. round baking pans with cooking spray and dust with flour. Pour batter into prepared pans.

3. Bake at 350° for 18-22 minutes or until a toothpick inserted near the center comes out clean. Cool for 10 minutes before removing from pans to a wire rack to cool completely.

4. For frosting, in a small bowl, combine cream cheese and butter until smooth. Add the lemon peel, lemonade concentrate and vanilla extract; mix well. Gradually beat in confectioners' sugar until smooth. Spread frosting between layers and over top and sides of cake. Refrigerate

for at least 1 hour before serving. Refrigerate leftovers.

PER SERVING *1 slice equals 352 cal., 12 g fat (7 g sat. fat), 58 mg chol., 237 mg sodium, 58 g carb., 1 g fiber, 5 g pro.*

Coconut Eggnog Pie

This family favorite came together by accident. One day I was trying to use up eggnog and coconut left over from other holiday goodies. I combined the two and discovered how well they go together!

—FAY MORELAND WICHITA FALLS, TX

PREP: 10 MIN. • **BAKE:** 55 MIN. + COOLING
MAKES: 10 SERVINGS

- 2 **large eggs**
- 1¼ **cups packed brown sugar**
- ¾ **cup eggnog**
- ½ **cup butter, melted**
- 2 **tablespoons all-purpose flour**
- 1 **teaspoon ground cinnamon**
  Dash salt
- 2½ **cups flaked coconut, divided**

COCONUT EGGNOG PIE

- 1 **extra-servings graham cracker crust (9 ounces)**
- ¼ **cup chopped walnuts or pecans**

1. Preheat oven to 425°. In a large bowl, beat the first seven ingredients until blended; stir in 2 cups coconut. Pour into crust; sprinkle with walnuts and remaining coconut. Bake on a lower oven rack 10 minutes.

2. Reduce the oven setting to 325°. Cover top loosely with foil. Bake for 45-50 minutes longer or until the filling is set. Cool on a wire rack. Refrigerate leftovers.

NOTE *To prepare a homemade graham cracker crust, mix 1½ cups graham cracker crumbs and ¼ cup sugar; stir in ⅓ cup melted butter. Press onto bottom and up sides of a greased 9-in. pie plate. Refrigerate 30 minutes.*

PER SERVING *1 piece equals 485 cal., 27 g fat (15 g sat. fat), 73 mg chol., 327 mg sodium, 58 g carb., 2 g fiber, 5 g pro.*

STRAWBERRY SHORTCAKE CUPS

Strawberry Shortcake Cups

Back when store-bought shortcake was unheard of, my grandmother made this from-scratch recipe. She passed it down to my mother, who later shared it with me, and I've since given it to my daughter.
—**ALTHEA HEERS** JEWELL, IA

PREP: 15 MIN. • **BAKE:** 15 MIN. + COOLING
MAKES: 8 SERVINGS

- 1 **quart fresh strawberries**
- 4 **tablespoons sugar, divided**
- 1½ **cups all-purpose flour**
- 1 **tablespoon baking powder**
- ½ **teaspoon salt**
- ¼ **cup cold butter, cubed**
- 1 **large egg**
- ½ **cup milk**
  Whipped cream

1. Mash or slice strawberries; place in a large bowl. Add 2 tablespoons sugar and set aside. In another bowl, combine flour, baking powder, salt and remaining sugar; cut in butter until crumbly. In a small bowl, beat the egg and milk; stir into flour mixture just until moistened.
2. Fill eight greased muffin cups two-thirds full. Bake at 425° for 12 minutes or until golden. Remove from the pan to cool on a wire rack.

3. Just before serving, split shortcakes in half horizontally. Spoon berries and whipped cream between layers and over tops of shortcakes.
PER SERVING *200 cal., 7 g fat (4 g sat. fat), 44 mg chol., 372 mg sodium, 30 g carb., 2 g fiber, 4 g pro.*

Chocolate-Banana Cream Pie

Adding chocolate to almost any dessert takes the awesome level up a notch. The banana and chocolate combo in this cream pie is pure yum!
—**DIANE NEMITZ** LUDINGTON, MI

PREP: 20 MIN. + CHILLING
BAKE: 25 MIN. + CHILLING
MAKES: 8 SERVINGS

- **Pastry for single-crust pie (9 inches)**
- ⅔ **cup plus ¼ cup sugar, divided**
- ½ **cup all-purpose flour**
- 1 **envelope unflavored gelatin**
- 1¼ **cups half-and-half cream**
- 3 **large egg yolks, lightly beaten**
- 1 **cup sour cream**
- 1 **teaspoon rum extract**
- 1 **teaspoon vanilla extract**
- 1 **ounce unsweetened chocolate, melted**
- 4 **medium bananas, sliced**
- ½ **cup heavy whipping cream**
  Shaved unsweetened chocolate, optional

1. On a floured surface, roll pastry dough to a ⅛-in.-thick circle; transfer to a 9-in. pie plate. Trim pastry to ½ in. beyond rim of plate; flute edge. Refrigerate 30 minutes. Preheat oven to 425°.
2. Line pastry with a double thickness of foil. Fill with pie weights, dried beans or uncooked rice. Bake on a lower oven rack until edges are golden brown, about 20-25 minutes. Remove foil and weights; bake until bottom is golden brown, about 4 minutes. Cool on a wire rack.
3. Meanwhile, in the top of a double boiler or a metal bowl over simmering water, mix ⅔ cup sugar, flour and gelatin. Whisk in half-and-half and egg yolks; cook, whisking constantly, until temperature reaches 160° and mixture is thick enough to coat a metal spoon. Remove from heat; whisk in sour cream and extracts. Transfer ¾ cup mixture to a small bowl; stir in melted chocolate until blended. Refrigerate vanilla and chocolate mixtures until set but not firm, about 30 minutes.
4. Spread chocolate mixture evenly over crust. Fold bananas into vanilla mixture; spread over chocolate layer. Refrigerate until firm, about 2 hours.
5. Beat cream until it begins to thicken. Add the remaining sugar; beat until stiff peaks form. Spread over top; if desired, sprinkle with shaved chocolate.

PASTRY FOR SINGLE-CRUST PIE (9 INCHES) *Combine 1¼ cups all-purpose flour and ¼ tsp. salt; cut in ½ cup cold butter until crumbly. Gradually add 3-5 Tbsp. ice water, tossing with a fork until dough holds together when pressed. Wrap in plastic wrap and refrigerate 1 hour.*
NOTE *Let pie weights cool before storing. Beans and rice may be reused for pie weights but not for cooking.*
PER SERVING *1 piece equals 562 cal., 30 g fat (19 g sat. fat), 159 mg chol., 201 mg sodium, 61 g carb., 3 g fiber, 11 g pro.*

Holiday Fruit Pie

My mom is an excellent pie maker, so I learned from the best. If this pie with cranberries and pineapple tastes a little tart, sprinkle sugar on the top crust.

—COURTNEY STULTZ WEIR, KS

PREP: 45 MIN. • **BAKE:** 45 MIN. + COOLING
MAKES: 8 SERVINGS

- 2 cups fresh or frozen cranberries, thawed
- ½ cup water
- ¼ cup honey
- 1 cup crushed pineapple, drained
- ¼ cup cornstarch
- 1 teaspoon ground cinnamon
- 1 medium apple, peeled and thinly sliced
  Pastry for double-crust pie (9 inches)

1. Preheat oven to 350°. In a small saucepan, combine cranberries, water and honey. Cook, uncovered, over medium heat until berries pop, about 15 minutes. Cool slightly.
2. In a large bowl, combine pineapple, cornstarch and cinnamon; stir in the cranberry mixture and apple. On a lightly floured surface, roll one half of pastry dough to a ⅛-in.-thick circle; transfer to a 9-in. pie plate. Trim pastry even with rim. Add filling.
3. Roll remaining dough to a ⅛-in.-thick circle. Place over filling. Trim, seal and flute edge. Cut slits in top. Bake 45-55 minutes or until crust is golden brown and filling is bubbly. Cover pie loosely with foil during the last 30 minutes if needed to prevent overbrowning. Remove foil. Cool on a wire rack.

PASTRY FOR DOUBLE-CRUST PIE (9 INCHES) *Combine 2½ cups all-purpose flour and ½ tsp. salt; cut in 1 cup cold butter until crumbly. Gradually add ⅓-⅔ cup ice water, tossing with a fork until dough holds together when pressed. Divide dough in half. Shape each into a disk; wrap in plastic wrap. Refrigerate 1 hour or overnight.*

PER SERVING *1 piece equals 430 cal., 23 g fat (14 g sat. fat), 60 mg chol., 311 mg sodium, 53 g carb., 3 g fiber, 5 g pro.*

My family gives this cranberry pie a big thumbs up! They even invite friends over to share it.

—LORRAINE CALAND SHUNIAH, ON

Cranberry Cheese Crumb Pie

PREP: 20 MIN. • **BAKE:** 45 MIN. + CHILLING
MAKES: 10 SERVINGS

- 1 sheet refrigerated pie pastry
- 8 ounces cream cheese, softened
- 1 can (14 ounces) sweetened condensed milk
- ¼ cup lemon juice
  CRANBERRY LAYER
- 1 can (14 ounces) whole-berry cranberry sauce
- 2 tablespoons cornstarch
- 1 tablespoon brown sugar
  TOPPING
- ½ cup all-purpose flour
- ¼ cup packed brown sugar
- ½ teaspoon ground cinnamon
- ¼ cup cold butter, cubed
- ¾ cup chopped pecans

1. Unroll pastry sheet into a 9-in. pie plate; flute edge. In a small bowl, beat cream cheese, milk and lemon juice until smooth. Spread evenly into crust.
2. In a small bowl, mix cranberry layer ingredients; spoon over cream cheese mixture. For topping, in another bowl, mix flour, brown sugar and cinnamon; cut in butter until crumbly. Stir in pecans. Sprinkle over cranberry layer.
3. Bake at 375° for 45-55 minutes or until crust and topping are golden brown. Cover edge loosely with foil during the last 10 minutes if needed to prevent overbrowning. Remove foil. Cool 1 hour on a wire rack; refrigerate at least 2 hours before serving.

PER SERVING *1 piece equals 512 cal., 27 g fat (12 g sat. fat), 55 mg chol., 260 mg sodium, 62 g carb., 2 g fiber, 7 g pro.*

HOLIDAY FRUIT PIE

**JULIE NOWAKOWSKI'S
BANANA CREAM BROWNIE
DESSERT** *PAGE 132*

Just Desserts

You'll want to **save room** for these delicious after-dinner sweets. From **light sorbets** to **creamy cheesecakes,** you're sure to find something that'll **satisfy every sweet tooth.**

GAIL PRATHER'S CARNIVAL CARAMEL APPLES *PAGE 135*

ALDENE BELCH'S STRAWBERRY PRETZEL DESSERT *PAGE 140*

EDNA HOFFMAN'S SLOW COOKER CINNAMON ROLL PUDDING *PAGE 139*

CRANBERRY-KISSED CHOCOLATE SILK

I combined fresh cranberry salad with the rich custard known as pots de creme, and the result is elegant compared to the usual desserts.
—**CARMELL CHILDS** FERRON, UT

EAT SMART **5 INGREDIENTS**

Raspberry-Banana Soft Serve

When I make this ice cream, I mix and match bananas for their ripeness. Very ripe ones add more banana flavor. Less ripe bananas lend a fluffier texture.
—**MELISSA HANSEN** MILWAUKEE, WI

PREP: 10 MIN. + FREEZING
MAKES: 2½ CUPS

  4 **medium ripe bananas**
 ½ **cup fat-free plain yogurt**
  1 **to 2 tablespoons maple syrup**
 ½ **cup frozen unsweetened raspberries**
     Fresh raspberries, optional

1. Thinly slice bananas; transfer to a large resealable plastic freezer bag. Arrange the slices in a single layer; freeze overnight.
2. Pulse bananas in a food processor until finely chopped. Add the yogurt, maple syrup and raspberries. Process just until smooth, scraping sides as needed. Serve immediately, adding fresh berries if desired.
CHOCOLATE-PEANUT BUTTER SOFT SERVE *Substitute 2 tablespoons each of creamy peanut butter and baking cocoa for the raspberries, then proceed as directed.*
PER SERVING *½ cup (calculated without fresh berries) equals 104 cal., 0 fat (0 sat. fat), 1 mg chol., 15 mg sodium, 26 g carb., 2 g fiber, 2 g pro.*
Diabetic Exchanges: *1 fruit, ½ starch.*

Cranberry-Kissed Chocolate Silk

PREP: 25 MIN. + CHILLING
MAKES: 6 SERVINGS

  1 **cup cranberry juice**
 ⅛ **teaspoon salt**
  4 **large eggs, beaten**
  1 **cup milk chocolate chips**
  1 **cup semisweet chocolate chips**
  1 **teaspoon vanilla extract**
  1 **cup fresh or frozen cranberries, thawed**
 ⅓ **cup sugar**
 ¾ **cup sweetened whipped cream**
  3 **tablespoons sliced almonds, toasted**

1. Place cranberry juice and salt in a small heavy saucepan; bring just to a boil. Remove from heat. In a small bowl, slowly whisk hot juice into eggs; return all to pan. Cook over low heat

2-3 minutes or until the mixture thickens and a thermometer reads 170°, stirring constantly.
2. Place egg mixture, chocolate chips and vanilla in a blender; let stand for 2 minutes. Cover and process until smooth. Pour into six dessert dishes. Refrigerate at least 4 hours, covering when completely cooled.
3. Place cranberries in a small food processor; pulse until finely chopped. Transfer berries to a small bowl; toss with sugar. Top each serving with the berries, whipped cream and almonds.
NOTE *To toast nuts, bake in a shallow pan in a 350° oven for 5-10 minutes or cook in a skillet over low heat until lightly browned, stirring occasionally.*
PER SERVING *473 cal., 27 g fat (15 g sat. fat), 151 mg chol., 129 mg sodium, 54 g carb., 4 g fiber, 9 g pro.*

RASPBERRY-BANANA SOFT SERVE

WATERMELON GRANITA

(5) INGREDIENTS

Semisweet Chocolate Mousse

A friend shared this rich, velvety mousse recipe with me. I love to cook and I have tons of recipes, but this one is a favorite.

—**JUDY SPENCER** SAN DIEGO, CA

PREP: 20 MIN. + CHILLING
MAKES: 2 SERVINGS

- ¼ cup semisweet chocolate chips
- 1 tablespoon water
- 1 large egg yolk, lightly beaten
- 1½ teaspoons vanilla extract
- ½ cup heavy whipping cream
- 1 tablespoon sugar
  Whipped cream, optional

1. In a small saucepan, melt chocolate chips with water; stir until smooth. Stir a small amount of the mixture into egg yolk; return all to the pan, stirring constantly. Cook and stir for 2 minutes or until slightly thickened. Remove from the heat; stir in the vanilla. Cool, stirring several times.

2. In a small bowl, beat the whipping cream until it begins to thicken. Add sugar; beat until soft peaks form. Fold in the cooled chocolate mixture. Cover and refrigerate at least 2 hours, then garnish with whipped cream if desired.

PER SERVING 1 cup equals 367 cal., 31 g fat (18 g sat. fat), 188 mg chol., 29 mg sodium, 21 g carb., 1 g fiber, 3 g pro.

(5) INGREDIENTS

Watermelon Granita

Say a sweet "ciao" to summer with this light and airy Italian treat! Serve in pretty glasses garnished with mint sprigs or wedges of cantaloupe.

—*TASTE OF HOME* TEST KITCHEN

PREP: 15 MIN. + FREEZING
MAKES: 8 SERVINGS

- 1¼ cups sugar
- 1¼ cups water
- 6 cups cubed watermelon
  Small watermelon wedges, optional

1. In a small saucepan, bring sugar and water to a boil. Cook and stir until the sugar is dissolved; set aside. In a blender, process the watermelon in batches until smooth. Strain; discard the pulp and seeds. Transfer to an 8-in. square dish; stir in the sugar mixture. Cool to room temperature.

2. Freeze for 1 hour; stir with a fork. Freeze for 2-3 hours longer or until completely frozen, stirring every 30 minutes. Stir granita with a fork just before serving; spoon into dessert dishes. Garnish with melon wedges if desired.

PER SERVING ⅔ cup equals 151 cal., 0 fat (0 sat. fat), 0 chol., 4 mg sodium, 41 g carb., 1 g fiber, trace pro.

SEMISWEET CHOCOLATE MOUSSE

FAST FIX

Cheesecake Phyllo Cups

I've been making these colorful cheesecake bites for years. Topped with kiwifruit and mandarin oranges, they are delicious.

—LORRAINE CHEVALIER MERRIMAC, MA

START TO FINISH: 25 MIN.
MAKES: 2½ DOZEN

- 4 ounces reduced-fat cream cheese
- ½ cup reduced-fat sour cream
  Sugar substitute equivalent to
    2 tablespoons sugar
- 1 teaspoon vanilla extract
- 2 packages (2.1 ounces each) frozen miniature phyllo tart shells, thawed
- 1 can (11 ounces) mandarin oranges slices, drained
- 1 kiwifruit, peeled, sliced and cut into quarters

1. In a small bowl, beat the cream cheese, sour cream, sugar substitute and vanilla until smooth.

2. Pipe or spoon into phyllo shells. Top each with an orange segment and kiwi piece. Refrigerate until serving.

NOTE *This recipe was tested with Splenda sugar blend.*

PER SERVING *1 each equals 46 cal., 2 g fat (1 g sat. fat), 4 mg chol., 29 mg sodium, 5 g carb., trace fiber, 1 g pro.*

Peanut Butter Custard Blast

Ooey-gooey and great is how friends and family describe my chocolate-peanut butter dessert. I appreciate its make-ahead convenience.

—MARILEE EVENSON WISCONSIN RAPIDS, WI

PREP: 30 MIN. • **COOK:** 25 MIN. + CHILLING
MAKES: 15 SERVINGS

- 2 cups Oreo cookie crumbs
- 2 tablespoons sugar
- ⅓ cup butter, melted

FILLING

- 1½ cups sugar
- ⅓ cup cornstarch
- 2 tablespoons all-purpose flour
- ½ teaspoon salt
- 6 cups 2% milk
- 6 large egg yolks, beaten
- 1 cup creamy peanut butter

TOPPING

- 2 cups heavy whipping cream
- 1 tablespoon confectioners' sugar
- 6 peanut butter cups, chopped
- ½ cup chopped salted peanuts
- 2 tablespoons chocolate syrup

1. Preheat the oven to 375°. In a small bowl, combine the cookie crumbs and sugar; stir in butter. Press onto bottom of a greased 13x9-in. baking dish. Bake for 8 minutes or until set. Cool on a wire rack.

2. For filling, in a large saucepan, combine sugar, cornstarch, flour and salt. Stir in milk until smooth. Cook and stir over medium-high heat until thickened and bubbly. Reduce heat; cook and stir 2 minutes. Remove from heat. Stir a small amount of the hot mixture into egg yolks; return all to pan, stirring constantly. Bring to a gentle boil; cook and stir 2 minutes.

3. Remove from heat. Stir 1 cup into peanut butter until smooth. Gently stir peanut butter mixture into the pan. Pour over crust. Cool to room temperature. Cover and refrigerate at least 2 hours.

4. For topping, in a large bowl, beat cream until it begins to thicken. Add confectioners' sugar; beat until stiff peaks form. Spread over peanut butter mixture. Sprinkle with peanut butter cups and peanuts, then drizzle with chocolate syrup.

TO MAKE AHEAD *After pouring the peanut butter custard over the crust, refrigerate overnight. Before serving, top with sweetened whipped cream, peanut butter candy, peanuts and chocolate syrup.*

PER SERVING *1 piece equals 585 cal., 37 g fat (16 g sat. fat), 144 mg chol., 396 mg sodium, 55 g carb., 3 g fiber, 12 g pro.*

PEANUT BUTTER CUSTARD BLAST

Quick & Easy Chocolate Sauce

Mom made this fudgy sauce to drizzle on cake. It's also pretty darn good over ice cream. It will keep for several weeks in the refrigerator.

—**MIKE MILLER** CRESTON, IA

START TO FINISH: 15 MIN.
MAKES: 2¼ CUPS

- 12 **ounces (2 cups) semisweet chocolate chips**
- 1 **cup heavy whipping cream**
- ¾ **cup sugar**

In a small saucepan, combine all of the ingredients. Stirring constantly, bring to a boil over medium heat; boil and stir for 2 minutes. Remove from heat.
PER SERVING *2 tablespoons equals 169 cal., 11 g fat (6 g sat. fat), 18 mg chol., 7 mg sodium, 21 g carb. (19 g sugars, 1 g fiber), 1 g pro.*

Marinated Oranges

I marinated oranges for a cake topping. Then I discovered they make a sweet, puckery dessert when paired with vanilla yogurt.

—**CAROL POINDEXTER** NORRIDGE, IL

PREP: 15 MIN. + MARINATING
MAKES: 4 SERVINGS

- 1 **cup orange juice**
- 1 **tablespoon sugar**
- 1 **tablespoon lemon juice**
- 1 **tablespoon grated orange peel (1 medium orange)**
- 1 **teaspoon grated lemon peel (1 small lemon)**
- 1 **teaspoon vanilla extract**
- 4 **medium oranges, peeled and thinly sliced (about 3 cups)**
  Vanilla yogurt, optional
  Grated lime peel, optional

Combine first six ingredients; pour over oranges. Cover; refrigerate for 2-3 hours. Serve with a slotted spoon. If desired, top with vanilla yogurt and grated lime peel.
PER SERVING *¾ cup equals 86 cal., 0 fat (0 sat. fat), 0 chol., 7 mg sodium, 20 g carb. (16 g sugars, 0 fiber), 1 g pro. Diabetic Exchange: 1½ fruit.*

MINIATURE PEANUT BUTTER CHEESECAKES

Miniature Peanut Butter Cheesecakes

These yummy treats with a peanut butter cup inside were handed down to me from my mother. They're perfect for holidays or any special occasion.

—**MARY ANN DELL** PHOENIXVILLE, PA

PREP: 20 MIN. • **BAKE:** 15 MIN. + CHILLING
MAKES: 6 SERVINGS

- ⅓ **cup graham cracker crumbs**
- 1 **tablespoon sugar**
- 5 **teaspoons butter, melted**
FILLING
- 4 **ounces cream cheese, softened**
- ¼ **cup sugar**
- 2 **teaspoons all-purpose flour**
- 2 **tablespoons beaten egg**
- ¼ **teaspoon vanilla extract**
- 6 **miniature peanut butter cups**

1. In a small bowl, combine cracker crumbs, sugar and butter. Press onto the bottoms of six paper-lined muffin cups; set aside.
2. In a small bowl, beat the cream cheese, sugar and flour until smooth. Add egg and vanilla; beat on low speed just until combined. Place a peanut butter cup in the center of each muffin cup; fill with cream cheese mixture.
3. Bake at 350° for 15-18 minutes or until center is set. Cool on a wire rack for 10 minutes before removing from pan to a wire rack to cool completely. Refrigerate for at least 2 hours.
PER SERVING *1 cheesecake equals 201 cal., 13 g fat (7 g sat. fat), 51 mg chol., 136 mg sodium, 19 g carb., trace fiber, 3 g pro.*

GLAZED CINNAMON APPLES

Banana Cream Brownie Dessert

I keep the ingredients for this extremely delicious dessert on hand because I make it often for potlucks and family gatherings. I'm always asked for the recipe. After one bite, you'll understand why.

—JULIE NOWAKOWSKI LASALLE, IL

PREP: 20 MIN. • **BAKE:** 30 MIN. + COOLING
MAKES: 12-15 SERVINGS

- 1 package fudge brownie mix (13-inch x 9-inch pan size)
- 1 cup (6 ounces) semisweet chocolate chips, divided
- ¾ cup dry roasted peanuts, chopped, divided
- 3 medium firm bananas
- 1⅔ cups cold milk
- 2 packages (5.1 ounces each) instant vanilla pudding mix
- 1 carton (8 ounces) frozen whipped topping, thawed

1. Prepare brownie batter according to package directions for fudge-like brownies. Stir in ½ cup chocolate chips and ¼ cup peanuts. Spread into a greased 13x9-in. baking pan. Bake at 350° for 28-30 minutes or until a toothpick inserted near the center comes out clean. Cool on a wire rack.
2. Slice bananas; arrange in a single layer over brownies. Sprinkle with ¼ cup chips and ¼ cup peanuts.
3. Beat milk and pudding mixes on low speed for 2 minutes. Fold in the whipped topping. Spread over the top. Sprinkle with remaining chips and peanuts. Refrigerate until serving.
PER SERVING *1 piece equals 479 cal., 23 g fat (8 g sat. fat), 29 mg chol., 349 mg sodium, 66 g carb., 3 g fiber, 6 g pro.*

TOP TIP

To amp up the dessert's banana flavor, try using banana pudding mix instead of vanilla. You can use one or two packages, whichever fits your taste best.

SLOW COOKER
Glazed Cinnamon Apples

If you are seeking comfort food on the sweet side, this warm apple dessert made with cinnamon and nutmeg will satisfy your craving.

—MEGAN MAZE OAK CREEK, WI

PREP: 20 MIN. • **COOK:** 3 HOURS
MAKES: 7 SERVINGS

- 6 large tart apples
- 2 tablespoons lemon juice
- ½ cup packed brown sugar
- ½ cup sugar
- 2 tablespoons all-purpose flour
- 1 teaspoon ground cinnamon
- ¼ teaspoon ground nutmeg
- 6 tablespoons butter, melted
    Vanilla ice cream

1. Peel, core and cut each apple into eight wedges; transfer to a 3-qt. slow cooker. Drizzle with the lemon juice. Combine sugars, flour, cinnamon and nutmeg; sprinkle over apples. Drizzle with butter.
2. Cover and cook on low for 3-4 hours or until the apples are tender. Serve in dessert dishes with ice cream.
PER SERVING *⅔ cup (calculated without ice cream) equals 285 cal., 10 g fat (6 g sat. fat), 26 mg chol., 75 mg sodium, 52 g carb., 2 g fiber, 1 g pro.*

WE FLIP FOR CHIPS

Let the chocolate chips fall where they may...especially into easy treats. Our staffers share the ways they show off those oh-so-delectable morsels.

1 My almost-5-year-old's newest favorite breakfast indulgence: wrap up about a tablespoon of chocolate chips in a triangle of refrigerated crescent roll dough and bake as directed. It's just a little departure from chocolate chip pancakes.
—**AMANDA HARMATYS**
BUSINESS ANALYST, CONTENT TOOLS

2 I like to melt them down with a scoop (or two) of peanut butter and drizzle it over vanilla ice cream. Instant peanut butter fudge sauce!
—**HOLLI FLETCHER**
RECEPTIONIST

3 Mix chocolate chips with Golden Grahams and mini marshmallows for a quick s'mores snack mix.
—**MELISSA HANSEN**
PREP COOK

4 Chocolate and cheese. Yes, indeed. Melt dark chocolate chips in the microwave, then dip chunks of your favorite aged Parmesan or aged cheddar partially into the chocolate. Cool on waxed paper. Eat. Swoon.
—**JEANNE AMBROSE**
EDITOR

5 My 2-year-old is in love with Minnie Mouse; therefore, she loves anything that's mini. I bake mini vanilla cupcakes, adding mini chocolate chips to both the batter and frosting. Then I sprinkle more mini chips on top for good measure. My daughter toddles around the kitchen so excited while they bake yelling, "Minnie!"
—**ELIZABETH HARRIS**
CONTRIBUTING ASSOCIATE EDITOR

6 My chocolate-swirled meringues wow everyone. Beat 4 room temperature egg whites and ¼ tsp. cream of tartar to form stiff peaks. Beat in a cup of sugar a little at a time. Fold in ¾ cup chocolate chips, melted, until the mixture is *barely* marbled. Make twelve 2½-in.-wide mounds on a parchment paper-lined baking sheet. Bake 40 minutes at 275°.
—**KRISTIN BOWKER**
ART DIRECTOR

7 I always love adding them to my banana and zucchini breads.
—**CINDY SOBCZAK**
ADMINISTRATIVE COORDINATOR, HR

8 I make a concoction called cheesecake bowl. Beat softened cream cheese with half-and-half and sugar (or Splenda) until light and creamy. I add almond extract and sometimes citrus zest. Top with toasted nuts and chocolate chips.
—**GINA NISTICO**
FOOD EDITOR

9 Melt chocolate chips, then dip clementine segments and sprinkle them with sea salt and red pepper flakes. Now I want some for a snack!
—**JULIANNE SCHNUCK**
DESIGNER

10 While brownies are still warm from the oven, pour chocolate chips on top and let them melt. Then spread all over for an easy frosting.
—**SHANNON ROUM**
FOOD STYLIST

Strawberry Cheesecake Ice Cream

Light and refreshing, my dreamy, creamy ice cream is perfect for warm afternoons. It's great in cones, and it doesn't melt as fast as regular ice cream.

—DEBRA GOFORTH NEWPORT, TN

PREP: 10 MIN. + FREEZING
MAKES: 2 QUARTS

- 1 package (8 ounces) cream cheese, softened
- ⅓ cup refrigerated French vanilla nondairy creamer
- ¼ cup sugar
- 1 teaspoon grated lemon peel
- 1 carton (16 ounces) frozen whipped topping, thawed
- 2 packages (10 ounces each) frozen sweetened sliced strawberries, thawed

In a large bowl, beat the cream cheese, creamer, sugar and lemon peel until blended. Fold in the whipped topping and strawberries. Transfer to a freezer container; freeze for 4 hours or until firm. Remove from freezer 10 minutes before serving.

PER SERVING *½ cup equals 181 cal., 10 g fat (8 g sat. fat), 16 mg chol., 44 mg sodium, 19 g carb., 1 g fiber, 1 g pro.*

RAINBOW SHERBET DESSERT

STRAWBERRY CHEESECAKE ICE CREAM

Rainbow Sherbet Dessert

Macaroons, pecans and layers of fruity sherbet combine in this beautiful, special dessert. Garnish it with fresh strawberries and just listen to folks ooh and ahh when you bring it out.

—KATHRYN DUNN AXTON, VA

PREP: 30 MIN. + FREEZING
MAKES: 12 SERVINGS

- 12 macaroon cookies, crumbled
- 2 cups heavy whipping cream
- 3 tablespoons confectioners' sugar
- 1 teaspoon vanilla extract
- ¾ cup chopped pecans, toasted
- 1 pint each raspberry, lime and orange sherbet, softened

1. Preheat the oven to 350°. Sprinkle the cookie crumbs onto an ungreased baking sheet. Bake for 5-8 minutes or until golden brown. Cool completely.
2. In a large bowl, beat cream until it begins to thicken. Add confectioners' sugar and vanilla; beat until stiff peaks form. Combine the cookie crumbs and pecans; fold in whipped cream. Spread half of cream mixture onto the bottom of an ungreased 9-in. springform pan. Freeze 30 minutes.
3. Gently spread raspberry sherbet over cream layer. Layer with the lime and orange sherbets; spread with the remaining cream mixture. Cover and freeze until firm. Remove from the freezer 10 minutes before serving. Remove sides of pan.

PER SERVING *1 slice equals 387 cal., 26 g fat (13 g sat. fat), 54 mg chol., 38 mg sodium, 37 g carb., 4 g fiber, 3 g pro.*

Carnival Caramel Apples

With four kids (one child whose birthday is November 1), we celebrate Halloween in style at our house. These caramel apples are a tried-and-true favorite.

—GAIL PRATHER BETHEL, MN

PREP: 20 MIN. • **COOK:** 25 MIN. + STANDING
MAKES: 10-12 APPLES

- ½ cup butter, cubed
- 2 cups packed brown sugar
- 1 cup light corn syrup
  Dash salt
- 1 can (14 ounces) sweetened condensed milk
- 1 teaspoon vanilla extract
- 10 to 12 Popsicle sticks
- 10 to 12 medium tart apples, washed and dried
- 1 cup salted peanuts, chopped

1. In a large heavy saucepan, melt the butter; add the brown sugar, corn syrup and salt. Cook and stir over medium heat until the mixture comes to a boil, about 10-12 minutes. Stir in milk. Cook and stir until a candy thermometer reads 248° (firm-ball stage). Remove from the heat; stir in vanilla.

2. Insert Popsicle sticks into apples. Dip each apple into the hot caramel mixture; turn to coat. Dip bottom of apples into peanuts. Place on greased waxed paper; let stand until set.

SWEET-SALTY CARAMEL APPLES
Omit peanuts. Dip bottoms and sides of caramel apple into crushed pretzels.

CHOCOLATE CARAMEL APPLES
Drizzle caramel apples with melted white baking chocolate and melted semisweet chocolate.

NOTE *We recommend that you test your candy thermometer before each use by bringing water to a boil; the thermometer should read 212°. Adjust your recipe temperature up or down based on your test.*

PER SERVING *1 caramel apple equals 526 cal., 17 g fat (7 g sat. fat), 32 mg chol., 231 mg sodium, 94 g carb., 4 g fiber, 6 g pro.*

Bread Pudding with Nutmeg

I always make my bread pudding recipe for my dad on his birthday and holidays. He says it tastes exactly like the bread pudding he enjoyed as a child.

—DONNA POWELL MONTGOMERY CITY, MO

PREP: 15 MIN. • **BAKE:** 40 MIN.
MAKES: 6 SERVINGS

- 2 large eggs
- 2 cups scalded milk
- ¼ cup butter, cubed
- ¾ cup sugar
- ¼ teaspoon salt
- 1 teaspoon ground cinnamon
- ½ teaspoon ground nutmeg
- 1 teaspoon vanilla extract
- 4½ to 5 cups soft bread cubes (about 9 slices)
- ½ cup raisins, optional

VANILLA SAUCE
- ⅓ cup sugar
- 2 tablespoons cornstarch
- ¼ teaspoon salt
- 1⅔ cups cold water
- 3 tablespoons butter
- 2 teaspoons vanilla extract
- ¼ teaspoon ground nutmeg

1. In a large bowl, lightly beat eggs. Combine milk and butter; add to eggs along with sugar, spices and vanilla. Add the bread cubes and, if desired, raisins; stir gently.

2. Pour into a well-greased 11x7-in. baking dish. Bake at 350° for 40-45 minutes or until a knife inserted 1 in. from edge comes out clean.

3. Meanwhile, for sauce, combine the sugar, cornstarch and salt in a medium saucepan. Stir in water until smooth. Bring to a boil over medium heat; cook and stir 2 minutes or until thickened. Remove from heat. Stir in the butter, vanilla and nutmeg, and serve with warm pudding.

PER SERVING *1 piece equals 419 cal., 19 g fat (11 g sat. fat), 118 mg chol., 534 mg sodium, 56 g carb., 1 g fiber, 7 g pro.*

BREAD PUDDING WITH NUTMEG

MAKEOVER PEANUT BUTTER
CUP CHEESECAKE

6. Microwave the remaining fudge topping on high 30 seconds or until warmed; spread over cheesecake. Garnish with peanut butter cups. Refrigerate overnight.

PER SERVING *1 slice equals 316 cal., 16 g fat (6 g sat. fat), 47 mg chol., 361 mg sodium, 32 g carb., 1 g fiber, 12 g pro.*

Rhubarb Crisp

I found this recipe in a box of Quaker Oats about 20 years ago. It's quick, and it's easier to make than pie. It's versatile, too, because you can add apples in the fall or strawberries in the spring. I usually pop it in the oven shortly before we sit down to eat so it's still warm for dessert.

—C.E. ADAMS CHARLESTOWN, NH

PREP: 15 MIN. • **BAKE:** 45 MIN.
MAKES: 8 SERVINGS

- ¾ **cup sugar**
- 3 **tablespoons cornstarch**
- 3 **cups sliced fresh rhubarb or frozen rhubarb, thawed**
- 2 **cups sliced peeled apples or sliced strawberries**
- 1 **cup quick-cooking or old-fashioned oats**
- ½ **cup packed brown sugar**
- ½ **cup butter, melted**
- ⅓ **cup all-purpose flour**
- 1 **teaspoon ground cinnamon**
  Vanilla ice cream, optional

1. In a large bowl, combine sugar and cornstarch. Add rhubarb and apples or strawberries; toss to coat. Spoon into an 8-in. square baking dish.

2. Combine the oats, brown sugar, butter, flour and cinnamon until the mixture resembles coarse crumbs. Sprinkle over fruit. Bake at 350° for 45 minutes or until bubbly and the fruit is tender. Serve warm, with ice cream if desired.

NOTE *If using frozen rhubarb, measure rhubarb while still frozen, then thaw completely. Drain in a colander, but do not press liquid out.*

PER SERVING *1 cup equals 320 cal., 12 g fat (7 g sat. fat), 31 mg chol., 124 mg sodium, 52 g carb., 3 g fiber, 3 g pro.*

Makeover Peanut Butter Cup Cheesecake

No one will ever guess this decadent, firmer-textured cheesecake has been lightened up. I promise!

—SHARON ANDERSON LYONS, IL

PREP: 30 MIN. • **BAKE:** 50 MIN. + CHILLING
MAKES: 16 SERVINGS

- ¾ **cup graham cracker crumbs**
- 2 **tablespoons sugar**
- 2 **tablespoons butter, melted**
- ¾ **cup creamy peanut butter**
FILLING
- 2 **packages (8 ounces each) fat-free cream cheese**
- 1 **package (8 ounces) reduced-fat cream cheese**
- 1 **cup (8 ounces) reduced-fat sour cream**
- ¾ **cup sugar**
- 2 **large eggs, lightly beaten**
- 1½ **teaspoons vanilla extract**
- ¾ **cup hot fudge ice cream topping, divided**
- 6 **peanut butter cups, cut into small wedges**

1. In a small bowl, combine cracker crumbs, sugar and butter. Press onto the bottom of a 9-in. springform pan coated with cooking spray.

2. Place pan on a baking sheet. Bake at 350° for 10 minutes. Cool on a wire rack. In a microwave-safe bowl, heat peanut butter on high for 30 seconds or until softened. Spread over crust to within 1 in. of edges.

3. In a large bowl, beat cream cheese, sour cream and sugar until smooth. Add eggs; beat on low speed just until combined. Stir in vanilla. Pour 1 cup into a bowl; set aside. Pour remaining filling over peanut butter layer.

4. Heat ¼ cup fudge topping in the microwave on high for 30 seconds or until thin; fold into the reserved cream cheese mixture. Carefully pour over filling; cut through with a knife to swirl.

5. Return pan to baking sheet. Bake for 50-60 minutes or until the center is almost set. Cool on a wire rack for 10 minutes. Carefully run a knife around edge of the pan to loosen; cool for 1 hour longer.

Strawberry Sorbet Sensation

PREP: 20 MIN. + FREEZING
MAKES: 8 SERVINGS

- 2 cups strawberry sorbet, softened if necessary
- 1 cup cold fat-free milk
- 1 package (1 ounce) sugar-free instant vanilla pudding mix
- 1 carton (8 ounces) frozen reduced-fat whipped topping, thawed
  Sliced fresh strawberries

1. Line an 8x4-in. loaf pan with foil. Spread sorbet onto bottom of pan; place in freezer 15 minutes.
2. In a small bowl, whisk the milk and pudding mix for 2 minutes. Let stand for 2 minutes or until soft-set. Fold whipped topping into pudding; spread over sorbet. Freeze, covered, 4 hours or overnight.
3. Remove from freezer 10-15 minutes before serving. Unmold the dessert onto a serving plate; remove foil. Cut into slices. Serve with strawberries.

PER SERVING *1 slice equals 153 cal., 3 g fat (3 g sat. fat), 1 mg chol., 163 mg sodium, 27 g carb., 2 g fiber, 1 g pro.* **Diabetic Exchanges:** *2 starch, 1/2 fat.*

GREAT PUMPKIN DESSERT

On hot days in Colorado, we chill out with slices of this berries-and-cream dessert. The layered effect is so much fun. Use any flavor of sorbet you like.
—**KENDRA DOSS** COLORADO SPRINGS, CO

STRAWBERRY SORBET SENSATION

Great Pumpkin Dessert

Here's a crowd-pleasing alternative to pumpkin pie. I always get compliments and requests for the recipe—and it's so easy to make!
—**LINDA GUYOT** FOUNTAIN VALLEY, CA

PREP: 5 MIN. • **BAKE:** 1 HOUR
MAKES: 12-16 SERVINGS

- 1 can (15 ounces) solid-pack pumpkin
- 1 can (12 ounces) evaporated milk
- 3 large eggs
- 1 cup sugar
- 4 teaspoons pumpkin pie spice
- 1 package yellow cake mix (regular size)
- ¾ cup butter, melted
- 1½ cups chopped walnuts
  Vanilla ice cream or whipped cream

1. In a large bowl, beat the first five ingredients until smooth.
2. Transfer to a greased 13x9-in. baking dish. Sprinkle with cake mix and drizzle with butter. Top with walnuts.
3. Bake at 350° for 1 hour or until a knife inserted near the center comes out clean. Serve with ice cream or whipped cream.

PER SERVING *1 piece equals 385 cal., 21 g fat (8 g sat. fat), 70 mg chol., 326 mg sodium, 44 g carb., 3 g fiber, 8 g pro.*

Zucchini Cobbler

Here's my surprise dessert! No one guesses that the secret ingredient is zucchini. Everyone who tries it tells me tastes like apples.

—JOANNE FAZIO CARBONDALE, PA

PREP: 35 MIN. • **BAKE:** 35 MIN.
MAKES: 16-20 SERVINGS

- 8 cups chopped seeded peeled zucchini (from about 3 pounds)
- ⅔ cup lemon juice
- 1 cup sugar
- 1 teaspoon ground cinnamon
- ½ teaspoon ground nutmeg

CRUST

- 4 cups all-purpose flour
- 2 cups sugar
- 1½ cups cold butter, cubed
- 1 teaspoon ground cinnamon

1. In a large saucepan over medium-low heat, cook and stir zucchini and lemon juice for 15-20 minutes or until the zucchini is tender. Add the sugar, cinnamon and nutmeg; cook 1 minute longer. Remove from the heat; set aside.
2. For crust, combine the flour and sugar in a bowl; cut in butter until the mixture resembles coarse crumbs. Stir ½ cup into zucchini mixture. Press half of remaining crust mixture into a greased 15x10x1-in. baking pan. Spread zucchini over top; crumble the remaining crust mixture over zucchini. Sprinkle with cinnamon.
3. Bake at 375° for 35-40 minutes or until golden and bubbly.
PER SERVING *1 piece equals 337 cal., 14 g fat (9 g sat. fat), 37 mg chol., 141 mg sodium, 51 g carb., 1 g fiber, 3 g pro.*

White Chocolate Raspberry Cheesecake

As the wife of a dairy farmer, I have some experience making cheesecake. I rank this white chocolate-raspberry version among my very best.

—WENDY BARKMAN BREEZEWOOD, PA

PREP: 25 MIN.
BAKE: 1 HOUR 20 MIN. + CHILLING
MAKES: 12 SERVINGS

- 1½ cups graham cracker crumbs
- ¼ cup sugar
- ⅓ cup butter, melted

FILLING

- 3 packages (8 ounces each) cream cheese, softened
- ¾ cup sugar
- ⅓ cup sour cream
- 3 tablespoons all-purpose flour
- 1 teaspoon vanilla extract
- 3 large eggs, lightly beaten
- 1 package (10 to 12 ounces) white baking chips
- ¼ cup seedless raspberry jam

1. In a small bowl, combine the graham cracker crumbs, sugar and butter. Press mixture onto the bottom of a greased 9-in. springform pan; set aside.
2. In a large bowl, beat the cream cheese and sugar until smooth. Beat in sour cream, flour and vanilla. Add the eggs; beat on low speed just until combined. Fold in the baking chips. Pour over crust.
3. In a microwave, melt raspberry jam; stir until smooth. Drop jam by teaspoonfuls over batter; cut through batter with a knife to swirl.
4. Place pan on a double thickness of heavy-duty foil (about 18 in. square). Securely wrap foil around pan. Place in a large baking pan; add 1 in. of hot water to larger pan.
5. Bake at 325° for 80-85 minutes or until center is just set. Cool on a wire rack for 10 minutes. Carefully run a knife around edge of pan to loosen; cool for 1 hour longer. Cover and refrigerate overnight. Remove the sides of the pan.
PER SERVING *1 slice equals 403 cal., 23 g fat (13 g sat. fat), 97 mg chol., 211 mg sodium, 45 g carb., trace fiber, 6 g pro.*

WHITE CHOCOLATE
RASPBERRY CHEESECAKE

BLUEBERRY
ICE CREAM

[5] INGREDIENTS
Blueberry Ice Cream

The blueberries that grow wild on our property spark many recipe ideas. Our 10 children, 19 grandkids and four great-grandchildren think this ice cream is tops for summertime taste.

—**ALMA MOSHER** MOHANNES, NB

PREP: 15 MIN. + CHILLING
PROCESS: 20 MIN./BATCH + FREEZING
MAKES: ABOUT 1¾ QUARTS

- 4 **cups fresh or frozen blueberries**
- 2 **cups sugar**
- 2 **tablespoons water**
- 4 **cups half-and-half cream**

1. In a large saucepan, combine the blueberries, sugar and water. Bring to a boil. Reduce heat; simmer, uncovered, until sugar is dissolved and berries are softened. Press mixture through a fine-mesh strainer into a bowl; discard pulp. Stir in cream. Cover and refrigerate overnight.

2. Fill cylinder of ice cream freezer two-thirds full; freeze according to the manufacturer's directions. (Refrigerate any remaining mixture until ready to freeze.) Transfer ice cream to freezer containers, allowing headspace for expansion. Freeze 2-4 hours or until firm. Repeat with any remaining ice cream mixture.

PER SERVING *½ cup equals 226 cal., 7 g fat (5 g sat. fat), 34 mg chol., 35 mg sodium, 37 g carb., 1 g fiber, 3 g pro.*

Peach Cobbler

I created this recipe with a few tips from my mom and grandma. Because it's so quick and easy, this cobbler can be made in minutes to suit any occasion. I've used it for a light snack, dessert, and a breakfast fruit dish.

—**MARTHA BETTEN** NORTH MANCHESTER, IN

PREP: 15 MIN. • **BAKE:** 25 MIN.
MAKES: 6-8 SERVINGS

- ½ **cup butter, melted**
- 1 **can (15¼ ounces) sliced peaches, drained**
- 1¼ **cups sugar, divided**
- 1 **cup all-purpose flour**
- 1 **cup milk**
- 2 **teaspoons baking powder**
- ¼ **teaspoon salt**

Pour butter into a shallow 2-qt. baking dish and set aside. Drain the peaches, reserving ¼ cup juice. In a saucepan, bring the peaches and juice just to a boil. Meanwhile, in a bowl, combine 1 cup sugar, flour, milk, baking powder and salt; mix well. Pour over the butter in baking dish. Spoon hot peaches over batter. Sprinkle with remaining sugar. Bake at 400° for 25 minutes or until cake tests done. Serve warm.

PER SERVING *1 cup equals 328 cal., 13 g fat (8 g sat. fat), 34 mg chol., 282 mg sodium, 52 g carb., 1 g fiber, 3 g pro.*

Delicious Angel Food Dessert

This is one of my favorite desserts. I brought it to a family reunion, and everyone raved about it.

—**JESSIE BRADLEY** BELLA VISTA, AR

PREP: 20 MIN. + CHILLING
MAKES: 15 SERVINGS

- 2 **cans (20 ounces each) unsweetened crushed pineapple, drained**
- 4 **medium firm bananas, sliced**
- 1 **loaf-shaped angel food cake (10½ ounces), cut into 1-inch cubes**
- 3 **cups cold fat-free milk**
- 2 **packages (1 ounce each) sugar-free instant vanilla pudding mix**
- 1 **carton (8 ounces) frozen reduced-fat whipped topping, thawed**
- ⅓ **cup chopped pecans, toasted**

1. Place the pineapple in a large bowl; gently fold in bananas. Place the cake cubes in a 13x9-in. dish. Spoon fruit over cake.

2. In another large bowl, whisk milk and pudding mixes for 2 minutes. Let stand for 2 minutes or until soft-set. Spread pudding over fruit. Carefully spread whipped topping over pudding. Sprinkle with the pecans, then cover and refrigerate for at least 2 hours before serving.

PER SERVING *210 cal., 4 g fat (2 g sat. fat), 1 mg chol., 291 mg sodium, 40 g carb., 2 g fiber, 4 g pro.*

SLOW COOKER
Slow Cooker Cinnamon Roll Pudding

A slow cooker turns day-old cinnamon rolls into a comforting, old-fashioned dessert. It tastes wonderful topped with lemon or vanilla sauce or whipped cream.

—**EDNA HOFFMAN** HEBRON, IN

PREP: 15 MIN. • **COOK:** 3 HOURS
MAKES: 6 SERVINGS

- 8 **cups cubed day-old unfrosted cinnamon rolls**
- 4 **large eggs**
- 2 **cups milk**
- ¼ **cup sugar**
- ¼ **cup butter, melted**
- ½ **teaspoon vanilla extract**
- ¼ **teaspoon ground nutmeg**
- 1 **cup raisins**

Place cubed cinnamon rolls in a 3-qt. slow cooker. In a small bowl, whisk the eggs, milk, sugar, butter, vanilla and nutmeg. Stir in raisins. Pour over cinnamon rolls; stir gently. Cover and cook on low for 3 hours or until a knife inserted near the center comes out clean.

NOTE *8 slices of cinnamon or white bread, cut into 1-inch cubes, may be substituted for the cinnamon rolls.*
PER SERVING *570 cal., 27 g fat (10 g sat. fat), 226 mg chol., 468 mg sodium, 72 g carb., 3 g fiber, 13 g pro.*

Blueberry Biscuit Cobbler

With a buttery biscuit topping and warm, thick blueberry filling, this home-style cobbler sure doesn't taste light.

—MARY RELYEA CANASTOTA, NY

PREP: 20 MIN. • **BAKE:** 30 MIN.
MAKES: 8 SERVINGS

- 4 **cups fresh or frozen blueberries, thawed**
- ¾ **cup sugar, divided**
- 3 **tablespoons cornstarch**
- 2 **tablespoons lemon juice**
- ¼ **teaspoon ground cinnamon**
- ⅛ **teaspoon ground nutmeg**
- 1 **cup all-purpose flour**
- 2 **teaspoons grated lemon peel**
- ¾ **teaspoon baking powder**
- ¼ **teaspoon salt**
- ¼ **teaspoon baking soda**
- 3 **tablespoons cold butter**
- ¾ **cup buttermilk**

1. In a large bowl, combine berries, ½ cup sugar, cornstarch, lemon juice, cinnamon and nutmeg. Transfer the mixture to a 2-qt. baking dish coated with cooking spray.

2. In a small bowl, combine the flour, grated lemon peel, baking powder, salt, baking soda and remaining sugar; cut in the butter until mixture resembles coarse crumbs. Stir in the buttermilk just until moistened. Drop batter by tablespoonfuls onto berry mixture.

3. Bake cobbler, uncovered, at 375° for 30-35 minutes or until golden brown. Serve warm.

PER SERVING *231 cal., 5 g fat (3 g sat. fat), 12 mg chol., 220 mg sodium, 45 g carb., 2 g fiber, 3 g pro.* **Diabetic Exchanges:** *2 starch, 1 fruit, 1 fat.*

DID YOU KNOW?

Instead of buying buttermilk for this recipe, you can place 2¼ teaspoons of white vinegar or lemon juice in a liquid measuring cup and add enough milk to measure ¾ cup. Stir, then let stand for 5 minutes. Or, you can substitute ¾ cup yogurt for the buttermilk.

STRAWBERRY PRETZEL DESSERT

Strawberry Pretzel Dessert

A salty pretzel crust nicely contrasts with cream cheese and gelatin layers.

—ALDENE BELCH FLINT, MI

PREP: 20 MIN. • **BAKE:** 10 MIN. + CHILLING
MAKES: 12-16 SERVINGS

- 2 **cups crushed pretzels (about 8 ounces)**
- ¾ **cup butter, melted**
- 3 **tablespoons sugar**

FILLING
- 2 **cups whipped topping**
- 1 **package (8 ounces) cream cheese, softened**
- 1 **cup sugar**

TOPPING
- 2 **packages (3 ounces each) strawberry gelatin**
- 2 **cups boiling water**
- 2 **packages (16 ounces each) frozen sweetened sliced strawberries, thawed**
   Additional whipped topping, optional

1. In a bowl, combine the pretzels, butter and sugar. Press mixture into an ungreased 13x9-in. baking dish. Bake at 350° for 10 minutes. Cool on a wire rack.

2. For filling, in a small bowl, beat whipped topping, cream cheese and sugar until smooth. Spread over the pretzel crust. Refrigerate until chilled.

3. For topping, dissolve gelatin in boiling water in a large bowl. Stir in strawberries; chill until partially set. Carefully spoon over the filling. Chill for 4-6 hours or until firm. Cut into squares; serve with whipped topping if desired.

PER SERVING *1 piece equals 295 cal., 15 g fat (10 g sat. fat), 39 mg chol., 305 mg sodium, 38 g carb., 1 g fiber, 3 g pro.*

Oat Apple Crisp

When making this crisp, I use a yellow cake mix instead of flour. It's different from a traditional crisp, but in the most delicious way possible.

—RUBY HODGE RICHLAND CENTER, WI

PREP: 25 MIN. • **BAKE:** 45 MIN.
MAKES: 8 SERVINGS

- 7 cups thinly sliced peeled tart apples (about 7 medium)
- 1 cup sugar
- 1 tablespoon all-purpose flour
- 1 teaspoon ground cinnamon
  Dash salt
- ¼ cup water
- 1 package (9 ounces) yellow cake mix
- ¾ cup quick-cooking oats
- ⅓ cup butter, softened
- ¼ cup packed brown sugar
- ¼ teaspoon baking powder
- ¼ teaspoon baking soda
  Vanilla ice cream

1. Place apples in a greased 2½ qt. shallow baking dish. In a small bowl, combine the sugar, flour, cinnamon and salt; sprinkle over apples. Drizzle with water. In a large bowl, combine the cake mix, oats, butter, brown sugar, baking powder and baking soda , then sprinkle over apples.
2. Bake crisp, uncovered, at 350° for 45-50 minutes or until the apples are tender and topping is golden brown. Serve warm with ice cream.
PER SERVING (calculated without ice cream) equals 394 cal., 10 g fat (6 g sat. fat), 20 mg chol., 335 mg sodium, 76 g carb., 2 g fiber, 2 g pro.

Deluxe Pumpkin Cheesecake

With its unique gingersnap crust and rich, luscious swirls of pumpkin, this is the ultimate holiday dessert.

—SHARON SKILDUM MAPLE GROVE, MN

PREP: 35 MIN. • **BAKE:** 55 MIN. + CHILLING
MAKES: 12 SERVINGS

- 1 cup crushed gingersnap cookies (about 20 cookies)
- ⅓ cup finely chopped pecans
- ¼ cup butter, melted
- 4 packages (8 ounces each) cream cheese, softened, divided
- 1½ cups sugar, divided
- 2 tablespoons cornstarch
- 2 teaspoons vanilla extract
- 4 large eggs
- 1 cup canned pumpkin
- 2 teaspoons ground cinnamon
- 1½ teaspoons ground nutmeg

GARNISH

  Chocolate syrup, caramel ice cream topping, whipped topping and additional crushed gingersnap cookies, optional

1. Preheat oven to 350°. Place a greased 9-in. springform pan on a double thickness of heavy-duty foil (about 18 in. square). Securely wrap foil around pan.
2. In a small bowl, combine the cookie crumbs, pecans and butter. Press onto the bottom of prepared pan. Place on a baking sheet. Bake for 8-10 minutes or until set. Cool on a wire rack.
3. For filling, in a large bowl, beat 1 package of cream cheese, ½ cup sugar and cornstarch until smooth, about 2 minutes. Beat in remaining cream cheese, one package at a time, until smooth. Add remaining sugar and vanilla. Add eggs; beat on low speed just until combined.
4. Place 2 cups filling in a small bowl; stir in the pumpkin, cinnamon, and nutmeg. Remove ¾ cup pumpkin filling; set aside. Pour the remaining pumpkin filling over crust; top with remaining plain filling. Cut through with a knife to swirl. Drop reserved pumpkin filling by spoonfuls over cheesecake; cut through with a knife to swirl.
5. Place the springform pan in a large baking pan; add 1 in. of hot water to the larger pan. Bake for 55-65 minutes or until center is just set and top appears dull. Remove the springform pan from the water bath. Cool on a wire rack for 10 minutes. Gently run a knife around the edge of the pan to loosen; cool for 1 hour longer. Refrigerate overnight.
6. Garnish with chocolate syrup, caramel sauce, whipped topping and crushed gingersnaps if desired.
PER SERVING 1 slice equals 500 cal., 35 g fat (18 g sat. fat), 155 mg chol., 390 mg sodium, 41 g carb., 8 g pro.

DELUXE PUMPKIN CHEESECAKE

Creme de Menthe Squares

This layered bar hits all the sweet spots: It's airy, creamy, crunchy and the perfect mix of cool mint and chocolate. It has a vintage dessert appeal that no one in our family can resist.

—MARILYN BLANKSCHIEN

CLINTONVILLE, WI

PREP: 30 MIN. + CHILLING
MAKES: 9 SERVINGS

- 1¼ **cups finely crushed Oreo cookies (about 14 cookies)**
- 2 **tablespoons butter, melted**
- 1 **teaspoon unflavored gelatin**
- 1¾ **cups cold 2% milk, divided**
- 20 **large marshmallows**
- 3 **tablespoons green creme de menthe**
- 3 **ounces cream cheese, softened**
- 1 **package (3.9 ounces) instant chocolate pudding mix**
- 1 **cup heavy whipping cream**

1. In a small bowl, mix the crushed cookies and melted butter. Reserve 3 tablespoons for topping. Press the remaining mixture onto bottom of a greased 8-in. square baking dish. Refrigerate 30 minutes.

2. In a large microwave-safe bowl, sprinkle gelatin over ½ cup cold milk; let stand 1 minute. Microwave on high 30-40 seconds. Stir until the gelatin is completely dissolved. Next add the marshmallows and cook 1-2 minutes longer or until the marshmallows are puffed; stir until smooth. Stir in the creme de menthe and refrigerate for 15-20 minutes or until cold but not set, stirring often.

3. Meanwhile, in a small bowl, beat cream cheese gradually until smooth. In another bowl, whisk pudding mix and remaining cold milk. Gradually beat into cream cheese.

4. In a large bowl, beat cream until soft peaks form. Fold cream into the marshmallow mixture. Spoon half of the mixture over prepared crust; refrigerate 10 minutes. Layer with pudding mixture and remaining marshmallow mixture; top with reserved crumbs. Refrigerate for 2 hours or until set.

PER SERVING *1 piece equals 371 cal., 21 g fat (11 g sat. fat), 58 mg chol., 232 mg sodium, 43 g carb., 1 g fiber, 4 g pro.*

CREME DE MENTHE
SQUARES

ROASTED BANANA &
PECAN CHEESECAKE

We keep bananas on hand, but with just two of us in the house they ripen faster than we can eat them. That makes them perfect for roasting and baking into this cheesecake with a nutty crust.
—**PATRICIA HARMON** BADEN, PA

Roasted Banana & Pecan Cheesecake

PREP: 45 MIN. + COOLING
BAKE: 45 MIN. + CHILLING
MAKES: 12 SERVINGS

- 3 **medium ripe bananas, unpeeled**
- 1¾ **cups crushed pecan shortbread cookies**
- 3 **tablespoons butter, melted**

FILLING

- 2 **packages (8 ounces each) cream cheese, softened**
- 1 **package (8 ounces) reduced-fat cream cheese**
- ½ **cup sugar**
- ¼ **cup plus 2 tablespoons packed brown sugar, divided**
- 1 **teaspoon vanilla extract**
- 2 **tablespoons spiced rum, optional**
- 4 **large eggs, lightly beaten**
- ½ **cup chopped pecans**
- ½ **teaspoon ground cinnamon**
- 12 **pecan halves, toasted**
  Chocolate syrup

1. Preheat oven to 400°. Place the unpeeled bananas in an 8-in.-square baking dish. Bake 10-12 minutes or until banana peels are black. Cool to room temperature. Reduce oven setting to 325°.

2. Place a greased 9-in. springform pan on a double thickness of heavy-duty foil (about 18 in. square). Wrap foil securely around pan. Place on a baking sheet.

3. In a small bowl, mix cookie crumbs and melted butter. Press onto bottom and 1 in. up sides of prepared pan. Bake for 8-10 minutes or until set, then cool on a wire rack.

4. In a large bowl, beat cream cheese, sugar and ¼ cup brown sugar until smooth. Beat in vanilla and, if desired, rum. Add the eggs; beat on low speed just until blended. Remove ½ cup of cream cheese mixture to a small bowl. Pour remaining filling into crust.

5. Peel and place roasted bananas in a food processor; process until smooth.

Add to reserved cream cheese mixture; stir in chopped pecans, cinnamon and remaining brown sugar. Pour over the plain cream cheese mixture, then cut through cream cheese mixture with a knife to swirl.

6. Place springform pan in a larger baking pan; add 1 in. of hot water to larger pan. Bake for 45-55 minutes or until center is just set and top appears dull. Remove springform pan from the water bath. Cool cheesecake on a wire rack 10 minutes. Loosen sides from pan with a knife; remove foil. Cool for 1 hour longer. Refrigerate overnight, covering when completely cooled.

7. Remove rim from the pan. Top the cheesecake with pecan halves; drizzle with chocolate syrup.

NOTE *To toast nuts, bake in a shallow pan in a 350° oven for 5-10 minutes or cook in a skillet over low heat until lightly browned, stirring occasionally.*
PER SERVING *1 slice (calculated without chocolate syrup) equals 430 cal., 30 g fat (14 g sat. fat), 126 mg chol., 308 mg sodium, 33 g carb., 2 g fiber, 8 g pro.*

(5)INGREDIENTS
Orange Creamsicles

Yogurt adds creaminess, calcium and a hint of tang to these sweet three-ingredient treats.
—**LAURIE PAYTON** COTTONWOOD, CA

PREP: 5 MIN. + FREEZING • **MAKES:** 10 POPS

- 2 **cups (16 ounces) plain yogurt**
- 1 **can (6 ounces) frozen orange juice concentrate, thawed**
- 2 **teaspoons vanilla extract**
- 10 **Popsicle molds or paper cups (3 ounces each) and Popsicle sticks**

In a small bowl, combine the yogurt, orange juice concentrate and vanilla. Fill each mold or cup with ¼ cup of yogurt mixture; top with holders or insert sticks into cups. Freeze.
PER SERVING *1 pop equals 59 cal., 2 g fat (1 g sat. fat), 6 mg chol., 23 mg sodium, 9 g carb., trace fiber, 2 g pro.*
Diabetic Exchange: *½ starch.*

CHERYL JOHNSON'S
BACON & EGG POTATO BAKE
PAGE 153

Breakfast & Brunch

You're guaranteed to **start the day off right** when you awake to any of these rise-and-shine **breakfast dishes.** Whether you're feeding a crowd or just a few, **you can't go wrong** with these **eye-opening** specialties.

AMELIA MEAUX'S SAUSAGE BRUNCH BRAID
PAGE 155

MARY LAJOIE'S BLUEBERRY FRUIT SMOOTHIE
PAGE 161

KAREN SCHROEDER'S FRUITY BAKED OATMEAL
PAGE 151

vanilla until blended; gently stir into flour mixture (do not overmix).

3. Spread batter onto bottom and ½ in. up sides of the prepared pan. Spread filling over the crust, leaving a ½-in. border around edge of pan. Spoon strawberry mixture over top; sprinkle with reserved crumb mixture.

4. Bake 50-60 minutes or until edges are golden brown. Cool on a wire rack for 20 minutes. Loosen sides from pan with a knife. Cool completely. Remove rim from pan. Refrigerate leftovers.

FREEZE OPTION *Securely wrap the cooled cake in plastic and foil, then freeze. To use, thaw in refrigerator.*

PER SERVING *1 slice equals 320 cal., 15 g fat (9 g sat. fat), 75 mg chol., 274 mg sodium, 41 g carb., 1 g fiber, 6 g pro.*

(5) INGREDIENTS FAST FIX

Fruit Smoothies

These smoothies pack a powerhouse of nutrition, so they're a great way to start the day. They also make a yummy snack paired with cinnamon graham crackers. Enjoy them any time of day.

—**TERESA DUNLAP** LIMA, OH

RHUBARB & STRAWBERRY COFFEE CAKE

START TO FINISH: 5 MIN.
MAKES: 2½ CUPS

- 1¼ cups milk
- 1 cup frozen unsweetened strawberries
- ½ cup frozen unsweetened sliced peaches
- 1 small ripe banana, halved
- 3 tablespoons sugar

Place all ingredients in a blender; cover and process until smooth. Pour into chilled glasses; serve immediately.

RASPBERRY PEACH SMOOTHIES *Substitute 1 cup frozen unsweetened raspberries for the strawberries.*

STRAWBERRY PINEAPPLE SMOOTHIES *Substitute ½ cup unsweetened crushed pineapple for the peaches. If necessary, add a few ice cubes while processing to thicken the drink.*

PER SERVING *1¼ cups equals 257 cal., 5 g fat (3 g sat. fat), 21 mg chol., 77 mg sodium, 49 g carb., 4 g fiber, 6 g pro.*

FREEZE IT

Rhubarb & Strawberry Coffee Cake

Eat cake for breakfast! I like that motto and you will, too, when you try this vanilla coffee cake that boasts a cream cheese filling and strawberry-rhubarb sauce.

—**DANIELLE ULAM** HOOKSTOWN, PA

PREP: 50 MIN. • **BAKE:** 50 MIN. + COOLING
MAKES: 12 SERVINGS

- 1½ teaspoons cornstarch
- 3 tablespoons sugar
- ¾ cup chopped fresh strawberries
- ¾ cup chopped fresh or frozen rhubarb
- 1 tablespoon water

FILLING
- 1 package (8 ounces) cream cheese, softened
- ¼ cup sugar
- 1 large egg, lightly beaten

CAKE
- 2 cups all-purpose flour
- ¾ cup sugar

- ½ cup cold butter, cubed
- ½ teaspoon baking powder
- ½ teaspoon baking soda
- ¼ teaspoon salt
- 1 large egg, lightly beaten
- ¾ cup fat-free sour cream
- 1 teaspoon vanilla extract

1. Preheat oven to 350°. Line bottom of a greased 9-in. springform pan with parchment paper; grease paper. In a small saucepan, mix cornstarch and sugar; stir in strawberries, rhubarb and water. Bring to a boil. Reduce heat; simmer, uncovered, 6-8 minutes or until thickened, stirring occasionally. For filling, in a small bowl, beat cream cheese and sugar until smooth, then beat in egg.

2. In a large bowl, combine flour and sugar; cut in the butter until crumbly. Reserve ¾ cup for topping. Stir baking powder, baking soda and salt into the remaining flour mixture. In a small bowl, whisk the egg, sour cream and

FARMER'S CASSEROLE

Farmer's Casserole

Between family and friends, we average 375 visitors a year to our home! This casserole is very handy for overnight guests. You can put it together the night before, let the flavors blend, and then bake it in the morning.
—**NANCY SCHMIDT** CENTER, CO

PREP: 10 MIN. + CHILLING • **BAKE:** 55 MIN.
MAKES: 6 SERVINGS

- 3 **cups frozen shredded hash brown potatoes**
- ¾ **cup shredded Monterey Jack cheese**
- 1 **cup cubed fully cooked ham**
- ¼ **cup chopped green onions**
- 4 **large eggs**
- 1 **can (12 ounces) evaporated milk**
- ¼ **teaspoon pepper**
- ⅛ **teaspoon salt**

1. Place potatoes in an 8-in. baking dish. Sprinkle with cheese, ham and onions. Whisk the eggs, milk, pepper and salt; pour over all. Cover dish and refrigerate several hours or overnight.

2. Remove from the refrigerator 30 minutes before baking. Preheat oven to 350° and bake, uncovered, for 55-60 minutes or until a knife inserted near center comes out clean.
PER SERVING *1 piece equals 252 cal., 14 g fat (7 g sat. fat), 187 mg chol., 531 mg sodium, 14 g carb., 1 g fiber, 17 g pro.*

Turkey Puff Pancake

This puff pancake is similar to a tart shell. Covered with mushrooms and turkey, it browns beautifully. I like to add water chestnuts for extra crunch.
—**PATRICIA MILLMANN** WAUWATOSA, WI

PREP: 10 MIN. • **BAKE:** 20 MIN.
MAKES: 4 SERVINGS

- 3 **tablespoons butter**
- 2 **large eggs**
- ¾ **cup 2% milk**
  Dash cayenne pepper
- ¾ **cup all-purpose flour**

TOPPING
- 2 **tablespoons butter**
- ¾ **cup sliced fresh mushrooms**
- 1 **small onion, chopped**
- 2 **tablespoons all-purpose flour**
- ¾ **cup turkey or chicken broth**
- ¼ **cup 2% milk**
- 2 **cups shredded cooked turkey**
- ¼ **teaspoon salt**
- ¼ **teaspoon pepper**
- 2 **tablespoons grated Parmesan cheese**

1. Preheat oven to 400°. Place the butter in a 9-in. pie plate. Place in oven 3-4 minutes or until melted. Meanwhile, in a small bowl, whisk eggs, milk and cayenne. Whisk flour into the egg mixture until blended. Pour into prepared pie plate. Bake 18-20 minutes or until golden brown and center is set.

2. Meanwhile, in a large skillet, heat butter over medium-high heat. Add mushrooms and onion; cook and stir 4-6 minutes or until tender. Stir in the flour until blended; gradually add the broth and milk. Bring to a boil, stirring constantly; cook and stir 1-2 minutes or until thickened. Stir in turkey, salt and pepper.

3. Cut the pancake into wedges. Spoon turkey mixture over wedges; sprinkle with Parmesan cheese and serve immediately.
PER SERVING *1 wedge equals 450 cal., 24 g fat (13 g sat. fat), 201 mg chol., 610 mg sodium, 26 g carb., 1 g fiber, 30 g pro.*

TURKEY PUFF PANCAKE

SHAKSHUKA

EAT SMART **FAST FIX** ▶

Shakshuka

Shakshuka is a meatless one-skillet dish that consists of eggs poached in a sauce of tomatoes, onions and cumin. I learned how to make it while traveling, and it's been my favorite way to eat eggs since.

—**EZRA WEEKS** CALGARY, AB

START TO FINISH: 30 MIN.
MAKES: 4 SERVINGS

- 2 tablespoons olive oil
- 1 medium onion, chopped
- 1 garlic clove, minced
- 1 teaspoon ground cumin
- 1 teaspoon pepper
- ½ to 1 teaspoon chili powder
- ½ teaspoon salt
- 1 teaspoon Sriracha Asian hot chili sauce or hot pepper sauce, optional
- 2 medium tomatoes, chopped
- 4 large eggs
    Chopped fresh cilantro
    Whole pita breads, toasted

1. In a large skillet, heat the oil over medium heat. Add onion; cook and stir 4-6 minutes or until tender. Add the garlic, seasonings and, if desired, hot chili sauce; cook 30 seconds more. Add tomatoes and cook 3-5 minutes or until the mixture is thickened, stirring occasionally.
2. With back of spoon, make four wells in vegetable mixture; break an egg into each well. Cook, covered, 4-6 minutes or until egg whites are completely set and yolks begin to thicken but are not hard. Sprinkle with cilantro; serve with pita bread.
PER SERVING (calculated without pita bread) equals 159 cal., 12 g fat (3 g sat. fat), 186 mg chol., 381 mg sodium, 6 g carb., 2 g fiber, 7 g pro. **Diabetic Exchanges:** 1½ fat, 1 medium-fat meat, 1 vegetable.

Sausage-Apple Breakfast Bread

I added sausage to a sweet quick bread to make it a little extra hearty. Serve it warm alongside scrambled eggs or fresh fruit.

—**ANITA HUNTER** STILWELL, KS

PREP: 25 MIN. • **BAKE:** 30 MIN. + COOLING
MAKES: 12 SERVINGS

- 1 pound bulk pork sausage
- 1 cup all-purpose flour
- 1 cup whole wheat flour
- 2 teaspoons baking powder
- ½ teaspoon salt
- 2 large eggs
- ½ cup packed brown sugar
- ½ cup apple cider or juice
- ½ cup canola oil
- 2 medium apples, peeled and shredded (about 1½ cups)

TOPPING
- ¼ cup old-fashioned oats
- ¼ cup packed brown sugar
- 2 tablespoons all-purpose flour
- 2 tablespoons cold butter
    Maple syrup, optional

1. Preheat oven to 350°. Grease and flour a 9-in. round baking pan. In a skillet, cook sausage over medium heat 6-8 minutes or until no longer pink, breaking into crumbles; drain.
2. In a bowl, whisk flours, baking powder and salt. In another bowl, whisk eggs, brown sugar, apple cider and oil until blended. Add to the flour mixture; stir just until moistened. Fold in the apples and half of the sausage. Transfer to prepared pan.
3. In a small bowl, mix oats, brown sugar and flour; cut in butter until crumbly. Stir in remaining sausage. Sprinkle over the batter. Bake for 30-35 minutes or until a toothpick inserted in center comes out clean. Cool in the pan for 10 minutes before removing to a wire rack. Serve warm. If desired, drizzle with maple syrup. Refrigerate leftovers.
PER SERVING 1 slice (calculated without syrup) equals 354 cal., 21 g fat (5 g sat. fat), 57 mg chol., 427 mg sodium, 35 g carb., 2 g fiber, 8 g pro.

SAUSAGE-APPLE BREAKFAST BREAD

Yogurt Pancakes

Get your day off to a great start with these yummy pancakes. If you're short on time, make a batch on the weekend and freeze until you're ready to serve.
—**CHERYLL BABER** HOMEDALE, ID

START TO FINISH: 30 MIN.
MAKES: 12 PANCAKES

- 2 **cups all-purpose flour**
- 2 **tablespoons sugar**
- 2 **teaspoons baking powder**
- 1 **teaspoon baking soda**
- 2 **large eggs, lightly beaten**
- 2 **cups (16 ounces) plain yogurt**
- ¼ **cup water**
  Semisweet chocolate chips, dried cranberries, sliced ripe bananas and coarsely chopped pecans, optional

1. In a small bowl, combine the flour, sugar, baking powder and baking soda. In another bowl, whisk eggs, yogurt and water. Stir into dry ingredients just until moistened.
2. Pour batter by ¼ cupfuls onto a hot griddle coated with cooking spray. Sprinkle with optional ingredients if desired. Turn when bubbles form on top, and cook until the second side is golden brown.
FREEZE OPTION *Arrange the cooled pancakes in a single layer on baking sheets. Freeze overnight or until frozen. Transfer to a resealable plastic freezer bag. May be frozen for up to 2 months. To use, microwave on high for 40-50 seconds or until heated through.*
PER SERVING *2 pancakes (calculated without optional ingredients) equals 242 cal., 5 g fat (2 g sat. fat), 81 mg chol., 403 mg sodium, 40 g carb., 1 g fiber, 9 g pro.* **Diabetic Exchange:** *3 starch.*

SLOW COOKER CHORIZO BREAKFAST CASSEROLE

SLOW COOKER 🍲
Slow Cooker Chorizo Breakfast Casserole

My kids ask for this hearty slow-cooked casserole for breakfast *and* dinner. We love the Southwestern twist, and it's even better topped with chopped avocado, salsa and a spritz of lime juice. We also enjoy it with white country gravy.
—**CINDY PRUITT** GROVE, OK

PREP: 25 MIN.
COOK: 4 HOURS + STANDING
MAKES: 8 SERVINGS

- 1 **pound fresh chorizo or bulk spicy pork sausage**
- 1 **medium onion, chopped**
- 1 **medium sweet red pepper, chopped**
- 2 **jalapeno peppers, seeded and chopped**
- 1 **package (30 ounces) frozen shredded hash brown potatoes, thawed**
- 1½ **cups (6 ounces) shredded Mexican cheese blend**
- 12 **large eggs**
- 1 **cup 2% milk**
- ½ **teaspoon pepper**

1. In a large skillet, cook chorizo, onion, red pepper and jalapenos over medium heat 7-8 minutes or until cooked through and vegetables are tender, breaking the chorizo into crumbles. Drain; cool slightly.
2. In a greased 5-qt. slow cooker, layer a third of the potatoes, chorizo mixture and cheese. Repeat the layers twice. In a large bowl, whisk the eggs, milk and pepper until blended; pour over top.
3. Cook on low 4-4½ hours or until eggs are set and a thermometer reads 160°. Uncover and let stand 10 minutes before serving.
NOTE *Wear disposable gloves when cutting hot peppers; the oils can burn skin. Avoid touching your face.*
PER SERVING *1½ cups equals 512 cal., 32 g fat (12 g sat. fat), 350 mg chol., 964 mg sodium, 25 g carb., 2 g fiber, 30 g pro.*

SLOW COOKER
Hash Brown Egg Brunch

Slow cookers aren't just for dinner fare. I prep this recipe the night before and let it cook for four hours while I sleep. By the time the kids get up, a hot meal is waiting.
—BARB KEITH EAU CLAIRE, WI

PREP: 20 MIN. • **COOK:** 4 HOURS
MAKES: 10 SERVINGS

- 1 package (30 ounces) frozen shredded hash brown potatoes, thawed
- 1 pound bacon strips, cooked and crumbled
- 1 medium onion, chopped
- 1 medium green pepper, chopped
- 1½ cups (6 ounces) shredded cheddar cheese
- 12 large eggs
- 1 cup 2% milk
- ½ teaspoon salt
- ½ teaspoon pepper

1. In a greased 5-qt. slow cooker, layer a third of each of the following: potatoes, bacon, onion, green pepper and cheese. Repeat layers twice. In a large bowl, whisk eggs, milk, salt and pepper; pour over layers.
2. Cook on high 30 minutes. Reduce heat to low; cook another 3½-4 hours or until a thermometer reads 160°.
PER SERVING *1 cup equals 315 cal., 17 g fat (8 g sat. fat), 289 mg chol., 589 mg sodium, 20 g carb., 2 g fiber, 20 g pro.*

HASH BROWN
EGG BRUNCH

UPSIDE-DOWN PEAR PANCAKE

EAT SMART FAST FIX
Upside-Down Pear Pancake

The fragrant fruit that grows on the pear tree in my yard inspires me to bake all sorts of goodies. This easy upside-down pancake is a favorite. The recipe works best with a firm pear that's not fully ripe.
—HELEN NELANDER BOULDER CREEK, CA

START TO FINISH: 30 MIN.
MAKES: 2 SERVINGS

- ½ cup all-purpose flour
- ½ teaspoon baking powder
- 1 large egg
- ¼ cup 2% milk
- 1 tablespoon butter
- 1 teaspoon sugar
- 1 medium pear, peeled and thinly sliced lengthwise
  Confectioners' sugar

1. Preheat oven to 375°. Whisk flour and baking powder. In a separate bowl, whisk the egg and milk until blended. Add to dry ingredients, stirring just until combined.
2. Meanwhile, in an ovenproof skillet, melt the butter over medium-low heat. Sprinkle with sugar. Add pear slices in a single layer; cook 5 minutes. Spread prepared batter over pears. Cover and cook until top is set, about 5 minutes.
3. Transfer pan to oven and bake until edges are lightly brown, 8-10 minutes. Invert onto a serving plate. Top with confectioners' sugar. Serve warm.
PER SERVING *½ pancake equals 274 cal., 9 g fat (5 g sat. fat), 111 mg chol., 197 mg sodium, 41 g carb. (12 g sugars, 4 g fiber), 8 g pro.* **Diabetic Exchanges:** *2 starch, 1½ fat, 1 medium-fat meat, ½ fruit.*

Fruity Baked Oatmeal

This is my husband's favorite breakfast treat and the ultimate comfort food. It's warm, filling and always a hit with guests.
—**KAREN SCHROEDER** KANKAKEE, IL

PREP: 15 MIN. • **BAKE:** 35 MIN.
MAKES: 9 SERVINGS

- 3 **cups quick-cooking oats**
- 1 **cup packed brown sugar**
- 2 **teaspoons baking powder**
- 1 **teaspoon salt**
- ½ **teaspoon ground cinnamon**
- 2 **large eggs, lightly beaten**
- 1 **cup fat-free milk**
- ½ **cup butter, melted**
- ¾ **cup chopped peeled tart apple**
- ⅓ **cup chopped fresh or frozen peaches**
- ⅓ **cup fresh or frozen blueberries**
  Additional fat-free milk, optional

1. Preheat oven to 350°. In a large bowl, combine oats, brown sugar, baking powder, salt and cinnamon. Combine eggs, milk and butter; add to the dry ingredients. Stir in apple, peaches and blueberries.

2. Pour into an 8-in. square baking dish coated with cooking spray. Bake, uncovered, 35-40 minutes or until a knife inserted near center comes out clean. Cut into squares. Serve with milk if desired.

NOTE *If using frozen blueberries, use without thawing to avoid discoloring the batter.*

PER SERVING *1 piece (calculated without additional milk) equals 322 cal., 13 g fat (7 g sat. fat), 75 mg chol., 492 mg sodium, 46 g carb., 3 g fiber, 7 g pro.*

DID YOU KNOW?

Old-fashioned oats and quick-cooking oats are interchangeable in most recipes; just consider the differences between the two. Both have been flattened with large rollers, but quick-cooking oats are cut into smaller pieces first. As a result, they cook faster and offer a more delicate texture. If you prefer a heartier texture, use old-fashioned oats.

FAST FIX
Eggs Benedict with Homemade Hollandaise

Legend has it that eggs Benedict—poached eggs served on an English muffin with hollandaise—was first served at the famous Delmonico's restaurant in New York City. Here's my take on the brunch classic.
—**BARBARA PLETZKE** HERNDON, VA

START TO FINISH: 30 MIN.
MAKES: 8 SERVINGS

- 4 **large egg yolks**
- 2 **tablespoons water**
- 2 **tablespoons lemon juice**
- ¾ **cup butter, melted**
  Dash white pepper
ASSEMBLY
- 8 **large eggs**
- 4 **English muffins, split and toasted**
- 8 **slices Canadian bacon, warmed**
  Paprika

1. For hollandaise sauce, in top of a double boiler or a metal bowl over simmering water, whisk the egg yolks, water and lemon juice until blended; cook, whisking constantly, until the mixture is just thick enough to coat a metal spoon and the temperature reaches 160°. Remove from heat. Very slowly drizzle in warm melted butter, whisking constantly. Whisk in pepper. Transfer to a small bowl if necessary. Place the small bowl in a larger bowl of warm water. Keep warm, stirring occasionally, until ready to serve, up to 30 minutes.

2. Place 2-3 in. of water in a large saucepan or skillet with high sides. Bring to a boil and adjust the heat to maintain a gentle simmer. Break an egg into a small bowl. Holding bowl close to surface of water, slip egg into water. Repeat with 3 remaining eggs.

3. Cook, uncovered, 2-4 minutes or until whites are completely set and yolks begin to thicken but are not hard. Using a slotted spoon, lift eggs out of water, one at a time.

4. Top each muffin half with a slice of bacon, a poached egg and 2 tablespoons sauce; sprinkle with paprika. Serve immediately.

PER SERVING *345 cal., 26 g fat (14 g sat. fat), 331 mg chol., 522 mg sodium, 15 g carb., 1 g fiber, 13 g pro.*

EGGS BENEDICT WITH HOMEMADE HOLLANDAISE

PRETTY AUTUMN SOUP

Fruit-Filled Puff Pancake

My husband and I often make a meal of this fruity puff pancake. The combination of cinnamon, blueberries and bananas is delicious. It's healthy, too.
—**LEANNE SENGER** OREGON CITY, OR

START TO FINISH: 25 MIN.
MAKES: 4 SERVINGS

- 3 large eggs
- ½ cup 2% milk
- ⅓ cup all-purpose flour
- ¼ teaspoon salt
- 3 tablespoons sugar, divided
- 1 tablespoon butter
- 1½ cups fresh or frozen blueberries, thawed
- 1 medium ripe banana, sliced
- ¼ teaspoon ground cinnamon

1. Preheat oven to 400°. In a large bowl, whisk eggs, milk, flour, salt and 1 tablespoon sugar until smooth. Place butter in a 9-in. pie plate. Place in oven 2-3 minutes or until melted.
2. Tilt pie plate to coat evenly with butter. Pour batter into hot plate. Bake 10-12 minutes or until sides are puffed and golden brown.
3. Meanwhile, combine blueberries and banana slices in a bowl. Remove pancake from oven and top with fruit. Mix cinnamon and remaining sugar; sprinkle over top. Cut into wedges; serve immediately.
PER SERVING *1 slice equals 232 cal., 8 g fat (4 g sat. fat), 171 mg chol., 240 mg sodium, 34 g carb., 2 g fiber, 8 g pro.* **Diabetic Exchanges:** *1 starch, 1 medium-fat meat, 1 fruit, ½ fat.*

Asparagus-Mushroom Frittata

PREP: 25 MIN. • **BAKE:** 20 MIN.
MAKES: 8 SERVINGS

- 8 large eggs
- ½ cup whole-milk ricotta cheese
- 2 tablespoons lemon juice
- ½ teaspoon salt
- ¼ teaspoon pepper
- 1 tablespoon olive oil
- 1 package (8 ounces) frozen asparagus spears, thawed
- 1 large onion, halved and thinly sliced
- ½ cup finely chopped sweet red or green pepper
- ¼ cup sliced baby portobello mushrooms

1. Preheat oven to 350°. In a large bowl, whisk eggs, ricotta cheese, lemon juice, salt and pepper. In a 10-in. ovenproof skillet, heat oil over medium heat. Add asparagus, onion, red pepper and mushrooms; cook and stir 6-8 minutes or until onion and pepper are tender.
2. Remove from heat and remove asparagus from skillet. Reserve eight spears; cut remaining asparagus into 2-in. pieces. Return cut asparagus to skillet; stir in egg mixture. Arrange reserved asparagus spears over eggs to resemble spokes of a wheel.
3. Bake, uncovered, 20-25 minutes or until eggs are completely set. Let stand 5 minutes. Cut into wedges.
PER SERVING *1 wedge equals 135 cal., 8 g fat (3 g sat. fat), 192 mg chol., 239 mg sodium, 7 g carb., 1 g fiber, 9 g pro.* **Diabetic Exchanges:** *1 medium-fat meat, 1 vegetable, ½ fat.*

> My Sicilian Aunt Paulina inspired this fluffy frittata. I remember visiting her garden, picking fresh veggies and watching her cook. Her wild asparagus frittata was my favorite.
> —CINDY ESPOSITO BLOOMFIELD, NJ

ASPARAGUS-MUSHROOM FRITTATA

Bacon & Egg Potato Bake

Frozen hash browns make this bacon and egg casserole a breeze to prepare. Make it the night before, keep it in the refrigerator overnight and bake the next morning.

—**CHERYL JOHNSON** PLYMOUTH, MN

PREP: 20 MIN. • **BAKE:** 45 MIN.
MAKES: 8 SERVINGS

- 1 package (30 ounces) frozen cubed hash brown potatoes, thawed
- 1 pound bacon strips, cooked and crumbled
- 1 cup (4 ounces) shredded cheddar cheese, divided
- ¼ to ½ teaspoon salt
- 8 large eggs
- 2 cups milk
  Paprika

1. In a large bowl, combine the hash browns, bacon, ½ cup cheese and salt. Spoon into a greased 13x9-in. baking dish. In another large bowl, beat eggs and milk until blended; pour over hash brown mixture. Sprinkle with paprika.
2. Bake, uncovered, at 350° for 45-50 minutes or until a knife inserted near the center comes out clean. Sprinkle with remaining cheese.
NOTE *This dish may be prepared in advance, covered and refrigerated overnight. Remove from refrigerator 30 minutes before baking.*
PER SERVING *1 cup equals 354 cal., 19 g fat (8 g sat. fat), 227 mg chol., 649 mg sodium, 23 g carb., 1 g fiber, 21 g pro.*

Southern Brunch Pastry Puff

My family jumps out of bed when the wonderful aroma butter fresh-baked pastry, sausage and eggs hits their noses. This recipe is true morning magic.
—**MISTY LEDDICK** CHESTER, SC

PREP: 30 MIN. • **BAKE:** 30 MIN. + STANDING
MAKES: 8 SERVINGS

- 2 cups plus 1 tablespoon water, divided
- ½ cup quick-cooking grits
- 1 cup (4 ounces) shredded cheddar cheese
- ¼ cup butter, cubed
- 2 tablespoons prepared pesto
- ½ teaspoon salt, divided
- ¼ teaspoon coarsely ground pepper, divided
- ½ pound bulk pork sausage
- ¼ cup finely chopped sweet red pepper
- 7 large eggs, divided use
- 1 package (17.3 ounces) frozen puff pastry, thawed

1. Preheat oven to 375°. In a small saucepan, bring 2 cups of water to a boil. Slowly stir in the grits. Reduce heat to medium-low; cook, covered, for about 5 minutes or until thickened, stirring occasionally. Remove from heat. Stir in the shredded cheddar cheese, butter, pesto, ¼ teaspoon salt and ⅛ teaspoon pepper until blended.
2. Meanwhile, in a large skillet, cook sausage and red pepper over medium heat for 4-6 minutes or until sausage is no longer pink and the red pepper is tender, breaking up sausage into crumbles. Drain.
3. In a small bowl, whisk six eggs and the remaining salt and pepper until blended. Return sausage to the skillet. Pour in egg mixture; cook and stir until eggs are thickened and no liquid egg remains.
4. Unfold each puff pastry sheet onto a 12x10-in. sheet of parchment paper. Spread grits to within ½ in. of pastry edges. Spoon sausage mixture over half of grits on each pastry. Fold the pastries over the sausage mixture to enclose; press edges with a fork to seal. Transfer to a baking sheet.
5. In a small bowl, whisk remaining egg and water; brush over pastries. If desired, top with additional ground pepper. Bake 30-35 minutes or until golden brown. Let stand 10 minutes. Cut each pastry into four pieces.
PER SERVING *1 piece equals 587 cal., 39 g fat (14 g sat. fat), 208 mg chol., 766 mg sodium, 43 g carb., 5 g fiber, 18 g pro.*

SOUTHERN BRUNCH PASTRY PUFF

Overnight Ham and Egg Casserole

You'll love how easy it is to assemble this savory egg casserole. Even better, you can put it together the night before to free up your time the next morning.

—JENNIFER HOWELL FORT COLLINS, CO

PREP: 10 MIN. + CHILLING
BAKE: 1 HOUR + STANDING
MAKES: 9 SERVINGS

- 4 **cups frozen shredded hash brown potatoes, thawed**
- 1 **cup cubed fully cooked ham**
- 1 **can (4 ounces) chopped green chilies**
- ½ **cup shredded Monterey Jack cheese**
- ½ **cup shredded cheddar cheese**
- 6 **large eggs**
- 1 **can (12 ounces) evaporated milk**
- ¼ **teaspoon pepper**
  Salsa, optional

1. In a greased 8-in. square baking dish, layer the hash browns, ham, chilies and cheeses. In a large bowl, whisk the eggs, milk and pepper; pour over the casserole. Cover and refrigerate overnight.
2. Remove from refrigerator about 30 minutes before baking and bake, uncovered, at 350° for 1 hour or until a knife inserted near the center comes out clean. Let stand for 5-10 minutes. Serve with salsa if desired.
PER SERVING *1 piece equals 203 cal., 11 g fat (6 g sat. fat), 175 mg chol., 407 mg sodium, 11 g carb., 1 g fiber, 14 g pro.*

CARAMELIZED ONION, BACON AND KALE STRATA

OVERNIGHT HAM AND EGG CASSEROLE

Caramelized Onion, Bacon and Kale Strata

When I have company, this strata is my go-to recipe. I created it one winter in Massachusetts to help me get through the snowstorms and shoveling.

—LINDA DALTON COCONUT CREEK, FL

PREP: 1 HOUR + CHILLING
BAKE: 40 MIN. + STANDING
MAKES: 6 SERVINGS

- 6 **bacon strips, chopped**
- 2 **medium onions, chopped**
- 4 **large eggs**
- 1¾ **cups 2% milk or half-and-half cream**
- 2 **tablespoons butter, melted**
- 1 **tablespoon Dijon mustard**
- ½ **teaspoon salt**
- ¼ **teaspoon pepper**
- 8 **cups cubed Italian bread**
- 1 **cup fresh baby kale or spinach**
- ½ **cup shredded fontina cheese**
- ¼ **cup crumbled Gorgonzola cheese**

1. In a large skillet, cook bacon over medium-low heat until crisp, stirring occasionally. Remove with a slotted spoon; drain on paper towels. Discard drippings, reserving 2 tablespoons in pan.
2. Add onions to drippings; cook and stir over medium-high heat for 2-4 minutes or until softened. Reduce the heat to medium-low and cook for 20-30 minutes or until deep golden brown, stirring occasionally.
3. In a large bowl, whisk eggs, milk, melted butter, mustard, salt and pepper until blended. Stir in bread, kale, cheeses, caramelized onions and bacon. Transfer to a greased 8-in. square baking dish. Cover and refrigerate 1 hour or overnight.
4. Preheat the oven to 325°. Remove strata from the refrigerator while oven heats. Bake, uncovered, 40-45 minutes or until a knife inserted near the center comes out clean. Let stand 10 minutes before serving.
PER SERVING *1 piece equals 391 cal., 22 g fat (10 g sat. fat), 167 mg chol., 886 mg sodium, 31 g carb., 2 g fiber, 17 g pro.*

Fresh Fruit Bowl

Slightly sweet and chilled, this summer salad is a refreshing accompaniment to any grilled entree—and glorious colors make it a pretty addition to any table.
—**MARION KIRST** TROY, MI

PREP: 15 MIN. + CHILLING
MAKES: 3-4 QUARTS

- 8 to 10 cups fresh melon cubes
- 1 to 2 tablespoons white corn syrup
- 1 pint fresh strawberries, halved
- 2 cups fresh pineapple chunks
- 2 oranges, sectioned
  Fresh mint leaves, optional

In a large bowl, combine melon cubes and corn syrup. Cover and refrigerate overnight. Just before serving, stir in remaining fruit. Garnish with fresh mint leaves if desired.

PER SERVING ¾ cup equals 55 cal., trace fat (trace sat. fat), 0 chol., 9 mg sodium, 13 g carb., 2 g fiber, 1 g pro.

Sausage Brunch Braid

I needed something stunning for a party, and this crescent braid did the trick. It's an edible centerpiece for a breakfast or appetizer buffet.
—**AMELIA MEAUX** CROWLEY, LA

PREP: 30 MIN. • **BAKE:** 20 MIN.
MAKES: 8 SERVINGS

- ¾ pound bulk pork sausage
- 1 small onion, chopped
- ¼ cup chopped celery
- ¼ cup chopped green pepper
- 1 garlic clove, minced
- 3 ounces cream cheese, cubed
- 1 green onion, chopped
- 2 tablespoons minced fresh parsley
- 1 tube (8 ounces) refrigerated crescent rolls
- 1 large egg, lightly beaten

1. Preheat oven to 350°. In a large skillet, cook the first five ingredients over medium heat 6-8 minutes or until sausage is no longer pink and vegetables are tender, breaking up sausage into crumbles. Drain. Add the cream cheese, green onion and parsley; cook and stir over low heat until cheese is melted.

2. Unroll crescent dough onto a greased baking sheet. Roll into a 12x10-in. rectangle, pressing the perforations to seal. Spoon sausage mixture lengthwise down center third of rectangle. On each long side, cut ¾-in.-wide strips 3 in. into center. Starting at one end, fold alternating strips at an angle across filling; seal ends. Brush with egg.

3. Bake for 20-25 minutes or until golden brown. Refrigerate leftovers.
PER SERVING 1 slice equals 249 cal., 18 g fat (7 g sat. fat), 50 mg chol., 449 mg sodium, 14 g carb., trace fiber, 7 g pro.

Lemon-Raspberry Ricotta Pancakes

I was raised in a home where stacks of freshly cooked pancakes were the norm every Sunday morning. I keep the tradition alive, making pancakes with almond milk, ricotta and raspberries.
—**ANITA ARCHIBALD** AURORA, ON

START TO FINISH: 30 MIN.
MAKES: 24 PANCAKES

- 1½ cups cake or all-purpose flour
- ¼ cup sugar
- 2 teaspoons baking powder
- ¼ teaspoon salt
- ¼ teaspoon ground cinnamon
- 1 cup unsweetened almond milk
- 1 cup part-skim ricotta cheese
- 3 large eggs, separated
- 2 teaspoons grated lemon peel
- 3 tablespoons lemon juice
- 1 teaspoon almond extract
- 1 cup fresh or frozen raspberries
  Whipped cream, maple syrup and additional raspberries

1. In a large bowl, whisk flour, sugar, baking powder, salt and cinnamon. In another bowl, whisk almond milk, ricotta, egg yolks, lemon peel, lemon juice and extract until blended. Add to dry ingredients, stirring just until moistened. In a clean small bowl, beat egg whites until stiff but not dry. Fold into batter. Gently stir in raspberries.

2. Lightly grease a griddle and heat over medium heat. Pour batter by ¼ cupfuls onto griddle. Cook until bubbles on top begin to pop and the bottoms are golden brown. Turn; cook until the second side is golden brown. Serve with whipped cream, syrup and additional raspberries.
PER SERVING 3 pancakes (calculated without toppings) equals 203 cal., 5 g fat (2 g sat. fat), 79 mg chol., 254 mg sodium, 31 g carb., 2 g fiber, 8 g pro. **Diabetic Exchanges:** 2 starch, 1 medium-fat meat.

LEMON-RASPBERRY RICOTTA PANCAKES

FAST FIX

Sweet Berry Bruschetta

Folks enjoy this fruity change of pace. Unlike traditional bruschetta, it's sweet instead of savory, and the French bread is delicious toasted on the grill. No matter how I serve it, there are never leftovers.

—PATRICIA NIEH PORTOLA VALLEY, CA

START TO FINISH: 20 MIN.
MAKES: 10 PIECES

- 10 slices French bread (½ inch thick)
  Cooking spray
- 5 teaspoons sugar, divided
- 6 ounces fat-free cream cheese
- ½ teaspoon almond extract
- ¾ cup fresh blackberries
- ¾ cup fresh raspberries
- ¼ cup slivered almonds, toasted
- 2 teaspoons confectioners' sugar

1. Place bread on an ungreased baking sheet; lightly coat with cooking spray. Sprinkle with 2 teaspoons sugar. Broil 3-4 in. from the heat for 1-2 minutes or until lightly browned.

2. In a small bowl, combine cream cheese, extract and remaining sugar. Spread over toasted bread and top with berries and almonds. Dust the bruschetta with confectioners' sugar and serve immediately.

PER SERVING *1 piece equals 92 cal., 2 g fat (trace sat. fat), 1 mg chol., 179 mg sodium, 14 g carb., 2 g fiber, 4 g pro.* **Diabetic Exchanges:** *1 starch, ½ fat.*

Streusel-Topped Blueberry Waffle Casserole

I had company coming and wanted to treat them to a new breakfast casserole. So I created this one that uses frozen waffles and is topped with a pecan streusel. My neighbors and husband were happy taste testers.

—JOAN HALLFORD NORTH RICHLAND HILLS, TX

PREP: 30 MIN. + CHILLING
BAKE: 40 MIN. + STANDING
MAKES: 12 SERVINGS

- 1 package (8 ounces) cream cheese, softened

STREUSEL-TOPPED
BLUEBERRY WAFFLE CASSEROLE

- ¼ cup packed brown sugar
- 15 frozen waffles, thawed and cut into 1-inch pieces
- 1½ cups fresh or frozen blueberries
- 8 large eggs
- 1½ cups 2% milk
- 6 tablespoons butter, melted
- 1 teaspoon vanilla extract
- ½ teaspoon ground cinnamon
STREUSEL
- ½ cup packed brown sugar
- ⅓ cup all-purpose flour
- 1 teaspoon ground cinnamon
- ¼ cup butter, softened
- ½ cup chopped pecans

1. In a small bowl, beat cream cheese and brown sugar until blended. Place half of the waffle pieces in a greased 13x9-in. baking dish, then drop cream cheese mixture by tablespoonfuls over waffles. Layer with blueberries and remaining waffles.

2. In a large bowl, whisk eggs, milk, melted butter, vanilla and cinnamon until blended; pour over the waffles. Refrigerate, covered, overnight.

3. Preheat oven to 350°. Remove casserole from refrigerator while oven heats. In a small bowl, mix brown sugar, flour and cinnamon; cut in butter until crumbly. Stir in the pecans; sprinkle over top. Bake, uncovered, 40-45 minutes or until set and top is golden. Let stand for 10 minutes before serving.

PER SERVING *1 piece equals 446 cal., 27 g fat (12 g sat. fat), 179 mg chol., 490 mg sodium, 41 g carb., 2 g fiber, 10 g pro.*

Apple-Cheddar Pancakes with Bacon

After tasting a scrumptious grilled apple and cheese sandwich, I decided to try the same flavors in pancakes. My sister suggested they'd be even better with bacon, and she was right.

—**KIM KORVER** ORANGE CITY, IA

PREP: 15 MIN. • **COOK:** 5 MIN./BATCH
MAKES: 16 PANCAKES

- 2 **large eggs**
- 1 **cup 2% milk**
- 2 **cups biscuit/baking mix**
- 8 **bacon strips, cooked and crumbled**
- 2 **large apples, peeled and shredded**
- 1½ **cups (6 ounces) shredded cheddar cheese**
  Butter and maple syrup, optional

1. In a large bowl, whisk eggs and milk until blended. Add biscuit mix and bacon; stir just until moistened. Fold in apples and cheese.
2. Lightly grease a griddle; heat over medium heat. Drop batter by ¼ cupfuls onto griddle, spreading batter with the back of a spoon as necessary. Cook until bubbles on top begin to pop and bottoms are golden brown. Turn; cook until second side is golden brown. If desired, serve with butter and syrup.
PER SERVING *2 pancakes (calculated without butter and syrup) equals 303 cal., 16 g fat (7 g sat. fat), 79 mg chol., 685 mg sodium, 27 g carb., 1 g fiber, 13 g pro.*

APPLE-CHEDDAR
PANCAKES WITH BACON

On a whim, I stuffed eggs into potato shells as a way to use up leftover baked potatoes. Now it's the brunch dish people ask for the most.

—**LISA RENSHAW** KANSAS CITY, MO

FIESTA EGG & POTATO BOATS

Fiesta Egg & Potato Boats

PREP: 40 MIN. • **BAKE:** 30 MIN.
MAKES: 8 SERVINGS

- 4 **large baking potatoes (about 3 pounds)**
- ¼ **cup butter, softened**
- ¼ **cup sour cream**
- 1 **to 2 tablespoons Sriracha Asian hot chili sauce**
- ½ **teaspoon salt**
- ¼ **teaspoon pepper**
- 8 **large eggs**
- 8 **bacon strips, cooked and crumbled**
- 1 **jar (4 ounces) diced pimientos, drained**
- 1 **cup (4 ounces) shredded pepper jack cheese**
- 4 **green onions, sliced (about ½ cup)**

1. Preheat oven to 375°. Scrub the potatoes; pierce several times with a fork. Place on a microwave-safe plate. Microwave, uncovered, on high 10-12 minutes or until tender, turning once.
2. When cool enough to handle, cut each potato lengthwise in half. Scoop out pulp, leaving ¼-in.-thick shells. In a small bowl, mash pulp together with butter, sour cream, hot chili sauce, salt and pepper.
3. Place potato shells on a parchment paper-lined 15x10x1-in. baking pan. Spoon the potato mixture into potato shells, creating a ¾-in.-deep well and building up sides with potato mixture as needed. Break one egg into each well. Bake for 25-30 minutes or until the egg whites are completely set and yolks begin to thicken but are not hard. Top with bacon, pimientos and cheese; bake for 2-4 minutes longer or until the cheese is melted. Sprinkle with green onions.
PER SERVING *1 stuffed potato half equals 384 cal., 20 g fat (10 g sat. fat), 230 mg chol., 571 mg sodium, 35 g carb., 5 g fiber, 17 g pro.*

Crustless Spinach Quiche

I served this at a church luncheon and laughed when a gentleman said, "This is good, and I don't even like broccoli!" I informed him it was actually spinach inside, not broccoli. He replied, "I don't like spinach, either, but this is good!"

—MELINDA CALVERLEY JANESVILLE, WI

PREP: 25 MIN. • **BAKE:** 40 MIN.
MAKES: 6-8 SERVINGS

- 1 cup chopped onion
- 1 cup sliced fresh mushrooms
- 1 tablespoon vegetable oil
- 1 package (10 ounces) frozen chopped spinach, thawed and well drained
- ⅔ cup finely chopped fully cooked ham
- 5 large eggs
- 3 cups (12 ounces) shredded Muenster or Monterey Jack cheese
- ⅛ teaspoon pepper

In a large skillet, saute onion and mushrooms in oil until tender. Add spinach and ham; cook and stir until the excess moisture is evaporated. Cool slightly. Beat eggs; add cheese and mix well. Stir in spinach mixture and pepper; blend well. Spread evenly into a greased 9-in. pie plate or quiche dish. Bake at 350° for 40-45 minutes or until a knife inserted near the center comes out clean.

PER SERVING 1 piece equals 255 cal., 19 g fat (10 g sat. fat), 180 mg chol., 482 mg sodium, 5 g carb., 2 g fiber, 17 g pro.

BUTTERMILK BISCUIT SAUSAGE PINWHEELS

(5) INGREDIENTS

Buttermilk Biscuit Sausage Pinwheels

Serve these delicious biscuits with scrambled eggs and fruit for a quick but filling breakfast or brunch. Use lean pork sausage for best results.

—GLADYS FERGUSON ROSSVILLE, GA

PREP: 15 MIN. + CHILLING • **BAKE:** 25 MIN.
MAKES: ABOUT 9 SERVINGS

- ¼ cup shortening
- 2 cups unsifted self-rising flour
- 1 cup buttermilk
- 1 pound raw bulk pork sausage, room temperature

With a pastry blender, cut shortening into flour. Add buttermilk; mix. On a lightly floured surface, knead for a few seconds, adding flour if necessary. Roll out on a lightly floured surface into a 12x9-in. rectangle. Spread the sausage over the dough. Roll up, jelly roll-style, starting from the short side. Chill. Cut into ½-in. slices. Place, cut side down, on a lightly greased baking sheet. Bake pinwheels at 425° for 25 minutes or until lightly browned.

PER SERVING 2 biscuits equals 312 cal., 20 g fat (6 g sat. fat), 35 mg chol., 768 mg sodium, 23 g carb., 1 g fiber, 10 g pro.

CRUSTLESS SPINACH QUICHE

CHEESY POTATO EGG BAKE

Cheesy Potato Egg Bake

Breakfast for dinner: It's brinner! This cozy egg bake with potato crowns hits the spot.
—AMY LENTS
GRAND FORKS, ND

PREP: 20 MIN. • **BAKE:** 45 MIN.
MAKES: 12 SERVINGS

- 1 **pound bulk lean turkey breakfast sausage**
- 1¾ **cups sliced baby portobello mushrooms, chopped**
- 4 **cups fresh spinach, coarsely chopped**
- 6 **large eggs**
- 1 **cup 2% milk**
  Dash seasoned salt
- 2 **cups (8 ounces) shredded cheddar cheese**
- 6 **cups frozen potato crowns**

1. Preheat oven to 375°. In a large skillet, cook sausage over medium heat 5-7 minutes or until no longer pink, breaking into crumbles. Add mushrooms and spinach; cook for 2-4 minutes more or until mushrooms are tender and the spinach is wilted.
2. Spoon sausage mixture into a greased 13x9-in. baking dish. In a large bowl, whisk eggs, milk and seasoned salt until blended; pour over sausage mixture. Layer with cheese and potato crowns.
3. Bake, uncovered, 45-50 minutes or until eggs are set and top is crisp.

PER SERVING *1 piece equals 315 cal., 20 g fat (7 g sat. fat), 154 mg chol., 910 mg sodium, 16 g carb., 2 g fiber, 20 g pro.*

FAST FIX ▶

Banana-Hazelnut Pain Perdu Duet

The ultimate breakfast at our house is French toast filled with warm bananas and Nutella. Pass it around with confectioners' sugar, maple syrup and fresh mint.
—CHARLENE CHAMBERS ORMOND BEACH, FL

START TO FINISH: 30 MIN.
MAKES: 4 SERVINGS

- 8 **slices French bread (½ inch thick)**
- ¼ **cup cream cheese, softened**
- ¼ **cup Nutella**
- 1 **medium banana, halved lengthwise and sliced**
- 4 **teaspoons brown sugar**
- 4 **large eggs**
- 1 **cup 2% milk**
- ¼ **cup hazelnut liqueur**
- 2 **teaspoons ground cinnamon**
- 2 **teaspoons vanilla extract**
- 2 **tablespoons butter**
  Optional toppings: confectioners' sugar, maple syrup, fresh mint leaves, additional banana slices and additional Nutella

1. On each of four bread slices, spread cream cheese and Nutella to within ½ in. of edges. Top with banana slices, brown sugar and remaining bread. In a shallow bowl, whisk the eggs, milk, liqueur, cinnamon and vanilla.
2. In a large skillet, heat butter over medium-low heat. Dip both sides of sandwiches in egg mixture, allowing each side to soak 30 seconds. Place sandwiches in skillet; toast each side 4-5 minutes or until golden brown. Serve with toppings as desired.
PER SERVING *1 stuffed French toast (calculated without optional toppings) equals 468 cal., 23 g fat (10 g sat. fat), 222 mg chol., 347 mg sodium, 48 g carb., 3 g fiber, 13 g pro.*

BANANA-HAZELNUT PAIN PERDU DUET

EAT SMART **SLOW COOKER**

Raisin Nut Oatmeal

There's no better feeling than waking up to a hot, ready-to-eat breakfast. The oats, fruit and spices in this homey meal cook together while you sleep.
—**VALERIE SAUBER** ADELANTO, CA

PREP: 10 MIN. • **COOK:** 7 HOURS
MAKES: 6 SERVINGS

- 3½ cups fat-free milk
- 1 large apple, peeled and chopped
- ¾ cup steel-cut oats
- ¾ cup raisins
- 3 tablespoons brown sugar
- 4½ teaspoons butter, melted
- ¾ teaspoon ground cinnamon
- ½ teaspoon salt
- ¼ cup chopped pecans

In a 3-qt. slow cooker coated with cooking spray, combine the first eight ingredients. Cover and cook on low for 7-8 hours or until liquid is absorbed. Spoon oatmeal into bowls; sprinkle with pecans.

NOTE *You may substitute 1½ cups quick-cooking oats for the steel-cut oats and increase the fat-free milk to 4½ cups.*

PER SERVING *¾ cup with 2 teaspoons pecans equals 289 cal., 9 g fat (3 g sat. fat), 10 mg chol., 282 mg sodium, 47 g carb., 4 g fiber, 9 g pro.*

For our Christmas brunch, I combine eggs, sausage and spinach into a snappy casserole. Sometimes I mix in fresh peppers or green chilies, so play with it.
—**KAREN WEEKLEY** WASHINGTON, WV

EGGS FLORENTINE CASSEROLE

RAISIN NUT OATMEAL

Eggs Florentine Casserole

PREP: 20 MIN. • **BAKE:** 30 MIN. + STANDING
MAKES: 12 SERVINGS

- 1 pound bulk pork sausage
- 2 tablespoons butter
- 1 large onion, chopped
- 1 cup sliced fresh mushrooms
- 1 package (10 ounces) frozen chopped spinach, thawed and squeezed dry
- 12 large eggs
- 2 cups 2% milk
- 1 cup (4 ounces) shredded Swiss cheese
- 1 cup (4 ounces) shredded sharp cheddar cheese
- ¼ teaspoon paprika

1. Preheat oven to 350°. In a large skillet, cook sausage over medium heat 6-8 minutes or until no longer pink, breaking into crumbles; drain and transfer to a greased 13x9-in. baking dish.

2. In the same skillet, heat butter over medium-high heat. Add the onion and mushrooms; cook and stir 3-5 minutes or until tender. Stir in spinach. Spoon vegetable mixture over sausage.

3. In a large bowl, whisk the eggs and milk until blended; pour egg mixture over vegetables. Sprinkle with cheeses and paprika and bake, uncovered, for 30-35 minutes or until the center is set and a thermometer inserted in center reads 165°. Let stand for 10 minutes before serving.

PER SERVING *1 piece equals 271 cal., 20 g fat (9 g sat. fat), 226 mg chol., 344 mg sodium, 6 g carb., 1 g fiber, 16 g pro.*

CHERRY-ALMOND COFFEE CAKE

(5) INGREDIENTS FAST FIX
Savory Apple-Chicken Sausage

These sausages taste great and make an elegant brunch dish. The recipe can be doubled or tripled for a crowd, and the sausage freezes well cooked or raw.

—ANGELA BUCHANAN LONGMONT, CO

START TO FINISH: 25 MIN.
MAKES: 8 PATTIES

- 1 large tart apple, peeled and diced
- 2 teaspoons poultry seasoning
- 1 teaspoon salt
- ¼ teaspoon pepper
- 1 pound ground chicken

1. In a large bowl, combine the apple, poultry seasoning, salt and pepper. Crumble chicken over mixture and mix well. Shape into eight 3-in. patties.
2. In a large skillet coated with cooking spray, cook patties over medium heat for 5-6 minutes on each side or until no longer pink. Drain if necessary.
PER SERVING *1 sausage patty equals 92 cal., 5 g fat (1 g sat. fat), 38 mg chol., 328 mg sodium, 4 g carb., 1 g fiber, 9 g pro.* **Diabetic Exchange:** *1 medium-fat meat.*

(5) INGREDIENTS FAST FIX
Blueberry Fruit Smoothie

Transport yourself back to the days of soda fountains with this more nutritious, fruit-filled alternative. You'll love its gorgeous color.

—MARY LAJOIE ORWELL, VT

START TO FINISH: 5 MIN.
MAKES: 3 SERVINGS

- 1 cup reduced-fat vanilla ice cream
- 1 cup fresh or frozen blueberries
- ½ cup chopped peeled fresh peaches or frozen unsweetened sliced peaches
- ½ cup pineapple juice
- ¼ cup vanilla yogurt

In a blender, combine all ingredients; cover and process until smooth. Pour into chilled glasses; serve immediately.
PER SERVING *¾ cup equals 149 cal., 2 g fat (1 g sat. fat), 7 mg chol., 57 mg sodium, 30 g carb., 2 g fiber, 3 g pro.* **Diabetic Exchanges:** *2 fruit, ½ fat.*

Cherry-Almond Coffee Cake

If you crave cheesecake, then you'll love this coffee cake that's almost as rich and creamy. I bake it every Christmas morning, but it's good any time of year. Feel free to use any kind of fruit preserves you like.

—SUE TORN GERMANTOWN, WI

PREP: 15 MIN. • **BAKE:** 50 MIN. + COOLING
MAKES: 12 SERVINGS

- 2½ cups all-purpose flour
- 1 cup sugar, divided
- ¾ cup cold butter, cubed
- ½ teaspoon baking powder
- ½ teaspoon baking soda
- ¼ teaspoon salt
- 1 cup (8 ounces) sour cream
- 2 large eggs, divided use
- 1 teaspoon almond extract
- 1 package (8 ounces) cream cheese, softened
- 1 cup cherry preserves
- ½ cup sliced almonds

1. Preheat oven to 350°. In a large bowl, mix flour and ¾ cup sugar; cut in butter until crumbly. Reserve ½ cup of the crumb mixture for topping. Add baking powder, baking soda and salt to remaining crumb mixture. Stir in sour cream, 1 egg and extract until blended.
2. Spread onto bottom of a greased 9-in. springform pan. In a small bowl, beat the cream cheese and remaining sugar until smooth. Add remaining egg and beat on low speed just until blended. Pour into pan and spoon the preserves over the top. Sprinkle with reserved crumb mixture and almonds.
3. Bake 50-60 minutes or until top is golden brown. Cool on a wire rack 15 minutes. Loosen sides from pan with a knife; remove rim from pan. Serve warm or cold. Refrigerate leftovers.
PER SERVING *1 slice equals 468 cal., 24 g fat (14 g sat. fat), 96 mg chol., 298 mg sodium, 56 g carb., 1 g fiber, 6 g pro.*

ZUCCHINI-CORNMEAL PANCAKES

Quinoa Granola

My kids love this healthy, tasty granola. It makes a great breakfast treat or anytime snack.

—CINDY REAMS
PHILIPSBURG, PA

PREP: 5 MIN. • **COOK:** 1 HOUR + COOLING
MAKES: 6 CUPS

- ¼ cup honey
- 2 tablespoons coconut or canola oil
- 1 teaspoon ground cinnamon
- 3 cups old-fashioned oats
- 1 cup uncooked quinoa
- 1 cup flaked coconut
- 1 cup chopped mixed dried fruit
- 1 cup chopped pecans

1. In a 3- or 4-qt. slow cooker, combine honey, oil and cinnamon. Gradually stir in oats and quinoa until well blended. Cook, covered, on high for 1 to 1½ hours, stirring well every 20 minutes.

2. Stir in the coconut, dried fruit and pecans. Spread evenly on waxed paper or baking sheets and cool completely. Store in airtight containers.

PER SERVING *½ cup equals 317 cal., 14 g fat (6 g sat. fat), 0 chol., 38 mg sodium, 44 g carb., 5 g fiber, 6 g pro.*

FAST FIX
Zucchini-Cornmeal Pancakes

My mom has made these treasured family hotcakes for years. They're delicious for breakfast, lunch or dinner. Serve with fresh fruit, yogurt and honey on top.

—KATHERINE WOLLGAST FLORISSANT, MO

START TO FINISH: 25 MIN.
MAKES: 8 PANCAKES

- 2 cups shredded zucchini
- 1 cup all-purpose flour
- ½ cup grated Parmesan cheese
- ⅓ cup yellow cornmeal
- ¼ cup sugar
- 1½ teaspoons baking powder
- 1 teaspoon salt
- ¼ teaspoon pepper
- 2 large eggs
- ⅓ cup 2% milk
- ¼ cup finely chopped onion
  Butter and maple syrup, optional

1. Place zucchini in a colander to drain; squeeze well to remove excess liquid. Pat dry.

2. Whisk the flour, cheese, cornmeal, sugar, baking powder, salt and pepper. In another bowl, whisk together the eggs, milk and onion. Add to the dry ingredients, stirring just until moistened. Fold in zucchini.

3. Lightly grease a griddle with cooking spray; preheat over medium heat. Pour batter by ¼ cupfuls onto griddle. Cook until bubbles on top begin to pop and bottoms are golden brown. Turn; cook until second side is golden brown. If desired, serve with butter and syrup.

PER SERVING *2 pancakes equals 314 cal., 6 g fat (3 g sat. fat), 103 mg chol., 973 mg sodium, 52 g carb., 2 g fiber, 12 g pro.*

QUINOA GRANOLA

Slow-Cooked Blueberry French Toast

Your slow cooker can be your best friend on a busy morning. Just get this recipe going, run some errands and come back to the aroma of French toast, ready to eat!

—ELIZABETH LORENZ PERU, IN

PREP: 30 MIN. + CHILLING • **COOK:** 3 HOURS
MAKES: 12 SERVINGS (2 CUPS SYRUP)

- 8 large eggs
- ½ cup plain yogurt
- ⅓ cup sour cream
- 1 teaspoon vanilla extract
- ½ teaspoon ground cinnamon
- 1 cup 2% milk
- ⅓ cup maple syrup
- 1 loaf (1 pound) French bread, cubed
- 1½ cups fresh or frozen blueberries
- 12 ounces cream cheese, cubed

BLUEBERRY SYRUP
- 1 cup sugar
- 2 tablespoons cornstarch
- 1 cup cold water
- ¾ cup fresh or frozen blueberries, divided
- 1 tablespoon butter
- 1 tablespoon lemon juice

1. In a large bowl, whisk eggs, yogurt, sour cream, vanilla and cinnamon. Gradually whisk in milk and maple syrup until blended.

2. Place half of the bread in a greased 5- or 6-qt. slow cooker; layer with half of the blueberries, cream cheese and egg mixture. Repeat the layers, then Refrigerate, covered, overnight.

3. Remove from the refrigerator 30 minutes before cooking. Cook, covered, on low 3-4 hours or until a knife inserted near the center comes out clean.

4. For syrup, in a small saucepan, mix the sugar and cornstarch; stir in water until smooth. Stir in ¼ cup blueberries. Bring to a boil; cook and stir until berries pop, about 3 minutes. Remove from heat; stir in the butter, lemon juice and remaining berries. Serve warm with French toast.

PER SERVING *1 cup with about 2 tablespoons sauce equals 390 cal., 17 g fat (9 g sat. fat), 182 mg chol., 371 mg sodium, 49 g carb., 2 g fiber, 12 g pro.*

Caramel Nut Breakfast Cake

I first tasted this incredible coffee cake when a kind neighbor brought it by. It was so good, my brother-in-law tried hiding it from us so he wouldn't have to share.

—ARLENE ISAAC CROOKED CREEK, AB

PREP: 25 MIN. • **BAKE:** 25 MIN.
MAKES: 18 SERVINGS

- 1 package white cake mix (regular size)
- 2 large eggs
- ⅔ cup water
- ½ cup all-purpose flour
- ¼ cup canola oil

TOPPING
- 1 cup packed brown sugar
- ¾ cup chopped pecans
- ¼ cup butter, melted

DRIZZLE
- 1 cup confectioners' sugar
- 1 tablespoon light corn syrup
- 1 tablespoon water

1. Preheat oven to 350°. Reserve 1 cup cake mix for topping. In a large bowl, combine the eggs, water, flour, oil and remaining cake mix; beat on low speed for 30 seconds. Beat on medium speed for 2 minutes. Transfer to a greased 13x9-in. baking pan.

2. In a small bowl, combine brown sugar, pecans and reserved cake mix; stir in butter until crumbly. Sprinkle over batter. Bake 25-30 minutes or until a toothpick inserted in center comes out clean. In a small bowl, mix confectioners' sugar, corn syrup and water until smooth; drizzle over the still-warm cake. Serve warm.

PER SERVING *1 piece equals 281 cal., 12 g fat (3 g sat. fat), 27 mg chol., 208 mg sodium, 43 g carb., 1 g fiber, 3 g pro.*

CARAMEL NUT BREAKFAST CAKE

**COLLEEN DELAWDER'S
BOURBON CANDIED BACON
DEVILED EGGS** *PAGE 169*

Potluck Pleasers

Set yourself apart from the **crowd** when you prepare the **standout** favorites in this chapter. **Mix and match** dishes or follow the **delectable** menus to make **potluck magic** at your next gathering.

JOAN HALLFORD'S WATERMELON-STRAWBERRY COOLER *PAGE 172*

KELLY WILLIAMS' SWEET TEA BARBECUED CHICKEN *PAGE 173*

ERRIKA PERRY'S GROUND BEEF TACO DIP *PAGE 176*

Pack a Picnic

Blue skies and a big basket of **mountain-high sandwiches,** crunchy **fried chicken** and **cool salads** make hungry people happy.

Pigeon River Chicken

For a picnic on the Pigeon River, we made chicken marinated in yogurt with a touch of cayenne. It's delectable warm or cold.

—**LIB JICHA** WAYNESVILLE, NC

PREP: 25 MIN. + MARINATING • **COOK:** 15 MIN.
MAKES: 12 SERVINGS

- 2 **cups (16 ounces) plain yogurt**
- 2 **tablespoons hot pepper sauce**
- 3 **teaspoons salt**
- 2 **broiler/fryer chickens (3 to 4 pounds each), cut up**

COATING

- 2 **cups all-purpose flour**
- 3 **tablespoons paprika**
- 4 **teaspoons cayenne pepper**
- 2 **teaspoons salt**
- 2 **teaspoons pepper**
- 1 **teaspoon dried thyme**
  Oil for deep-fat frying

1. In a large resealable plastic bag, combine the yogurt, pepper sauce and 3 teaspoons salt. Add chicken; seal bag and turn to coat. Refrigerate 8 hours or overnight.
2. Drain chicken, discarding marinade. In a shallow bowl, mix flour and seasonings. Add chicken, a few pieces at a time, and toss to coat; shake off excess. Transfer to a 15x10x1-in. pan; let stand 20 minutes.
3. In a Dutch oven or other deep skillet, heat ½ in. of oil over medium heat to 350°. Fry chicken, uncovered, 7-8 minutes per side or until coating is dark golden brown and meat is no longer pink, turning occasionally. Drain on paper towels.
PER SERVING *608 cal., 42 g fat (7 g sat. fat), 109 mg chol., 1,031 mg sodium, 19 g carb., 1 g fiber, 37 g pro.*

TOP TIP

My son and I go to the beach a lot during the summer. I pack frozen drinks, which first act as ice packs, then as beverages when they melt.
—**MELANIE M.** BEDEQUE, PEI

PIGEON RIVER CHICKEN

Bright carrots and radishes pop in this citrusy salad. My husband likes it with anything from the grill. I like to pile it on tacos.
—CHRISTINA BALDWIN COVINGTON, LA

RADISH, CARROT & CILANTRO SALAD

CRUNCHY RAMEN SALAD

Radish, Carrot & Cilantro Salad

PREP: 20 MIN. + CHILLING • **MAKES:** 12 SERVINGS (⅔ CUP EACH)

- 36 radishes, thinly sliced
- 1½ pounds medium carrots, thinly sliced
- 6 green onions, chopped
- ¼ cup coarsely chopped fresh cilantro

DRESSING

- 1 teaspoon grated lemon peel
- 1 teaspoon grated orange peel
- 3 tablespoons lemon juice
- 3 tablespoons orange juice
- 2 tablespoons extra virgin olive oil
- ½ teaspoon salt
- ¼ teaspoon pepper

In a large bowl, combine radishes, carrots, onions and cilantro. In a small bowl, whisk dressing ingredients until blended. Pour over salad; toss to coat. Refrigerate, covered, at least 1 hour before serving.

PER SERVING *⅔ cup equals 51 cal., 2 g fat (trace sat. fat), 0 chol., 145 mg sodium, 7 g carb., 2 g fiber, 1 g pro.* **Diabetic Exchanges:** *1 vegetable, ½ fat.*

FAST FIX
Crunchy Ramen Salad

For potlucks and picnics, this salad's a knockout. I tote the veggies in a bowl, dressing in a jar and noodles in a bag. Then shake them up together when it's time to eat.
—LJ PORTER BAUXITE, AR

START TO FINISH: 25 MIN. • **MAKES:** 16 SERVINGS (¾ CUP EACH)

- 1 tablespoon plus ½ cup olive oil, divided
- ½ cup slivered almonds
- ½ cup sunflower kernels
- 2 packages (14 ounces each) coleslaw mix
- 12 green onions, chopped (about 1½ cups)
- 1 medium sweet red pepper, chopped
- ⅓ cup cider vinegar
- ¼ cup sugar
- ⅛ teaspoon pepper
- 2 packages (3 ounces each) chicken ramen noodles

1. In a large skillet, heat 1 tablespoon oil over medium heat. Add almonds and sunflower kernels; cook until toasted, about 4 minutes. Cool.

2. In a large bowl, combine coleslaw mix, onions and red pepper. In a small bowl, whisk vinegar, sugar, pepper, contents of ramen seasoning packets and remaining oil. Pour over salad; toss to coat. Refrigerate until serving. Break noodles into small pieces. Just before serving, stir in noodles, almonds and sunflower kernels.

PER SERVING *¾ cup equals 189 cal., 13 g fat (2 g sat. fat), 0 chol., 250 mg sodium, 16 g carb., 3 g fiber, 4 g pro.*

JUDY'S MACARONI SALAD

COBB SALAD SUB

⑤ INGREDIENTS
Judy's Macaroni Salad

After finding this vintage macaroni salad years ago, I tweaked the flavor and bumped up the pickles. Tuck it inside your picnic basket.

—**ELIZABETH KIRCHGATTER** MAYSVILLE, KY

PREP: 20 MIN. + CHILLING
MAKES: 12 SERVINGS (¾ CUP EACH)

- 2½ cups uncooked elbow macaroni
- 1½ cups mayonnaise
- ¼ cup sweet pickle juice
- ½ teaspoon salt
- ¼ teaspoon pepper
- 1 cup (4 ounces) shredded cheddar cheese
- 6 hard-cooked large eggs, chopped
- 6 sweet pickles, chopped

1. Cook macaroni according to package directions. Drain macaroni; rinse with cold water and drain well.
2. In a large bowl, combine mayonnaise, pickle juice, salt and pepper. Stir in cheese, eggs and pickles. Add macaroni; toss gently to coat. Refrigerate, covered, at least 2 hours or until chilled.
PER SERVING *¾ cup equals 347 cal., 28 g fat (6 g sat. fat), 113 mg chol., 413 mg sodium, 15 g carb., 1 g fiber, 8 g pro.*

TOP TIP

We have a cooler that plugs into the car's power jack. I pack perishables in that—pasta or potato salad, fresh fruit and sandwiches. I pack a big thermos of ice water, too.
—**ANN S.** LAWRENCE, MA

FAST FIX
Cobb Salad Sub

When we need a quick meal to share, we turn Cobb salad into a sandwich masterpiece. Sometimes I swap in tortillas for the bread and make wraps instead.
—**KIMBERLY GRUSENDORF** MEDINA, OH

START TO FINISH: 15 MIN.
MAKES: 12 SERVINGS

- 1 loaf (1 pound) unsliced Italian bread
- ½ cup balsamic vinaigrette or dressing of your choice
- 5 ounces fresh baby spinach (about 6 cups)
- 1½ pounds sliced deli ham
- 4 hard-cooked large eggs, finely chopped
- 8 bacon strips, cooked and crumbled
- ½ cup crumbled Gorgonzola cheese
- 1 cup cherry tomatoes, chopped

Cut loaf of bread in half; hollow out top and bottom, leaving a ¾-in. shell (discard removed bread or save for another use). Brush vinaigrette over bread halves. Layer spinach, ham, eggs, bacon, cheese and tomatoes on bread bottom. Replace top. Cut in half lengthwise; cut crosswise five times to make 12 total pieces.
PER SERVING *1 slice equals 233 cal., 10 g fat (3 g sat. fat), 97 mg chol., 982 mg sodium, 17 g carb., 1 g fiber, 18 g pro.*

Bourbon Candied Bacon Deviled Eggs

At our house, it doesn't get any better than deviled eggs with bacon—bourbon candied bacon, that is. See if you can resist them. We can't.

—**COLLEEN DELAWDER** HERNDON, VA

PREP: 20 MIN. • **BAKE:** 25 MIN.
MAKES: 2 DOZEN

- 2 tablespoons brown sugar
- ¾ teaspoon Dijon mustard
- ½ teaspoon maple syrup
- ⅛ teaspoon salt
- 2 teaspoons bourbon, optional
- 4 thick-sliced bacon strips

EGGS

- 12 hard-cooked large eggs
- ¾ cup mayonnaise
- 1 tablespoon maple syrup
- 1 tablespoon Dijon mustard
- ¼ teaspoon pepper
- ¼ teaspoon ground chipotle pepper
  Minced fresh chives

1. Preheat oven to 350°. In a small bowl, mix brown sugar, ¾ teaspoon mustard, ½ teaspoon syrup and salt. If desired, stir in bourbon. Coat bacon with brown sugar mixture. Place on a rack in a foil-lined 15x10x1-in. baking pan. Bake 25-30 minutes or until crisp. Cool completely.

2. Cut eggs in half lengthwise. Remove yolks, reserving whites. In a small bowl, mash yolks. Add mayonnaise, 1 tablespoon syrup, 1 tablespoon mustard and both types of pepper; stir until smooth. Chop bacon finely; fold half into egg yolk mixture. Spoon or pipe into egg whites. Sprinkle with remaining bacon and chives. Refrigerate, covered, until serving.

PER SERVING *1 stuffed egg half equals 107 cal., 9 g fat (2 g sat. fat), 97 mg chol., 142 mg sodium, 2 g carb., 0 fiber, 4 g pro.*

FAST FIX

Layered BLT Dip

When I throw a party for friends, I whip up this addictive layered three-cheese dip. Somehow, it's always gone within the first 20 minutes.

—**JADE BENNETT** KINGWOOD, TX

START TO FINISH: 25 MIN.
MAKES: 20 SERVINGS (¼ CUP EACH)

- 1 package (8 ounces) cream cheese, softened
- ½ cup mayonnaise
- ¼ cup grated Parmesan cheese
- 1 cup finely chopped lettuce
- 8 bacon strips, cooked and crumbled
- 4 plum tomatoes, chopped
- 4 green onions, chopped
- 1½ cups (6 ounces) shredded cheddar cheese
  Toasted French bread baguette slices

In a small bowl, beat cream cheese, mayonnaise and Parmesan cheese until blended; spread into a large shallow dish. Layer with lettuce, bacon, tomatoes, onions and cheddar cheese. Refrigerate until serving. Serve with bread slices.

PER SERVING *¼ cup (calculated without baguette) equals 137 cal., 13 g fat (5 g sat. fat), 27 mg chol., 204 mg sodium, 2 g carb., trace fiber, 4 g pro.*

LAYERED BLT DIP

Potluck on the Porch

Come and get roasted **okra**, tangy **chowchow** and chicken in **sweet tea barbecue** sauce. You don't have to be a **Southerner** to cook like one.

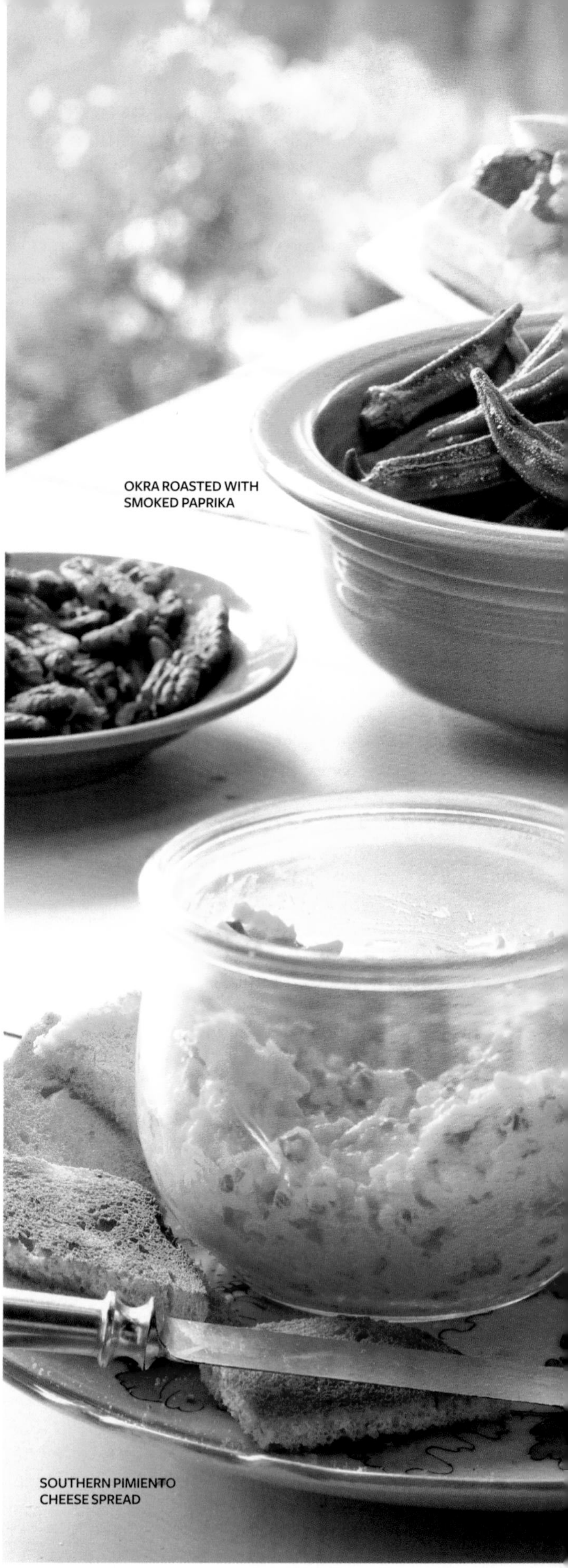

Okra Roasted with Smoked Paprika

When you want to cook okra without frying it, roast it with lemon juice for a lighter version. The smoked paprika gives it even more roasty oomph.

—**LEE EVANS** QUEEN CREEK, AZ

PREP: 5 MIN. • **COOK:** 30 MIN. • **MAKES:** 12 SERVINGS

- 3 **pounds fresh okra, whole**
- 3 **tablespoons olive oil**
- 3 **tablespoons lemon juice**
- 1½ **teaspoons smoked paprika**
- ¼ **teaspoon garlic powder**
- ¾ **teaspoon salt**
- ½ **teaspoon pepper**

Preheat oven to 400°. Toss together all ingredients. Arrange in a 15x10x1-in. baking pan; roast until okra is tender and lightly browned, 30-35 minutes.
PER SERVING *⅔ cup equals 57 cal., 4 g fat (1 g sat. fat), 0 chol., 155 mg sodium, 6 g carb., 3 g fiber, 2 g pro.* **Diabetic Exchanges:** *1 vegetable, ½ fat.*

OKRA ROASTED WITH SMOKED PAPRIKA

Southern Pimiento Cheese Spread

Pimiento cheese is the ultimate Southern comfort food. We serve it as a dip for crackers, chips and celery or slather it on burgers and hot dogs.

—**EILEEN BALMER** SOUTH BEND, IN

PREP: 10 MIN. + CHILLING • **MAKES:** 1¼ CUPS

- 1½ **cups (6 ounces) shredded cheddar cheese**
- 1 **jar (4 ounces) diced pimientos, drained and finely chopped**
- ⅓ **cup mayonnaise**
  Assorted crackers

Combine cheese, pimientos and mayonnaise. Refrigerate for at least 1 hour. Serve with crackers.
PER SERVING *2 tablespoons (calculated without crackers) equals 116 cal., 11 g fat (4 g sat. fat), 21 mg chol., 144 mg sodium, 1 g carb., trace fiber, 4 g pro.*

SOUTHERN PIMIENTO CHEESE SPREAD

Green Tomato Chowchow

My grandmom's long-cherished chowchow has Pennsylvania Dutch roots. Her pickled relish of cabbage, onions and peppers is tart and sweet with a smidge of spice.
—**SHARON TIPTON** CASSELBERRY, FL

PREP: 10 MIN. • **COOK:** 1 HOUR • **MAKES:** 40 SERVINGS

- 3 pounds green tomatoes (about 5 medium)
- 2 tablespoons salt
- 1 medium head cabbage
- 1 pound medium onions (about 3 medium)
- 1 pound green and sweet red peppers (about 3 medium), seeded
- 1 jalapeno pepper, seeded and chopped, optional
- 4 cups cider vinegar
- 2¾ cups sugar
- 4 teaspoons mixed pickling spices

1. Chop tomatoes. Transfer to a strainer and sprinkle with salt; let stand 10 minutes. Meanwhile, chop cabbage, onions and green and red peppers. Place in a Dutch oven. Add drained tomatoes to pan and, if desired, jalapeno.
2. Stir in the vinegar and sugar. Place pickling spices on a double thickness of cheesecloth. Gather corners to enclose spices; tie securely with string. Add to pan. Bring to a boil. Reduce heat; simmer, uncovered, until thickened, stirring occasionally, 1 to 1½ hours. Discard spice bag. Cool to room temperature; refrigerate leftovers.
PER SERVING ¼ cup equals 80 cal., 0 fat (0 sat. fat), 0 chol., 276 mg sodium, 19 g carb. (17 g sugars, 1 g fiber), 1 g pro.

GREEN TOMATO CHOWCHOW

(5) INGREDIENTS FAST FIX ▶
Southern Buttermilk Biscuits

The recipe for these four-ingredient biscuits has been handed down for many generations.
—**FRAN THOMPSON** TARBORO, NC

START TO FINISH: 30 MIN.
MAKES: 9 BISCUITS

- ½ cup cold butter, cubed
- 2 cups self-rising flour
- ¾ cup buttermilk
  Melted butter

1. In a large bowl, cut butter into flour until mixture resembles coarse crumbs. Stir in buttermilk just until moistened. Turn onto a lightly floured surface; knead 3-4 times. Pat or lightly roll to ¾-in. thickness. Cut with a floured 2½-in. biscuit cutter.
2. Place biscuits on a greased baking sheet. Bake at 425° for 11-13 minutes or until golden brown. Brush tops with butter. Serve warm.
NOTE As a substitute for each cup of self-rising flour, place 1½ teaspoons baking powder and ½ teaspoon salt in a measuring cup. Add all-purpose flour to measure 1 cup.
PER SERVING 1 biscuit equals 197 cal., 11 g fat (7 g sat. fat), 28 mg chol., 451 mg sodium, 22 g carb., 1 g fiber, 1 g pro.

Cast-Iron Peach Crostata

While the crostata, an open-faced fruit tart, is actually Italian, my version's peach filling is American all the way.

—**LAUREN KNOELKE** MILWAUKEE, WI

PREP: 45 MIN. + CHILLING • **COOK:** 45 MIN.
MAKES: 10 SERVINGS

- 1½ cups all-purpose flour
- 2 tablespoons plus ¾ cup packed brown sugar, divided
- 1¼ teaspoons salt, divided
- ½ cup cold unsalted butter, cubed
- 2 tablespoons shortening
- 3 to 5 tablespoons ice water
- 8 cups sliced peaches (about 7-8 medium)
- 1 tablespoon lemon juice
- 3 tablespoons cornstarch
- ½ teaspoon ground cinnamon
- ¼ teaspoon ground nutmeg
- 1 large egg, beaten
- 2 tablespoons sliced almonds
- 1 tablespoon coarse sugar
- ⅓ cup water
- 1 cup fresh raspberries, optional

1. Mix flour, 2 tablespoons brown sugar and 1 teaspoon salt; cut in butter and shortening until crumbly. Gradually add ice water, tossing with a fork until dough holds together when pressed. Shape into a disk; wrap in plastic wrap. Refrigerate 1 hour or overnight.

2. Combine the peaches and lemon juice. Add the remaining brown sugar, cornstarch, spices and remaining salt; toss gently. Let stand 30 minutes.

3. Preheat oven to 400°. On a lightly floured surface, roll dough into a 13-in. circle; transfer to a 10-in. cast-iron skillet, letting excess hang over edge.

Using a slotted spoon, transfer peaches into pastry, reserving liquid. Fold pastry edge over filling, pleating as you go, leaving center uncovered. Brush folded pastry with beaten egg; sprinkle with almonds and coarse sugar. Bake until crust is dark golden and filling bubbly, 45-55 minutes.

4. In a small saucepan, combine reserved liquid and water; bring to a boil. Simmer until thickened, 1-2 minutes; serve warm with pie. If desired, top with fresh raspberries.

PER SERVING *1 slice equals 322 cal., 13 g fat (7 g sat. fat), 43 mg chol., 381 mg sodium, 49 g carb., 3 g fiber, 4 g pro.*

CAST-IRON PEACH CROSTATA

EAT SMART (5)INGREDIENTS

Watermelon-Strawberry Cooler

My family gulps this frosty cooler because we simply adore watermelon. The strawberries give it an extra pop. This is a perfect drink for the Texas heat.

—**JOAN HALLFORD**
NORTH RICHLAND HILLS, TX

PREP: 10 MIN. + CHILLING
MAKES: 10 SERVINGS (1 CUP EACH)

- 2 cups water
- ½ cup lemon juice
- 12 cups cubed watermelon (about 3½ pounds)
- 2 cups fresh strawberries or raspberries
- ⅔ cup sugar
- 1½ teaspoons minced fresh mint
  Small watermelon wedges and fresh mint leaves

1. Place 1 cup water, ¼ cup lemon juice, 6 cups watermelon, 1 cup berries, ⅓ cup sugar and ¾ teaspoon minced mint in a blender; cover and process until smooth. Transfer to a large pitcher. Repeat with remaining water, lemon juice, fruit, sugar and the minced mint.

2. Refrigerate 1 hour or until cold. If desired, press through a fine-mesh strainer. Serve with watermelon wedges and mint leaves.

PER SERVING *1 cup equals 119 cal., trace fat (trace sat. fat), 0 chol., 2 mg sodium, 30 g carb., 1 g fiber, 1 g pro.*

Southern Corn Bread Salad

To feed a crowd, I make this eye-popping corn bread salad. It's beautiful in a trifle bowl and instant sunshine by the spoonful.

—**DEBBIE JOHNSON** CENTERTOWN, MO

PREP: 30 MIN. + CHILLING
MAKES: 16 SERVINGS (¾ CUP EACH)

- 1 package (8½ ounces) corn bread/muffin mix
- 1 cup (8 ounces) sour cream
- 1 cup mayonnaise
- 1 envelope ranch salad dressing mix
- 3 large tomatoes, seeded and chopped
- ½ cup chopped sweet red pepper
- ½ cup chopped green pepper
- 1 cup thinly sliced green onions, divided
- 2 cans (15 ounces each) pinto beans, rinsed and drained
- 2 cups (8 ounces) shredded cheddar cheese
- 10 bacon strips, cooked and crumbled
- 3½ cups frozen corn, thawed

1. Prepare and bake corn bread mix according to package directions, using an 8-in. square baking dish. Crumble when cool.

2. Mix sour cream, mayonnaise and salad dressing mix until blended. In a separate bowl, combine tomatoes, peppers and ½ cup green onions.

3. In a 3-qt. glass bowl, layer half of each: corn bread, beans, tomato mixture, cheese, bacon, corn and dressing. Repeat layers. Top with remaining green onions. Refrigerate 3 hours.

PER SERVING *¾ cup equals 367 cal., 23 g fat (7 g sat. fat), 46 mg chol., 607 mg sodium, 29 g carb., 4 g fiber, 11 g pro.*

TOP TIP

To quickly seed a tomato, cut it into wedges. Swipe your finger over each wedge to remove the gel pocket and seeds. This is nice for when you don't need perfectly seeded tomatoes.

SOUTHERN CORN BREAD SALAD

WATERMELON-STRAWBERRY COOLER

SWEET TEA BARBECUED CHICKEN

Marinades sometimes use coffee or espresso, and that inspired me to try sweet tea and apple juice to perk up barbecued chicken.

—**KELLY WILLIAMS** FORKED RIVER, NJ

Sweet Tea Barbecued Chicken

PREP: 15 MIN. • **COOK:** 1 HOUR
MAKES: 8 SERVINGS

- 1 cup unsweetened apple juice
- 1 cup water
- 2 teaspoons seafood seasoning
- 1 teaspoon paprika
- 1 teaspoon garlic powder
- 1 teaspoon coarsely ground pepper
- 1 broiler/fryer chicken (4 to 5 pounds), cut up
- 1 cup barbecue sauce
- ½ cup sweet tea

1. Preheat oven to 350°. Pour apple juice and water into a large shallow roasting pan. Mix seafood seasoning, paprika, garlic powder and pepper; rub over chicken. Place in roasting pan.

2. Bake, covered, until juices run clear and a thermometer reads 170° to 175°, about 50-60 minutes. Transfer chicken to a foil-lined 15x10x1-in. baking pan. Whisk barbecue sauce and sweet tea; brush over chicken.

3. Place chicken on greased grill rack; grill over medium heat 3-4 minutes per side, brushing occasionally with remaining sauce.

PER SERVING *1 piece equals 374 cal., 17 g fat (5 g sat. fat), 104 mg chol., 608 mg sodium, 19 g carb., 1 g fiber, 33 g pro.*

Time to Tailgate

One of the best things about **football?** The **food!** Here's game-time grub from the wives of players and coaches for the **Green Bay Packers**.

Spicy BBQ Chicken Wings

For zesty appetizers that win big every time, I glaze chicken wings with barbecue sauce, a little heat and a team of spices.

PREP: 25 MIN. + CHILLING • **COOK:** 45 MIN. • **MAKES:** 16 SERVINGS

- 4 **pounds chicken wings**
- 2 **cups white vinegar**
- 2 **cups water**
- 1 **cup all-purpose flour**
- 1 **tablespoon adobo seasoning**
- 1 **teaspoon garlic salt**
- 1 **teaspoon coarsely ground pepper**
- 1 **teaspoon kosher salt**
- 1 **teaspoon onion powder**
  Canola oil for frying
- 1 **cup honey barbecue sauce**
- 1 **cup hickory smoke-flavored barbecue sauce**
- ¼ **cup honey**
- 1 **jalapeno pepper, seeded and minced**

1. Using a sharp knife, cut through the two wing joints; discard wing tips. Place wings in a large bowl; add vinegar and water. Refrigerate, covered, 45 minutes. Drain and rinse, discarding vinegar mixture. Combine flour and seasonings; add chicken, tossing to coat.

2. Preheat oven to 375°. In a deep skillet, heat 1 in. oil to 375°. Fry wings, a few at a time, 3-4 minutes on each side or until golden brown. Drain on paper towels; cool 10 minutes.

3. In a small saucepan over medium heat, cook and stir barbecue sauces, honey and jalapeno. Bring to a boil; reduce heat and simmer, stirring occasionally, to allow flavors to blend, 10-15 minutes. Dip wings in sauce; place on greased foil-lined baking pans. Bake until glazed, about 10 minutes.

PER SERVING *2 pieces equals 317 cal., 19 g fat (3 g sat. fat), 36 mg chol., 816 mg sodium, 23 g carb. (16 g sugars, 0 fiber), 12 g pro.*

EAT SMART

Skinny Quinoa Veggie Dip

This good-for-you recipe might be ideal for the athlete in training, but it has plenty of flavor to satisfy the whole roster.

PREP: 20 MIN. • **COOK:** 15 MIN. • **MAKES:** 32 SERVINGS

- 2 **cans (15 ounces) black beans, rinsed and drained**
- 1½ **teaspoons ground cumin**

SPICY BBQ
CHICKEN WINGS
AUDI PERRY
WIFE OF NICK PERRY,
LINEBACKER

1½ teaspoons paprika
½ teaspoon cayenne pepper
1⅔ cups water, divided
   Salt and pepper to taste
⅔ cup quinoa, rinsed
5 tablespoons lime juice, divided
2 medium ripe avocados, peeled and coarsely chopped
2 tablespoons plus ¾ cup sour cream, divided
¼ cup minced fresh cilantro
3 plum tomatoes, chopped
¾ cup finely chopped peeled and seeded cucumber
¾ cup finely chopped zucchini
¼ cup finely chopped red onion
   Cucumber slices

1. Pulse beans, cumin, paprika, cayenne and ⅓ cup water in food processor until smooth. Add salt and pepper to taste.
2. In a small saucepan, cook quinoa with remaining 1⅓ cups water according to package directions. Fluff with fork; sprinkle with 2 tablespoons lime juice. Set aside. Meanwhile, mash together avocados, 2 tablespoons sour cream, cilantro and remaining lime juice.
3. In a 2½-qt. dish, layer bean mixture, quinoa, avocado mixture, remaining sour cream, tomatoes, chopped cucumber, zucchini and onion. Serve with cucumber slices.
PER SERVING *¼ cup equals 65 cal., 3 g fat (1g sat. fat), 4 mg chol., 54 mg sodium, 8 g carb. (1 g sugars, 2 g fiber), 2 g pro. Diabetic Exchanges: ½ starch, ½ fat.*

Tailgate Toffee Bars

Make a one-handed grab for this tender cake studded with toffee bits. Victory is extra sweet with a treat this good.

PREP: 15 MIN. • **BAKE:** 35 MIN. + COOLING • **MAKES:** 2 DOZEN

2 cups all-purpose flour
2 cups packed brown sugar
½ cup cold butter, cut into ¼-in. cubes
1 cup 2% milk
1 large egg
1 teaspoon baking soda
½ teaspoon almond or vanilla extract
3 Heath candy bars (1.4 ounces each), chopped
1 cup sliced almonds

1. Using a pastry blender or two forks, combine flour, brown sugar and butter until crumbly. Set aside 1 cup mixture.
2. In a separate bowl, whisk milk, egg, baking soda and extract. Stir into flour mixture until combined; pour into a greased and floured 13x9-in. pan. Top with chopped Heath bars, almonds and reserved flour mixture. Bake at 350° until a toothpick inserted in center comes out clean, about 30 minutes. Cool on a wire rack.
PER SERVING *1 bar equals 199 cal., 8 g fat (4 g sat. fat), 20 mg chol., 108 mg sodium, 30 g carb. (22 g sugars, 1 g fiber), 3 g pro.*

TAILGATE TOFFEE BARS
NICOLETTE BURNETT
WIFE OF MORGAN BURNETT, SAFETY

SKINNY QUINOA VEGGIE DIP
JENNIFER GIZZI
WIFE OF CHRIS GIZZI, STRENGTH & CONDITIONING ASSISTANT

GROUND BEEF TACO DIP
ERRIKA PERRY
WIFE OF DARREN PERRY,
SECONDARY –SAFETIES COACH

SLOW COOKER
ARTICHOKE-SPINACH DIP
ALYSSA JANIS
WIFE OF JEFF JANIS,
WIDE RECEIVER

PER SERVING *½ cup equals 116 cal., 7 g fat (3 g sat. fat), 30 mg chol., 378 mg sodium, 7 g carb. (2 g sugars, 0 fiber), 7g pro.*

SLOW COOKER 🍲

Slow Cooker Artichoke-Spinach Dip

Little extras like crumbled feta and red wine vinegar take this creamy dip of artichoke hearts, spinach and Parmesan to the next level. Just throw the whole nine yards into a slow cooker and this dip is good to go on game day.

PREP: 20 MIN. • **COOK:** 2 HOURS
MAKES: 24 SERVINGS

- 2 cans (14 ounces each) water-packed artichoke hearts, drained and chopped
- 1 package (10 ounces) frozen chopped spinach, thawed and squeezed dry
- 1 cup (8 ounces) sour cream
- 1 small onion, chopped
- 2 garlic cloves, minced
- ¾ cup grated Parmesan cheese
- ¾ cup 2% milk
- ½ cup crumbled feta cheese
- ⅓ cup mayonnaise
- 1 tablespoon red wine vinegar
- ¼ teaspoon coarsely ground pepper
- 1 package (8 ounces) cream cheese, cubed
- Sweet red pepper slices and tortilla chip scoops

1. Combine first 11 ingredients until well blended. Add cream cheese.
2. Place artichoke mixture in a greased 3- or 4-qt. slow cooker; cook, covered, on low about 2 hours. Stir; cover and keep warm. Serve with red pepper slices and tortilla chip scoops.
PER SERVING *¼ cup equals 112 cal., 9 g fat (4g sat. fat), 22 mg chol., 217 mg sodium, 4 g carb. (1 g sugars, 0 fiber), 4 g pro.*

FAST FIX ▶

Ground Beef Taco Dip

It's not a football party without taco dip. This version made with spicy ground beef and fresh toppings does not disappoint the diehards. It's full of classic flavors and is a little extra-filling for game-day appetites.

START TO FINISH: 25 MIN.
MAKES: 24 SERVINGS

- 1 pound lean ground beef (90% lean)
- ¾ cup water
- 2 envelopes taco seasoning, divided
- 1 container (16 ounces) fat-free sour cream
- 1 package (8 ounces) cream cheese, softened
- 2 cups shredded iceberg lettuce
- 1 cup (4 ounces) shredded cheddar cheese
- 3 medium tomatoes, finely chopped
- 1 medium green pepper, finely chopped
- 1 can (2¼ ounces) sliced ripe olives, drained

1. In a large skillet, cook and crumble beef over medium heat until no longer pink, 4-6 minutes; drain. Add water and one envelope taco seasoning; cook until thickened. Cool slightly.
2. Beat sour cream, cream cheese and remaining taco seasoning until blended. Spread in a 3-qt. dish; add ground beef. Top with lettuce, cheddar, tomatoes, pepper and olives.

Go Team!

OUR FACEBOOK FANS GET PUMPED UP FOR TAILGATE SNACKS *AND* THE SCHOOL THEY'RE CHEERING FOR. TACKLE A FEW OF THEIR FAVORITES AND SEE WHY.

1 UNIVERSITY OF TENNESSEE

We have country ribs, éclair cake, and tables of cheese balls, cheese wafers and cheese soup. **Anything orange goes.**

—*Beth Tuesburg, Roanoke, VA*

2 NORTHWESTERN UNIVERSITY

We do ours to the nines with a candelabra and tablecloth. We cook a turkey at home and carve it there—and there's always a bottle of champagne to share with everyone.

—*Bonnie Hawkins, Elkhorn, WI* Field Editor

3 TEXAS CHRISTIAN UNIVERSITY

It wouldn't be a tailgate if we didn't have my Jalapeno Bombers. Big jalapenos (seeded) filled with cream cheese, wrapped in bacon and baked. What a way to cheer on my alma mater.

—*Joan Hallford, North Richland Hills, TX* Field Editor

4 CLEMSON UNIVERSITY

Gotta have fried chicken and potato salad!

—*Nancy Lak, Bremen, GA*

5 UNIVERSITY OF MICHIGAN

The dip I like to make most of all is a mix of two packages of cream cheese and a jar of salsa. Top with shredded cheddar cheese. Let's go Blue!

—*Ashley Ooley Jones, South Boardman, MI*

6 MICHIGAN STATE UNIVERSITY

We put up three big tents and long banquet tables brimming with snacks, and of course there's our special coney sauce that's slathered on snappy grilled hot dogs.

—*Teri Rasey, Cadillac, MI* Field Editor

7 UNIVERSITY OF OKLAHOMA

Breakfast burritos show up at all our tailgating parties. Go Sooners!

—*Darla German, Tulsa, OK*

8 TEXAS A&M

A typical Aggie tailgate includes brisket, sausage and dips of all kinds, like corn dips, salsa and our favorite cheesy queso.

—*Cassie O'Haver, Houston, TX*

9 UNIVERSITY OF IOWA

The night before, we make BLT dip so it's ready to grab as we head out the door. Go Hawkeyes!

—*Virginia Clayton Roudabush, Mount Vernon, IA*

10 UNIVERSITY OF NEW HAMPSHIRE

Wildcat fans don't hold back when it comes to tailgating. Grilled romaine salad, bacon-wrapped chicken bites with BBQ sauce, roasted shrimp with cocktail sauce, low and slow baby back ribs, sweet and hot chili, and, for dessert, hot fudge brownie sundaes.

—*Anne Ormond, Dover, NH* Field Editor

ERIC OLSSON'S
CREOLE ROASTED TURKEY WITH
HOLY TRINITY STUFFING *PAGE 199*

Holiday & Seasonal Celebrations

Every **season** brings **special times** you'll want to **celebrate.** Turn here for the **extra-festive menu ideas** that will make each **holiday** truly memorable.

**VELMA BECK'S
COOL AND CREAMY
WATERMELON PIE** *PAGE 184*

**LILY JULOW'S
ROASTED SQUASH,
CARROTS & WALNUTS** *PAGE 197*

**BEVERLY LAUNIUS'
SPRITZ COOKIES**
PAGE 207

Springtime Brunch

Get your family **hopping right to the table** with **irresistible** entrees, **sparkling** sips, fresh fruit and cute treats the kids will **love.**

FAST FIX

Fresh Fruit Salad with Honey-Orange Dressing

I first made this fruit salad for my husband's surprise party on his 73rd birthday. It's been a hit ever since. The night before serving, I combine the oranges, pineapple, grapes and strawberries in a large plastic bag, then refrigerate until ready to serve. I also make the dressing the night before.

—**LEA ANN SCHALK** GARFIELD, AR

START TO FINISH: 30 MIN. • **MAKES:** 16 SERVINGS (¾ CUP EACH)

- ½ cup honey
- ⅓ cup thawed orange juice concentrate
- 1 tablespoon canola oil
- 1 teaspoon poppy seeds

SALAD

- 3 cups sliced fresh strawberries
- 2 cups seedless red grapes, halved
- 2 cups cubed fresh pineapple
- 2 medium navel oranges, peeled and coarsely chopped
- 2 medium apples, chopped
- 2 ripe medium bananas, sliced

1. In a small bowl, whisk honey, orange juice concentrate, oil and poppy seeds until blended. In a large bowl, combine strawberries, grapes, pineapple and oranges.
2. Just before serving, stir in apples and bananas. Pour dressing over salad; toss to coat.
PER SERVING ¾ cup equals 115 cal., 1 g fat (0 sat. fat), 0 chol., 4 mg sodium, 28 g carb., 2 g fiber, 1 g pro.

TOP TIP

When making a fruit salad, I toss the juice from a small can of pineapple with my sliced apples and bananas. The juice keeps the fruit from browning. And bits of pineapple in the salad give it a tropical zing.
—**FRAN A.** ROHNERT PARK, CA

CARROT GARDEN ICE CREAM DESSERT

Carrot Garden Ice Cream Dessert

When I was a kid, my mom made an ice cream dessert topped with gummy worms. I've riffed on it with carrots made out of frosting.

—**KAREN ENNS** KAMLOOPS, BC

PREP: 15 MIN. + FREEZING • **MAKES:** 12 SERVINGS

- 1 package (15½ ounces) Oreo cookies
- 1½ quarts vanilla ice cream
- 1 carton (8 ounces) frozen whipped topping, thawed
- ½ cup canned vanilla frosting
  Orange paste food coloring
- 2 to 3 pieces pull-apart green apple licorice

1. Finely crush half of the cookies; coarsely crush the remaining cookies.
2. In a large bowl, beat ice cream, whipped topping and finely crushed cookies until blended. Spread into an 8-in. square dish; sprinkle with crushed cookies. Freeze until firm.
3. Tint frosting orange; pipe carrot tops in rows over dessert. Cut green apple licorice into 1-in. pieces; separate strands, leaving one end intact. Place on carrots to form stems.
PER SERVING 414 cal., 20 g fat (10 g sat. fat), 29 mg chol., 228 mg sodium, 56 g carb., 2 g fiber, 3 g pro.

Mascarpone-Stuffed French Toast with Berry Topping

I love to make this rich and delicious French toast for my family. With a warm, creamy filling of mascarpone cheese and a sauce of mixed berries, it's an easy breakfast treat that looks like you spent all morning preparing it.

—PAMELA SHANK PARKERSBURG, WV

PREP: 20 MIN. • **COOK:** 10 MIN./BATCH
MAKES: 6 SERVINGS (4 CUPS SAUCE)

- ½ **cup sugar**
- 3 **tablespoons cornstarch**
- ¼ **teaspoon salt**
- ½ **cup cold water**
- 1 **package (12 ounces) frozen unsweetened mixed berries**
- 2 **cups coarsely chopped fresh strawberries or blueberries**
- 1 **loaf (1 pound) challah or egg bread, cut into 12 slices**
- 6 **tablespoons mascarpone cheese**
- 6 **large eggs**
- 1½ **cups heavy whipping cream**
- ¾ **cup 2% milk**
- 3 **teaspoons ground cinnamon**
- ¾ **teaspoon vanilla extract**
- 4 **tablespoons butter**

1. In a large saucepan, combine sugar, cornstarch and salt. Whisk in water. Stir in frozen berries. Bring to a boil; cook and stir 1-2 minutes or until thickened. Remove from heat; stir in fresh berries.

2. On each of six bread slices, spread 1 tablespoon mascarpone to within ½ in. of edges. Top with the remaining bread. In a shallow bowl, whisk eggs, cream, milk, cinnamon and vanilla.

3. In a large skillet, heat 2 tablespoons butter over medium heat. Dip both sides of sandwiches in egg mixture, allowing each side to soak 2 minutes. Place three sandwiches in skillet; toast 4-5 minutes on each side or until golden brown. Repeat with remaining butter and sandwiches. Serve with warm berry sauce.

PER SERVING *826 cal., 53 g fat (29 g sat. fat), 365 mg chol., 571 mg sodium, 72 g carb., 4 g fiber, 18 g pro.*

MARSCARPONE-STUFFED FRENCH
TOAST WITH BERRY TOPPING

SPRING STRAWBERRY SANGRIA

Spring Strawberry Sangria

Wine-infused berries make a delightful addition to this sparkling drink. I love serving this during the beginning of spring to celebrate the new season.

—**GINA QUARTERMAINE** ALEXANDRIA, VA

PREP: 10 MIN. + CHILLING
MAKES: 10 SERVINGS (ABOUT 2 QUARTS)

- 4 cups dry white wine, chilled
- ½ pound fresh strawberries, hulled and sliced
- ¼ cup sugar
- 2 cups club soda, chilled
- 2 cups champagne, chilled

1. In a pitcher, combine the wine, strawberries and sugar. Refrigerate at least 1 hour.

2. Just before serving, stir in club soda and champagne.

PER SERVING ¾ cup equals 136 cal., 0 fat (0 sat. fat), 0 chol., 15 mg sodium, 10 g carb., 0 fiber, 0 pro.

FAST FIX ▶

Southwestern Eggs Benedict with Avocado Sauce

I frequently make this spicy spin-off of classic Eggs Benedict for my husband, who loves breakfast. I like the heat from the jalapenos and also that the avocado sauce is a healthier substitute for the typical hollandaise.

—**KARA SCOW** MCKINNEY, TX

START TO FINISH: 30 MIN.
MAKES: 6 SERVINGS

- 1 medium ripe avocado, peeled and cubed
- ½ cup water
- ½ cup reduced-fat sour cream
- ¼ cup fresh cilantro leaves
- 2 tablespoons ranch salad dressing mix
- 2 tablespoons lime juice
- 2 tablespoons pickled jalapeno slices
- 1 garlic clove, chopped
- ¼ teaspoon salt
- ⅛ teaspoon pepper
- 6 slices whole wheat bread, toasted
- 12 slices deli ham
- 6 slices Monterey Jack cheese
- 2 teaspoons white vinegar
- 6 large eggs

1. Preheat oven to 425°. Place first 10 ingredients in a blender; cover and process until smooth.

2. Place toast on a baking sheet. Top each with two slices ham and one slice cheese. Bake 6-8 minutes or until the cheese is melted.

3. Meanwhile, place 2-3 in. of water in a large saucepan or skillet with high sides; add vinegar. Bring to a boil; adjust heat to maintain gentle simmer. Break cold eggs, one at a time, into a small bowl; holding bowl close to surface of water, slip egg into pan.

4. Cook, uncovered, 3-5 minutes or until whites are completely set and yolks begin to thicken but are not hard. Using a slotted spoon, lift eggs out of water. Serve immediately with ham and cheese toasts and avocado mixture.

PER SERVING 345 cal., 19 g fat (8 g sat. fat), 232 mg chol., 1,069 mg sodium, 19 g carb., 3 g fiber, 25 g pro.

SOUTHWESTERN EGGS BENEDICT WITH AVOCADO SAUCE

Ham & Cheese Breakfast Muffins

Ever since we began making these muffins, they have been a huge hit with family and friends. They are simple to make, are tasty warm or cold and never stay around for long.

—**LAURA NEWCOMER** BOWDOIN, ME

PREP: 15 MIN. • **BAKE:** 20 MIN.
MAKES: 20 MUFFINS

- 3 cups all-purpose flour
- 3 teaspoons baking powder
- ½ teaspoon baking soda
- ¼ teaspoon salt
  Dash pepper
- 2 large eggs
- 1⅓ cups buttermilk
- ⅓ cup canola oil
- 1 cup finely chopped fully cooked ham
- 1 cup (4 ounces) shredded cheddar cheese
- ¾ cup finely chopped onion

1. Preheat oven to 400°. In a large bowl, whisk flour, baking powder, baking soda, salt and pepper. In another bowl, whisk eggs, buttermilk and oil until blended. Add to flour mixture; stir just until moistened. Fold in ham, cheese and onion.
2. Fill greased or foil-lined muffin cups three-fourths full. Bake for 18-22 minutes or until a toothpick inserted in center comes out clean. Cool 5 minutes before removing from pans to wire racks. Serve warm.
PER SERVING *1 muffin equals 149 cal., 7 g fat (2 g sat. fat), 29 mg chol., 281 mg sodium, 16 g carb., 1 g fiber, 6 g pro.*

DID YOU KNOW?

Many muffin recipes are made using the stirred batter technique. Dry and wet ingredients are combined in separate bowls, then mixed just until blended. The batter may even have some lumps. Mix-ins such as cheese or veggies are gently folded in with as little mixing as possible. Light mixing ensures a tender finished product with a fine crumb, not one that is tough or chewy.

STRAWBERRY BLISS

Strawberry Bliss

A homemade puff pastry crust is topped with a soft-set pudding layer that offers a hint of strawberry flair. Because this dessert needs to chill for at least an hour, it's a great choice for your next make-ahead gathering.

—**CANDACE RICHTER** STEVENS POINT, WI

PREP: 30 MIN. • **BAKE:** 20 MIN. + CHILLING
MAKES: 12 SERVINGS

- 1 cup water
- ½ cup butter, cubed
- 1 cup all-purpose flour
- 4 large eggs
- 1 package (8 ounces) cream cheese, softened
- ½ cup sugar
- 5 tablespoons seedless strawberry jam
- 3 cups cold milk
- 1 package (5.1 ounces) instant vanilla pudding mix
- ½ cup heavy whipping cream
- 3 cups quartered fresh strawberries

1. Preheat oven to 400°. In a large saucepan, bring water and butter to a rolling boil. Add flour all at once and beat until blended. Cook over medium heat, stirring vigorously until mixture pulls away from sides of pan and forms a ball. Remove from heat; let stand 5 minutes.
2. Add eggs, one at a time, beating well after each addition. Continue beating until mixture is smooth and shiny.
3. Spread into a greased 15x10x1-in. baking pan. Bake 20-25 minutes or until puffed and golden brown (surface will be uneven). Cool completely in pan on a wire rack.
4. In a large bowl, beat cream cheese, sugar and jam until smooth. Beat in milk and pudding mix until smooth. In a small bowl, beat cream until stiff peaks form; fold into pudding mixture. Spread over crust. Refrigerate at least 1 hour.
5. Just before serving, top with strawberries.
PER SERVING *1 piece equals 377 cal., 22 g fat (13 g sat. fat), 131 mg chol., 332 mg sodium, 40 g carb., 1 g fiber, 7 g pro.*

Fourth of July Treats

Celebrate **the red, white and blue** with cool, creamy **sweets** guaranteed to bring enthusiastic **oohs and ahhs.**

Cool and Creamy Watermelon Pie

This simple pie is so refreshing, it never lasts long on warm summer days. Watermelon and a few convenience items make a delightful dessert that's easy to whip up.

—**VELMA BECK** CARLINVILLE, IL

PREP: 15 MIN. + CHILLING • **MAKES:** 6-8 SERVINGS

- 1 package (3 ounces) watermelon gelatin
- ¼ cup boiling water
- 1 carton (12 ounces) frozen whipped topping, thawed
- 2 cups cubed seeded watermelon
- 1 graham cracker crust (9 inches)

In a large bowl, dissolve gelatin in boiling water. Cool to room temperature. Whisk in whipped topping; fold in watermelon. Spoon into crust. Refrigerate for 2 hours or until set.

PER SERVING *1 piece equals 272 cal., 12 g fat (8 g sat. fat), 0 chol., 147 mg sodium, 36 g carb., 1 g fiber, 2 g pro.*

Patriotic Ice Cream Cupcakes

Create flavor fireworks with these frosty cupcakes. The little treats feature red velvet cake, blue moon ice cream, a creamy white topping and sparkling accents.

—**TASTE OF HOME** TEST KITCHEN

PREP: 30 MIN. + FREEZING • **BAKE:** 15 MIN. + COOLING
MAKES: 3 DOZEN

- 1 package red velvet cake mix (regular size)
- 1 quart blue moon ice cream, softened
- 3 cups heavy whipping cream
- 1½ cups marshmallow creme
  Red, white and blue sprinkles
  Blue colored sugar

1. Prepare cake mix batter according to package directions for cupcakes.
2. Fill paper-lined muffin cups half full. Bake at 350° for 11-14 minutes or until a toothpick inserted near the center comes out clean. Cool for 10 minutes before removing from pans to wire racks to cool completely.
3. Working quickly, spread ice cream over cupcakes. Freeze for at least 1 hour.

4. In a large bowl, combine cream and marshmallow creme; beat until stiff peaks form. Pipe over cupcakes; decorate with sprinkles and colored sugar. Freeze for 4 hours or until firm.

NOTE *As a substitute for blue moon ice cream, tint softened vanilla ice cream with blue food coloring.*

PER SERVING *1 cupcake equals 202 cal., 13 g fat (6 g sat. fat), 50 mg chol., 137 mg sodium, 20 g carb., trace fiber, 3 g pro.*

PATRIOTIC ICE CREAM CUPCAKES

Red, White 'n' Blue Salad

PREP: 30 MIN. + CHILLING • **MAKES:** 16 SERVINGS

- 1 package (3 ounces) berry blue gelatin
- 2 cups boiling water, divided
- 2½ cups cold water, divided
- 1 cup fresh blueberries
- 1 envelope unflavored gelatin
- 1 cup heavy whipping cream
- 6 tablespoons sugar
- 2 cups (16 ounces) sour cream
- 1 teaspoon vanilla extract
- 1 package (3 ounces) raspberry gelatin
- 1 cup fresh raspberries
  Whipped topping and additional berries, optional

1. Dissolve berry blue gelatin in 1 cup boiling water; stir in 1 cup cold water. Add blueberries. Pour into a 3-qt. serving bowl. Refrigerate until firm, about 1 hour.

2. In a saucepan, sprinkle unflavored gelatin over ½ cup cold water; let stand for 1 minute. Add cream and sugar; cook and stir over low heat until dissolved. Cool to room temperature. Whisk in sour cream and vanilla. Spoon over blue layer. Refrigerate until firm.

3. Dissolve raspberry gelatin in remaining hot water; stir in remaining cold water. Add raspberries. Spoon over cream layer. Chill until set. Top with whipped topping and berries if desired.

PER SERVING *179 cal., 11 g fat (7 g sat. fat), 40 mg chol., 46 mg sodium, 18 g carb., 1 g fiber, 3 g pro.*

Our striking "flag" salad drew plenty of attention at our Independence Day party. I use gelatin to help create the shimmering stripes.
—**LAURIE NEVERMAN** DENMARK, WI

RED, WHITE 'N' BLUE SALAD

Outdoor Adventure

Grab some **foil** and a **cast-iron skillet.** Stoke the **fire** for recipes cooked in wide-open spaces. Take 'em camping or on a trip to the **backyard.**

ECLAIRS ON THE GRILL

(5) INGREDIENTS
Eclairs on the Grill

My best camping treat is a simple eclair on a stick. This is the one that makes people watch what you're doing and beg to be included.

—**BONNIE HAWKINS** ELKHORN, WI

PREP: 5 MIN. • **GRILL:** 5 MIN./BATCH • **MAKES:** 6 SERVINGS

> Stick or wooden dowel (⅝-inch diameter and 24 inches long)
1 tube (8 ounces) refrigerated seamless crescent dough sheet
3 snack-size cups (3¼ ounces each) vanilla or chocolate pudding
½ cup chocolate frosting
> Whipped cream in a can

1. Prepare campfire or grill for high heat. Wrap one end of a stick or wooden dowel with foil. Unroll crescent dough and cut into six 4-in. squares. Wrap one piece of dough around prepared stick; pinch end and seam to seal.

2. Cook over campfire or grill 5-7 minutes or until golden brown, turning occasionally. When dough is cool enough to handle, remove from stick. Finish cooling. Repeat with remaining dough.

3. Place pudding in a resealable plastic bag; cut a small hole in one corner. Squeeze bag to press mixture into each shell. Spread with frosting; top with whipped cream.

PER SERVING *1 eclair equals 293 cal., 12 g fat (4 g sat. fat), 0 chol., 418 mg sodium, 43 g carb., trace fiber, 4 g pro.*

BLUEBERRY-CINNAMON CAMPFIRE BREAD

EAT SMART
Blueberry-Cinnamon Campfire Bread

PREP: 10 MIN. • **COOK:** 30 MIN. + STANDING • **MAKES:** 8 SERVINGS

1 loaf (1 pound) cinnamon-raisin bread
6 large eggs
1 cup 2% milk or half-and-half cream
2 tablespoons maple syrup
1 teaspoon vanilla extract
½ cup chopped pecans, toasted
2 cups fresh blueberries, divided

A neighboring camper made a bread so tempting that I had to ask for the details. Here's my version, best enjoyed with a steaming cup of coffee by the campfire.

—**JOAN HALLFORD** NORTH RICHLANDS, TX

1. Prepare campfire or grill for low heat. Arrange bread slices on a greased double thickness of heavy-duty foil (about 24x18 in.). Bring foil up the sides, leaving the top open. Whisk eggs, milk, syrup and vanilla. Pour over bread; sprinkle with nuts and 1 cup blueberries. Fold edges over top, crimping to seal.

2. Place on a grill grate over campfire or grill until egg is cooked through, about 30-40 minutes. Remove from heat; let stand 10 minutes. Sprinkle with remaining blueberries; serve with additional maple syrup if desired.

OVEN DIRECTIONS *Preheat oven to 350°. Place foil packet on a 15x10x1-in. baking pan. Bake 25-30 minutes or until heated through. Let stand 10 minutes before serving. Sprinkle with remaining blueberries; serve with syrup.*

PER SERVING *2 slices equals 266 cal., 10 g fat (2 g sat. fat), 142 mg chol., 185 mg sodium, 36 g carb., 5 g fiber, 12 g pro.* **Diabetic Exchanges:** *2 starch, 1 medium-fat meat, ½ fruit, ½ fat.*

FREEZE IT FAST FIX

Egg & Spinach Breakfast Burritos

When we camp out, we want our meals ready in a hurry. We make these hearty burritos at home, freeze them and reheat over the campfire.

—**KRISTEN JOHNSON** WAUKESHA, WI

START TO FINISH: 30 MIN. • **MAKES:** 10 SERVINGS

- 1 **pound bulk lean turkey breakfast sausage**
- 1 **tablespoon canola oil**
- 1 **cup frozen cubed hash brown potatoes, thawed**
- 1 **small red onion, chopped**
- 1 **small sweet red pepper, chopped**
- 6 **cups (about 4 ounces) fresh spinach, coarsely chopped**
- 6 **large eggs, beaten**
- 10 **multigrain tortillas (8 inches), warmed**
- ¾ **cup crumbled queso fresco or feta cheese**
  Guacamole and salsa, optional

1. In a nonstick skillet, cook sausage over medium heat until no longer pink, 4-6 minutes, breaking into crumbles; remove from pan.

2. In same skillet, heat oil. Add potatoes, onion and pepper; cook, stirring, until tender, 5-7 minutes. Add spinach; stir until wilted, 1-2 minutes. Add sausage and eggs; cook and stir until no liquid egg remains.

3. Spoon ½ cup filling across center of each tortilla; sprinkle with cheese. Fold bottom and sides over filling and roll up. If desired, serve with guacamole and salsa.

FREEZE OPTION *Cool filling before making burritos. Individually wrap burritos in foil and freeze in a resealable plastic freezer bag. Freeze up to 1 month. To use, partially thaw overnight in refrigerator or cooler. Prepare campfire or grill for medium heat. Place foil-wrapped burritos on a grill grate over a campfire or on grill. Grill until heated through, 25-30 minutes, turning occasionally.*

PER SERVING *1 burrito equals 333 cal., 15 g fat (5 g sat. fat), 166 mg chol., 882 mg sodium, 27 g carb., 6 g fiber, 22 g pro.*

EGG & SPINACH BREAKFAST BURRITOS

CAMPERS FAVORITE DIP

GRILLED SPICY
CORN ON THE COB

2 **cups shredded cheddar cheese**
2 **thinly sliced green onions, optional**
   Tortilla chip scoops

1. Prepare campfire or grill for medium-low heat. Spread cream cheese in the bottom of a 9-in. disposable foil pie pan. Top with chili; sprinkle with cheese.

2. Place pan on a grill grate over a campfire or on grill until cheese is melted, 5-8 minutes. If desired, sprinkle with green onion. Serve with corn chips.

PER SERVING *¼ cup equals 250 cal., 17 g fat (7 g sat. fat), 32 mg chol., 403 mg sodium, 15 g carb., 2 g fiber, 9 g pro.*

(5)INGREDIENTS FAST FIX

Grilled Peaches 'n' Berries

Highlight the natural sweetness of peak summertime fruit with brown sugar, butter and a squeeze of lemon juice. Foil packets make this a go-anywhere dessert.
—**SHARON BICKETT** CHESTER, SC

START TO FINISH: 30 MIN.
MAKES: 3 SERVINGS

3 **medium ripe peaches, halved and pitted**
1 **cup fresh blueberries**
2 **tablespoons brown sugar**
2 **tablespoons butter**
1 **tablespoon lemon juice**

1. Place two peach halves, cut side up, on each of three double thicknesses of heavy-duty foil (12 in. square). Top with blueberries, brown sugar, butter and lemon juice. Fold foil around mixture and seal tightly.

2. Grill, covered, over medium-low heat for 18-20 minutes or until tender. Open the foil carefully to allow steam to escape.

PER SERVING *172 cal., 8 g fat (5 g sat. fat), 20 mg chol., 81 mg sodium, 27 g carb., 3 g fiber, 1 g pro.*

FAST FIX

Grilled Spicy Corn on the Cob

During a family picnic, we added jalapenos and hot pepper sauce to our homegrown corn. Now we spice up the ears every chance we get.
—**BERNADETTE WALKER** WACO, TX

START TO FINISH: 25 MIN.
MAKES: 4 SERVINGS

4 **large ears sweet corn, husks removed**
¼ **cup butter, melted**
2 **teaspoons dried thyme**
1 **tablespoon hot pepper sauce**
1 **teaspoon chicken bouillon granules**
¼ **cup chopped seeded jalapeno peppers**

1. Place each ear of corn on a double thickness of heavy-duty foil (about 18x12 in.). Combine butter, thyme, hot pepper sauce and bouillon granules.

Brush over corn; sprinkle each with 1 tablespoon jalapenos. Seal tightly.

2. Grill, covered, over medium heat until the corn is tender, about 15-20 minutes. Open carefully to allow steam to escape.

NOTE *Wear disposable gloves when cutting hot peppers; the oils can burn skin. Avoid touching your face.*

PER SERVING *1 ear of corn equals 229 cal., 13 g fat (7 g sat. fat), 30 mg chol., 335 mg sodium, 28 g carb., 4 g fiber, 5 g pro.*

(5)INGREDIENTS FAST FIX

Campers Favorite Dip

Our family craves this cheesy chili dip so much we often make two batches. If you're not grilling out, bake the dip in the oven or microwave it.
—**VALORIE EBIE** BEL AIRE, KS

START TO FINISH: 15 MIN.
MAKES: 3½ CUPS

1 **package (8 ounces) reduced-fat cream cheese**
1 **can (15 ounces) chili with beans**

EASY AS PIE

Call them mountain pies, hobo pies, pudgy pies or just darn good. These toasty classics are made with simple stuff but bring the happiest memories.

MILKY WAY PUDGY PIE

My favorite is made with white bread, chopped Milky Way candy bars, graham cracker crumbs and marshmallows. So irresistible!
—Ashlan Potts, Ontario, Canada

APPLE-CINNAMON PUDGY PIE

I remember the first time I tasted a pie-iron pie. My sister buttered two slices of white bread while I peeled a Macintosh apple. She sliced it thin, arranged it on the bread and poured liberal amounts of white sugar and cinnamon over the top. I couldn't believe the sweet magic that came out of that fire!
—Monica Kronemeyer DeRegt, Abbotsford, BC

REUBEN PUDGY PIE

Our favorite pudgy pie recipe is the Reuben: Corned beef, sauerkraut and Swiss cheese! We always use buttered bread.
—Kim Goetz, Andover, MN

Sweet Horseradish Glazed Ribs

If you like to prep ahead of camping, roast these ribs, wrap them and finish with a sweet, savory sauce at your campfire or grill.
—**RALPH JONES** SAN DIEGO, CA

PREP: 10 MIN. + CHILLING
COOK: 2 ¼ HOURS • **MAKES:** 8 SERVINGS

- 3 racks pork baby back ribs (about 8 pounds)
- 1½ teaspoons salt, divided
- 1½ teaspoons coarsely ground pepper, divided
- 2 bottles (12 ounces each) beer or 3 cups unsweetened apple juice
- 1 jar (12 ounces) apricot preserves
- ¼ cup prepared horseradish, drained
- 2 tablespoons honey or maple syrup
- 1 teaspoon liquid smoke, optional

1. Preheat oven to 325°. If necessary, remove thin membrane from ribs and discard. Sprinkle 1 teaspoon each salt and pepper over ribs. Transfer to a large shallow roasting pan, bone side down; add beer or juice. Bake, covered, until tender, 2-3 hours.
2. Meanwhile, puree the preserves, horseradish, honey, remaining salt and pepper and, if desired, liquid smoke in a blender.
3. Drain ribs. Place 1 rib rack on a large piece of aluminum foil. Brush with apricot-horseradish mixture; wrap tightly. Repeat with remaining ribs. Refrigerate up to 2 days.
4. Prepare campfire or grill for medium heat. Remove ribs from foil; grill until browned, 10-15 minutes, turning occasionally.
PER SERVING *1 pound equals 690 cal., 42 g fat (15 g sat. fat), 163 mg chol., 674 mg sodium, 33 g carb., 0 fiber, 45 g pro.*

EAT SMART **FAST FIX**

Lemon-Dill Salmon Packets

Grilling salmon in foil is an easy technique I use with foods that cook quickly, like fish, shrimp, bite-size meats and fresh veggies. The options are endless—and the cleanup is easy.
—**A.J. WEINHOLD** MCARTHUR, CA

START TO FINISH: 25 MIN. • **MAKES:** 4 SERVINGS

- 1 tablespoon butter, softened
- 4 salmon fillets (6 ounces each)
- ½ teaspoon salt
- ¼ teaspoon pepper
- ½ medium onion, sliced
- 4 garlic cloves, sliced
- 4 fresh dill sprigs
- 1 tablespoon minced fresh basil
- 1 medium lemon, sliced

1. Prepare campfire or grill for medium heat. Spread butter in the center of each of four pieces of a double thickness of foil (about 12 in. square). Place one salmon fillet in the center of each; sprinkle with salt and pepper. Top with onion, garlic, dill, basil and lemon. Fold foil around fillets; seal.

SWEET HORSERADISH GLAZED RIBS

2. Place packets on a grill grate over a campfire or grill. Cook 8-10 minutes or until fish just begins to flake easily with a fork. Open carefully to allow steam to escape.

PER SERVING *1 fillet equals 305 cal., 19 g fat (5 g sat. fat), 93 mg chol., 405 mg sodium, 4 g carb., 1 g fiber, 29 g pro. Diabetic Exchanges: 5 lean meat, 1 fat.*

FAST FIX
Grilled Zucchini & Pesto Pizza
In the great outdoors, we surprise our campmates because they don't think it's possible to have standout pizza in the backwoods. This one with zucchini proves our point.
—**JESSEE ARRIAGA** RENO, NV

START TO FINISH: 20 MIN. • **MAKES:** 6 SERVINGS

- 4 **naan flatbreads**
- ½ **cup prepared pesto**
- 2 **cups (8 ounces) shredded part-skim mozzarella cheese**
- 1 **medium zucchini, thinly sliced**
- 1 **small red onion, thinly sliced**
- ¼ **pound thinly sliced hard salami, chopped**
- ½ **cup fresh basil leaves, thinly sliced**
- ¼ **cup grated Romano cheese**

1. Over each naan, spread 2 tablespoons pesto; top with ½ cup mozzarella, ⅓ cup zucchini, ¼ cup onion and one-quarter of the salami.
2. Grill, covered, over medium-low heat until mozzarella has melted and vegetables are tender, 4-6 minutes. Rotate naan halfway through grilling for evenly browned crust.
3. Remove from heat. Top each naan with basil and Romano; cut into thirds.

PER SERVING *2 pieces equals 391 cal., 24 g fat (9 g sat. fat), 51 mg chol., 1,276 mg sodium, 25 g carb., 1 g fiber, 20 g pro.*

(5)INGREDIENTS SLOW COOKER
Root Beer Apple Baked Beans

PREP: 20 MIN. • **COOK:** 45 MIN. • **MAKES:** 12 SERVINGS

- 6 **thick-sliced bacon strips, chopped**
- 4 **cans (16 ounces each) baked beans**
- 1 **can (21 ounces) apple pie filling**
- 1 **can (12 ounces) root beer**
- 1 **teaspoon ground ancho chili pepper, optional**
- 1 **cup shredded smoked cheddar cheese, optional**

1. Prepare campfire or grill for medium heat, using 32-36 charcoal briquettes or large wood chips.
2. In a 10-in. Dutch oven, cook bacon over campfire until crisp. Remove; discard drippings. Return bacon to pan; stir in baked beans, pie filling, root beer and, if desired, ancho chili pepper.
3. Cover Dutch oven. When briquettes or wood chips are covered with ash, place Dutch oven on top of 16-18 briquettes. Place 16-18 briquettes on pan cover. Cook 30-40 minutes to allow flavors to blend. If desired, sprinkle servings with cheese.

PER SERVING *¾ cup equals 255 cal., 5 g fat (2 g sat. fat), 16 mg chol., 778 mg sodium, 47 g carb., 9 g fiber, 10 g pro.*

GRILLED ZUCCHINI & PESTO PIZZA

All nine men in our family love roughing it outdoors. My bean dish with bacon and apples is a "must" to keep their outdoor energy going.
—**NANCY HEISHMAN** LAS VEGAS, NV

ROOT BEER APPLE BAKED BEANS

Spooky Soup Night

Double, double, **boil and bubble** your way to steamy **bowls** filled with fall veggies, fresh herbs and cozy spices. Add some **frightfully fun** sides.

FAST FIX ▶
Mummy-Wrapped Brie

My baked Brie appetizer is good enough to wake the dead. You can assemble it in advance and bake it right before the party if you have lots of prep to do.
—**MARION LOWERY** MEDFORD, OR

START TO FINISH: 30 MIN. • **MAKES:** 10 SERVINGS

- 1 package (17.3 ounces) frozen puff pastry, thawed
- ¼ cup apricot jam
- 1 round (16 ounces) Brie cheese
- 1 large egg
- 1 tablespoon water
  Apple slices
- 2 dried cranberries or raisins

1. Preheat oven to 400°. Unfold one sheet of puff pastry. On a lightly floured surface, roll pastry into a 14-in. square. Cut off corners to make a circle. Spread jam into a 4½-in. circle in center of pastry. Place Brie on top; fold pastry over cheese, trimming as necessary, and pinch edges to seal. Beat egg and water; brush over pastry.

2. Place on an ungreased baking sheet, seam side down. Roll remaining pastry into a 14-in. square. Cut four 1-in. strips; cut strips in half crosswise. Wrap strips around Brie, trimming as necessary. Discard scraps. Bake 10 minutes; brush again with egg wash. Bake until crust is golden brown, 10-15 minutes more. For eyes, cut two circles from apple slices; place on top of Brie. Top each circle with a dried cranberry. Serve warm with apple slices.

PER SERVING (calculated without apples) 372 cal., 24 g fat (10 g sat. fat), 64 mg chol., 426 mg sodium, 28 g carb. (4 g sugars, 3 g fiber), 13 g pro.

Bloody Mary Soup

After entertaining, I had leftover Bloody Mary mix. I added chicken broth and veggies to come up with a blockbuster soup. Make it with your favorite mix.
—**JOANNA JOHNSON** FLOWER MOUND, TX

PREP: 10 MIN. • **COOK:** 30 MIN. • **MAKES:** 16 SERVINGS

- 1 tablespoon olive oil
- 1 large onion, chopped
- 1 medium green pepper, chopped
- 5 garlic cloves, chopped
- 3 cans (14½ ounces each) stewed tomatoes, chopped
- 1 bottle (33.8 ounces) spicy Bloody Mary mix
- 1 carton (32 ounces) chicken broth
- 1 tablespoon Worcestershire sauce
- 1 teaspoon salt
- ½ teaspoon hot pepper sauce
- ½ teaspoon coarsely ground pepper
- 6 ounces fresh baby spinach (about 7½ cups)
  Additional Worcestershire and hot pepper sauce
  Pimiento-stuffed olives, optional

BLOODY MARY SOUP

MUMMY-WRAPPED BRIE

1. In a Dutch oven, heat oil over medium-high heat. Add onion and pepper; cook and stir until vegetables are tender, 8-10 minutes. Add the garlic and cook until fragrant, about 30 seconds. Stir in tomatoes; cook 2 minutes.

2. Add next six ingredients; bring to a boil. Reduce heat; simmer, covered, 10 minutes.

3. Stir in spinach; cook until it wilts, about 5 minutes. Soup will be chunky. Serve immediately with additional Worcestershire and hot pepper sauce. If desired, add olives to resemble eyes.

PER SERVING *1 cup equals 64 cal., 1 g fat (0 sat. fat), 1 mg chol., 805 mg sodium, 12 g carb. (8 g sugars, 1 g fiber), 2 g pro.*

QUICK BUTTERMILK CORN BREAD

WHITE BEAN & CHICKEN ENCHILADA SOUP

Quick Buttermilk Corn Bread

The tattered recipe card for this corn bread proves it's been a family favorite for years.
—**JUDY SELLGREN** GRAND RAPIDS, MI

START TO FINISH: 30 MIN. • **MAKES:** 8-9 SERVINGS

- 1¼ cups cornmeal
- 1 cup all-purpose flour
- ⅔ cup packed brown sugar
- ⅓ cup sugar
- 1 teaspoon baking soda
- ½ teaspoon salt
- 1 large egg
- 1 cup buttermilk
- ¾ cup canola oil

In large bowl, combine first six ingredients. Whisk the egg, buttermilk and oil; stir into dry ingredients until moistened. Place in a greased 9-in. round or square baking pan (pan will be full). Bake at 425° for 20-25 minutes or until a toothpick inserted near the center comes out clean. Cool 5 minutes.

PER SERVING *1 piece equals 390 cal., 19 g fat (3 g sat. fat), 25 mg chol., 314 mg sodium, 50 g carb., 2 g fiber, 5 g pro.*

White Bean & Chicken Enchilada Soup

I made this soup to please my daughters' craving for creaminess, my husband's for spice and mine for white beans. Garnish with jalapenos, sour cream and green onions.
—**DARCY GONZALEZ** PALMDALE, CA

PREP: 15 MIN. • **COOK:** 20 MIN. • **MAKES:** 8 SERVINGS

- 4 cans (15½ ounces each) great northern beans, rinsed and drained
- 1 to 1¼ pounds boneless skinless chicken breasts, cubed
- ½ medium onion, chopped
- 1 garlic clove, minced
- 2 cups frozen corn
- 1 can (10¾ ounces) condensed cream of chicken soup, undiluted
- 1 carton (32 ounces) reduced-sodium chicken broth
- 1 tablespoon ground cumin
- 2 seeded and chopped jalapeno peppers, divided
- 1 teaspoon pepper
- 2 green onions, chopped
  Sour cream, shredded cheddar cheese and tortilla chips

1. In a large stockpot, combine first eight ingredients. Add 1 chopped jalapeno and ground pepper. Simmer, covered, until chicken is no longer pink, 15-20 minutes.

2. Serve with remaining chopped jalapeno; top with green onions, sour cream, cheese and tortilla chips.

PER SERVING *1½ cups equals 301 cal., 5 g fat (1 g sat. fat), 41 mg chol., 1,121 mg sodium, 37 g carb. (1 g sugars, 12 g fiber), 25 g pro.*

PUMPKIN-LENTIL SOUP

Pumpkin-Lentil Soup

I was really craving a hot delicious soup—something filling and healthy. I looked around my kitchen for a few ingredients, then created this recipe. Pumpkin adds creamy richness and body.

—AMY BLOM MARIETTA, GA

PREP: 15 MIN. • **COOK:** 45 MIN.
MAKES: 6 SERVINGS

- 3 **cups water**
- 3 **cups reduced-sodium chicken broth**
- ⅔ **cup dried lentils, rinsed**
- 2 **large garlic cloves, minced**
- 1 **tablespoon ground cumin**
- 2 **teaspoons dried oregano**
- 1 **can (15 ounces) pinto beans, rinsed and drained**
- 1 **can (15 ounces) black beans, rinsed and drained**
- 1 **can (15 ounces) solid-pack pumpkin**
- ½ **cup mild salsa**
- ½ **teaspoon salt**
- 5 **cups fresh spinach, lightly packed**

1. In a 6-qt. stockpot, bring first six ingredients to a boil. Cook, covered, over medium heat until lentils are tender, 20-25 minutes.

2. Stir in beans, pumpkin, salsa and salt until blended; return to a boil. Reduce heat; simmer, uncovered, 20 minutes, stirring occasionally. Stir in spinach; cook until wilted, 3-5 minutes.

PER SERVING *1⅓ cups equals 244 cal., 1 g fat (0 sat. fat), 0 chol., 857 mg sodium, 44 g carb. (6 g sugars, 11 g fiber), 15 g pro.*

(5) INGREDIENTS

Bacon Cheddar Muffins

Cheddar cheese and bacon add hearty flavor to these delectable muffins. Calling for just a few ingredients, they're quick to stir up and handy to eat on the run.

—SUZANNE MCKINLEY LYONS, GA

PREP: 15 MIN. • **BAKE:** 20 MIN. + COOLING
MAKES: ABOUT 1 DOZEN

- 2 **cups biscuit/baking mix**
- ⅔ **cup 2% milk**
- ¼ **cup canola oil**
- 1 **large egg**
- 1 **cup (4 ounces) finely shredded sharp cheddar cheese**
- 8 **bacon strips, cooked and crumbled**

1. In a large bowl, combine the biscuit mix, milk, oil and egg just until moistened. Fold in cheddar cheese and bacon. Fill greased muffin cups three-fourths full.

2. Bake at 375° for 20 minutes or until a toothpick inserted near the center comes out clean. Cool for 10 minutes; remove from pan to a wire rack. Serve warm. Refrigerate leftovers.

PER SERVING *1 muffin equals 194 cal., 13 g fat (5 g sat. fat), 33 mg chol., 388 mg sodium, 13 g carb., trace fiber, 6 g pro.*

ADD A SIDE OF CREEPY CROSTINI

Spread toasted bread with Boursin cheese; top with two thinly sliced radishes, then top each radish slice with a caper to make eyes. Add a snip of chive above each radish to form the eyebrows.

Anti-Vampire Potion (Butternut Squash & Garlic Soup)

I remember making this velvety soup with my mom. Butternut squash gives it warm color, and garlic wards off any unfriendly spirits. Try using whipping cream for an extra smooth texture.

—STEVEN EDER LEBANON, PA

PREP: 15 MIN. • **COOK:** 25 MIN.
MAKES: 6 SERVINGS

- 2 **tablespoons butter**
- 1 **medium onion, chopped**
- 8 **garlic cloves, chopped**
- 1 **teaspoon ground cinnamon**
- ¼ to ½ **teaspoon ground nutmeg**
- 4 **cups peeled butternut squash, cut in 1-in. cubes**
- 2 **cups vegetable stock**
- 2 **cups half-and-half cream**
  Salt and pepper to taste
- 8 **cooked bacon strips, chopped**
- 1 **package (5.2 ounces) Boursin Garlic & Fine Herbs Gournay Cheese, crumbled**

1. In a large saucepan, melt butter over medium heat. Add onion and garlic; cook until tender, 3-4 minutes. Add cinnamon and nutmeg; cook 2 minutes.

2. Stir in the squash and vegetable stock. Bring to a boil. Reduce heat; simmer, covered, until squash is tender, 15-20 minutes.

3. Use an immersion blender or pulse soup in batches in blender until smooth. Return to pan; add half-and-half cream and salt and pepper to taste. Heat through, but do not boil. Serve immediately with bacon and crumbled cheese.

NOTE *Boursin Garlic & Fine Herbs Gournay Cheese has a firmer texture than the spreadable cheese product.*
PER SERVING *1 cup equals 388 cal., 28 g fat (17 g sat. fat), 92 mg chol., 697 mg sodium, 21 g carb. (7 g sugars, 3 g fiber), 12 g pro.*

Autumn Bisque

I like cozy comfort-food soups that taste creamy—but without the cream. This one's full of good stuff like rutabagas, leeks, fresh herbs and almond milk.

—MERRY GRAHAM NEWHALL, CA

PREP: 25 MIN. • **COOK:** 50 MIN.
MAKES: 14 CUPS (3½ QUARTS)

BUTTER-HERB BALL
- ¼ **cup buttery spread**
- 2 **teaspoons minced chives**
- 2 **teaspoons minced fresh parsley**
- ½ **teaspoon grated lemon peel**

BISQUE
- 2 **tablespoons olive oil**
- 2 **large rutabagas, peeled and cubed**
- 3 **medium leeks (white portion only), chopped**
- 1 **large celery root, peeled and cubed**
- 1 **large carrot, cubed**
- 3 **garlic cloves, minced**
- 7 **cups vegetable stock**
- 2 **teaspoons minced fresh thyme**
- 1½ **teaspoons minced fresh rosemary**
- 1 **teaspoon salt**
- ½ **teaspoon coarsely ground pepper**
- 2 **cups almond milk**
- 2 **tablespoons minced chives**

1. Combine buttery spread, chives, parsley and lemon peel; shape into 14 balls. Freeze in a single layer on a plate; transfer to a freezer-safe container. May be frozen up to 2 months.

2. For bisque, heat oil over medium heat in a Dutch oven. Add rutabagas, leeks, celery root and carrot; cook and stir 8 minutes. Add the garlic; cook 2 minutes longer. Stir in stock and seasonings; bring to a boil. Reduce heat; cover and simmer until vegetables are tender, 30-35 minutes.

3. Cool slightly. In a blender, pulse soup in batches until smooth. Return to pan. Stir in milk; heat through. To serve, sprinkle each portion with chives; top with a butter-herb ball.

PER SERVING *1 cup equals 125 cal., 6 g fat (1 g sat. fat), 0 chol., 576 mg sodium, 17 g carb. (8 g sugars, 4 g fiber), 2 g pro.* **Diabetic Exchanges:** *1 starch, ½ fat.*

AUTUMN BISQUE

Turkey Day Feast

Looking for a **new dish** for your Thanksgiving table? **Feast your eyes** on delectable turkey, bountiful sides and a **pretty raisin pie.**

APPLE-CRANBERRY STUFFING

(5)INGREDIENTS FAST FIX

Spinach & Pearl Onions

When I was a culinary student, this creamy dish wowed me, and I don't even like spinach. This side is a keeper!

—**CHELSEA PUCHEL** PICKENS, SC

START TO FINISH: 25 MIN. • **MAKES:** 8 SERVINGS

- ¼ cup butter, cubed
- 1 package (14.4 ounces) frozen pearl onions, thawed and drained
- 2 cups heavy whipping cream
- ½ cup grated Parmesan cheese
- ½ teaspoon salt
- ¼ teaspoon pepper
- 10 ounces fresh baby spinach (about 13 cups)

1. In a large skillet, heat butter over medium heat. Add pearl onions; cook and stir 6-8 minutes or until tender. Stir in cream. Bring to a boil; cook 6-8 minutes or until liquid is reduced by half.

2. Stir in cheese, salt and pepper. Add the spinach and cook, covered, 3-5 minutes or until spinach is wilted, stirring occasionally.

PER SERVING *½ cup equals 307 cal., 30 g fat (18 g sat. fat), 102 mg chol., 328 mg sodium, 8 g carb., 1 g fiber, 5 g pro.*

Apple-Cranberry Stuffing

I leave out the giblets my mom used in stuffing and bump up the apples, wild rice and cranberries instead.

—**MIRANDA ALLISON** SIMPSONVILLE, SC

PREP: 20 MIN. • **BAKE:** 40 MIN.
MAKES: 16 SERVINGS (¾ CUP EACH)

- ½ cup butter, cubed
- ½ cup chopped sweet onion
- 1 celery rib, chopped
- 12 cups seasoned stuffing cubes (about 20 ounces)
- 2 medium apples, finely chopped
- 2 cups cooked wild rice
- 1½ cups dried cranberries
- 3 teaspoons dried parsley flakes
- 1 teaspoon salt
- 1 teaspoon poultry seasoning
- ½ teaspoon pepper
- 1½ to 2 cups chicken broth

1. Preheat oven to 350°. In a 6-qt. stockpot, heat butter over medium heat. Add onion and celery; cook and stir 4-5 minutes or until tender. Add stuffing cubes, apples, rice, cranberries and seasonings; toss. Stir in enough broth to reach desired moistness.

2. Transfer to a greased 13x9-in. baking dish. Bake, covered, 30 minutes. Bake, uncovered, 10-15 minutes longer or until lightly browned.

PER SERVING *¾ cup equals 261 cal., 8 g fat (4 g sat. fat), 16 mg chol., 819 mg sodium, 45 g carb., 4 g fiber, 5 g pro.*

SPINACH & PEARL ONIONS

Roasted Squash, Carrots & Walnuts

After the turkey's done, I dial up the oven temperature and roast carrots and sweet butternut squash for this yummy side. Roasting the vegetables frees me up to start the gravy while the turkey rests.

—**LILY JULOW** LAWRENCEVILLE, GA

PREP: 15 MIN. • **BAKE:** 35 MIN. • **MAKES:** 8 SERVINGS

- 2 **pounds carrots (about 12 medium)**
- 1 **medium butternut squash (3 pounds), peeled and cubed**
- ¼ **cup packed brown sugar**
- ¼ **cup olive oil**
- 2 **teaspoons kosher salt**
- ½ **teaspoon ground cinnamon**
- ¼ **teaspoon ground nutmeg**
- 1 **cup chopped walnuts**

1. Preheat oven to 400°. Cut carrots in half lengthwise, then in half crosswise.
2. In a large bowl, toss squash and carrots with brown sugar, oil, salt, cinnamon and nutmeg. Transfer to two greased foil-lined 15x10x1-in. baking pans. Roast 30 minutes, stirring occasionally.
3. Sprinkle walnuts over vegetables. Roast 5-10 minutes longer or until vegetables are tender.
PER SERVING *305 cal., 17 g fat (2 g sat. fat), 0 chol., 567 mg sodium, 40 g carb., 10 g fiber, 5 g pro.*

Citrus & Herb Roasted Turkey Breast

Brining turkey breast with lemon, rosemary and orange juice makes it so moist and flavorful. It's the star attraction at our table.
—**FAY MORELAND** WICHITA FALLS, TX

PREP: 1 HOUR + CHILLING • **BAKE:** 2 HOURS + STANDING
MAKES: 10 SERVINGS

- 4 **cups water**
- ¾ **cup kosher salt**
- ¾ **cup sugar**
- 2 **medium lemons, quartered**
- 6 **fresh rosemary sprigs**
- 6 **fresh thyme sprigs**
- 8 **garlic cloves, halved**
- 1 **tablespoon coarsely ground pepper**
- 2 **cups cold apple juice**
- 2 **cups cold orange juice**
- 2 **large oven roasting bags**
- 1 **bone-in turkey breast (5 to 6 pounds)**

HERB BUTTER
- ⅓ **cup butter, softened**
- 4 **teaspoons grated lemon peel**
- 1 **tablespoon minced fresh rosemary**
- 1 **tablespoon minced fresh thyme**
- 1½ **teaspoons coarsely ground pepper**

SEASONED SALT BUTTER
- ¼ **cup butter, melted**
- 1½ **teaspoons seasoned salt**

1. In a 6-qt. stockpot, combine the first eight ingredients. Bring to a boil. Remove from heat. Add cold juices to brine; cool to room temperature.
2. Place one oven roasting bag inside the other. Place turkey breast inside both bags; pour in cooled brine. Seal bags, pressing out as much air as possible, and turn to coat. Place in a roasting pan. Refrigerate 8 hours or overnight, turning occasionally.
3. In a small bowl, beat herb butter ingredients until blended. Remove turkey from brine; rinse and pat dry. Discard brine. Place turkey on a rack in a 15x10x1-in. baking pan. With fingers, carefully loosen skin from turkey breast; rub herb butter under the skin. Secure skin to underside of breast with toothpicks. Refrigerate, covered, 18-24 hours.
4. Preheat oven to 425°. In a small bowl, mix butter and seasoned salt; brush over outside of turkey. Roast for 15 minutes.
5. Reduce oven setting to 325°. Roast 1¾-2¼ hours longer or until a thermometer reads 170°. (Cover loosely with foil if turkey browns too quickly.) Remove turkey from oven; tent with foil. Let stand 15 minutes before carving.
PER SERVING *6 ounces cooked turkey equals 411 cal., 23 g fat (10 g sat. fat), 151 mg chol., 482 mg sodium, 1 g carb., trace fiber, 48 g pro.*

CITRUS & HERB ROASTED TURKEY BREAST

Corn & Onion Souffle

I changed my dependable cheese souffle recipe to prepare it with corn. If you're souffle challenged, remember to hold off from adding the egg whites until just before you slip it in the oven.

—LILY JULOW LAWRENCEVILLE, GA

PREP: 25 MIN. • **BAKE:** 45 MIN.
MAKES: 10 SERVINGS

- 6 large eggs
- 2 tablespoons plus ½ cup cornmeal, divided
- 2 cups fresh or frozen corn, thawed
- 2 cups 2% milk
- 1 tablespoon sugar
- ¾ cup heavy whipping cream
- ½ cup butter, melted
- 1 tablespoon canola oil
- 1 cup chopped sweet onion
- 3 ounces cream cheese, softened
- 1 teaspoon plus ⅛ teaspoon salt, divided
- ½ teaspoon freshly ground pepper
- ⅛ teaspoon baking soda

1. Separate eggs; let stand at room temperature 30 minutes. Grease a 2½-qt. souffle dish; dust lightly with 2 tablespoons cornmeal.

2. Preheat oven to 350°. Place corn, milk and sugar in a blender; cover and process until smooth. Add cream and melted butter; cover and process 15-30 seconds longer.

3. In a large saucepan, heat oil over medium heat. Add onion; cook and stir 4-6 minutes or until tender. Stir in the corn mixture, cream cheese, 1 teaspoon salt, pepper and remaining cornmeal until heated through. Remove to a large bowl.

4. Whisk a small amount of hot mixture into egg yolks; return all to bowl, whisking constantly.

5. Beat egg whites with baking soda and remaining salt on high speed until stiff but not dry. With a spatula, gently stir a fourth of egg whites into corn mixture. Fold in remaining whites. Transfer to prepared dish. Bake for 45-50 minutes or until the top is deep golden brown and puffed and center appears set. Serve immediately.

PER SERVING 325 cal., 25 g fat (13 g sat. fat), 174 mg chol., 463 mg sodium, 19 g carb., 1 g fiber, 8 g pro.

Raisin Pecan Pie

I remember my grandmother Voltie and great aunt Ophelia making this Southern-style pie for Thanksgiving. It was always one of the many cakes and pies lined up for dessert.

—ANGIE PRICE BRADFORD, TN

PREP: 20 MIN. + CHILLING
BAKE: 35 MIN. + COOLING
MAKES: 8 SERVINGS

- Pastry for single-crust pie (9 inches)
- ½ cup boiling water
- ½ cup golden raisins
- 3 large eggs
- 1½ cups sugar
- ½ cup butter, melted
- 2 teaspoons cider vinegar
- 1 teaspoon vanilla extract
- ½ teaspoon ground cinnamon
- ½ teaspoon ground cloves
- ¼ teaspoon ground nutmeg
- ½ cup chopped pecans

1. On a lightly floured surface, roll dough to a ⅛-in.-thick circle; transfer to a 9-in. pie plate. Trim pastry to ½ in. beyond rim of plate; flute edge. Refrigerate 30 minutes. Preheat oven to 350°.

2. Pour boiling water over raisins in a small bowl; let stand 5 minutes. Drain. In a large bowl, beat eggs, sugar, melted butter, vinegar, vanilla and spices until blended. Stir in pecans and drained raisins. Pour into pastry shell.

3. Bake on a lower oven rack 35-40 minutes or until filling is set. Cool on a wire rack. Refrigerate leftovers.

PASTRY FOR SINGLE-CRUST PIE (9 INCHES) *Combine 1¼ cups all-purpose flour and ¼ teaspoon salt; cut in ½ cup cold butter until crumbly. Gradually add 3-5 tablespoons ice water, tossing with a fork until dough holds together when pressed. Wrap in plastic wrap and refrigerate 1 hour.*

PER SERVING *1 piece equals 524 cal., 30 g fat (16 g sat. fat), 130 mg chol., 275 mg sodium, 61 g carb., 2 g fiber, 6 g pro.*

RAISIN PECAN PIE

Creole Roasted Turkey with Holy Trinity Stuffing

I jazz up turkey Creole-style with the trinity of onions, bell peppers and celery—plus a stuffing that gets hotter and hotter the longer it sits.

—ERIC OLSSON MACOMB, MI

PREP: 15 MIN.
BAKE: 3 HOURS 35 MIN. + STANDING
MAKES: 16 SERVINGS

- 1 **large onion, cut into 1-inch pieces**
- 1 **medium green pepper, cut into 1-inch pieces**
- 2 **celery ribs, chopped**
- 10 **pepperoncini**
- 3 **garlic cloves, minced**
- 1 **turkey (14 to 16 pounds)**
- 1 **cup butter, softened**
- 3 **tablespoons Creole seasoning**

1. Preheat oven to 400°. Place onion, pepper, celery, pepperoncini and garlic in turkey cavity. Tuck wings under turkey; tie drumsticks together. Place on a rack in a shallow roasting pan, breast side up. In a small bowl, beat butter and Creole seasoning; rub over turkey. Roast, uncovered, 20 minutes.
2. Reduce oven setting to 325°. Roast for 3¼-3¾ hours longer or until a thermometer inserted in thickest part of thigh reads 170°-175°. (Cover loosely with foil if turkey browns too quickly.)
3. Remove turkey from oven; tent with foil. Let stand 20 minutes before carving. Skim fat from pan drippings; serve drippings with turkey and vegetable mixture.

PER SERVING *9 ounces cooked turkey with ¼ cup vegetable mixture equals 575 cal., 33 g fat (14 g sat. fat), 245 mg chol., 702 mg sodium, 2 g carb., trace fiber, 64 g pro.*

DID YOU KNOW?

The mixing of celery, onion and green bell pepper is a classic Creole combination called holy trinity or Cajun mirepoix. Standard mirepoix uses carrots instead of green pepper.

SWEET POTATO, ORANGE & PINEAPPLE CRUNCH

I combined my two absolute favorite sweet potato casseroles in the world to create my own version for the holiday table.

—LISA VARNER EL PASO, TX

Sweet Potato, Orange & Pineapple Crunch

PREP: 35 MIN. • **BAKE:** 40 MIN.
MAKES: 12 SERVINGS (½ CUP EACH)

- 2 **pounds sweet potatoes, peeled and cubed (about 6 cups)**
- ¾ **cup sugar**
- 1 **can (8 ounces) crushed pineapple, drained**
- 2 **large eggs, lightly beaten**
- ½ **cup sour cream or plain yogurt**
- ½ **teaspoon grated orange peel**
- ¼ **cup orange juice**
- ¼ **cup butter, melted**
- 1 **teaspoon vanilla extract**

TOPPING

- 1 **cup flaked coconut**
- 1 **cup chopped pecans**
- 1 **cup packed brown sugar**
- ½ **cup all-purpose flour**
- ¼ **cup butter, melted**

1. Preheat oven to 350°. Place sweet potatoes in a large saucepan; add water to cover. Bring to a boil over high heat. Reduce the heat to medium; cook, uncovered, 10-15 minutes or until tender. Drain.
2. Place sweet potatoes in a large bowl; mash potatoes. Stir in sugar, pineapple, eggs, sour cream, orange peel, juice, butter and vanilla; transfer to a greased 13x9-in. baking dish. For topping, in a large bowl, mix coconut, pecans, brown sugar and flour. Add butter; mix until crumbly. Sprinkle over top.
3. Bake, uncovered, 40-45 minutes or until heated through and topping is golden brown.

PER SERVING *½ cup equals 432 cal., 20 g fat (9 g sat. fat), 58 mg chol., 110 mg sodium, 62 g carb., 4 g fiber, 4 g pro.*

Christmas Dinner

Hang the **wreath,** clear off the **buffet** and whip up a big batch of holiday **cheer.** Tell the family to come on **home for Christmas.**

EAT SMART

Spinach Salad with Raspberries & Candied Walnuts

I created a bright spinach salad with raspberries for Christmas dinner. Even those who turn up their noses at spinach change their minds after the first bite.

—**LORY AUCELLUZZO** SIMI VALLEY, CA

PREP: 15 MIN. • **BAKE:** 25 MIN. + COOLING • **MAKES:** 8 SERVINGS

- 1 **large egg white**
- ¾ **teaspoon vanilla extract**
- 2 **cups walnut halves**
- ½ **cup sugar**

DRESSING
- ¼ **cup canola oil**
- 2 **tablespoons cider vinegar**
- 1 **tablespoon sugar**
- 1½ **teaspoons light corn syrup**
- 1 **teaspoon poppy seeds**
- ¼ **teaspoon salt**
- ¼ **teaspoon ground mustard**

SALAD
- 8 **ounces fresh baby spinach (about 10 cups)**
- 1½ **cups fresh raspberries**

1. Preheat oven to 300°. In a small bowl, whisk egg white and vanilla until frothy. Stir in walnuts. Sprinkle with sugar; toss to coat evenly. Spread in a single layer in a greased 15x10x1-in. baking pan.

2. Bake 25-30 minutes or until lightly browned, stirring every 10 minutes. Spread on waxed paper to cool completely.

3. In a small bowl, whisk dressing ingredients until blended. Place spinach in a large bowl. Drizzle with dressing; toss to coat. Sprinkle with raspberries and 1 cup candied walnuts (save remaining walnuts for another use).

PER SERVING *1½ cups equals 171 cal., 13 g fat (1 g sat. fat), 0 chol., 100 mg sodium, 12 g carb., 3 g fiber, 3 g pro.* **Diabetic Exchanges:** *1½ fat, 1 starch, 1 vegetable.*

QUICK & EASY AU GRATIN POTATOES

ROASTED ITALIAN GREEN BEANS & TOMATOES

Roasted Italian Green Beans & Tomatoes

When you roast green beans and tomatoes, their flavors really shine through. The vibrant colors light up our holiday table.

—**BRITTANY ALLYN** MESA, AZ

START TO FINISH: 25 MIN. • **MAKES:** 8 SERVINGS

- 1½ pounds fresh green beans, trimmed and halved
- 1 tablespoon olive oil
- 1 teaspoon Italian seasoning
- ½ teaspoon salt
- 2 cups grape tomatoes, halved
- ½ cup grated Parmesan cheese

1. Preheat oven to 425°. Place green beans in a 15x10x1-in. baking pan coated with cooking spray. Mix the oil, Italian seasoning and salt; drizzle over beans. Toss to coat. Roast 10 minutes, stirring once.

2. Add tomatoes to pan. Roast 4-6 minutes longer or until beans are crisp-tender and tomatoes are softened. Sprinkle with cheese.

PER SERVING ¾ cup equals 70 cal., 3 g fat (1 g sat. fat), 4 mg chol., 231 mg sodium, 8 g carb., 3 g fiber, 4 g pro. **Diabetic Exchanges:** 1 vegetable, ½ fat.

Quick & Easy au Gratin Potatoes

On Christmas night, a friend serves these creamy, cheesy potatoes when we gather together to celebrate with lifelong friends and our grown children.

—**CAROL BLUE** BARNESVILLE, PA

PREP: 10 MIN. • **BAKE:** 50 MIN.
MAKES: 12 SERVINGS (¾ CUP EACH)

- 2 cups (16 ounces) sour cream
- 1 can (10¾ ounces) condensed cream of chicken soup, undiluted
- ½ teaspoon salt
- ¼ teaspoon pepper
- 1 package (30 ounces) frozen shredded hash brown potatoes, thawed
- 2 cups (8 ounces) shredded cheddar cheese
- 1 small onion, chopped
- 2 cups crushed cornflakes
- ¼ cup butter, melted

1. Preheat oven to 350°. In a large bowl, mix sour cream, condensed soup, salt and pepper; stir in potatoes, cheese and onion. Transfer to a greased 13x9-in. baking dish.

2. In a small bowl, mix crushed cornflakes and melted butter; sprinkle over potato mixture. Bake, uncovered, 50-60 minutes or until golden brown.

PER SERVING ¾ cup equals 394 cal., 22 g fat (14 g sat. fat), 70 mg chol., 680 mg sodium, 36 g carb., 2 g fiber, 11 g pro.

SPINACH SALAD WITH RASPBERRIES & CANDIED WALNUTS

Italian Herb-Crusted Pork Loin

I like to change things up during the holidays by roasting pork loin with my favorite herbs and veggies. This dish is a showpiece that really dazzles my family.

—KIM PALMER KINGSTON, GA

PREP: 15 MIN. + CHILLING
BAKE: 50 MIN. + STANDING
MAKES: 8 SERVINGS

- 3 **tablespoons olive oil**
- 5 **garlic cloves, minced**
- 1 **teaspoon salt**
- 1 **teaspoon each dried basil, thyme and rosemary, crushed**
- ½ **teaspoon Italian seasoning**
- ½ **teaspoon pepper**
- 1 **boneless pork loin roast (3 to 4 pounds)**
- 8 **medium carrots, halved lengthwise**
- 2 **medium onions, quartered**

1. In a small bowl, mix oil, garlic and seasonings; rub over roast. Arrange carrots and onions on the bottom of a 13x9-in. baking pan. Place roast over vegetables, fat side up. Refrigerate, covered, 1 hour.

2. Preheat oven to 475°. Roast meat and vegetables 20 minutes.

3. Reduce oven setting to 425°. Roast 30-40 minutes longer or until a thermometer reads 145° and vegetables are tender. Remove roast from oven; tent with foil. Let stand 20 minutes before slicing.

PER SERVING *295 cal., 13 g fat (4 g sat. fat), 85 mg chol., 388 mg sodium, 9 g carb., 2 g fiber, 34 g pro.* **Diabetic Exchanges:** *5 lean meat, 1 vegetable, 1 fat.*

READER RAVE

This is an excellent roast. It comes out moist, tender and flavorful. I made different veggies and cooked them separately...red cabbage with apples and mashed potatoes.

--ANNRMS TASTEOFHOME.COM

ITALIAN HERB-CRUSTED PORK LOIN

CRANBERRY PESTO

Cranberry Pesto

I updated a classic Italian pesto to include cranberries and walnuts. It's so good slathered on pork loin, pasta or even turkey sandwiches.

—AYSHA SCHURMAN AMMON, ID

START TO FINISH: 10 MIN.
MAKES: 1¼ CUPS

- ⅔ **cup loosely packed basil leaves**
- ½ **cup dried cranberries**
- ¼ **cup chopped walnuts**
- 1 **green onion, chopped**
- 3 **garlic cloves, coarsely chopped**
- ½ **teaspoon pepper**
- ¼ **teaspoon salt**
- ⅔ **cup olive oil**

Place the first seven ingredients in a food processor; pulse until coarsely chopped. Continue processing while gradually adding oil in a steady stream. Store in an airtight container in the refrigerator for up to 1 week.

PER SERVING *2 tablespoons equals 168 cal., 16 g fat (2 g sat. fat), 0 chol., 60 mg sodium, 6 g carb., 1 g fiber, 1 g pro.*

Pina Colada Bundt Cake

We named this Bundt cake a pina colada—because it has coconut, rum and pineapple. It's a dazzling finish to a big holiday spread.

—DEBRA KEIL OWASSO, OK

PREP: 15 MIN. • **BAKE:** 45 MIN. + COOLING
MAKES: 12 SERVINGS

- 1 **package white cake mix (regular size)**
- 1 **package (3.4 ounces) instant coconut cream pudding mix**
- 1 **cup canola oil**
- ¾ **cup water**
- 2 **large eggs**
- ¼ **cup rum**
- 1 **cup drained crushed pineapple**

GLAZE

- 2 **cups confectioners' sugar, divided**
- 2 **tablespoons unsweetened pineapple juice**
- ¼ **cup cream of coconut**
- 1 **tablespoon rum**
- ¼ **cup flaked coconut**

1. Grease and flour a 10-in. fluted tube pan. In a large bowl, combine cake mix, pudding mix, oil, water, eggs and rum; beat on low speed 30 seconds. Beat on medium 2 minutes. Stir in pineapple. Transfer batter to prepared pan. Bake at 350° for 45-50 minutes or until a toothpick inserted in center comes out clean. Cool cake for 15 minutes before removing to a wire rack.

2. In a small bowl, mix 1 cup confectioners' sugar and pineapple juice; brush over warm cake. Cool cake completely.

3. In another bowl, mix cream of coconut, rum and remaining confectioners' sugar; drizzle over cake. Sprinkle with coconut.

NOTE *This recipe was tested with Coco Lopez cream of coconut. Look for it in the liquor section. To remove cakes easily, use solid shortening to grease plain and fluted tube pans.*

PER SERVING *1 slice equals 495 cal., 25 g fat (5 g sat. fat), 31 mg chol., 357 mg sodium, 64 g carb., 1 g fiber, 3 g pro.*

PINA COLADA BUNDT CAKE

BLACKBERRY BRANDY SLUSH

Triple Ginger Cookies

PREP: 20 MIN. + CHILLING
BAKE: 15 MIN./BATCH + COOLING
MAKES: ABOUT 2½ DOZEN

- ½ **cup butter, softened**
- ½ **cup packed brown sugar**
- 1 **large egg**
- 3 **tablespoons molasses**
- ½ **teaspoon grated fresh gingerroot**
- 2¼ **cups all-purpose flour**
- ½ **teaspoon baking powder**
- ½ **teaspoon ground ginger**
- ¼ **teaspoon salt**
- ¼ **teaspoon baking soda**

ICING

- ½ **cup confectioners' sugar**
- 2 **to 3 teaspoons water**
- ¼ **cup finely chopped crystallized ginger**

1. Preheat oven to 350°. In a large bowl, cream butter and brown sugar until light and fluffy. Beat in egg, molasses and fresh ginger. In another bowl, whisk flour, baking powder, ground ginger, salt and baking soda; gradually beat into creamed mixture. Refrigerate, covered, 2 hours or until firm enough to handle.
2. Shape tablespoonfuls of dough into balls; place 1-in. apart on ungreased baking sheets. Flatten slightly with bottom of a glass. Bake 12-14 minutes or until set and edges begin to brown. Remove from pans to wire racks to cool completely.
3. For icing, in a small bowl, mix the confectioners' sugar and enough water to reach desired consistency. Drizzle over cookies; sprinkle with chopped crystallized ginger.
PER SERVING *1 cookie equals 97 cal., 3 g fat (2 g sat. fat), 15 mg chol., 64 mg sodium, 16 g carb., trace fiber, 1 g pro.*

TOP TIP

Dark brown sugar contains more molasses than light or golden brown sugar. The types are generally interchangeable in recipes. But if you prefer a bolder flavor, choose dark brown sugar.

[5]INGREDIENTS

Blackberry Brandy Slush

We wanted a grown-up twist on a favorite slushy, so we spiked it with blackberry brandy. Here's a refreshing must-have for your next party.
—**LINDSEY SPINLER** SOBIESKI, WI

PREP: 10 MIN. + FREEZING
MAKES: 28 SERVINGS (1 CUP EACH)

- 8 **cups water**
- 2 **cups sugar**
- 3 **cups blackberry brandy**
- 1 **can (12 ounces) frozen lemonade concentrate, thawed**
- 1 **can (12 ounces) frozen grape juice concentrate, thawed**
- 14 **cups lemon-lime soda, chilled**

1. In a large bowl, stir water and sugar until sugar is dissolved. Stir in brandy and juice concentrates. Transfer to freezer containers; freeze overnight.
2. To serve, place about ½ cup brandy mixture in each glass; top with ½ cup of soda.
PER SERVING *1 cup equals 235 cal., trace fat (trace sat. fat), 0 chol., 18 mg sodium, 51 g carb., trace fiber, trace pro.*

My dad loved ginger cookies. I've tinkered with the recipe my grandma handed down by using fresh, ground and crystallized ginger for more pizzazz.
—**TRISHA KRUSE** EAGLE, ID

TRIPLE GINGER COOKIES

Merry Sweets

Spread **yuletide cheer** with platters and tins of these sweet treets. **Create smiles** by the dozen when you share these **cookies** and treats.

Snow Day Cookies

Clear your pantry to bake up these chocolate chip cookies loaded with goodies. We add oats, M&M's, pretzels and even potato chips.

—**BRITTNEY MUSGROVE** DALLAS, GA

PREP: 25 MIN. • **BAKE:** 15 MIN./BATCH • **MAKES:** ABOUT 2½ DOZEN

- 1 **cup butter, softened**
- 1¼ **cups packed brown sugar**
- 2 **large eggs**
- 3 **teaspoons vanilla extract**
- 2 **teaspoons 2% milk**
- 2 **cups old-fashioned oats**
- 1¾ **cups all-purpose flour**
- 1 **teaspoon baking soda**
- ½ **teaspoon salt**
- 1½ **cups coarsely crushed potato chips**
- 1½ **cups coarsely crushed pretzels**
- 1 **cup (6 ounces) semisweet chocolate chips**
- ¾ **cup milk chocolate M&M's**

1. Preheat oven to 350°. In a large bowl, cream butter and brown sugar until light and fluffy. Beat in eggs, vanilla and milk. In another bowl, whisk oats, flour, baking soda and salt; gradually beat into creamed mixture. Stir in potato chips, pretzels, chocolate chips and M&M's.
2. Drop dough by scant ¼ cupfuls 2 in. apart onto ungreased baking sheets; flatten slightly. Bake 14-16 minutes or until edges are golden brown (centers will be light). Cool on pans 2 minutes. Remove to wire racks to cool.
PER SERVING *1 cookie equals 226 cal., 11 g fat (6 g sat. fat), 29 mg chol., 223 mg sodium, 31 g carb., 1 g fiber, 3 g pro.*

Pumpkin Cookies with Penuche Frosting

For our parties, we have pumpkin cookies with penuche, a caramel-flavored frosting of brown sugar, butter and milk. We sometimes use home-canned pumpkin.

—**PRISCILLA ANDERSON** SALT LAKE CITY, UT

PREP: 25 MIN. • **BAKE:** 10 MIN./BATCH + COOLING
MAKES: ABOUT 7 DOZEN

- 1 **cup butter, softened**
- ½ **cup sugar**
- ½ **cup packed brown sugar**
- 1 **large egg**
- 1 **cup canned pumpkin**
- 2 **teaspoons vanilla extract**
- 2 **cups all-purpose flour**
- 1 **teaspoon baking powder**
- 1 **teaspoon baking soda**
- 1 **teaspoon ground cinnamon**
- ½ **teaspoon salt**
- ¾ **cup chopped pecans**

FROSTING

- ¼ **cup packed brown sugar**
- 3 **tablespoons butter**
- ¼ **cup 2% milk**
- 2½ **to 3 cups confectioners' sugar**

1. Preheat oven to 350°. In a large bowl, cream butter and sugars until light and fluffy. Beat in egg, pumpkin and vanilla. In another bowl, whisk flour, baking powder, baking soda, cinnamon and salt; gradually beat into creamed mixture. Stir in pecans.
2. Drop dough by rounded teaspoonfuls 2 in. apart onto ungreased baking sheets. Bake 9-11 minutes or until edges are light brown. Remove from pans to wire racks to cool completely.
3. For frosting, in a small saucepan, bring brown sugar and butter to a boil. Cook and stir over medium heat 1 minute. Remove from heat; cool 10 minutes. Transfer to a large bowl; beat in milk. Gradually beat in enough confectioners' sugar to achieve spreading consistency. Frost cookies.
PER SERVING *1 cookie equals 69 cal., 3 g fat (2 g sat. fat), 9 mg chol., 56 mg sodium, 9 g carb., trace fiber, 1 g pro.*

PUMPKIN COOKIES WITH PENUCHE FROSTING

SPRITZ COOKIES

French Christmas Cookies

I make batches of these and store them in the freezer, but they always seem to disappear before I've even had a chance to add the chocolate topping.

—JUDY WILDER MANKATO, MN

PREP: 20 MIN. • **BAKE:** 10 MIN./BATCH + COOLING
MAKES: ABOUT 2½ DOZEN

- ½ cup butter, softened
- 1 cup packed brown sugar
- 1 cup 2% milk
- 2¾ cups graham cracker crumbs
- 2 cups finely chopped walnuts
- 2 cups milk chocolate chips

TOPPING
- ½ cup milk chocolate chips, melted

1. Preheat oven to 375°. In a large bowl, cream butter and brown sugar until light and fluffy. Beat in milk. Gradually beat cracker crumbs into creamed mixture. Stir in walnuts and 2 cups chocolate chips.

2. Fill 2-in. foil baking cup liners three-fourths full. Place 1 in. apart in 15x10x1-in. baking pans. Bake 10-12 minutes or until set. Remove from pans to wire racks to cool completely.

3. Drizzle with melted chocolate; let stand until set. Store in an airtight container in the refrigerator.

PER SERVING *1 cookie equals 224 cal., 13 g fat (5 g sat. fat), 12 mg chol., 85 mg sodium, 24 g carb., 1 g fiber, 3 g pro.*

Spritz Cookies

These tender little cookies are like eye-catching gems on my Christmas cookie tray. The dough is easy to work with, so it's fun to make these into a variety of festive shapes.

—BEVERLY LAUNIUS SANDWICH, IL

PREP: 20 MIN. • **BAKE:** 10 MIN./BATCH + COOLING
MAKES: ABOUT 7½ DOZEN

- 1 cup butter, softened
- 1¼ cups confectioners' sugar
- ½ teaspoon salt
- 1 large egg
- 1 teaspoon vanilla extract
- ½ teaspoon almond extract
- 2½ cups all-purpose flour

GLAZE
- 1 cup confectioners' sugar
- 2 to 3 tablespoons water
  Colored sugar and sprinkles

1. Preheat oven to 375°. In a large bowl, cream butter, confectioners' sugar and salt until light and fluffy. Beat in egg and extracts. Gradually beat flour into creamed mixture.

2. Using a cookie press fitted with a disk of your choice, press dough 2 in. apart onto ungreased baking sheets. Bake 6-8 minutes or until set (do not brown). Remove to wire racks to cool completely.

3. In a small bowl, mix confectioners' sugar and enough water to reach desired consistency. Dip cookies in glaze; decorate as desired. Let stand until set.

PER SERVING *1 cookie equals 43 cal., 2 g fat (1 g sat. fat), 7 mg chol., 30 mg sodium, 6 g carb., trace fiber, trace pro.*

FRENCH CHRISTMAS COOKIES

SCANDINAVIAN
ALMOND BARS

Snickerdoodle Crisps

This classic cookie from New England can be made two ways: soft or crunchy. My version spiced with cinnamon, ginger and nutmeg is crispy to perfection.

—**JENNI SHARP** MILWAUKEE, WI

PREP: 20 MIN. + CHILLING
BAKE: 10 MIN./BATCH
MAKES: ABOUT 5 DOZEN

- 1 **cup butter, softened**
- 2 **cups sugar**
- 2 **large eggs**
- 2 **teaspoons vanilla extract**
- 3 **cups all-purpose flour**
- 4 **teaspoons ground cinnamon**
- 2 **teaspoons ground ginger**
- ¾ **teaspoon ground nutmeg**
- ½ **teaspoon ground allspice**
- 2 **teaspoons cream of tartar**
- 1 **teaspoon baking soda**
- ½ **teaspoon salt**

SPICED SUGAR
- ⅓ **cup sugar**
- 1 **teaspoon ground cinnamon**
- ¾ **teaspoon ground ginger**
- ¼ **teaspoon ground nutmeg**
- ¼ **teaspoon ground allspice**

1. Cream butter and sugar until light and fluffy. Beat in eggs and vanilla. In another bowl, whisk flour, spices, cream of tartar, baking soda and salt; gradually beat into creamed mixture.
2. Divide dough in half; shape each into an 8-in.-long roll. Wrap in plastic wrap; refrigerate 2 hours or until firm.
3. Preheat oven to 350°. In a small bowl, mix spiced sugar ingredients. Unwrap and cut dough crosswise into ¼-in. slices; press cookies into sugar mixture to coat both sides or sprinkle sugar mixture over cookies. Place 2 in. apart on greased baking sheets. Bake 7-9 minutes or until edges are light brown. Cool on pans 2 minutes. Remove to wire racks to cool.
FREEZE OPTION *Freeze wrapped logs in a resealable plastic freezer bag. To use, unwrap frozen logs and cut into slices. If necessary, let dough stand a few minutes at room temperature before cutting. Bake as directed.*
PER SERVING *1 cookie equals 84 cal., 3 g fat (2 g sat. fat), 14 mg chol., 68 mg sodium, 13 g carb., trace fiber, 1 g pro.*

Scandinavian Almond Bars

Delicate and crisp with a rich butter and almond flavor, these cookies are irresistible. They're a tradition for us and definitely always worth making.

—**MELVA BAUMER** MILLMONT, PA

PREP: 20 MIN.
BAKE: 20 MIN./BATCH + COOLING
MAKES: ABOUT 4 DOZEN

- ½ **cup butter, softened**
- 1 **cup sugar**
- 1 **large egg**
- ½ **teaspoon almond extract**
- 1¾ **cups all-purpose flour**
- 2 **teaspoons baking powder**
- ¼ **teaspoon salt**
- 1 **tablespoon 2% milk**
- ½ **cup sliced almonds, chopped**

ICING
- 1 **cup confectioners' sugar**
- ¼ **teaspoon almond extract**
- 1 **to 2 tablespoons 2% milk**

1. Preheat oven to 325°. In a large bowl, cream butter and sugar until light and fluffy. Beat in egg and extract. In another bowl, whisk flour, baking powder and salt; gradually beat into creamed mixture.
2. Divide dough into four portions. Roll or pat each portion into a 12x3-in. rectangle. Place 5 in. apart on greased baking sheets. Brush with milk; sprinkle with almonds.
3. Bake 18-20 minutes or until firm and edges are light brown. Cool on pans 5 minutes; cut diagonally into 1-in. slices. Remove to wire racks to cool completely.
4. In a small bowl, mix confectioner's sugar, extract and enough milk to reach desired consistency; drizzle over bars.
PER SERVING *1 cookie equals 67 cal., 3 g fat (1 g sat. fat), 9 mg chol., 46 mg sodium, 10 g carb., trace fiber, 1 g pro.*

Coffee Shortbread

PREP: 15 MIN.
BAKE: 20 MIN./BATCH + COOLING
MAKES: ABOUT 2½ DOZEN

- 1 cup butter, softened
- ½ cup packed brown sugar
- ¼ cup sugar
- 2 tablespoons instant coffee granules
- ¼ teaspoon salt
- 2 cups all-purpose flour
- ½ cup semisweet chocolate chips
- 2 teaspoons shortening, divided
- ½ cup white baking chips

1. Preheat oven to 300°. In a large bowl, cream butter, sugars, coffee granules and salt until light and fluffy; gradually beat flour into creamed mixture.

2. On a lightly floured surface, roll dough to ¼-in. thickness. Cut with floured 2-in. cookie cutters. Place 2 in. apart on ungreased baking sheets.

3. Bake 20-22 minutes or until set. Remove to wire racks to cool completely. In a microwave, melt chocolate chips and 1 teaspoon shortening; stir until smooth. Repeat with baking chips and remaining shortening. Drizzle over cookies; refrigerate until set. Store cookies between pieces of waxed paper in an airtight container.

PER SERVING *1 cookie equals 137 cal., 8 g fat (5 g sat. fat), 17 mg chol., 73 mg sodium, 15 g carb., trace fiber, 1 g pro.*

When you need a treat for brunch, bake some of these coffee-flavored shortbreads. The chocolate drizzle is surprisingly easy.
—**DIXIE TERRY** GOREVILLE, IL

COFFEE SHORTBREAD

Crackle Cookies

Because these tender cookies crack on top, my granddaughter thinks I make a mistake when I bake them. They're very close to Mama's wonderful recipe for chocolate cookies.

—**RUTH CAIN** HARTSELLE, AL

PREP: 20 MIN. + CHILLING
BAKE: 10 MIN./BATCH
MAKES: ABOUT 1½ DOZEN

- ½ cup sugar
- 2 tablespoons canola oil
- 1 ounce unsweetened chocolate, melted and cooled
- ½ teaspoon vanilla extract
- 1 large egg
- ½ cup all-purpose flour
- ½ teaspoon baking powder
- ⅛ teaspoon salt
  Confectioners' sugar

1. In a bowl, beat sugar, oil, chocolate and vanilla until blended. Beat in egg. In another bowl, whisk flour, baking powder and salt; gradually beat into sugar mixture. Refrigerate, covered, 2 hours or until firm enough to handle.
2. Preheat oven to 350°. With sugared hands, shape dough into 1-in. balls; roll in confectioners' sugar. Place 2 in. apart on greased baking sheets. Bake 10-12 minutes or until set. Remove from pans to wire racks to cool.
PER SERVING *1 cookie equals 60 cal., 3 g fat (1 g sat. fat), 10 mg chol., 32 mg sodium, 9 g carb., trace fiber, 1 g pro.*

CRACKLE COOKIES

Snowman Cookies

I wrap these chocolate-capped snowmen in colored tissue and place them in holiday containers. Like real snowmen, they don't last long.

—**BETTY TABB** MIFFLINTOWN, PA

PREP: 20 MIN. + CHILLING
BAKE: 20 MIN./BATCH + COOLING
MAKES: 4 DOZEN

- 1 cup butter, softened
- 1 package (8 ounces) cream cheese, softened
- 2 cups sugar
- 1 large egg
- 1 teaspoon vanilla extract
- ¼ teaspoon almond extract
- ¼ teaspoon coconut extract
- 3½ cups all-purpose flour
- 1 teaspoon baking powder
  Miniature semisweet chocolate chips, and green and red M&M's minis

FROSTING
- 1 cup confectioners' sugar
- ⅛ teaspoon coconut extract
- 2 to 4 teaspoons 2% milk
  Red and/or green food coloring
  Miniature milk chocolate kisses, unwrapped

1. In a large bowl, cream butter, cream cheese and sugar until light and fluffy. Beat in egg and extracts. In another bowl, whisk flour and baking powder; gradually beat into creamed mixture. Refrigerate, covered, overnight.
2. Preheat oven to 325°. Shape dough into forty-eight 1-in. balls, forty-eight ¾-in. balls and forty-eight ½-in. balls. On ungreased baking sheets, place one ball of each size, side by side, for each snowman.
3. Bake 18-20 minutes or until light brown. Remove from oven; cool on pans 2 minutes. Press on chocolate chips for eyes and M&M's for buttons. Carefully remove from pans to wire racks to cool completely.
4. For frosting, in a small bowl, beat confectioners' sugar, extract and enough milk to reach a piping consistency. If two colors of frosting are desired, transfer half of the frosting to another bowl and tint with a different food coloring.
5. Cut a small hole in a corner of a food-safe plastic bag; fill with frosting. Pipe scarves on snowmen. Use frosting to attach chocolate kisses for hats.
PER SERVING *1 cookie equals 139 cal., 6 g fat (4 g sat. fat), 20 mg chol., 60 mg sodium, 20 g carb., trace fiber, 2 g pro.*

SNOWMAN COOKIES

Slice 'n' Bake Lemon Gems

Cookies are meant to brighten someone's day. I like to make a lot of these lemony treats so I can fill the dessert tray with happiness.

—**DELORES EDGECOMB** ATLANTA, NY

PREP: 25 MIN. + CHILLING
BAKE: 10 MIN./BATCH + COOLING
MAKES: ABOUT 2 DOZEN

- ¾ **cup butter, softened**
- ½ **cup confectioners' sugar**
- 1 **tablespoon grated lemon peel**
- 1 **cup all-purpose flour**
- ½ **cup cornstarch**
- ¼ **cup colored sugar or nonpareils**

ICING

- 1 **cup confectioners' sugar**
- ½ **teaspoon grated lemon peel**
- 2 **tablespoons lemon juice**

1. In a small bowl, cream butter and confectioners' sugar until light and fluffy. Beat in lemon peel. In another bowl, whisk flour and cornstarch; gradually beat into creamed mixture. Refrigerate, covered, 1 hour or until easy to handle.

2. Shape into a 7-in.-long roll (about 1¾-in. diameter); roll in colored sugar. Wrap in plastic wrap; refrigerate 2-3 hours or until firm.

3. Preheat oven to 375°. Unwrap and cut dough crosswise into ¼-in. slices. Place 1 in. apart on ungreased baking sheets. Bake 9-11 minutes or until set and edges are light brown. Cool on pans 1 minute. Remove to wire racks to cool completely.

4. In a small bowl, mix the icing ingredients; spread over cookies. Let stand until set.

PER SERVING *1 cookie equals 117 cal., 6 g fat (4 g sat. fat), 15 mg chol., 46 mg sodium, 16 g carb., trace fiber, 1 g pro.*

DID YOU KNOW?

You can often use lemon and lime juice and peel interchangeably in recipes to achieve a different flavor. To substitute orange, though, you'll need to keep a little lemon or lime to spark up the flavor.

Date-Nut Pinwheels

Pinwheel cookies with dates and walnuts are a family treasure. There are a few steps when prepping, so I sometimes freeze the dough and bake the cookies later.

—**FRIEDA WHITELEY** LISBON, CT

PREP: 30 MIN. + CHILLING
BAKE: 10 MIN./BATCH
MAKES: ABOUT 9 DOZEN

- 1 **cup butter, softened**
- 1 **cup sugar**
- 1 **cup packed brown sugar**
- 2 **large eggs**
- 4 **cups all-purpose flour**
- ½ **teaspoon baking soda**

FILLING

- 2 **packages (8 ounces each) pitted dates**
- 1 **cup water**
- ½ **cup sugar**
- ½ **cup chopped walnuts**

1. In a large bowl, cream butter and sugars until light and fluffy. Beat in eggs. In another bowl, whisk flour and baking soda; gradually beat into creamed mixture. Divide dough into three portions. Shape each into a disk; wrap in plastic wrap. Refrigerate 1 hour or until firm enough to roll.

2. For filling, place dates, water and sugar in a large saucepan. Bring to a boil. Reduce heat; simmer, uncovered, until dates are tender and liquid is almost evaporated. Stir in walnuts; cool completely.

3. Roll each portion between two sheets of waxed paper into a 12x10-in. rectangle. Refrigerate 30 minutes. Remove waxed paper. Spread a third of the filling over each rectangle. Roll up tightly jelly-roll style, starting with a long side. Wrap in plastic wrap. Refrigerate until firm.

4. Preheat oven to 350°. Unwrap and cut dough crosswise into ⅓-in. slices. Place 2 in. apart on greased baking sheets. Bake 10-12 minutes or until set. Remove cookies from pans to wire racks to cool.

PER SERVING *1 cookie equals 67 cal., 2 g fat (1 g sat. fat), 8 mg chol., 21 mg sodium, 12 g carb., 1 g fiber, 1 g pro.*

DATE-NUT PINWHEELS

White Velvet Cutouts

We give these cutouts as sweet gifts. One year, we baked a batch a week all through December to be sure we'd have plenty for ourselves, too.

—**KIM HINKLE** WAUSEON, OH

PREP: 25 MIN. + CHILLING
BAKE: 10 MIN./BATCH + COOLING
MAKES: ABOUT 5½ DOZEN

- 2 **cups butter, softened**
- 1 **package (8 ounces) cream cheese, softened**
- 2 **cups sugar**
- 2 **large egg yolks**
- 1 **teaspoon vanilla extract**
- 4½ **cups all-purpose flour**

FROSTING
- 3 **tablespoons butter, softened**
- 1 **tablespoon shortening**
- ½ **teaspoon vanilla extract**
- 3½ **cups confectioners' sugar**
- 4 **to 5 tablespoons 2% milk**
  Food coloring, optional

1. In a large bowl, cream butter, cream cheese and sugar until light and fluffy. Beat in egg yolks and vanilla. Gradually beat flour into creamed mixture. Divide dough in half. Shape each into a disk; wrap in plastic wrap. Refrigerate 2 hours or until firm enough to roll.
2. Preheat oven to 350°. On a lightly floured surface, roll each portion of dough to ¼-in. thickness. Cut with floured 3-in. cookie cutters. Place 1 in. apart on greased baking sheets. Bake 10-12 minutes or until set (do not brown). Cool on pans 5 minutes. Remove to wire racks to cool completely.
3. For frosting, in a bowl, beat butter, shortening and vanilla until blended. Beat in confectioners' sugar and enough milk to reach spreading consistency; beat 3 minutes or until light and fluffy. If desired, beat in food coloring. Frost cookies. (Keep frosting covered with a damp towel to prevent it from drying out.)
PER SERVING *1 cookie equals 149 cal., 8 g fat (5 g sat. fat), 26 mg chol., 62 mg sodium, 19 g carb., trace fiber, 1 g pro.*

EGGNOG THUMBPRINTS

WHITE VELVET CUTOUTS

Eggnog Thumbprints

These cute cookie bites always get a recipe request. They make special holiday gifts and freeze well, too.
—**MARY ANN LUDWIG** EDWARDSVILLE, IL

PREP: 30 MIN. + CHILLING
BAKE: 10 MIN./BATCH + COOLING
MAKES: ABOUT 4 DOZEN

- ⅔ cup butter, softened
- ½ cup sugar
- 2 large egg yolks
- 1 teaspoon vanilla extract
- 1½ cups all-purpose flour
- ¼ teaspoon salt
- ⅛ teaspoon ground nutmeg
- 2 large egg whites
- 1 cup finely chopped walnuts

FILLING

- ¼ cup butter, softened
- ¼ teaspoon rum extract
- 1 cup confectioners' sugar
- 1 to 2 teaspoons 2% milk
- 1 to 2 drops yellow food coloring, optional
  Additional ground nutmeg

1. In a large bowl, cream butter and sugar until light and fluffy. Beat in egg yolks and vanilla. In another bowl, whisk flour, salt and nutmeg; gradually beat into creamed mixture. Refrigerate, covered, 1 hour or until firm enough to handle.

2. Preheat oven to 350°. Shape dough into 1-in. balls. In a shallow bowl, whisk egg whites until foamy. Place walnuts in a separate shallow bowl. Dip balls in egg whites; roll in walnuts.

3. Place 2 in. apart on greased baking sheets. Press a ½-in.-deep indentation in center of each with your thumb. Bake 10-12 minutes or until center is set. Carefully remove from pans to wire racks to cool completely.

4. For filling, in a small bowl, beat butter and extract until creamy. Beat in confectioners' sugar alternately with enough milk to reach spreading consistency. If desired, beat in food coloring. Fill each cookie with ½ teaspoon filling. Sprinkle with additional nutmeg.

PER SERVING *1 cookie equals 82 cal., 5 g fat (2 g sat. fat), 17 mg chol., 42 mg sodium, 8 g carb., trace fiber, 1 g pro.*

PEPPERMINT MELTAWAYS

Peppermint Meltaways

I often cover a plate of my minty bites with red or green plastic wrap and a bright bow in one corner. And yes, they really do melt in your mouth!
—**DENISE WHEELER** NEWAYGO, MI

PREP: 30 MIN. + CHILLING
BAKE: 10 MIN./BATCH + COOLING
MAKES: ABOUT 2½ DOZEN

- 1 cup butter, softened
- ½ cup confectioners' sugar
- ½ teaspoon peppermint extract
- 1¼ cups all-purpose flour
- ½ cup cornstarch

FROSTING

- 2 tablespoons butter, softened
- 2 tablespoons 2% milk
- ¼ teaspoon peppermint extract
- 2 to 3 drops red food coloring, optional
- 1½ cups confectioners' sugar
- ½ cup crushed peppermint candies

1. In a small bowl, cream butter and confectioners' sugar until light and fluffy. Beat in extract. In another bowl, whisk the flour and the cornstarch; gradually beat into creamed mixture. Refrigerate, covered, 30 minutes or until firm enough to handle.

2. Preheat oven to 350°. Shape dough into 1-in. balls; place 2 in. apart on ungreased baking sheets. Bake for 9-11 minutes or until the bottoms are light brown. Remove from pans to wire racks to cool completely.

3. In a small bowl, beat butter until creamy. Beat in milk, extract and, if desired, food coloring. Gradually beat in confectioners' sugar until smooth. Spread over cookies; sprinkle with crushed candies. Store cookies in an airtight container.

PER SERVING *1 cookie equals 126 cal., 7 g fat (4 g sat. fat), 18 mg chol., 56 mg sodium, 15 g carb., trace fiber, 1 g pro.*

Eggnog Cream with Spiced Pecan Raisin Dunkers

PREP: 30 MIN. + CHILLING • **BAKE:** 10 MIN./BATCH
MAKES: 16 SERVINGS

- 1 **package spice cake mix (regular size)**
- ½ **cup canola oil**
- 2 **large eggs**
- 1 **cup chopped pecans or walnuts**
- ¾ **cup golden raisins**

EGGNOG CREAM

- 1 **package (8 ounces) cream cheese, softened**
- 2 **jars (7 ounces each) marshmallow creme**
- 1 **teaspoon rum extract**
- ¾ **teaspoon ground nutmeg**
- ¼ **teaspoon ground cinnamon**
- 1 **carton (8 ounces) frozen whipped topping, thawed**
  Additional ground nutmeg

1. Preheat oven to 375°. In a large bowl, beat cake mix, oil and eggs until well blended. Stir in pecans and raisins.

2. Divide dough in half. On baking sheets, roll each portion between two sheets of parchment paper into a 12x8-in. rectangle. Refrigerate 30 minutes. Meanwhile, In a large bowl, beat cream cheese, marshmallow creme, extract, nutmeg and cinnamon until smooth; fold in whipped topping. Refrigerate, covered, until serving.

3. Remove top sheet of parchment paper from dough. Cut each dough rectangle in half lengthwise; cut crosswise into 1-in. strips. Transfer to parchment paper-lined baking sheets. (Refrigerate any remaining strips until ready to bake.) Bake 8-10 minutes or until edges are golden brown. Cool on pans 4 minutes. Remove to wire racks to cool.

4. Sprinkle eggnog cream with additional nutmeg; serve with dunkers.

PER SERVING *⅓ cup eggnog cream with 3 dunkers equals 448 cal., 24 g fat (8 g sat. fat), 42 mg chol., 318 mg sodium, 54 g carb., 2 g fiber, 4 g pro.*

I have a thing for eggnog and other creamy desserts like s'mores, puddings, mousses and dips. So I turned them into one yummy dip with homemade dunkers. —**ARLENE ERLBACH** MORTON GROVE, IL

EGGNOG CREAM WITH SPICED PECAN RAISIN DUNKERS

Chocolate-Dipped Pretzel Wreath

Give chocolate and pretzels the holiday treatment they deserve when you shape them as a wreath. Make one for the house and more to give away.

—**SHANNON ROUM** MILWAUKEE, WI

START TO FINISH: 30 MIN. • **MAKES:** 24 SERVINGS

> 2 packages (10 to 12 ounces each) white baking chips
> 1 package (10 ounces) pretzel rods, halved
> 1½ cups green and red sprinkles

In a microwave, melt white baking chips; stir until smooth. Dip pretzels in chocolate, allowing excess to drip off. Add sprinkles; place on waxed paper until set. Arrange pretzels in a circle on a decorative serving plate.

PER SERVING *1 pretzel equals 231 cal., 10 g fat (5 g sat. fat), 5 mg chol., 280 mg sodium, 32 g carb., trace fiber, 3 g pro.*

Hungarian Nut Rolls

It isn't officially Christmas until I've made this treasured recipe handed down by my husband's grandmother. The apple-walnut filling has the most amazing flavor. The loaves make wonderful home-baked gifts.

—**DONNA BARDOCZ** HOWELL, MI

PREP: 40 MIN. + RISING • **BAKE:** 30 MIN. + COOLING
MAKES: 4 LOAVES (12 SLICES EACH)

> 2 packages (¼ ounce each) active dry yeast
> ½ cup warm 2% milk (110° to 115°)
> ¼ cup plus 2 tablespoons sugar
> ¾ teaspoon salt
> 1 cup butter, softened
> 1 cup (8 ounces) sour cream
> 3 large eggs, lightly beaten
> 6 to 6½ cups all-purpose flour

FILLING
> 1¼ cups sugar
> ½ cup butter, cubed
> 1 large egg
> ½ teaspoon ground cinnamon
> 4½ cups ground walnuts
> 1 large apple, peeled and grated

ICING
> 2 cups confectioners' sugar
> 2 to 3 tablespoons 2% milk

1. In a large bowl, dissolve yeast in warm milk. Add the sugar, salt, butter, sour cream, eggs and 3 cups flour. Beat on medium speed for 3 minutes. Beat until smooth. Stir in enough remaining flour to form a soft dough (dough will be sticky).

2. Turn onto a floured surface; knead until smooth and elastic, about 6-8 minutes. Place in a greased bowl, turning once to grease top. Cover and let rise in a warm place until doubled, about 1 hour.

3. Meanwhile, in a large saucepan, combine the sugar, butter, egg and cinnamon. Cook and stir over medium heat until mixture is thick enough to coat the back of a spoon. Remove from the heat; gently stir in walnuts and apple. Cool completely.

4. Punch dough down. Turn onto a lightly floured surface; divide into four portions. Roll each into a 12x10-in. rectangle. Spread filling to within ½ in. of edges. Roll up jelly-roll style, starting with a long side; pinch seams to seal. Place seam side down on greased baking sheets. Cover and let rise until doubled, about 30 minutes.

5. Bake at 350° for 30-40 minutes or until lightly browned. Remove from pans to wire racks to cool. Combine icing ingredients; drizzle over loaves.

PER SERVING *1 slice equals 222 cal., 12 g fat (5 g sat. fat), 36 mg chol., 87 mg sodium, 26 g carb., 1 g fiber, 4 g pro.*

LOIS ENGER'S
CORNFLAKE-COATED
BAKED FRENCH TOAST PAGE 224

Family Best

Good **home-cooked meals** served up with love just can't be beat. In this chapter, **family cooks** share the **heartwarming stories**—and the **soul-satisfying dishes**—that bring their families to the table.

**ADAN FRANCO'S
SAUTEED SQUASH WITH
TOMATOES & ONIONS** *PAGE 219*

**LOIS ENGER'S
MINI HAM & CHEESE QUICHES**
PAGE 225

**CHRISTINA ADDISON'S
ORANGE SPICE CARROTS**
PAGE 223

Family Fiesta

Welcome to Sunday dinner at the Delgadillo house. The hibiscus tea's chilled, the tortilla chips are warm, and the home-cooked spread keeps this family dreaming of their Sunday tradition all week long. RECIPES BY **ADAN FRANCO** | MILWAUKEE, WI

It's Sunday afternoon, and the comforting aroma of beans and rice wafts through Grandma Delfina Delgadillo's bustling Milwaukee home. Each week, her family comes together around faith and a home-cooked Mexican meal. Young grandkids bound through the living room, cousins set the table, and aunts tote spicy chicken, cookies and tortillas to the kitchen to prepare for the come-as-you-are feast.

After church, nearly 20 people pop by Grandma's house, including the newest family member, *Taste of Home* set stylist Missy Franco. Missy and her husband, Adan, married in 2015, but she knew how close-knit his family was from the start. "The first time I met Adan's family was at a summer party for their grandma. Imagine being introduced to more than 75 people in one sitting!" Missy says, laughing. Adan's grandparents came to Milwaukee from Mexico, and as the family grew, the dinners became a touchstone. "My family gathers every Sunday afternoon for a meal," Adan says. "Birthdays blend with holidays and turn into picnics and parties."

Chicken tostadas and tamales are menu staples. But Missy is partial to dessert. "My favorite is the fruit salsa and cinnamon chips—and the cookies, too. I have a sweet tooth; need I say more?" Adan, a professional chef, credits these meals for more than delicious food. "My appreciation for cooking came from watching my mother and grandmother cook," he says. "Endless support—and rice—keep our family tradition alive every week!"

to a large bowl. Add sugar and remaining water, stirring until sugar is dissolved. If desired, stir in rum. Refrigerate until cold. Add mint sprigs if desired.

NOTE *This recipe was tested with Tazo passion tea bags.*
PER SERVING *¾ cup (calculated without rum) equals 67 cal., 0 fat (0 sat. fat), 0 chol., 2 mg sodium, 17 g carb., trace fiber, trace pro.*

GRILLED ONION & SKIRT STEAK TACOS

AGUA DE JAMAICA

⑤INGREDIENTS
Agua de Jamaica

PREP: 15 MIN. + CHILLING • **MAKES:** 6 SERVINGS

- 1 **cup dried hibiscus flowers or 6 hibiscus tea bags**
- 5 **cups water, divided**
- 1½ **teaspoons grated lime peel**
- ½ **cup sugar**
- 1 **cup rum, optional**
  Mint sprigs, optional

1. Rinse flowers in cold water. In a large saucepan, combine 3 cups water, flowers and lime peel. Bring to a boil. Reduce heat; simmer, uncovered, 10 minutes.
2. Remove from heat; let stand 15 minutes. Strain mixture, discarding flowers and lime peel; transfer

Grilled Onion & Skirt Steak Tacos

PREP: 15 MIN. + MARINATING • **GRILL:** 5 MIN. • **MAKES:** 8 SERVINGS

- 2 **beef skirt or flank steaks (1 pound each)**
- 1 **bottle (12 ounces) beer**
- ¼ **cup lime juice**
- 3 **tablespoons olive oil, divided**
- 8 **spring onions**
- 1¼ **teaspoons salt, divided**
- ¾ **teaspoon pepper, divided**
  Corn tortillas, minced fresh cilantro and lime wedges

1. Pound beef with a meat mallet to tenderize. In a large bowl, mix the beer, lime juice and 2 tablespoons oil until blended. Add beef to marinade; turn to coat. Refrigerate, covered, at least 30 minutes.

2. Meanwhile, cut partially through onions, leaving the tops intact. Drizzle with the remaining oil; sprinkle with ¼ teaspoon salt and ¼ teaspoon pepper.

3. Drain beef, discarding marinade, and sprinkle with the remaining salt and pepper. On a greased grill rack, grill the steaks and onions, covered, over medium heat or broil 4 in. from heat 2-4 minutes on each side or until meat reaches desired doneness (for medium-rare, a thermometer should read 145°; medium, 160°; well-done, 170°) and onions are crisp-tender.

4. Cut steak diagonally across the grain into thin slices. Serve with tortillas, onions, cilantro and lime wedges.

PER SERVING (calculated without tortillas, cilantro and lime wedges) equals 288 cal., 14 g fat (5 g sat. fat), 67 mg chol., 458 mg sodium, 7 g carb., 1 g fiber, 31 g pro.

Sauteed Squash with Tomatoes & Onions

START TO FINISH: 20 MIN. • **MAKES:** 8 SERVINGS

- 2 **tablespoons olive oil**
- 1 **medium onion, finely chopped**
- 4 **medium zucchini, chopped**
- 2 **large tomatoes, finely chopped**
- 1 **teaspoon salt**
- ¼ **teaspoon pepper**

1. In a large skillet, heat oil over medium-high heat. Add onion; cook and stir 2-4 minutes or until tender. Add zucchini; cook and stir 3 minutes.

2. Stir in the tomatoes, salt and pepper; cook and stir 4-6 minutes longer or until the squash is tender. Serve with a slotted spoon.

PER SERVING ¾ cup equals 60 cal., 4 g fat (1 g sat. fat), 0 chol., 306 mg sodium, 6 g carb., 2 g fiber, 2 g pro. *Diabetic Exchanges: 1 vegetable, ½ fat.*

SAUTEED SQUASH WITH TOMATOES & ONIONS

Fruit Salad Salsa with Cinnamon Tortilla Chips

PREP: 15 MIN. • **COOK:** 5 MIN./BATCH
MAKES: 6 CUPS SALSA (80 CHIPS)

- 2 **medium apples, finely chopped**
- 2 **medium nectarines or peaches, finely chopped**
- 2 **cups chopped fresh strawberries**
- 1 **cup fresh blueberries**
- 2 **tablespoons lemon juice**
  Dash salt

CHIPS
- ½ **cup sugar**
- 2 **tablespoons ground cinnamon**
- 10 **flour tortillas (8 inches)**
  Oil for frying

1. In a large bowl, combine the first six ingredients. Refrigerate until serving.
2. In a small bowl, mix the sugar and cinnamon. Cut each tortilla into eight wedges. In an electric skillet, heat 1 in. of oil to 375°. Fry chips, several at a time, 2-3 minutes on each side or until golden brown. Drain on paper towels.
3. Transfer the chips to a large bowl; sprinkle with sugar mixture and gently toss to coat. Serve with salsa.
PER SERVING *¼ cup salsa with 3 chips equals 122 cal., 4 g fat (1 g sat. fat), 0 chol., 104 mg sodium, 21 g carb., 2 g fiber, 2 g pro.*

FRUIT SALAD SALSA WITH CINNAMON TORTILLA CHIPS

MEXICAN CINNAMON COOKIES

Mexican Cinnamon Cookies

PREP: 25 MIN. + STANDING • **BAKE:** 10 MIN./BATCH
MAKES: 12 DOZEN

- 1 **large egg, separated**
- 2 **cups lard**
- 4 **cups all-purpose flour**
- 3 **teaspoons baking powder**
- 1½ **teaspoons ground cinnamon**
  Dash salt
- ¾ **cup sugar**

COATING
- ⅔ **cup sugar**
- 4 **teaspoons ground cinnamon**
  Confectioners' sugar

1. Place egg white in a small bowl; let stand at room temperature 30 minutes.
2. Preheat oven to 375°. In a large bowl, beat lard until creamy. In another bowl, whisk flour, baking powder, cinnamon and salt; gradually beat into lard.
3. Beat egg white on high speed until stiff peaks form. Gently whisk in sugar and egg yolk. Gradually beat into lard mixture. Turn onto a lightly floured surface; knead gently 8-10 times.
4. Divide dough into six portions. On a lightly floured surface, roll each portion into a 24-in.-long rope and cut diagonally into 1-in. pieces. Place 1 in. apart on ungreased baking sheets. Bake 8-10 minutes or until edges are light brown. Cool on pans 2 minutes.
5. In a small bowl, mix sugar and cinnamon. Roll warm cookies in cinnamon sugar mixture or confectioners' sugar. Cool on wire racks.
PER SERVING *1 cookie equals 47 cal., 3 g fat (1 g sat. fat), 4 mg chol., 10 mg sodium, 5 g carb., trace fiber, trace pro.*

Lime-Marinated Shrimp Salad

PREP: 25 MIN. + CHILLING • **MAKES:** 10 CUPS

- 1 large onion, quartered
- 2 to 4 serrano peppers, seeded and coarsely chopped
- 2 medium cucumbers, peeled, quartered and seeds removed
- 2 large tomatoes, cut into chunks
- 6 green onions, coarsely chopped (about ¾ cup)
- 2 pounds peeled and deveined cooked shrimp (26-30 per pound)
- ¾ cup lime juice
- ½ teaspoon salt
- ¼ teaspoon pepper
  Tortilla chips or tostada shells

1. Place the onion and peppers in a food processor; pulse until very finely chopped. Transfer to a large bowl. Place cucumbers, tomatoes and green onions in food processor; pulse until finely chopped. Add to bowl.

2. Place shrimp in food processor; pulse until chopped. Add shrimp, lime juice, salt and pepper to vegetable mixture; toss to coat. Refrigerate until cold. Serve with tortilla chips or tostada shells.

NOTE *Wear disposable gloves when cutting hot peppers; the oils can burn skin. Avoid touching your face.*
PER SERVING ½ *cup (calculated without chips) equals 61 cal., 1 g fat (trace sat. fat), 69 mg chol., 128 mg sodium, 4 g carb., 1 g fiber, 10 g pro.* **Diabetic Exchange:** *1 lean meat.*

LIME-MARINATED
SHRIMP SALAD

A Meat Loaf Story

Inspired by her favorite holiday movie, this fun-loving Ohio mom gives a third-generation family recipe a Tinseltown mashed-potato twist. **You'll eat your heart out, kid.**

RECIPES & STORY BY **CHRISTINA ADDISON** | BLANCHESTER, OH

I grew up watching *A Christmas Story* every Christmas Day after we opened presents, and now it's a tradition I've carried on with my family. I love making holiday-themed dishes, so I thought it was fitting to create a meat loaf recipe in honor of the movie.

I started with the meat loaf recipe my mother learned from her mom, then gave it my own twist based on the dinner the Parker family sits down to in the film.

We're going through a picky-eating stage with our 3-year-old. Sometimes he reminds me of Ralphie's little brother in the movie—there's no licking the plate, but when he really likes a meal he shovels in loads of food.

My son even recites the movie's famous quote, "You'll shoot your eye out, kid." He's starting to ask for a Red Ryder BB gun and I respond with that line, since he's only 3 years old. I definitely appreciate the meat loaf scene, as the mom has to think creatively to get smiles around the table and food in her kids' bellies—not to mention eat a little dinner herself.

FAST FIX
Easy Cheesy Biscuits

START TO FINISH: 30 MIN. • **MAKES:** 1 DOZEN

- 3 **cups all-purpose flour**
- 3 **teaspoons baking powder**
- 1 **tablespoon sugar**
- 1 **teaspoon salt**
- ¾ **teaspoon cream of tartar**
- ½ **cup cold butter**
- 1 **cup (4 ounces) shredded sharp cheddar cheese**
- 1 **garlic clove, minced**
- ¼ **to ½ teaspoon crushed red pepper flakes**
- 1¼ **cups 2% milk**

1. Preheat oven to 450°. In a large bowl, whisk flour, baking powder, sugar, salt and cream of tartar. Cut in butter until mixture resembles coarse crumbs. Stir in cheese, garlic and pepper flakes. Add milk; stir just until moistened.

2. Drop dough by heaping ¼ cupfuls 2 in. apart onto a greased baking sheet. Bake 18-20 minutes or until golden brown. Serve warm.

PER SERVING *1 biscuit equals 237 cal., 12 g fat (7 g sat. fat), 32 mg chol., 429 mg sodium, 26 g carb., 1 g fiber, 7 g pro.*

A CHRISTMAS STORY
MEAT LOAF

ORANGE SPICE
CARROTS

A Christmas Story Meat Loaf

PREP: 15 MIN. • **BAKE:** 50 MIN. + STANDING • **MAKES:** 6 SERVINGS

- 2 large eggs, lightly beaten
- ½ cup ketchup
- 1 medium onion, finely chopped
- 1 small green or sweet red pepper, finely chopped
- ⅔ cup crushed saltines (about 12)
- ½ teaspoon salt
- 1 teaspoon pepper
- 1½ pounds ground beef
- 4 cups hot mashed potatoes, divided
- 1 tablespoon minced fresh parsley

1. Preheat the oven to 375°. Place a rack in a 15x10x1-in. baking pan; place a 12x8-in. piece of foil in center of rack. In a large bowl, combine eggs, ketchup, onion, green pepper, crushed saltines, salt and pepper. Add beef; mix lightly but thoroughly. Place mixture over foil rectangle and shape into a 9x6-in. loaf. Bake 50-60 minutes or until a thermometer reads 160°. Let stand 10 minutes before slicing.

2. Transfer meat loaf to a serving plate, discarding the foil. Pipe or spread 1 cup mashed potatoes over meat loaf and sprinkle with parsley. Serve meat loaf with remaining mashed potatoes.

PER SERVING *1 slice with ½ cup mashed potatoes equals 436 cal., 20 g fat (7 g sat. fat), 132 mg chol., 1,105 mg sodium, 37 g carb., 3 g fiber, 26 g pro.*

`SLOW COOKER` 🍲
Orange Spice Carrots

PREP: 10 MIN. • **COOK:** 4 HOURS • **MAKES:** 6 SERVINGS

- 2 pounds medium carrots or baby carrots, cut into 1-inch pieces
- ½ cup packed brown sugar
- ½ cup orange juice
- 2 tablespoons butter
- ¾ teaspoon ground cinnamon
- ½ teaspoon salt
- ¼ teaspoon ground nutmeg
- 4 teaspoons cornstarch
- ¼ cup cold water

1. In a 3-qt. slow cooker, combine first seven ingredients. Cook, covered, on low 4-5 hours or until carrots are tender.

2. In a small bowl, mix cornstarch and water until smooth; gradually stir into carrot mixture until sauce is thickened.

PER SERVING *⅔ cup equals 187 cal., 4 g fat (3 g sat. fat), 10 mg chol., 339 mg sodium, 38 g carb., 4 g fiber, 2 g pro.*

Breakfast for Dinner

Full plates and big laughs always welcomed new Air Force cadets at Lois Enger's home. Her go-to French toast did more than fill hungry bellies—it **helped recruit a son-in-law to her family.** RECIPES & STORY BY **LOIS ENGER** | COLORADO SPRINGS, CO

FAMILY BEST

My husband and I began sponsoring Air Force Academy cadets in 1978. Before retiring, Rolf had been the academy's director of education, and earlier he'd been an Air Force officer. We provided a welcoming home away from home for young cadets who were on their own for the first time. They quickly became like family. I cooked for them often, and we'd host them through all four years of academy, throwing each a graduation party.

Breakfast for dinner was a favorite: comforting, warm, easy to make and loved by all. My French toast with cinnamon syrup became our tradition. Cadets often invited their friends, but no matter how many hungry guests piled into our home, I'd make the meal stretch. I'd throw together scrambled eggs, fruit or sweet rolls and they'd eat to their hearts' content.

In 2004 we decided it would be our last year to sponsor cadets. Fate intervened when we welcomed two more: Big Joe and Little Joe. Big Joe came over often, and soon we realized it wasn't just for my cooking—he loved visiting our daughter, Holly. Now married with their own family, Joe and Holly are continuing my tradition of serving baked French toast to their Air Force friends. We've been blessed to have cadets in our lives, and we're so glad we got to keep one.

FAST FIX
Cornflake-Coated Baked French Toast

START TO FINISH: 25 MIN. • **MAKES:** 6 SERVINGS (1 CUP SYRUP)

- 2 large eggs
- ½ cup 2% milk
- ½ teaspoon salt
- ½ teaspoon vanilla extract
- 1 cup cornflake crumbs
- 6 slices Texas toast
- ¼ cup butter, melted

CINNAMON SYRUP

- ⅔ cup sugar
- ⅓ cup light corn syrup
- 2 tablespoons water
- ½ teaspoon ground cinnamon
- ⅓ cup evaporated milk or 2% milk
- 1½ teaspoons butter
- ¼ teaspoon almond extract

1. Preheat oven to 450°. In a shallow bowl, whisk eggs, milk, salt and vanilla until blended. Place cornflake crumbs in another shallow bowl. Dip both sides of bread in egg mixture, then in cornflake crumbs, patting to help coating adhere.
2. Place in a greased 15x10x1-in. baking pan. Drizzle with melted butter. Bake 10-12 minutes or until golden brown.
3. For syrup, in a small saucepan, combine sugar, corn syrup, water and cinnamon; bring to a boil. Cook and stir 2 minutes. Remove from heat. Stir in milk, butter and extract. Serve with French toast.

PER SERVING *1 slice with 3 tablespoons syrup equals 419 cal., 13 g fat (7 g sat. fat), 91 mg chol., 619 mg sodium, 70 g carb., 1 g fiber, 8 g pro.*

CORNFLAKE-COATED BAKED FRENCH TOAST

GRAPEFRUIT, LIME &
MINT YOGURT PARFAIT

MINI HAM & CHEESE
QUICHES

FAST FIX
Mini Ham & Cheese Quiches

START TO FINISH: 30 MIN. • **MAKES:** 1 DOZEN

- 1 **cup salad croutons**
- 1 **cup (4 ounces) shredded cheddar cheese**
- 1 **cup chopped fully cooked ham**
- 4 **large eggs**
- 1½ **cups 2% milk**
- 1½ **teaspoons dried parsley flakes**
- ½ **teaspoon Dijon mustard**
- ¼ **teaspoon salt**
- ⅛ **teaspoon onion powder**
  Dash pepper

1. Preheat oven to 325°. Divide croutons, cheese and ham among 12 greased muffin cups. In a large bowl, whisk the remaining ingredients until blended. Divide egg mixture among prepared muffin cups.

2. Bake 15-20 minutes or until a knife inserted near the center comes out clean. Let stand for 5 minutes before removing from pan. Serve warm.

PER SERVING *1 mini quiche equals 107 cal., 6 g fat (3 g sat. fat), 81 mg chol., 328 mg sodium, 4 g carb., trace fiber, 8 g pro.*

EAT SMART ⑤INGREDIENTS FAST FIX
Grapefruit, Lime & Mint Yogurt Parfait

START TO FINISH: 15 MIN. • **MAKES:** 6 SERVINGS

- 4 **large grapefruit**
- 4 **cups (32 ounces) reduced-fat plain yogurt**
- 2 **teaspoons grated lime peel**
- 2 **tablespoons lime juice**
- 3 **tablespoons honey**
  Torn fresh mint leaves

1. Cut a thin slice from the top and bottom of each grapefruit; stand upright on a cutting board. With a knife, cut off peel and outer membrane from grapefruit. Cut along the membrane of each segment to remove fruit.

2. In a large bowl, mix yogurt, lime peel and juice. Layer half of the grapefruit sections and yogurt mixture into six parfait glasses. Repeat layers. Drizzle with honey; top with mint.

PER SERVING *1 parfait equals 207 cal., 3 g fat (2 g sat. fat), 10 mg chol., 115 mg sodium, 39 g carb., 3 g fiber, 10 g pro.*

ANDREA RIVERA'S
SUMMERTIME SPAGHETTI WITH
GRILLED MEATBALLS *PAGE 230*

Field Editor Favorites

Taste of Home Field Editors—**cooks just like you** from across the U.S. and Canada—love to share their treasured recipes. Savor these **special dishes** sure to become **your family's favorites** as well.

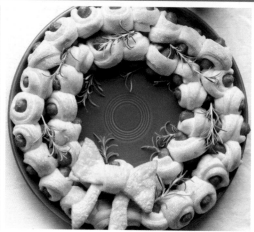

KIM FORNI'S SMOKED GOUDA & SWISS CHARD STRATA PAGE 233

JULIE PETERSON'S RING OF PIGGIES PAGE 237

DAWN LOWENSTEIN'S SPICY APPLESAUCE FRUIT BREAD PAGE 235

STRAWBERRY-CHICKEN
SALAD WITH
BUTTERED PECANS

Wild for Strawberries

Grab a pint or two, then hull, slice and nibble till your fingers turn pink. Field Editors share their best and brightest strawberry dishes, picked fresh for you.

Strawberry-Chicken Salad with Buttered Pecans

Having lived in several states in the South, I love tossing pecans into recipes for a little added flavor and crunch. Fresh berries and other nuts round out this hearty salad.
—**LISA VARNER** EL PASO, TX

START TO FINISH: 15 MIN.
MAKES: 6 SERVINGS

2 tablespoons butter
1 cup pecan halves
¼ teaspoon salt
⅛ teaspoon freshly ground pepper

DRESSING
2 tablespoons balsamic vinegar
2 tablespoons olive oil
1 tablespoon sugar
1 tablespoon orange juice
⅛ teaspoon freshly ground pepper

SALAD
1 package (5 ounces) spring mix salad greens
¾ pound sliced rotisserie chicken breast
1 cup sliced fresh strawberries
1 cup (4 ounces) shredded Swiss cheese
Salad croutons, optional

1. In a large heavy skillet, melt butter. Add pecans; cook over medium heat until nuts are toasted, about 4 minutes. Stir in salt and pepper.
2. In a small bowl, whisk dressing ingredients until blended. For salad, in a large bowl, combine salad greens, chicken, strawberries and cheese. Drizzle with dressing; toss to coat. Serve with buttered pecans and, if desired, croutons.
PER SERVING *(calculated without croutons) equals 392 cal., 30 g fat (8 g sat. fat), 77 mg chol., 210 mg sodium, 10 g carb., 3 g fiber, 24 g pro.*

CHOCOLATE-COVERED
STRAWBERRY COBBLER

SMOKY & SWEET
STRAWBERRY
CHIPOTLE JAM

Smoky & Sweet Strawberry Chipotle Jam

Strawberries and chipotle give this jam a sweet-spicy kick. We use it to baste chicken, beef ribs or pork, and it's unbelievably good over cream cheese.

—**REDAWNA KALYNCHUK** BARRHEAD, AB

PREP: 10 MIN.
COOK: 10 MIN. + PROCESSING
MAKES: 5 HALF-PINTS

- 1½ **pounds fresh strawberries, hulled**
- 2 **teaspoons grated lemon peel**
- 3 **tablespoons lemon juice**
- 2 **to 3 chipotle peppers in adobo sauce, finely chopped**
- ¼ **teaspoon salt**
- 1 **package (1¾ ounces) powdered fruit pectin**
- 3 **cups sugar**

1. Place half of the strawberries in a food processor; process until pureed. Chop remaining strawberries.
2. In a large saucepan, combine strawberries, lemon peel, lemon juice, peppers and salt. Stir in pectin. Bring to a full rolling boil over high heat, stirring constantly. Stir in sugar; return to a full rolling boil. Boil and stir 1 minute.
3. Remove from heat; skim off foam. Ladle hot mixture into five hot half-pint jars, leaving ¼-in. headspace. Remove air bubbles and adjust headspace, if necessary, by adding hot mixture. Wipe rims. Center lids on jars; screw on bands until fingertip tight.
4. Place jars into canner with simmering water, ensuring that they are completely covered with water. Bring to a boil; process for 10 minutes. Remove jars and cool.
NOTE *The processing time listed is for altitudes of 1,000 feet or less. Add 1 minute to the processing time for each 1,000 feet of additional altitude.*
PER SERVING *2 tablespoons equals 65 cal., trace fat (0 sat. fat), 0 chol., 20 mg sodium, 17 g carb., trace fiber, trace pro.*

Chocolate-Covered Strawberry Cobbler

This cobbler came about because I love chocolate-covered strawberries. Top it with whipped cream, either plain or with a little chocolate syrup stirred in.

—**ANDREA BOLDEN** UNIONVILLE, TN

PREP: 15 MIN. • **BAKE:** 35 MIN. + STANDING
MAKES: 12 SERVINGS

- 1 **cup butter, cubed**
- 1½ **cups self-rising flour**
- 2¼ **cups sugar, divided**
- ¾ **cup 2% milk**
- 1 **teaspoon vanilla extract**
- ⅓ **cup baking cocoa**
- 4 **cups fresh strawberries, quartered**
- 2 **cups boiling water**
  Whipped cream and additional strawberries

1. Preheat oven to 350°. Place butter in a 13x9-in. baking pan; heat pan in oven 3-5 minutes or until butter is melted. Meanwhile, in a large bowl, combine flour, 1¼ cups sugar, milk and vanilla until well blended. In a small bowl, mix cocoa and remaining sugar.
2. Remove baking pan from oven; add batter. Sprinkle with strawberries and cocoa mixture; pour boiling water evenly over top (do not stir). Bake 35-40 minutes or until a toothpick inserted into cake portion comes out clean. Let stand 10 minutes. Serve warm with whipped cream and additional strawberries.
PER SERVING *(calculated without whipped cream and additional strawberries) equals 368 cal., 16 g fat (10 g sat. fat), 42 mg chol., 316 mg sodium, 55 g carb., 2 g fiber, 3 g pro.*

Vine to Table

It's tomato time! Pile those sun-ripened beauts in your basket, 'cause these Field Editors know just how to use them.

EAT SMART **FAST FIX**
Curried Shrimp-Stacked Tomatoes

In Florida, we're known for tomatoes and Gulf shrimp, so we use both in this tasty lunch. They stack up fast and keep the kitchen cool.

—**JUDY BATSON** TAMPA, FL

START TO FINISH: 20 MIN.
MAKES: 4 SERVINGS

- 4 large heirloom tomatoes
- 6 tablespoons reduced-fat mayonnaise
- 1 teaspoon curry powder
- ¼ teaspoon salt
- ¼ teaspoon ground ginger
- 12 ounces peeled and deveined cooked shrimp (61-70 per pound)
- 1 celery rib, chopped
- ½ cup finely chopped cucumber
- 1 small navel orange, peeled and finely chopped
- 2 green onions, thinly sliced

1. Cut tomatoes into thick slices; place on paper towels to dry.
2. In a large bowl, combine the mayonnaise, curry powder, salt and ginger. Stir in remaining ingredients. Layer shrimp mixture between tomato slices.

PER SERVING *1 stacked tomato equals 217 cal., 9 g fat (1 g sat. fat), 137 mg chol., 435 mg sodium, 14 g carb., 3 g fiber, 20 g pro.* **Diabetic Exchanges:** *3 lean meat, 2 vegetable, 1 fat.*

Roasted Tomato Quiche

This cheesy quiche comes together quickly enough that I don't have to wake up really early to get it on the table, and that's a bonus.

—**ELISABETH LARSEN** PLEASANT GROVE, UT

PREP: 45 MIN. • **BAKE:** 40 MIN. + STANDING
MAKES: 6 SERVINGS

- 1 sheet refrigerated pie pastry
- 1 cup grape tomatoes
- 1 tablespoon olive oil
- ⅛ teaspoon plus ½ teaspoon salt, divided
- ⅛ teaspoon plus ¼ teaspoon pepper, divided
- ½ pound bulk Italian sausage
- 1 small onion, chopped
- 1 package (6 ounces) fresh baby spinach, chopped
- 1 cup (4 ounces) shredded part-skim mozzarella cheese
- 3 large eggs
- 1 cup half-and-half cream
- ½ teaspoon garlic powder

1. Unroll pastry into a 9-in. pie plate; flute edges. Line unpricked pastry with a double thickness of heavy-duty foil. Fill with dried beans, uncooked rice or pie weights.
2. Bake at 450° for 8 minutes. Remove foil and weights; bake crust 5 minutes longer. Cool on a wire rack.
3. Place tomatoes in a 15x10x1-in. baking pan. Drizzle with oil; sprinkle with ⅛ teaspoon salt and pepper. Bake at 450° until skins blister, about 8-10 minutes.
4. In a large skillet, cook sausage and onion over medium heat until sausage is no longer pink; drain. Remove sausage. In the same skillet, cook spinach until wilted, about 4-5 minutes.
5. Combine sausage, tomatoes, spinach and cheese; transfer to crust. Whisk eggs, cream, garlic powder and remaining salt and pepper; pour over top.
6. Bake at 375° until a knife inserted in center comes out clean, about 40-45 minutes. Cover edges with foil during the last 15 minutes to prevent overbrowning if necessary. Let stand 10 minutes before serving.

NOTE *Let pie weights cool before storing. Beans and rice may be reused for pie weights, but not for cooking.*
PER SERVING *1 piece equals 397 cal., 26 g fat (11 g sat. fat), 158 mg chol., 725 mg sodium, 23 g carb., 1 g fiber, 15 g pro.*

Summertime Spaghetti with Grilled Meatballs

After Hurricane Sandy, we were without power for two weeks. I learned what you can make on a grill, such as these smoky meatballs and tomato sauce.

—**ANDREA RIVERA** WESTBURY, NY

PREP: 25 MIN. • **COOK:** 10 MIN.
MAKES: 6 SERVINGS

- 12 ounces uncooked spaghetti
- **MEATBALLS**
- ½ cup finely chopped onion
- ¼ cup seasoned bread crumbs
- 1 large egg
- 2 tablespoons grated Parmesan cheese
- 1 tablespoon 2% milk
- ½ teaspoon garlic powder
- ½ teaspoon onion powder
- 1 pound ground beef

CURRIED SHRIMP-STACKED TOMATOES

SUMMERTIME SPAGHETTI WITH GRILLED MEATBALLS

OVEN-DRIED TOMATOES

ROASTED TOMATO QUICHE

TOMATO SAUCE

- 2 **pounds (4 to 5) large tomatoes, chopped**
- 3 **garlic cloves, minced**
- 1 **tablespoon olive oil**
- 1 **teaspoon sugar**
- ¾ **teaspoon salt**
- ½ **teaspoon dried oregano**
- ½ **teaspoon pepper**
- 2 **tablespoons minced fresh basil**

TOPPING

Shredded Parmesan cheese

1. Cook spaghetti according to package directions; drain.

2. Meanwhile, combine onion, bread crumbs, egg, Parmesan, milk and seasonings. Add beef; mix lightly. With wet hands, shape into 1½-in. balls. Place meatballs on greased grill rack; grill, covered, over medium heat until cooked through, about 10 minutes.

3. For sauce, combine tomatoes, garlic, oil, sugar, salt, oregano and pepper in an 11x7x2-in. disposable foil pan. Grill over medium heat until sauce begins

to simmer, about 10 minutes. Stir in basil.

4. Serve meatballs and sauce with spaghetti; top with shredded Parmesan.

PER SERVING *1 cup spaghetti with ½ cup sauce and 3 meatballs equals 446 cal., 14 g fat (5 g sat. fat), 79 mg chol., 470 mg sodium, 55 g carb., 4 g fiber, 25 g pro.*

Oven-Dried Tomatoes

We owned an organic greenhouse and business that included classes. I had 100 tomato varieties to work with, so I started oven-drying them and taught my students, too.

—SUE GRONHOLZ BEAVER DAM, WI

PREP: 15 MIN. • **BAKE:** 5 HOURS
MAKES: 4 SERVINGS

- 8 **plum tomatoes**
  Ice water
- ¼ **cup olive oil**
- ¼ **cup minced fresh basil**

- 4 **garlic cloves, minced**
- ½ **teaspoon salt**
- ¼ **teaspoon pepper**

1. Preheat oven to 250°. Fill a large saucepan two-thirds with water; bring to a boil. Cut a shallow "X" on the bottom of each tomato. Place tomatoes, a few at a time, in boiling water just until skin at the "X" begins to loosen, about 30 seconds. Remove and immediately drop into ice water. Pull off and discard skins.

2. Cut tomatoes in half lengthwise. Combine all ingredients; toss to coat. Transfer tomatoes, cut side up, to a greased 15x10x1-in. baking pan. Roast until tomatoes are soft and slightly shriveled, about 5 hours. Cool the tomatoes completely; refrigerate.

PER SERVING *4 tomato halves equals 147 cal., 14 g fat (2 g sat. fat), 0 chol., 302 mg sodium, 6 g carb., 2 g fiber, 1 g pro.* **Diabetic Exchanges:** *3 fat, 1 vegetable.*

FIELD EDITOR FAVORITES

Good Eggs

Wrap them in tortillas or tuck them into a bacon-studded strata. Field Editors take a crack at breakfasts worth crowing about.

Chorizo and Eggs Ranchero

For a festive Mexican breakfast, we do chorizo and huevos rancheros. Add refried beans and cheddar, and serve everything in bowls made of tortillas.

—**PAUL WILLIAMS** FORT MOHAVE, AZ

PREP: 25 MIN. + COOLING • **COOK:** 10 MIN.
MAKES: 2 SERVINGS

- 2 **flour tortillas (8 inches)**
  Cooking spray
- ¾ **cup refried beans**
- 4 **ounces fresh chorizo**
- 4 **large eggs, lightly beaten**
- ½ **cup mild salsa**
- ¼ **cup shredded cheddar cheese**

1. Preheat oven to 425°. Spritz both sides of tortillas with cooking spray. Press tortillas onto bottom and up sides of two 1½-qt. ovenproof bowls. Bake until edges are just browned, 8-10 minutes. Cool 5 minutes; remove from bowls. Cool completely.

2. Microwave beans, covered, on high until heated through, 1-2 minutes. Spread half in each tortilla bowl.

3. In a large nonstick skillet, cook and crumble chorizo over medium heat until cooked through, 4-6 minutes; spoon half in each tortilla bowl. Wipe out skillet. Add eggs; scramble, cooking until thickened and no liquid egg remains. Meanwhile, microwave salsa, covered, on high until heated through, 1 minute.

4. Spoon egg mixture over beans; top with salsa. Sprinkle with cheese.

PER SERVING *1 tortilla bowl equals 675 cal., 37 g fat (13 g sat. fat), 436 mg chol., 1728 mg sodium, 44 g carb. (3 g sugars, 5 g fiber), 37 g pro.*

CHORIZO AND
EGGS RANCHERO

SMOKED GOUDA &
SWISS CHARD STRATA

Smoked Gouda & Swiss Chard Strata

I shared this impressive strata with friends at their new home. For your special occasions, change up the veggies and cheese. I've used tomatoes, spinach and cheddar.

—KIM FORNI LACONIA, NH

PREP: 30 MIN. + CHILLING • **BAKE:** 1 HOUR
MAKES: 10 SERVINGS

- 10 bacon strips, chopped
- 1 pound Swiss chard, leaves chopped and stems julienned
- 1 large sweet onion, thinly sliced
- ½ cup chopped roasted sweet red peppers
- 12 slices white bread, toasted and cubed
- 2 cups (8 ounces) smoked Gouda or smoked Gruyere cheese, shredded
- 2 cups (8 ounces) Swiss cheese, shredded
- 10 large eggs
- 3½ cups 2% milk
- 2 teaspoons prepared mustard
- 1 teaspoon salt
- ½ teaspoon coarsely ground pepper
- ½ teaspoon cayenne pepper

1. In a large skillet, cook bacon over medium heat until crisp; drain on paper towels, reserving 1 tablespoon drippings. Cook chard stems and onion in reserved drippings over medium heat until tender, about 4 minutes. Add chard leaves and red pepper; cook 2 minutes. Drain.

2. Lightly grease a 13x9-in. baking dish. Layer with half of the bread cubes, half of the vegetable mixture and half of the cheeses. Repeat layers.

3. Mix remaining ingredients until well blended. Pour over layers; press down slightly. Sprinkle bacon over top. Cover and refrigerate several hours or overnight.

4. Preheat oven to 325°. Bake until puffy, lightly browned and set, about 1 hour.

PER SERVING *1 piece equals 509 cal., 31 g fat (14 g sat. fat), 257 mg chol., 1055 mg sodium, 28 g carb. (10 g sugars, 2 g fiber), 28 g pro.*

Spinach-Egg Breakfast Pizzas

I like my food pretty, and this breakfast pizza is eye-popping. Bring it to the table with a bowl of berries or grapes and cafe au lait.

—LILY JULOW LAWRENCEVILLE, GA

PREP: 20 MIN. • **BAKE:** 15 MIN.
MAKES: 4 SERVINGS

- Cornmeal
- 1 loaf (1 pound) frozen pizza dough, thawed
- 1 tablespoon plus additional extra virgin olive oil, divided
- 5 to 6 ounces fresh baby spinach
- ⅓ cup plus additional grated Parmesan cheese, divided
- 3 tablespoons sour cream
- 1 small garlic clove, minced
- ¼ teaspoon sea salt
- ⅛ teaspoon plus additional coarsely ground pepper, divided
- 4 large eggs

1. Preheat oven to 500°. Line two 15x10-in. baking pans with parchment paper; sprinkle lightly with cornmeal. Cut dough into four pieces; stretch and shape into 6- to 7-in. circles.

2. Meanwhile, in a large skillet, heat olive oil over medium-high heat. Add spinach; cook and stir until just starting to wilt, 1-2 minutes. Combine spinach with next five ingredients; spread spinach mixture over each pizza. Leave a slight border of raised dough along edge. Bake on a lower oven rack about 5 minutes.

3. Remove from oven; break an egg into center of each pizza. Return to lower oven rack, baking until the egg whites are set but yolks are still runny, about 6-10 minutes. Drizzle additional olive oil over pizzas; top each with additional Parmesan and pepper. Serve immediately.

PER SERVING *1 pizza equals 433 cal., 14 g fat (4 g sat. fat), 199 mg chol., 865 mg sodium, 55 g carb. (3 g sugars, 1 g fiber), 16 g pro.*

SPINACH-EGG
BREAKFAST PIZZAS

Sweetly Spiced

These Field Editors treat you to their prized desserts filled with cinnamon, nutmeg and ginger. Settle in and enjoy a nice big slice.

GINGER-WALNUT BUNDT CAKE

Ginger-Walnut Bundt Cake

My husband, Ken, loves this Bundt cake with its bits of crystallized ginger. Feel free to drizzle the cake with vanilla glaze instead of lemon.

—NANCY ZIMMERMAN
CAPE MAY COURT HOUSE, NJ

PREP: 20 MIN. • **BAKE:** 40 MIN. + COOLING
MAKES: 16 SERVINGS

- 1 cup packed brown sugar
- 1 cup hot brewed coffee
- 1 cup canola oil
- 1 cup light molasses
- ¼ cup sour cream
- 2 large eggs
- 3¾ cups all-purpose flour
- 5 teaspoons ground ginger
- 2½ teaspoons baking soda
- 1½ teaspoons ground cinnamon
- 1 teaspoon salt
- 1 cup chopped walnuts, toasted
- ¼ cup chopped crystallized ginger

GLAZE
- 2 cups confectioners' sugar
- 2 teaspoons grated lemon peel
- 3 to 4 tablespoons lemon juice
  Additional chopped crystallized ginger

1. Preheat oven to 350°. Grease and flour a 10-in. fluted tube pan. In a large bowl, beat brown sugar, coffee, oil, molasses and sour cream. Add eggs; beat until well blended. In another bowl, whisk flour, ground ginger, baking soda, cinnamon and salt; gradually beat into molasses mixture. Stir in walnuts and crystallized ginger.
2. Transfer batter to prepared pan. Bake 40-50 minutes or until a toothpick inserted in center comes out clean. Cool in pan 10 minutes

before removing to a wire rack to cool completely.
3. For glaze, in a small bowl, mix confectioners' sugar, lemon peel and enough lemon juice to reach a drizzling consistency. Drizzle over cake; sprinkle with additional crystallized ginger.

NOTE *To remove cakes easily, use solid shortening to grease plain and fluted tube pans. To toast nuts, bake in a shallow pan in a 350° oven for 5-10 minutes or cook in a skillet over low heat until lightly browned, stirring occasionally.*

PER SERVING *1 slice equals 465 cal., 20 g fat (2 g sat. fat), 26 mg chol., 369 mg sodium, 68 g carb., 1 g fiber, 5 g pro.*

Bagel Bread Pudding with Bourbon Sauce

I worked in a health club where bagels arrived daily, so I experimented with leftovers. I wasn't a bread pudding fan until I tried it with bagels.

—KATHY HAWKINS INGLESIDE, IL

PREP: 20 MIN. + CHILLING • **BAKE:** 40 MIN.
MAKES: 15 SERVINGS (1⅓ CUPS SAUCE)

- 4 large eggs
- 3¾ cups 2% milk
- 1 cup sugar
- ¾ cup butter, melted
- 2 teaspoons ground cinnamon
- 2 teaspoons vanilla extract
- 1 teaspoon ground nutmeg
- 6 cinnamon-raisin bagels, cubed (about 10 cups)
- 1⅓ cups raisins

SAUCE
- ½ cup 2% milk
- 1 teaspoon white vinegar
- 1 cup sugar
- 6 tablespoons butter, cubed
- 2 tablespoons bourbon
- 1 tablespoon light corn syrup
- 1 teaspoon vanilla extract
- ½ teaspoon baking soda

1. In a large bowl, whisk eggs, milk, sugar, melted butter, cinnamon, vanilla and nutmeg until blended. Stir in cubed bagels and raisins. Transfer to a greased 13x9-in. baking dish. Refrigerate, covered, several hours or overnight.

2. Preheat oven to 350°. Remove bread pudding from refrigerator; uncover and let stand while oven heats. Bake 40-45 minutes or until puffed, golden and a knife inserted in center comes out clean.

3. For sauce, mix milk and vinegar; let stand 5 minutes. In a small saucepan, combine remaining sauce ingredients; stir in milk mixture. Bring to a boil. Cook and stir until sugar is dissolved. Serve with warm bread pudding.

PER SERVING 442 cal., 17 g fat (10 g sat. fat), 91 mg chol., 346 mg sodium, 65 g carb., 2 g fiber, 8 g pro.

BAGEL BREAD PUDDING WITH BOURBON SAUCE

SPICY APPLESAUCE FRUIT BREAD

EAT SMART
Spicy Applesauce Fruit Bread

I've had this fruity quick bread in my recipe collection since 1975. I tweak it with spices and candied fruit, depending on the season.

—DAWN LOWENSTEIN
HUNTINGDON VALLEY, PA

PREP: 20 MIN. • **BAKE:** 30 MIN. + COOLING
MAKES: 2 LOAVES (12 SLICES EACH)

- 2 cups plus 2 tablespoons all-purpose flour, divided
- 2 teaspoons baking powder
- 1 teaspoon salt
- 1 teaspoon ground cinnamon
- 1 teaspoon ground nutmeg
- ½ teaspoon ground allspice
- ½ teaspoon ground cloves
- ½ teaspoon baking soda
- 2 large eggs
- 1¼ cups unsweetened applesauce
- ¾ cup sugar
- ¼ cup packed brown sugar
- ¼ cup butter, melted
- 1 tablespoon grated orange peel
- ½ cup dried cranberries or raisins
- ½ cup chopped candied citron

1. Preheat oven to 350°. In a large bowl, whisk 2 cups flour, baking powder, salt, spices and baking soda. In another bowl, whisk eggs, applesauce, sugars, melted butter and orange peel until blended. Add to flour mixture; stir just until moistened. In a small bowl, toss cranberries and candied citron with remaining flour; fold into batter.

2. Transfer to two greased 8x4-in. loaf pans. Bake 30-35 minutes or until a toothpick inserted in center comes out clean. Cool in pans 10 minutes before removing to wire racks to cool.

PER SERVING 1 slice equals 126 cal., 3 g fat (1 g sat. fat), 21 mg chol., 194 mg sodium, 25 g carb., 1 g fiber, 2 g pro. *Diabetic Exchanges:* 1½ starch, ½ fat.

Pigs in a Blanket

Go ahead and watch these pigs fly—off the table, that is. Three Field Editors reveal their own takes on the coziest of cocktail apps.

PIGS IN A PONCHO

(5) INGREDIENTS

Grandmother's Toad in a Hole

I have fond memories of my grandma's Yorkshire pudding wrapped around sausages, a puffy dish my kids called The Boat.

—**SUSAN KIEBOAM** STREETSBORO, OH

PREP: 10 MIN. + STANDING • **BAKE:** 25 MIN.
MAKES: 6 SERVINGS

- 3 **large eggs**
- 1 **cup 2% milk**
- ½ **teaspoon salt**
- 1 **cup all-purpose flour**
- 1 **package (12 ounces) uncooked maple breakfast sausage links**
- 3 **tablespoons olive oil**
  Butter and maple syrup, optional

1. Preheat oven to 400°. In a small bowl, whisk eggs, milk and salt. Whisk flour into egg mixture until blended. Let stand 30 minutes. Meanwhile, cook sausage according to package directions; cut each sausage into three pieces.

2. Place oil in a 12-in. nonstick ovenproof skillet. Place in oven for 3-4 minutes or until hot. Stir batter and pour into prepared skillet; top with sausage. Bake 20-25 minutes or until golden brown and puffed. Remove from skillet; cut into wedges. If desired, serve with butter and syrup.

PER SERVING *1 wedge (calculated without butter and syrup) equals 336 cal., 22 g fat (6 g sat. fat), 126 mg chol., 783 mg sodium, 20 g carb., 1 g fiber, 14 g pro.*

GRANDMOTHER'S TOAD IN A HOLE

Drain on paper towels. Discard toothpicks before serving. Serve with sour cream and salsa if desired.

PER SERVING *(calculated without sour cream and salsa) equals 726 cal., 50 g fat (14 g sat. fat), 50 mg chol., 1,494 mg sodium, 48 g carb., 5 g fiber, 21 g pro.*

⑤INGREDIENTS
Ring of Piggies

This charming plate of piggies looks like a festive holiday wreath when I drape fresh rosemary in the center. It makes a wonderful display for merry get-togethers.
—**JULIE PETERSON** CROFTON, MD

PREP: 20 MIN. • **BAKE:** 20 MIN.
MAKES: 3½ DOZEN

- 2 **tubes (8 ounces each) refrigerated crescent rolls**
- 42 **miniature smoked sausages**
  Fresh rosemary sprigs

RING OF PIGGIES

1. Preheat oven to 350°. Unroll crescent dough and separate each tube into eight triangles; cut 14 of the 16 triangles lengthwise into three triangles each. Place one sausage on the wide end of each smaller triangle; roll up tightly.
2. Arrange 24 appetizers, point side down, in a 10-in. circle on a parchment paper-lined baking sheet. Place the remaining appetizers in the center of the ring to form a 7-in. circle. Bake 16-18 minutes or until golden brown.
3. Shape remaining 2 dough triangles into a bow; place on another parchment paper-lined baking sheet. Bake for 10-12 minutes or until golden brown.
4. Cool 5 minutes before carefully removing to a serving platter, placing bow on bottom. Garnish wreath with rosemary sprigs, if desired.

PER SERVING *1 appetizer equals 72 cal., 5 g fat (2 g sat. fat), 6 mg chol., 181 mg sodium, 5 g carb., 0 fiber, 2 g pro.*

Pigs in a Poncho

For pigs in a blanket Mexican style, we add refried beans and chopped green chilies. Spice it up even more with some pepper jack, jalapenos and guacamole.
—**JENNIFER STOWELL** SMITHVILLE, MO

PREP: 25 MIN. • **COOK:** 5 MIN./BATCH
MAKES: 8 SERVINGS

- 8 **hot dogs**
- 1 **can (16 ounces) refried beans**
- 8 **flour tortillas (10 inches)**
- 1 **can (4 ounces) chopped green chilies**
- 1 **can (2¼ ounces) sliced ripe olives, drained**
- 2 **cups (8 ounces) shredded Monterey Jack cheese**
  Oil for frying
  Sour cream and salsa, optional

1. Heat hot dogs according to package directions. Spread beans over the center of each tortilla; layer with green chilies, olives and cheese. Place hot dog down center of tortilla. Fold bottom and sides of tortilla over filling and roll up; secure with a toothpick.
2. In a deep skillet or electric skillet, heat 1 in. of oil to 375°. Fry wraps in batches, seam side down, 2-3 minutes on each side or until golden brown.

MELANIE TRITTEN'S SAUSAGE ORECCHIETTE PASTA *PAGE 242*

Quick Fixes

When you need **dinner in a hurry,** these delightful dishes all cook up in 30 minutes or less. Terrifically tasty, they make **excellent family meals** or fun additions to casual parties and **get-togethers.**

COURTNEY STULTZ'S ARUGULA PESTO CHICKEN

PAGE 240

ANGIE ZIMMERMAN'S DILL PICKLE HAMBURGER PIZZA

PAGE 246

BRANDI CASTILLO'S BREADED BAKED TILAPIA

PAGE 251

Tropical Sweet and Spicy Pork Tenderloin

FAST FIX ▸

When we're craving something sweet and spicy, a pork tenderloin cooked with chipotle, barbecue sauce and pineapple really delivers.

—**CYNTHIA GERKEN** NAPLES, FL

START TO FINISH: 30 MIN.
MAKES: 4 SERVINGS

- 1 pork tenderloin (1 pound), cut into 1-in. cubes
- ¼ teaspoon salt
- ¼ teaspoon pepper
- 2 tablespoons olive oil
- 1 medium onion, chopped
- 1 medium green pepper, chopped
- 3 garlic cloves, minced
- 1 cup chicken stock
- 1 can (20 ounces) pineapple tidbits, drained
- 1 cup honey barbecue sauce
- ½ cup packed brown sugar
- 2 finely chopped chipotle peppers plus 2 teaspoons adobo sauce
- 2 tablespoons reduced-sodium soy sauce
  Hot cooked rice

1. Sprinkle pork with salt and pepper. In a large skillet, heat oil over medium-high heat. Add the pork; cook until browned, 4-6 minutes. Remove.

2. In same skillet, cook onion and pepper until softened, 2-4 minutes. Add garlic; cook 1 minute. Return pork to pan; stir in chicken stock. Cook, covered, until pork is tender, about 5 minutes.

3. Stir in the next five ingredients; simmer, uncovered, until sauce is thickened, about 5 minutes. Serve with rice.

PER SERVING *1½ cups equals 539 cal., 11 g fat (2 g sat. fat), 64 mg chol., 1,374 mg sodium, 82 g carb. (72 g sugars, 2 g fiber), 25 g pro.*

FAST FIX ▸

Arugula Pesto Chicken

We had an abundance of arugula in our garden, so I turned it into pesto. The bold green color reminds my son of something The Incredible Hulk would eat.

—**COURTNEY STULTZ** WEIR, KS

START TO FINISH: 25 MIN.
MAKES: 4 SERVINGS

- 4 cups fresh arugula or spinach
- 1 cup fresh basil leaves
- ¼ cup pine nuts
- 1 garlic clove, minced
- 1½ teaspoons sea salt, divided
- ¼ cup plus 1 tablespoon olive oil, divided
- 4 medium zucchini
- 1 rotisserie chicken, skin removed, shredded
- 2 plum tomatoes, chopped
- ¼ teaspoon pepper
  Grated Parmesan cheese, optional

1. Pulse arugula, basil, pine nuts, garlic and 1 teaspoon salt in a food processor until chopped. While processing, gradually add ¼ cup oil in a steady stream until mixture is smooth. Using a shredder or a spiralizer, shred zucchini lengthwise into long strands.

2. In a large skillet, heat remaining oil over medium heat. Add zucchini strands and chicken. Cook and stir until zucchini is crisp-tender, about 4 minutes.

3. Remove from heat. Add tomatoes, pesto, pepper and remaining salt; toss to coat. If desired, sprinkle with Parmesan cheese. Serve using a slotted spoon.

PER SERVING *1½ cups equals 488 cal., 32 g fat (5 g sat. fat), 110 mg chol., 836 mg sodium, 10 g carb., 3 g fiber, 41 g pro.*

TROPICAL SWEET AND
SPICY PORK TENDERLOIN

⑤INGREDIENTS FAST FIX
Weekday Beef Stew

Beef stew capped with flaky puff pastry adds comfort and joy to the weeknight menu. Make a salad and call your crowd to the table.

—**DANIEL ANDERSON** KENOSHA, WI

START TO FINISH: 30 MIN.
MAKES: 4 SERVINGS

- 1 **sheet frozen puff pastry, thawed**
- 1 **package (15 ounces) refrigerated beef roast au jus**
- 2 **cans (14½ ounces each) diced tomatoes, undrained**
- 1 **package (16 ounces) frozen vegetables for stew**
- ¾ **teaspoon pepper**
- 2 **tablespoons cornstarch**
- 1¼ **cups water**

1. Preheat oven to 400°. Unfold puff pastry. Using a 4-in. round cookie cutter, cut out four circles. Place 2 in. apart on a greased baking sheet. Bake 14-16 minutes or until golden brown.
2. Meanwhile, shred beef with two forks; transfer to a large saucepan. Add tomatoes, vegetables and pepper; bring to a boil. In a small bowl, mix cornstarch and water until smooth; stir into beef mixture. Return to a boil, stirring constantly; cook and stir 1-2 minutes or until thickened.
3. Ladle stew into four bowls; top each with a pastry round.
PER SERVING *1½ cups with 1 pastry round equals 604 cal., 25 g fat (8 g sat. fat), 73 mg chol., 960 mg sodium, 65 g carb., 9 g fiber, 32 g pro.*

DID YOU KNOW?

Imitation crabmeat is best when used in salads, appetizers, casseroles and soups. However, it can be substituted for real crab in equal proportions in other recipes if you keep in mind that the flavor and texture will be different from the real thing. In addition, since imitation crabmeat is already cooked, the cooking time in the recipe may need to be adjusted.

EASY CRAB CAKES

EAT SMART FAST FIX
Easy Crab Cakes

Canned crabmeat makes these delicate patties ideal for dinner when you are pressed for time. You can also form the crab mixture into four thick patties instead of eight cakes.

—**CHARLENE SPELOCK** APOLLO, PA

START TO FINISH: 25 MIN.
MAKES: 4 SERVINGS

- 1 **cup seasoned bread crumbs, divided**
- 2 **green onions, finely chopped**
- ¼ **cup finely chopped sweet red pepper**
- 1 **large egg, lightly beaten**
- ¼ **cup reduced-fat mayonnaise**
- 1 **tablespoon lemon juice**
- ½ **teaspoon garlic powder**
- ⅛ **teaspoon cayenne pepper**
- 2 **cans (6 ounces each) crabmeat, drained, flaked and cartilage removed**
- 1 **tablespoon butter**

1. In a large bowl, combine ⅓ cup bread crumbs, green onions, red pepper, egg, mayonnaise, lemon juice, garlic powder and cayenne; fold in the crab.
2. Place the remaining bread crumbs in a shallow bowl. Divide crab mixture into eight portions; shape into 2-in. balls. Gently coat in bread crumbs and shape into a ½-in.-thick patty.
3. In a large nonstick skillet, heat butter over medium-high heat. Add crab cakes; cook 3-4 minutes on each side or until golden brown.
PER SERVING *2 crab cakes equals 239 cal., 11 g fat (3 g sat. fat), 141 mg chol., 657 mg sodium, 13 g carb., 1 g fiber, 21 g pro.* **Diabetic Exchanges:** *3 lean meat, 2 fat, 1 starch.*

Sausage Orecchiette Pasta

I adapted this pasta to be like my favorite Italian restaurant version, only lighter—and tastier. I often use spicy sausage and broccoli rabe.
—**MELANIE TRITTEN** CHARLOTTE, NC

START TO FINISH: 25 MIN.
MAKES: 6 SERVINGS

- 4 cups uncooked orecchiette or small tube pasta
- 1 package (19½ ounces) Italian turkey sausage links, casings removed
- 3 garlic cloves, minced
- 1 cup white wine or chicken broth
- 4 cups small fresh broccoli florets
- 1 can (14½ ounces) diced tomatoes, drained
- ⅓ cup grated or shredded Parmesan cheese

1. Cook pasta according to package directions. Meanwhile, in a large skillet, cook sausage over medium heat 6-8 minutes or until no longer pink, breaking into crumbles. Add garlic; cook 1 minute longer. Add wine, stirring to loosen browned bits from pan. Bring to a boil; cook 1-2 minutes or until liquid is reduced by half.
2. Stir in the broccoli and tomatoes. Reduce heat; simmer, covered, for 4-6 minutes or until the broccoli is crisp-tender. Drain pasta; add to the skillet and toss to coat. Serve with Parmesan cheese.

PER SERVING 1⅔ cups equals 363 cal., 8 g fat (2 g sat. fat), 38 mg chol., 571 mg sodium, 48 g carb., 5 g fiber, 20 g pro. *Diabetic Exchanges: 3 lean meat, 2½ starch, 1 vegetable.*

READER RAVE

Everyone in my family enjoys this recipe. Try doubling it—I do for my family. Then I keep the leftovers in the fridge for my teenagers to heat up as a snack, since they're always hunting for something good to eat. The pasta is easy and tasty!
—**SNWILLIAMSON**
TASTEOFHOME.COM

BEEF & BACON GNOCCHI SKILLET

Try this gnocchi dish that tastes like bacon cheeseburgers. Go ahead and top it as you would a burger—with ketchup, mustard and pickles.
—**ASHLEY LECKER** GREEN BAY, WI

Beef & Bacon Gnocchi Skillet

START TO FINISH: 30 MIN.
MAKES: 6 SERVINGS

- 1 package (16 ounces) potato gnocchi
- 1¼ pounds lean ground beef (90% lean)
- 1 medium onion, chopped
- 8 cooked bacon strips, crumbled and divided
- 1 cup water
- ½ cup heavy whipping cream
- 1 tablespoon ketchup
- ¼ teaspoon salt
- ¼ teaspoon pepper
- 1½ cups (6 ounces) shredded cheddar cheese
- ½ cup chopped tomatoes
- 2 green onions, sliced

1. Preheat broiler. Cook gnocchi according to package directions; drain.
2. Meanwhile, in a large ovenproof skillet, cook beef and onion, crumbling beef, over medium heat until no longer pink, about 4-6 minutes. Drain.
3. Stir in half of the bacon; add the gnocchi, water, cream and ketchup. Bring to a boil. Cook, stirring, over medium heat until the sauce has thickened, 3-4 minutes. Add the seasonings. Sprinkle with cheese.
4. Broil 3-4 in. from heat until cheese has melted, 1-2 minutes. Top with tomatoes, green onions and remaining bacon.

NOTE *Look for potato gnocchi in the pasta or frozen foods section.*
PER SERVING 1 cup equals 573 cal., 31 g fat (16 g sat. fat), 136 mg chol., 961 mg sodium, 35 g carb. (7 g sugars, 2 g fiber), 36 g pro.

Shrimp Tortellini Pasta Toss

Cheese tortellini may taste indulgent, but when you bulk it up with peas and shrimp, it's actually a healthy, quick meal.

—*TASTE OF HOME* TEST KITCHEN

START TO FINISH: 20 MIN.
MAKES: 4 SERVINGS

- 1 **package (9 ounces) refrigerated cheese tortellini**
- 1 **cup frozen peas**
- 3 **tablespoons olive oil, divided**
- 1 **pound uncooked shrimp (31-40 per pound), peeled and deveined**
- 2 **garlic cloves, minced**
- ¼ **teaspoon salt**
- ¼ **teaspoon dried thyme**
- ¼ **teaspoon pepper**

1. Cook tortellini according to the package directions, adding peas during the last 5 minutes of cooking.

2. Meanwhile, in a large nonstick skillet, heat 2 tablespoons oil over medium-high heat. Add shrimp; cook and stir 2 minutes. Add garlic; cook 1-2 minutes longer or until shrimp turn pink.

3. Drain tortellini mixture; add to skillet. Stir in salt, thyme, pepper and remaining oil; toss to coat.

PER SERVING *1¼ cups equals 413 cal., 17 g fat (4 g sat. fat), 165 mg chol., 559 mg sodium, 36 g carb., 3 g fiber, 29 g pro.* **Diabetic Exchanges:** *4 lean meat, 2 starch, 2 fat.*

SHRIMP ASPARAGUS FETTUCCINE
Bring 4 quarts water to a boil. Add 9 ounces refrigerated fettuccine and 1 cup cut fresh asparagus. Boil for 2-3 minutes or until pasta is tender. Proceed with the recipe as written but replace thyme with ¾ tsp. dried basil.

SOY SHRIMP WITH RICE NOODLES
Cook 8.8 ounces thin rice noodles according to package directions, adding 1 cup frozen shelled edamame during the last 4 minutes of cooking. Proceed with the recipe as written but replace thyme with ¼ cup reduced-sodium soy sauce and omit salt.

Thai Red Curry Chicken & Vegetables

The key to this curry chicken is getting complex flavors without a heavy feel. For the veggies, I like colorful pea pods, sweet red peppers and water chestnuts.

—**DAVID DAHLMAN** CHATSWORTH, CA

START TO FINISH: 30 MIN.
MAKES: 4 SERVINGS

- 1½ **pounds boneless skinless chicken breasts, cut into 1½-inch pieces**
- 1⅓ **cups light coconut milk**
- 2 **tablespoons red curry paste**
- ½ **teaspoon salt**
- 3 **cups hot cooked brown rice**
- 1 **package (16 ounces) frozen stir-fry vegetable blend**

1. Preheat oven to 425°. Place chicken in a greased 8-in. square baking dish. In a small bowl, mix coconut milk, curry paste and salt; pour over chicken.

2. Bake, covered, 18-22 minutes or until chicken is no longer pink. Meanwhile, cook the vegetables according to package directions; drain. Serve chicken with rice and vegetables.

PER SERVING *1 cup chicken with ¾ cup rice and ¾ cup vegetables equals 511 cal., 14 g fat (6 g sat. fat), 94 mg chol., 606 mg sodium, 51 g carb., 5 g fiber, 41 g pro.* **Diabetic Exchanges:** *5 lean meat, 3 starch, 1 vegetable, 1 fat.*

SHRIMP TORTELLINI PASTA TOSS

Skillet Shepherd's Pie

This is the best shepherd's pie I've ever tasted. It's very quick to make, and I usually have most of the ingredients on hand. Round out the meal with fresh fruit.

—**TIRZAH SANDT** SAN DIEGO, CA

START TO FINISH: 30 MIN.
MAKES: 6 SERVINGS

- 1 **pound ground beef**
- 1 **cup chopped onion**
- 2 **cups frozen corn, thawed**
- 2 **cups frozen peas, thawed**
- 2 **tablespoons ketchup**
- 1 **tablespoon Worcestershire sauce**
- 2 **teaspoons minced garlic**
- 1 **tablespoon cornstarch**
- 1 **teaspoon beef bouillon granules**
- ½ **cup cold water**
- ½ **cup sour cream**
- 3½ **cups mashed potatoes (prepared with milk and butter)**
- ¾ **cup shredded cheddar cheese**

1. In a large skillet, cook beef and onion over medium heat until meat is no longer pink; drain. Stir in the corn, peas, ketchup, Worcestershire sauce and garlic. Reduce heat to medium-low; cover and cook for 5 minutes.

2. Combine the cornstarch, bouillon and water until well blended; stir into beef mixture. Bring to a boil over medium heat; cook and stir for 2 minutes or until thickened. Stir in sour cream and heat through (do not boil).

3. Spread mashed potatoes over the top; sprinkle with cheese. Cover and cook until potatoes are heated through and cheese is melted.

FREEZE OPTION *Prepare beef mixture as directed but do not add sour cream. Freeze cooled meat mixture in a freezer container. To use, partially thaw in refrigerator overnight. Heat through in a large skillet, stirring occasionally and adding a little water if necessary. Stir in sour cream and proceed as directed.*

PER SERVING *448 cal., 20 g fat (12 g sat. fat), 80 mg chol., 781 mg sodium, 45 g carb., 7 g fiber, 24 g pro.*

Grilled Salmon with Chorizo-Olive Sauce

Every one of the ingredients in this recipe brings a ton of flavor. Both chorizo and salmon cook in a hurry, and garlic and citrus go beautifully with them, too.

—**CHARLENE CHAMBERS**
ORMOND BEACH, FL

START TO FINISH: 25 MIN.
MAKES: 4 SERVINGS

- 3 **links (3 to 4 ounces each) fresh chorizo**
- 4 **green onions, chopped**
- 2 **garlic cloves, minced**
- 1 **can (14½ ounces) diced tomatoes, drained**
- ¼ **cup chopped pitted green olives**
- ½ **teaspoon grated orange peel**
- ¼ **teaspoon salt**
- ¼ **teaspoon pepper**
- 4 **salmon fillets (6 ounces each)**

1. Remove chorizo from casings. In a large ovenproof skillet on a stove or grill, cook and stir chorizo, green onions and the garlic over medium-high heat, crumbling sausage. Cook until sausage is no longer pink, 4-6 minutes; drain.

2. Reduce heat to medium. Add tomatoes, olives and orange peel; stir to combine. Sprinkle salt and pepper over salmon.

3. On a greased grill rack, grill salmon, covered, over medium heat 3-4 minutes per side, or until fish just begins to flake easily with a fork. Top with chorizo mixture.

PER SERVING *1 salmon fillet with ½ cup sauce equals 545 cal., 36 g fat (10 g sat. fat), 142 mg chol., 1,355 mg sodium, 7 g carb. (4 g sugars, 2 g fiber), 43 g pro.*

SKILLET
SHEPHERD'S PIE

SPICY CHICKEN
NUGGETS

(5) INGREDIENTS FAST FIX
Spicy Chicken Nuggets

We devour these golden brown chicken nuggets at least once a week. If you want to tone down the heat, skip the chipotle pepper.

—CHERYL COOK PALMYRA, VA

START TO FINISH: 30 MIN.
MAKES: 6 SERVINGS

- 1½ **cups panko (Japanese) bread crumbs**
- 1½ **cups grated Parmesan cheese**
- ½ **teaspoon ground chipotle pepper, optional**
- ¼ **cup butter, melted**
- 1½ **pounds boneless skinless chicken thighs, cut into 1½-inch pieces**

1. Preheat oven to 400°. In a shallow bowl, mix bread crumbs, cheese and, if desired, chipotle pepper. Place butter in a separate shallow bowl. Dip chicken pieces in butter, then in crumb mixture, patting to help coating adhere.
2. Place chicken pieces on a greased 15x10x1-in. baking pan; sprinkle with remaining crumb mixture. Bake for 20-25 minutes or until no longer pink.
PER SERVING *371 cal., 22 g fat (10 g sat. fat), 113 mg chol., 527 mg sodium, 13 g carb., 1 g fiber, 29 g pro.*

EAT SMART (5) INGREDIENTS FAST FIX
Asian Beef and Noodles

A yummy, economical dish, this recipe takes only five ingredients—all of which are easy to keep on hand. Serve with a dash of soy sauce and a side of fresh pineapple slices. You can also make it with ground turkey instead of beef.

—LAURA STENBERG WYOMING, MN

START TO FINISH: 20 MIN.
MAKES: 4 SERVINGS

- 1 **pound lean ground beef (90% lean)**
- 2 **packages (3 ounces each) Oriental ramen noodles, crumbled**
- 2½ **cups water**
- 2 **cups frozen broccoli stir-fry vegetable blend**
- ¼ **teaspoon ground ginger**
- 2 **tablespoons thinly sliced green onion**

1. In a large skillet, cook beef over medium heat until no longer pink; drain. Add the contents of one ramen noodle flavoring packet; stir until dissolved. Remove beef and set aside.
2. In the same skillet, combine the water, vegetables, ginger, noodles and contents of remaining flavoring packet. Bring to a boil. Reduce heat; cover and simmer for 3-4 minutes or until noodles are tender, stirring occasionally. Return beef to the pan and heat through. Stir in onion.
PER SERVING *1½ cups equals 377 cal., 15 g fat (7 g sat. fat), 56 mg chol., 624 mg sodium, 31 g carb., 3 g fiber, 27 g pro.* **Diabetic Exchanges:** *3 lean meat, 2 starch, 1 fat.*

ASIAN BEEF AND NOODLES

> I created this very tempting seafood pasta for my wife. It's a terrific meal served with crusty sourdough. If you don't like spice, skip the red pepper flakes.
> —GEORGE LEVINTHAL GOLETA, CA

FAST FIX

Sauteed Scallops & Shrimp Pasta

START TO FINISH: 30 MIN.
MAKES: 2 SERVINGS

- 8 uncooked shrimp (16–20 per pound), peeled and deveined
- 6 sea scallops (about 12 ounces)
- ½ teaspoon seafood seasoning
- 3 tablespoons unsalted butter, divided
- 1½ cups (about 3 to 4 ounces) small fresh mushrooms, halved
- ½ cup frozen peas, thawed
- ¼ cup finely chopped shallots
- ⅓ cup white wine or chicken broth
- 4 ounces uncooked angel hair pasta
- ¼ cup plus 1 tablespoon chopped fresh parsley, divided
- 2 large garlic cloves, minced
- ¼ to ½ teaspoon crushed red pepper flakes
- ¼ teaspoon salt
- 2 tablespoons grape-seed oil

1. Pat shrimp and scallops dry; sprinkle with seafood seasoning.
2. In a small skillet, melt 1 tablespoon butter over medium heat. Cook and stir mushrooms about 3 minutes. Add peas; cook until vegetables are tender, about 3-4 minutes. Remove. Add shallots and 1 tablespoon butter; cook and stir until they start to soften, 1-2 minutes. Stir in wine; reduce heat to medium-low and simmer, uncovered, until ready to serve.
3. Meanwhile, in a large saucepan, cook pasta according to package directions; drain, reserving ½ cup pasta water. Return pasta to pan. Over low heat, stir in ¼ cup parsley, garlic, pepper flakes, salt, mushroom mixture and remaining butter, adding enough reserved pasta water to moisten.
4. In a large skillet, heat grape-seed oil over medium-high heat. Add scallops and shrimp; sear until scallops are golden brown and firm and shrimp turn pink, about 2-3 minutes on each side. Combine with pasta and sauce; sprinkle with remaining parsley.

PER SERVING *1 serving equals 733 cal., 35 g fat (13 g sat. fat), 210 mg chol., 1263 mg sodium, 56 g carb. (3 g sugars, 3 g fiber), 47 g pro.*

FAST FIX

Dill Pickle Hamburger Pizza

My husband's favorite foods are pizza and cheeseburgers, so I combined the two in a pizza with mayo and dill pickle juice topping.
—ANGIE ZIMMERMAN EUREKA, IL

START TO FINISH: 30 MIN.
MAKES: 6 SERVINGS

- ½ pound ground beef
- 1 prebaked 12-inch pizza crust
- ½ cup ketchup
- ¼ cup prepared mustard
- 1½ cups (6 ounces) shredded cheddar cheese
- 2 cups shredded lettuce
- ½ cup chopped dill pickle
- ¼ cup chopped onion
- ½ cup mayonnaise
- 2 to 3 tablespoons dill pickle juice

1. Preheat oven to 425°. In a large skillet, crumble and cook beef over medium heat until no longer pink, about 3-4 minutes; drain.
2. Meanwhile, place crust on an ungreased baking sheet or pizza pan. Mix ketchup and mustard; spread over crust. Add ground beef; bake 5 minutes. Sprinkle with cheese; bake until cheese is bubbly and crust is lightly browned, 8-10 minutes more.
3. Top with shredded lettuce, dill pickle and onion. Whisk mayonnaise and enough pickle juice to reach desired consistency; drizzle over the pizza.

PER SERVING *1 slice equals 521 cal., 32 g fat (10 g sat. fat), 59 mg chol., 1,192 mg sodium, 36 g carb. (7 g sugars, 2 g fiber), 21 g pro.*

DILL PICKLE HAMBURGER PIZZA

Pizza Go Round

Pizza's saucy, spicy possibilities extend well beyond the crust. Our Facebook fans deliver the good times with their delicious twists on the classic.

1 My boys love **bubble pizza.** Start by cutting up packaged biscuit dough, and place it in a lightly greased baking dish. Top with pizza sauce and your favorite fixings, then bake. It bubbles and breaks into bite-size pieces.
MEGAN KOREN
WESTFORD, NY

2 **Pizza dip.** Spread an 8-oz. block of softened cream cheese into a pie plate. Drizzle some pizza sauce on top. Sprinkle a little shredded mozzarella over that, and top with pepperoni and olives. Bake, and serve warm with plenty of scoop-shaped corn chips.
ANNE ZECHEL RUBICON, WI

3 Take your favorite pizza ingredients and put them over tortilla chips in a large cast-iron skillet. Put it in the oven and bake till the **nachos** are warm and melty. Instead of salsa, you can put warmed pizza or marinara sauce on them.
KERRIE SIMMONDS
NAMPA, ID

4 **Pizza pasta.** It's just pasta, pepperoni, ground beef, onions, mushrooms and green pepper mixed with spaghetti sauce, then topped with cheese.
KENDRA HICKS
CAMDENTON, MO

5 Start with **a layer of fries,** then pour meat sauce over them. Top with your favorite pizza toppings and lots of cheese. Pop it under the broiler...heaven and heart attack in a pan!
CRAIG CUNNINGHAM
CHÂTEAUGUAY, QC

6 Butterfly boneless, skinless **chicken breasts,** stuff them with mozzarella and pepperoni, and then fold them up. I top the chicken with marinara, spicy salami, pepperoni and more cheese, then bake until done. Delicious!
VICTORIA PENFOLD
CRANBROOK, BC

7 I love making **pizza cheese balls** with sun-dried tomatoes.
RAY CARSON
CINCINNATI, OH

8 We take our leftover pizza toppers and **scramble them with eggs** the next morning. Works with any toppings!
ERIN BURNS
CHICAGO, IL

9 **Pizza oyster crackers!** Toss two (10-oz.) packages oyster crackers with ½ cup canola oil, ⅓ cup grated Parmesan cheese, ½ tsp. garlic powder and 3 Tbsp. pizza seasoning (I always have it in my cupboard). Bake 5 minutes at 350°. I store these in an airtight container so we have lots for snacking when my kids visit.
CAROL BETZ
GRAND RAPIDS, MI

10 Try your favorite pizza toppings **tossed into a salad.** It's a healthy version of pizza with all the flavors you enjoy! I like mine with salami, cheese cubes, onions, tomatoes, olives, mushrooms and pepperoncini. Splash on Italian dressing and toss on some homemade croutons.
LAUREN KREHMEYER
MEQUON, WI

SHRIMP & CORN STIR-FRY

EAT SMART **FAST FIX**
Shrimp & Corn Stir-Fry

I make this seafood stir-fry at summer's end when my garden has plenty of tomatoes, squash, garlic and corn. For a quick supper, we serve it over rice.
—**LINDSAY HONN** HUNTINGDON, PA

START TO FINISH: 20 MIN.
MAKES: 4 SERVINGS

- 2 **tablespoons olive oil**
- 2 **small yellow summer squash, sliced**
- 1 **small onion, chopped**
- 1 **pound uncooked shrimp (26–30 per pound), peeled and deveined**
- 1½ **cups fresh or frozen corn, thawed**
- 1 **cup chopped tomatoes**
- 4 **garlic cloves, minced**
- ½ **teaspoon salt**
- ¼ **teaspoon pepper**
- ¼ **teaspoon crushed red pepper flakes, optional**
- ¼ **cup chopped fresh basil**
  Hot cooked brown rice

1. In a large skillet, heat oil over medium-high heat. Add squash and onion; stir-fry until squash is crisp-tender, 2-3 minutes.
2. Add next six ingredients and, if desired, pepper flakes; stir-fry until shrimp turn pink, 3-4 minutes longer. Top with basil. Serve with rice.
PER SERVING *(calculated without rice) 239 cal., 9 g fat (1 g sat. fat), 138 mg chol., 443 mg sodium, 19 g carb. (8 g sugars, 3 g fiber), 22 g pro. Diabetic Exchanges: 3 lean meat, 1½ fat, 1 starch, 1 vegetable.*

EAT SMART **FAST FIX**
Saucy Beef & Cabbage Supper

My beef and cabbage supper began as a Reuben sandwich idea without the gluten. We also make it with smoked sausage. It's comforting on cooler days.
—**COURTNEY STULTZ** WEIR, KS

START TO FINISH: 30 MIN.
MAKES: 6 SERVINGS

- 1 **pound lean ground beef (90% lean)**
- 3 **tablespoons olive oil, divided**
- 8 **cups (about 1 small head) chopped cabbage**
- 5 **medium carrots, peeled and finely chopped**
- 1 **medium onion, chopped**
- 2 **large garlic cloves, minced**
- 1 **teaspoon sea salt**
- 1 **teaspoon pepper**
- ½ **teaspoon caraway seeds**
- ¼ **teaspoon ground allspice**
- ⅛ **teaspoon ground cloves**
- ½ **cup ketchup**
- 2 **teaspoons cider vinegar**

1. In a 6-qt. stockpot over medium heat, crumble and cook beef until meat is no longer pink, 5-7 minutes; drain.
2. Add 2 tablespoons olive oil; stir in next nine ingredients. Cook for 5-7 minutes, stirring frequently, until vegetables are crisp-tender.
3. Stir together ketchup, vinegar and remaining oil until smooth. Pour over meat and vegetables; cook 5 minutes more.
PER SERVING *1¼ cups equals 260 cal., 13 g fat (3 g sat. fat), 47 mg chol., 671 mg sodium, 20 g carb. (12 g sugars, 5 g fiber), 17 g pro. Diabetic Exchanges: 2 lean meat, 2 vegetable, 1½ fat, ½ starch.*

TOP TIP

To shred cabbage by hand, cut cabbage into wedges. Place cut side down on a cutting board. With a large sharp knife, cut into thin slices.

Peanut Butter Pork Curry

For an anniversary with my boyfriend, I cooked tenderloins Asian-style with peanut, coconut and curry flavors. Bonus: The butcher cubed the pork for me to save time.

—ANGELA ROBINSON FINDLAY, OH

START TO FINISH: 30 MIN.
MAKES: 6 SERVINGS

- 2 **pork tenderloins (¾ pound each), cubed**
- 1 **teaspoon salt, divided**
- ½ **teaspoon pepper**
- 1 **tablespoon olive oil**
- 1 **cup sliced fresh carrots**
- 1 **medium onion, chopped**
- 2 **garlic cloves, minced**
- 1 **can (14½ ounces) diced tomatoes, drained**
- 1 **cup chicken broth**
- 1 **cup cream of coconut or coconut milk**
- ½ **cup creamy peanut butter**
- 3 **teaspoons curry powder**
- ¼ **teaspoon cayenne pepper**
  Cooked brown rice

1. Sprinkle pork with ½ teaspoon salt and pepper. In a large nonstick skillet, heat oil over medium-high heat. Add pork; cook and stir until no longer pink, 4-6 minutes. Remove.
2. In same skillet, cook carrots and onion until softened, 4-6 minutes. Add the garlic; cook for 2 minutes. Return pork to skillet. Add tomatoes and broth. Reduce heat; simmer, covered, 6-8 minutes.
3. Stir in cream of coconut, peanut butter, curry, cayenne and remaining salt until smooth. Simmer, uncovered, until thickened slightly, about 2 minutes. Serve with brown rice.
PER SERVING *1 cup equals 463 cal., 24 g fat (9 g sat. fat), 64 mg chol., 837 mg sodium, 36 g carb. (29 g sugars, 4 g fiber), 29 g pro.*

Gnocchi with White Beans

Here's one of those no-muss, no-fuss recipes you can toss together in a single pan. It's also good with crumbled Italian chicken sausage if you need to please the meat lovers in your house.

—JULI MEYERS HINESVILLE, GA

START TO FINISH: 30 MIN.
MAKES: 6 SERVINGS

- 1 **tablespoon olive oil**
- 1 **medium onion, chopped**
- 2 **garlic cloves, minced**
- 1 **package (16 ounces) potato gnocchi**
- 1 **can (15 ounces) white kidney or cannellini beans, rinsed and drained**
- 1 **can (14½ ounces) Italian diced tomatoes, undrained**
- 1 **package (6 ounces) fresh baby spinach**
- ¼ **teaspoon pepper**
- ½ **cup shredded part-skim mozzarella cheese**
- 3 **tablespoons grated Parmesan cheese**

1. In a large skillet, heat oil over medium-high heat. Add onion; cook and stir until tender. Add garlic; cook 1 minute longer. Add gnocchi; cook and stir 5-6 minutes or until golden brown. Stir in beans, tomatoes, spinach and pepper; heat through.
2. Sprinkle with the cheeses; cover and remove from heat. Let stand 3-4 minutes or until cheese is melted.
NOTE *Look for potato gnocchi in the pasta or frozen foods section.*
PER SERVING *1 cup equals 307 cal., 6 g fat (2 g sat. fat), 13 mg chol., 789 mg sodium, 50 g carb., 6 g fiber, 13 g pro.*

GNOCCHI WITH WHITE BEANS

Ham & Mango Quesadillas

If you like the ease of quesadillas, especially on busy weeknights, you'll really love this fresh and fruity variation featuring mango-enhanced jarred salsa.
—*TASTE OF HOME* TEST KITCHEN

START TO FINISH: 25 MIN.
MAKES: 4 SERVINGS

- 1 tablespoon butter
- 4 flour tortillas (8 inches)
- 2 cups (8 ounces) shredded Monterey Jack cheese
- 1 medium mango, peeled and cubed, divided
- ¼ pound thick sliced deli ham, cut into ½-in. strips
- 6 teaspoons minced fresh cilantro, divided
- ¾ cup salsa
  Sour cream, optional

1. Spread butter over one side of each tortilla. Place tortillas, butter side down, on a griddle. Sprinkle each with ½ cup cheese, 3 tablespoons mango, ¼ cup ham and 1 teaspoon cilantro. Fold over and cook on low heat for 1-2 minutes on each side or until cheese is melted. Cut into wedges.

2. Combine salsa and the remaining mango and cilantro; serve with the quesadillas. Garnish with sour cream if desired.

PER SERVING *1 quesadilla with ¼ cup salsa (calculated without sour cream) equals 459 cal., 24 g fat (13 g sat. fat), 70 mg chol., 1,018 mg sodium, 38 g carb., 1 g fiber, 24 g pro.*

> My ribeye steak showcases flavors of Greece that my husband and I learned about while on a cruise. We like it with pita bread and hummus.
> —**MARY LOU COOK** WELCHES, OR

Grilled Steaks with Greek Relish

START TO FINISH: 30 MIN.
MAKES: 2 SERVINGS

- 2 plum tomatoes, seeded and chopped
- ½ cup chopped red onion
- ⅓ cup pitted Greek olives
- 2 tablespoons minced fresh cilantro
- 2 tablespoons lemon juice, divided
- 1 tablespoon olive oil
- 1 garlic clove, minced
- 1 beef ribeye steak (¾ pound)
- ½ cup crumbled feta cheese

1. For relish, in a small bowl, combine tomatoes, onion, olives, cilantro, 1 tablespoon lemon juice, oil and garlic.

2. Drizzle remaining lemon juice over steak. Grill steak, covered, over medium heat or broil 4 in. from heat for 5-7 minutes on each side or until meat reaches desired doneness (for medium-rare, a thermometer should read 145°; medium, 160°; well-done, 170°). Let stand 5 minutes before cutting in half. Serve with relish and cheese.

PER SERVING *4 ounces cooked steak with ⅔ cup relish and 2 tablespoons cheese equals 562 cal., 42 g fat (14 g sat. fat), 108 mg chol., 587 mg sodium, 10 g carb., 2 g fiber, 34 g pro.*

HAM & MANGO QUESADILLAS

Spinach Pizza

Looking for a fun twist on a traditional favorite? Veggies and Alfredo sauce add complexity to simple pizza.

—**DAWN BARTHOLOMEW** RALEIGH, NC

START TO FINISH: 25 MIN.
MAKES: 4-6 SERVINGS

- 1 **package (6½ ounces) pizza crust mix**
- ½ **cup Alfredo sauce**
- 2 **medium tomatoes**
- 4 **cups chopped fresh spinach**
- 2 **cups (8 ounces) shredded Italian cheese blend**

1. Prepare pizza dough according to package directions. With floured hands, press dough onto a greased 12-in. pizza pan.
2. Spread Alfredo sauce over dough to within 1 in. of edges. Thinly slice or chop tomatoes; top pizza with spinach, tomatoes and cheese.
3. Bake at 450° for 10-15 minutes or until cheese is melted and crust is golden brown.

PER SERVING *1 slice pizza equals 270 cal., 11 g fat (7 g sat. fat), 33 mg chol., 549 mg sodium, 27 g carb. (3 g sugars, 2 g fiber), 13 g pro.*

Breaded Baked Tilapia

So much flavor...so few ingredients! A quick and easy crumb coating makes this yummy tilapia recipe ideal for busy weeknights. Try the breading on cod for a change of pace.

—**BRANDI CASTILLO** SANTA MARIA, CA

START TO FINISH: 20 MIN.
MAKES: 4 SERVINGS

- ¾ **cup soft bread crumbs**
- ⅓ **cup grated Parmesan cheese**
- 1 **teaspoon garlic salt**
- 1 **teaspoon dried oregano**
- 4 **tilapia fillets (5 ounces each)**

1. Preheat oven to 425°. In a shallow bowl, combine bread crumbs, cheese, garlic salt and oregano. Coat fillets in crumb mixture. Place on a baking sheet coated with cooking spray.
2. Bake 8-12 minutes or until fish flakes easily with a fork.

MEDITERRANEAN PASTA CAESAR TOSS

PER SERVING *1 fillet equals 143 cal., 2 g fat (1 g sat. fat), 72 mg chol., 356 mg sodium, 2 g carb., trace fiber, 28 g pro. Diabetic Exchange: 4 lean meat.*

Mediterranean Pasta Caesar Toss

Get creative using convenience items for a fresh take on ravioli. Try this lightened-up pasta toss for an al fresco dinner, or double it for a family picnic.

—**LIBBY WALP** CHICAGO, IL

START TO FINISH: 30 MIN.
MAKES: 4 SERVINGS

- 1 **package (9 ounces) refrigerated cheese ravioli**
- 1 **cup frozen cut green beans, thawed**
- 1 **cup cherry tomatoes, halved**
- ¾ **teaspoon coarsely ground pepper**
- ⅓ **cup reduced-fat creamy Caesar salad dressing**
- 3 **tablespoons shredded Parmesan cheese**

1. In a large saucepan, cook the ravioli according to the package directions, adding beans during the last 3 minutes of cooking. Drain.
2. In a serving bowl, combine the ravioli mixture, tomatoes and pepper. Add dressing; toss to coat. Sprinkle with cheese.

PER SERVING *1 cup equals 264 cal., 10 g fat (4 g sat. fat), 28 mg chol., 649 mg sodium, 31 g carb., 3 g fiber, 12 g pro. Diabetic Exchanges: 1½ starch, 1 lean meat, 1 vegetable, 1 fat.*

**LEANN DOYLE'S
TURKEY SALISBURY STEAKS**
PAGE 259

Cooking Lighter

Savor all the **fantastic comfort foods** your family members crave...without all the extra calories, fat, sugar and salt. With these light recipes, **eating healthy never tasted so good!**

AMBER MASSEY'S BUFFALO CHICKEN MEATBALLS PAGE 263

MICHELE TUNGETT'S GRILLED TOMATO PIZZAS PAGE 262

LAURIE MARTIGNON'S MANDARIN PORK STIR-FRY PAGE 257

EAT SMART
One-Pot Beef & Pepper Stew

I love almost anything made with green peppers, tomatoes or green chilies. I improvised this quick, satisfying dish one night with things I had on hand.

—**SANDRA CLARK** SIERRA VISTA, AZ

PREP: 10 MIN. • **COOK:** 30 MIN.
MAKES: 8 SERVINGS

- 1 **pound lean ground beef (90% lean)**
- 3 **cans (14½ ounces each) diced tomatoes, undrained**
- 4 **large green peppers, coarsely chopped**
- 1 **large onion, chopped**
- 2 **cans (4 ounces each) chopped green chilies**
- 3 **teaspoons garlic powder**
- 1 **teaspoon pepper**
- ¼ **teaspoon salt**
- 2 **cups uncooked instant rice**
  Hot pepper sauce, optional

1. In a 6-qt. stockpot, cook beef over medium heat 6-8 minutes or until no longer pink, breaking into crumbles; drain. Add tomatoes, green peppers, onion, chilies, garlic powder, pepper and salt. Bring to a boil. Reduce heat; simmer, covered, 20-25 minutes or until vegetables are tender.

2. Prepare rice according to package directions. Serve with stew. If desired, add hot pepper sauce.

PER SERVING *1½ cups equals 244 cal., 5 g fat (2 g sat. fat), 35 mg chol., 467 mg sodium, 35 g carb., 5 g fiber, 15 g pro.* **Diabetic Exchanges:** *2 lean meat, 2 vegetable, 1½ starch.*

ONE-POT BEEF & PEPPER STEW

MAKEOVER	TYPICAL
145 Calories	**250** Calories
6g Fat	**12**g Fat
2g Saturated Fat	**8**g Saturated Fat

MAKEOVER LEMON POUND CAKE

EAT SMART
Makeover Lemon Pound Cake

I use fat-free Greek yogurt in this tender, buttery cake to trim the calories. It's a lovely light dessert for those warm summer evenings when you'd like to dine outside.

—**LAUREN GILMORE** PENNINGTON, NJ

PREP: 20 MIN. • **BAKE:** 50 MIN. + COOLING
MAKES: 1 LOAF (16 SLICES)

- ¼ **cup butter, softened**
- ¾ **cup sugar**
- 3 **large eggs**
- 2 **tablespoons canola oil**
- 2 **tablespoons lemon juice**
- 2 **teaspoons grated lemon peel**
- 1 **teaspoon vanilla extract**
- 2 **tablespoons poppy seeds, optional**
- 1½ **cups all-purpose flour**
- 2½ **teaspoons baking powder**
- ¾ **teaspoon salt**
- 1 **cup fat-free vanilla Greek yogurt**
  Candied lemon slices, optional

1. Preheat oven to 350°. Coat a 9x5-in. loaf pan with cooking spray.

2. In a large bowl, beat butter and sugar until crumbly. Add eggs, one at a time, beating well after each addition. Beat in oil, lemon juice, peel, vanilla and, if desired, poppy seeds. In another bowl, whisk flour, baking powder and salt; add to creamed mixture alternately with yogurt, beating after each addition just until combined.

3. Transfer to prepared pan. Bake 50-60 minutes or until a toothpick inserted in center comes out clean. Cool in pan 10 minutes before removing to a wire rack to cool completely. If desired, top with candied lemon slices.

PER SERVING *1 slice (calculated without candied lemon slices) equals 145 cal., 6 g fat (2 g sat. fat), 43 mg chol., 253 mg sodium, 20 g carb., trace fiber, 4 g pro.* **Diabetic Exchanges:** *1 starch, 1 fat.*

Smoked Trout Pate

This tasty spread is easy to make in a food processor, and it's a guaranteed winner at parties. The recipe is quite versatile, so feel free to substitute your own favorite smoked fish.

—**JUDY WALLE** TOLEDO, OH

START TO FINISH: 15 MIN.
MAKES: 2⅔ CUPS

- 1 **pound flaked smoked trout**
- 3 **ounces reduced-fat cream cheese**
- ½ **cup half-and-half cream**
- 1 **tablespoon horseradish sauce**
- 1 **tablespoon lemon juice**
- ⅛ **teaspoon pepper**
- 2 **teaspoons minced fresh parsley**
  Assorted crackers

Place first seven ingredients in a food processor; cover and process until blended. Transfer to a small bowl. Chill until serving. Serve pate with crackers.

PER SERVING *2 tablespoons pate (calculated without crackers) equals 55 cal., 3 g fat (1 g sat. fat), 16 mg chol., 174 mg sodium, 1 g carb., trace fiber, 5 g pro.*

Cabbage Roll Skillet

Have a happy helping of this quicker take on something our grandmothers would make. We serve it over brown rice. It also freezes well.

—**SUSAN CHICKNESS** PICTOU COUNTY, NS

PREP: 15 MIN. • **COOK:** 20 MIN.
MAKES: 6 SERVINGS

- 1 **can (28 ounces) whole plum tomatoes, undrained**
- 1 **pound extra-lean ground beef (95% lean)**
- 1 **large onion, chopped**
- 1 **can (8 ounces) tomato sauce**
- 2 **tablespoons cider vinegar**
- 1 **tablespoon brown sugar**
- 1 **teaspoon dried oregano**
- 1 **teaspoon dried thyme**
- ½ **teaspoon pepper**
- 1 **small head cabbage, thinly sliced (about 6 cups)**
- 1 **medium green pepper, cut into thin strips**
- 4 **cups hot cooked brown rice**

1. Drain plum tomatoes, reserving liquid; coarsely chop the tomatoes. In a large nonstick skillet, cook beef and onion over medium-high heat 6-8 minutes or until beef is no longer pink, breaking up beef into crumbles. Stir in tomato sauce, vinegar, brown sugar, seasonings and the tomatoes and reserved liquid.

2. Add cabbage and green pepper; cook, covered, 6 minutes, stirring occasionally. Cook, uncovered, 6-8 minutes longer or until cabbage is tender. Serve with rice.

PER SERVING *1⅓ cups with ⅔ cup rice equals 332 cal., 5 g fat (2 g sat. fat), 43 mg chol., 439 mg sodium, 50 g carb., 9 g fiber, 22 g pro.* **Diabetic Exchanges:** *3 starch, 3 lean meat.*

Microwave Egg Sandwich

Looking for a grab-and-go breakfast? This sandwich is high in protein, low in fat and will keep you full all morning.

—**BRENDA OTTO** REEDSBURG, WI

START TO FINISH: 15 MIN.
MAKES: 1 SERVING

- 1 **piece Canadian bacon**
- ¼ **cup egg substitute**
- 1 **tablespoon salsa**
- 1 **tablespoon shredded reduced-fat cheddar cheese**
- 1 **whole wheat English muffin, split, toasted**
- 3 **spinach leaves**

1. Place Canadian bacon on bottom of a 6-oz. ramekin or custard cup coated with cooking spray. Pour egg substitute over top. Microwave, uncovered, on high for 30 seconds; stir. Microwave 15-30 seconds or until egg is almost set. Top with salsa; sprinkle with cheese. Microwave just until cheese is melted, about 10 seconds.

2. Line bottom of English muffin with spinach. Place egg and Canadian bacon over spinach; replace English muffin top.

PER SERVING *1 sandwich equals 218 cal., 4 g fat (2 g sat. fat), 12 mg chol., 751 mg sodium, 30 g carb., 5 g fiber, 17 g pro.* **Diabetic Exchanges:** *2 starch, 2 lean meat.*

TOP TIP

Try using egg substitute instead of whole eggs if you're watching your cholesterol. Using ¼ cup egg substitute instead of 1 whole egg saves 210 mg cholesterol per serving. Egg substitute works great in many recipes, especially in frittatas, omelets and quiches. However, replacing the eggs in baked goods with egg substitute may not produce the best results.

MICROWAVE EGG SANDWICH

BAKED CHICKEN CHALUPAS

Baked Chicken Chalupas

I wanted an easy and healthy alternative to deep-fried chalupas. I tried this baked method, and they turned out amazing!

—**MAGDALENA FLORES** ABILENE, TX

PREP: 20 MIN. • **BAKE:** 15 MIN.
MAKES: 6 SERVINGS

- 6 **corn tortillas (6 inches)**
- 2 **teaspoons olive oil**
- ¾ **cup shredded part-skim mozzarella cheese**
- 2 **cups chopped cooked chicken breast**
- 1 **can (14½ ounces) diced tomatoes with mild green chilies, undrained**
- 1 **teaspoon garlic powder**
- 1 **teaspoon onion powder**
- 1 **teaspoon ground cumin**
- ¼ **teaspoon salt**
- ¼ **teaspoon pepper**
- ½ **cup finely shredded cabbage**

1. Preheat oven to 350°. Place tortillas on an ungreased baking sheet. Brush each tortilla with oil; sprinkle with cheese.
2. Place the chicken, tomatoes and seasonings in a large skillet; cook and stir over medium heat 6-8 minutes or until most of the liquid is evaporated. Spoon mixture over tortillas. Bake 15-18 minutes or until tortillas are crisp and the cheese is melted. Top with cabbage.
PER SERVING *1 chalupa equals 206 cal., 6 g fat (2 g sat. fat), 45 mg chol., 400 mg sodium, 17 g carb., 3 g fiber, 19 g pro.* **Diabetic Exchanges:** *2 lean meat, 1 starch, ½ fat.*

Shrimp & Vegetable Boil

When my kids were small, they enjoyed selecting the ingredients for this dish. If you don't have any shrimp on hand, you can substitute chicken or crab with equally good results.

—**JOYCE GUTH** MOHNTON, PA

PREP: 20 MIN. • **COOK:** 30 MIN.
MAKES: 6 SERVINGS

- 4 **cups water**
- 4 **cups chicken broth**
- 2 **teaspoons salt**
- 2 **teaspoons ground nutmeg**
- ½ **teaspoon sugar**
- 2 **pounds red potatoes (about 8 medium), cut into wedges**
- 1 **medium head cauliflower, broken into florets**
- 2 **large onions, quartered**
- 3 **medium carrots, sliced**
- 1 **pound fresh peas, shelled (about 1 cup)**
- 2 **pounds uncooked shell-on shrimp (26-30 per pound), deveined**
- 6 **ounces fresh baby spinach (about 8 cups)**
- 1 **tablespoon minced fresh parsley**
  Salt and pepper to taste

1. In a stockpot, combine the first five ingredients; add the potatoes, cauliflower, onions, carrots and peas. Bring to a boil. Reduce heat; simmer, uncovered, 12-15 minutes or until vegetables are tender.
2. Stir in shrimp and spinach; cook 3-5 minutes longer or until shrimp turn pink. Drain; transfer to a large serving bowl. Sprinkle with parsley; season with salt and pepper.
PER SERVING *2⅔ cups equals 367 cal., 3 g fat (1 g sat. fat), 185 mg chol., 721 mg sodium, 50 g carb., 11 g fiber, 35 g pro.* **Diabetic Exchanges:** *4 lean meat, 3 starch.*

DID YOU KNOW?

Shrimp are available fresh or frozen (raw or cooked, peeled or in the shell) or canned. Shrimp in the shell (fresh or frozen) are available in different varieties and sizes (medium, large, extra large, jumbo). Uncooked shrimp will have shells that range in color from gray or brown to pink or red. Fresh shrimp should have a firm texture with a mild odor.

SHRIMP & VEGETABLE BOIL

Mandarin Pork Stir-Fry

When my husband and I were dating, he told me he liked Asian food. I got a wok and discovered the joy of dishes like this pork stir-fry. See photo on page 253.

—**LAURIE MARTIGNON** NIAGARA, WI

START TO FINISH: 25 MIN.
MAKES: 4 SERVINGS

- **2** cups uncooked instant rice
- **1** tablespoon cornstarch
- **½** teaspoon garlic powder
- **½** teaspoon ground ginger
- **½** cup orange juice
- **¼** cup water
- **2** tablespoons soy sauce
- **1** pork tenderloin (1 pound), cut into 2-inch strips
- **2** tablespoons canola oil
- **1** package (14 ounces) frozen sugar snap peas
- **1** can (11 ounces) mandarin oranges, drained

1. Cook rice according to package directions. Meanwhile, in a small bowl, combine cornstarch, garlic powder and ginger. Stir in orange juice until smooth. Stir in water and soy sauce; set aside.

2. In a large wok or skillet, stir-fry pork in oil until juices run clear; remove to a platter and keep warm. In the same skillet, stir-fry peas until tender. Return pork to skillet. Stir orange juice mixture; add to skillet. Cook and stir for 2 minutes or until thickened. Gently stir in oranges. Serve with rice.

PER SERVING *1 cup pork mixture with 1 cup cooked rice equals 473 cal., 11 g fat (2 g sat. fat), 63 mg chol., 514 mg sodium, 61 g carb., 5 g fiber, 30 g pro.*

Lemon Chicken Pasta

This dish reminds me of the lemony chicken and rice my mom used to make. In my version, I saute breaded chicken breasts and serve them over pasta.

—**AILEEN RIVERA** BRONX, NY

PREP: 30 MIN. • **COOK:** 15 MIN.
MAKES: 6 SERVINGS

- **4** boneless skinless chicken breast halves (6 ounces each)

LEMON
CHICKEN PASTA

- **1** teaspoon salt, divided
- **¼** teaspoon plus ⅛ teaspoon pepper, divided
- **½** cup all-purpose flour
- **8** ounces uncooked capellini or angel hair pasta
- **3** tablespoons olive oil, divided
- **¼** cup peeled and thinly sliced garlic cloves (about 12 cloves)
- **1** cup white wine or chicken broth
- **2** tablespoons lemon juice
- **½** cup grated Parmigiano-Reggiano cheese
- **⅓** cup plus 3 tablespoons minced fresh parsley, divided
  Lemon wedges, optional

1. Pound chicken breasts with a meat mallet to ¼-in. thickness. Sprinkle with ½ teaspoon salt and ¼ teaspoon pepper. Place flour in a shallow bowl. Dip chicken in flour to coat both sides; shake off excess.

2. Cook pasta according to package directions for al dente. Meanwhile, in a large skillet, heat 2 tablespoons oil over medium heat. Add chicken; cook 2-3 minutes on each side or until no longer pink. Remove and keep warm.

3. In same pan, heat remaining oil over medium heat; add garlic. Cook and stir 30-60 seconds or until garlic is lightly browned. Add wine to pan; increase heat to medium-high. Cook, stirring to loosen browned bits from pan, until liquid is reduced by half. Stir in lemon juice.

4. Drain pasta, reserving ½ cup pasta water; place in a large bowl. Add cheese, ⅓ cup parsley, half of the garlic mixture, and remaining salt and pepper; toss to combine, adding enough reserved pasta water to moisten pasta. Serve with chicken. Drizzle with remaining garlic mixture; sprinkle with remaining parsley. If desired, serve with lemon wedges.

PER SERVING *403 cal., 12 g fat (3 g sat. fat), 68 mg chol., 577 mg sodium, 35 g carb., 2 g fiber, 31 g pro.* **Diabetic Exchanges:** *4 lean meat, 2 starch, 1½ fat.*

Philly Cheesesteak Rolls

You'll love my light take on classic Philly cheesesteak. These rolls boast tender meat, creamy cheese and sweet-and-tangy veggies.

—**PAIGE DAY** NORTH AUGUSTA, SC

PREP: 30 MIN. • **BAKE:** 15 MIN.
MAKES: 4 SERVINGS

- ½ **pound sliced fresh mushrooms**
- 1 **medium onion, halved and sliced**
- 1 **small green pepper, cut into thin strips**
- 1 **beef top round steak (1 pound)**
- 4 **wedges The Laughing Cow light Swiss cheese**
- ¼ **teaspoon pepper**
- 3 **cups hot mashed potatoes (made with fat-free milk)**

1. Preheat oven to 450°. Place a large nonstick skillet coated with cooking spray over medium-high heat. Add mushrooms, onion and green pepper; cook and stir 8-10 minutes or until tender. Remove from pan; cool slightly.
2. Cut steak into four pieces; pound with a meat mallet to ¼-in. thickness. Spread with cheese. Sprinkle with pepper; top with onion mixture. Roll up from a short side; secure with toothpicks.
3. Transfer rolls to a foil-lined 15x10x1-in. baking pan. Bake 15-20 minutes or until meat reaches desired doneness (for medium-rare, a thermometer should read 145°; medium, 160°; well-done, 170°). Let stand 5 minutes. Serve with mashed potatoes.

PER SERVING *1 roll with ¾ cup mashed potatoes equals 364 cal., 10 g fat (3 g sat. fat), 68 mg chol., 822 mg sodium, 34 g carb., 4 g fiber, 33 g pro.* **Diabetic Exchanges:** *4 lean meat, 2 starch, 1 vegetable.*

PHILLY CHEESESTEAK ROLLS

ITALIAN SPAGHETTI WITH CHICKEN & ROASTED VEGETABLES

Italian Spaghetti with Chicken & Roasted Vegetables

Whenever I get a craving for homemade tomato sauce, I make a zesty batch to toss with chicken, veggies and pasta.

—**CARLY CURTIN** ELLICOTT CITY, MD

PREP: 25 MIN. • **COOK:** 25 MIN.
MAKES: 6 SERVINGS

- 3 **plum tomatoes, seeded and chopped**
- 2 **medium zucchini, cubed**
- 1 **medium yellow summer squash, cubed**
- 2 **tablespoons olive oil, divided**
- 2 **teaspoons Italian seasoning, divided**
- 8 **ounces uncooked whole wheat spaghetti**
- 1 **pound boneless skinless chicken breasts, cubed**
- ½ **teaspoon garlic powder**
- ½ **cup reduced-sodium chicken broth**
- ⅓ **cup dry red wine or additional reduced-sodium chicken broth**
- 4 **cans (8 ounces each) no-salt-added tomato sauce**
- 1 **can (6 ounces) tomato paste**
- ¼ **cup minced fresh basil**
- 2 **tablespoons minced fresh oregano**
- ¼ **teaspoon salt**
- 6 **tablespoons shredded Parmesan cheese**

1. Preheat oven to 425°. In a large bowl, combine tomatoes, zucchini and squash. Add 1 tablespoon oil and 1 teaspoon Italian seasoning. Transfer to a 15x10x1-in. baking pan coated with cooking spray. Bake 15-20 minutes or until tender.
2. Meanwhile, cook spaghetti according to package directions. Sprinkle chicken with garlic powder and remaining Italian seasoning. In a large nonstick skillet, heat remaining oil over medium heat. Add chicken; cook until no longer pink. Remove from skillet.
3. Add broth and wine to skillet; stir to loosen browned bits from pan. Stir in the tomato sauce, tomato paste, basil, oregano and salt. Bring to a boil. Return chicken to skillet. Reduce the heat; simmer, covered 4-6 minutes or until sauce is slightly thickened.
4. Drain spaghetti. Add spaghetti and vegetables to tomato mixture; heat through. Sprinkle with cheese.

PER SERVING *1⅔ cups with 1 tablespoon cheese equals 379 cal., 9 g fat (2 g sat. fat), 45 mg chol., 345 mg sodium, 49 g carb., 8 g fiber, 26 g pro.* **Diabetic Exchanges:** *2½ starch, 2 lean meat, 2 vegetable, 1 fat.*

Turkey Salisbury Steaks

My mom often made Salisbury steak. I developed my own recipe using turkey, and it's now one of my husband's favorites. See photo on page 252.

—**LEANN DOYLE** PATCHOGUE, NY

PREP: 20 MIN. • **COOK:** 15 MIN.
MAKES: 4 SERVINGS

- ⅔ cup seasoned bread crumbs, divided
- ⅓ cup finely chopped onion
- 2 teaspoons low-sodium Worcestershire sauce
- 2 teaspoons A.1. steak sauce
- 1 garlic clove, minced
- ½ teaspoon dried basil
- ½ teaspoon dried oregano
- ¼ teaspoon garlic powder
- ¼ teaspoon pepper
- 1 pound extra-lean ground turkey
- 1½ teaspoons olive oil

SAUCE

- 2 tablespoons olive oil
- 2 tablespoons all-purpose flour
- 1½ cups reduced-sodium beef broth
- 1 tablespoon low-sodium Worcestershire sauce
- 1 tablespoon A.1. steak sauce
- 1 can (4 ounces) sliced mushrooms, drained

1. In a bowl, combine ⅓ cup bread crumbs, onion, Worcestershire sauce, steak sauce, garlic and seasonings. Add turkey; mix lightly but thoroughly. Shape mixture into four ½-in.-thick oval patties. Place remaining bread crumbs in a shallow bowl. Press the patties into crumbs, patting to help coating adhere.

2. In a nonstick skillet coated with cooking spray, heat 1½ teaspoons oil over medium heat. Add patties; cook 3-4 minutes on each side or until a thermometer reads 165°. Remove from pan.

3. In same pan, heat 2 tablespoons oil over medium heat. Stir in flour until smooth; gradually whisk in broth, Worcestershire sauce and steak sauce. Bring to a boil, stirring constantly; cook and stir 1-2 minutes or until thickened. Stir in mushrooms. Return patties to pan. Reduce heat; simmer, covered, 2-3 minutes or until heated through.

PER SERVING *1 patty with ⅓ cup sauce equals 291 cal., 11 g fat (1 g sat. fat), 47 mg chol., 703 mg sodium, 18 g carb., 2 g fiber, 32 g pro.* **Diabetic Exchanges:** *3 lean meat, 2 fat, 1 starch.*

FAST FIX

Makeover Cheddar Biscuits

These biscuits have a cheesy richness that everybody is going to love. Serve them with steaming bowls of chili or a hearty beef soup.

—*TASTE OF HOME* TEST KITCHEN

START TO FINISH: 30 MIN.
MAKES: 15 BISCUITS

- 1 cup all-purpose flour
- 1 cup cake flour
- 1½ teaspoons baking powder
- ¾ teaspoon salt
- ½ teaspoon garlic powder, divided
- ¼ teaspoon baking soda
- 4 tablespoons cold butter, divided
- ⅓ cup finely shredded cheddar cheese
- 1 cup buttermilk
- ½ teaspoon dried parsley flakes

1. In a large bowl, combine the flours, baking powder, salt, ¼ teaspoon garlic powder and baking soda. Cut in 3 tablespoons butter until mixture resembles coarse crumbs; add cheese. Stir in buttermilk just until moistened.

2. Drop by two tablespoonfuls 2 in. apart onto baking sheets coated with cooking spray. Bake at 425° for 10-12 minutes or until golden brown. Melt remaining butter; stir in parsley and remaining garlic powder. Brush over biscuits. Serve warm.

PER SERVING *1 biscuit equals 106 cal., 4 g fat (3 g sat. fat), 11 mg chol., 233 mg sodium, 14 g carb., trace fiber, 3 g pro.*

MAKEOVER CHEDDAR BISCUITS

MAKEOVER	TYPICAL
106 Calories	150 Calories
4g Fat	8g Fat
233g Sodium	350g Sodium

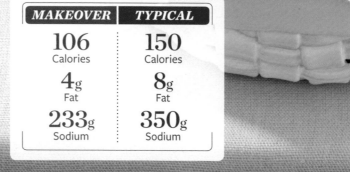

Lemon-Basil Chicken Rotini

My husband and sons like to have meat with their meals, but I prefer more veggies. This combo is colorful and healthy, and it keeps everyone happy.

—ANNA-MARIE WILLIAMS
LEAGUE CITY, TX

PREP: 25 MIN. • **COOK:** 20 MIN.
MAKES: 6 SERVINGS

- 3 cups uncooked white fiber rotini or whole wheat rotini
- 2 teaspoons olive oil
- 1 pound boneless skinless chicken breasts, cut into ¾-inch strips
- 1½ cups sliced fresh mushrooms
- 1½ cups shredded carrots
- 4 garlic cloves, thinly sliced
- 1 cup reduced-sodium chicken broth
- 3 ounces reduced-fat cream cheese
- 1 tablespoon lemon juice
- 1½ cups frozen peas (about 6 ounces), thawed
- ⅓ cup shredded Parmesan cheese
- ¼ cup minced fresh basil
- 2 teaspoons grated lemon peel
- ¼ teaspoon salt
- ¼ teaspoon pepper
- ¼ teaspoon crushed red pepper flakes

1. Cook rotini according to package directions. Meanwhile, in a large nonstick skillet, heat oil over medium heat. Add chicken; cook and stir until no longer pink. Remove from pan.

2. Add mushrooms and carrots to same skillet; cook and stir until tender. Add garlic; cook 1 minute longer. Stir in chicken broth, cream cheese and lemon juice; stir until cheese is melted.

3. Drain the rotini; add to vegetable mixture. Stir in the chicken, peas, Parmesan cheese, basil, grated lemon peel, salt, pepper and pepper flakes; heat through.

PER SERVING *1¼ cups equals 308 cal., 8 g fat (4 g sat. fat), 56 mg chol., 398 mg sodium, 31 g carb., 6 g fiber, 27 g pro.* ***Diabetic Exchanges:*** *3 lean meat, 2 starch, ½ fat.*

Slow Cooker Beef Tostadas

I dedicate these slow-simmered tostadas to my husband, the only Italian man I know who can't get enough of Mexican flavors. Pile on your best toppings!

—TERESA DEVONO RED LION, PA

PREP: 20 MIN. • **COOK:** 6 HOURS
MAKES: 6 SERVINGS

- 1 large onion, chopped
- ¼ cup lime juice
- 1 jalapeno pepper, seeded and minced
- 1 serrano pepper, seeded and minced
- 1 tablespoon chili powder
- 3 garlic cloves, minced
- ½ teaspoon ground cumin
- 1 beef top round steak (about 1½ pounds)
- 1 teaspoon salt
- ½ teaspoon pepper
- ¼ cup chopped fresh cilantro
- 12 corn tortillas (6 inches)
  Cooking spray

TOPPINGS

- 1½ cups shredded lettuce
- 1 medium tomato, finely chopped
- ¾ cup shredded sharp cheddar cheese
- ¾ cup reduced-fat sour cream, optional

1. Place the first seven ingredients in a 3- or 4-qt. slow cooker. Cut steak in half and sprinkle with salt and pepper; add to slow cooker. Cook, covered, on low 6-8 hours or until meat is tender.

2. Remove meat; cool slightly. Shred meat with two forks. Return beef to slow cooker and stir in cilantro; heat through. Spritz both sides of tortillas with cooking spray. Place in a single layer on baking sheets; broil 1-2 minutes on each side or until crisp. Spoon beef mixture over tortillas; top with lettuce, tomato, cheese and, if desired, sour cream.

NOTE *Wear disposable gloves when cutting hot peppers; the oils can burn skin. Avoid touching your face.*

PER SERVING *2 tostadas equals 372 cal., 13 g fat (6 g sat. fat), 88 mg chol., 602 mg sodium, 30 g carb., 5 g fiber, 35 g pro.* ***Diabetic Exchanges:*** *4 lean meat, 2 starch, ½ fat.*

SLOW COOKER
BEEF TOSTADAS

LIGHTENED-UP
VEGGIE PIZZA SQUARES

Lightened-Up Veggie Pizza Squares

This hearty, creamy and full-bodied veggie pizza, served as an appetizer, is sure to bring compliments from your guests.

—SANDRA SHAFER MOUNTAIN VIEW, CA

PREP: 30 MIN. + CHILLING
MAKES: 2 DOZEN

- 2 **tubes (8 ounces each) refrigerated reduced-fat crescent rolls**
- 1 **package (8 ounces) reduced-fat cream cheese**
- 1 **package (8 ounces) fat-free cream cheese**
- ½ **cup plain yogurt**
- ⅓ **cup reduced-fat mayonnaise**
- ¼ **cup fat-free milk**
- 1 **tablespoon dill weed**
- ½ **teaspoon garlic salt**
- 1 **cup shredded carrots**
- 1 **cup fresh cauliflowerets, chopped**
- 1 **cup fresh broccoli florets, chopped**
- 1 **cup julienned green pepper**
- 1 **cup sliced fresh mushrooms**
- 2 **cans (2¼ ounces each) sliced ripe olives, drained**
- ¼ **cup finely chopped sweet onion**

1. Unroll both tubes of crescent dough and pat into an ungreased 15x10x1-in. baking pan; seal seams and perforations. Bake at 375° for 10-12 minutes or until golden brown. Cool completely on a wire rack.
2. In a small bowl, beat the cream cheeses, yogurt, mayonnaise, milk, dill and garlic salt until smooth. Spread over crust. Sprinkle with carrots, cauliflower, broccoli, green

pepper, mushrooms, olives and onion. Cover and refrigerate for at least 1 hour. Cut into squares. Refrigerate leftovers.
THE SKINNY *Typical Veggie Pizza Squares use a mixture of full-fat cream cheese, mayonnaise and heavy cream. The lighter version subs in milk and yogurt, and it uses a lower-fat crust.*
PER SERVING *1 piece equals 128 cal., 7 g fat (2 g sat. fat), 9 mg chol., 365 mg sodium, 11 g carb., 1 g fiber, 4 g pro. Diabetic Exchanges: 1 starch, 1 fat.*

EAT SMART   FREEZE IT

Pigs in a Pool

My kids love sausage and pancakes, but making them for breakfast on a busy weekday was out of the question. My homemade version of pigs in a blanket is a great alternative to the packaged kind, and they freeze like a dream.

—LISA DODD GREENVILLE, SC

PREP: 45 MIN. • **BAKE:** 20 MIN.
MAKES: 4 DOZEN

- 1 **pound reduced-fat bulk pork sausage**
- 2 **cups all-purpose flour**
- ¼ **cup sugar**
- 1 **tablespoon baking powder**
- 1 **teaspoon salt**
- ½ **teaspoon ground cinnamon**
- ¼ **teaspoon ground nutmeg**
- 1 **large egg, lightly beaten**
- 2 **cups fat-free milk**
- 2 **tablespoons canola oil**
- 2 **tablespoons honey**
  Maple syrup, optional

1. Preheat oven to 350°. Coat mini-muffin cups with cooking spray.
2. Shape sausage into forty-eight ¾-in. balls. Place meatballs on a rack coated with cooking spray in a shallow baking pan. Bake 15-20 minutes or until cooked through. Drain on paper towels. In a large bowl, whisk flour, sugar, baking powder, salt and spices. In another bowl, whisk egg, milk, oil and honey until blended. Add to flour mixture; stir just until moistened.
3. Place a sausage ball into each mini-muffin cup; cover with batter. Bake 20-25 minutes or until lightly browned. Cool 5 minutes before removing from pans to wire racks. Serve warm with syrup if desired.
FREEZE OPTION *Freeze cooled muffins in resealable plastic freezer bags. To use, microwave each muffin on high for 20-30 seconds or until heated through.*
PER SERVING *4 mini muffins (calculated without syrup) equals 234 cal., 10 g fat (3 g sat. fat), 45 mg chol., 560 mg sodium, 26 g carb., 1 g fiber, 10 g pro. Diabetic Exchanges: 1½ starch, 1 medium-fat meat, ½ fat.*

PIGS IN A POOL

MAKEOVER	TYPICAL
363 Calories	**700** Calories
15g Fat	**40**g Fat
115mg Sodium	**1,500**mg Sodium

GRILLED
TOMATO PIZZAS

EAT SMART
Grilled Tomato Pizzas

This grilled pizza with a tangy balsamic glaze tastes as if it were baked in wood-burning oven. I slashed the fat and sodium in a big way with a from-scratch crust layered with snappy toppings.

—**MICHELE TUNGETT** ROCHESTER, IL

PREP: 30 MIN. + RISING
GRILL: 5 MIN./BATCH
MAKES: 6 SERVINGS

- 1 **package (¼ ounce) active dry yeast**
- 1 **cup warm water (110° to 115°)**
- 2 **tablespoons plus ¼ cup olive oil, divided**
- 1 **tablespoon honey**
- ¼ **teaspoon salt**
- 2 **to 3 cups all-purpose flour**
   Cooking spray
- 6 **cups cherry tomatoes, halved**
- 1 **cup fresh basil, torn**
- ½ **cup balsamic glaze**
   Shaved Parmesan cheese, optional

1. Dissolve the yeast in warm water. Combine 2 tablespoons oil, honey, salt, yeast mixture and 1½ cups flour; beat on medium speed until smooth. Stir in enough remaining flour to form a soft dough (dough will be sticky). Turn onto a floured surface; knead until smooth and elastic, about 6-8 minutes. Place in a greased bowl, turning once to grease top. Cover; let rise in a warm place until doubled, about 1 hour.
2. Punch down dough; divide into six portions. On a lightly floured surface, roll each portion into an 8x6-in. rectangle. Transfer each to a greased 14-in. piece of heavy-duty foil. Cover; let rest 10 minutes. Spritz with cooking spray.
3. Carefully invert dough onto greased grill rack; peel off foil. Grill, covered, over medium heat until golden brown, about 2-3 minutes. Turn; grill until second side begins to brown, about 1-2 minutes.
4. Remove from grill. Brush with olive oil; top with cherry tomatoes. Grill, covered, until crust is golden brown and tomatoes are heated through, about 2-4 minutes, rotating halfway through cooking to ensure an evenly browned crust.
5. Top with basil; drizzle with the balsamic glaze. If desired, top with Parmesan cheese.
PER SERVING *1 pizza equals 363 cal., 15 g fat (2 g sat. fat), 0 chol., 115 mg sodium, 53 g carb., 3 g fiber, 6 g pro.*

Walnut-Crusted Ginger Salmon

For those who aren't wild about fish, this gingery salmon is a game-changer. Baking on foil makes for extra-easy cleanup.

—**BECKY WALCH** ORLAND, CA

START TO FINISH: 25 MIN.
MAKES: 4 SERVINGS

- 1 **tablespoon brown sugar**
- 1 **tablespoon reduced-sodium soy sauce**
- 1 **tablespoon Dijon mustard**
- 1 **teaspoon ground ginger**
- ¼ **teaspoon salt**
- 4 **salmon fillets (6 ounces each)**
- ⅓ **cup chopped walnuts**

1. Preheat oven to 425°. In a small bowl, mix the brown sugar, soy sauce, mustard, ginger and salt until blended. Brush over the fillets; sprinkle with chopped walnuts.
2. Transfer to a foil-lined 15x10x1-in. baking pan coated with cooking spray. Bake 12-15 minutes or until fish just begins to flake easily with a fork.
THE SKINNY *Reduced-sodium soy sauce makes this recipe suitable for those watching their salt intake. With the Dijon and ginger flavors, you won't even notice the difference.*
PER SERVING *1 fillet equals 349 cal., 22 g fat (4 g sat. fat), 85 mg chol., 468 mg sodium, 6 g carb., 1 g fiber, 31 g pro. Diabetic Exchanges: 5 lean meat, 1½ fat.*

WALNUT-CRUSTED GINGER SALMON

Makeover Penne alla Vodka

This makeover of my favorite pasta recipe is still as creamy and rich as the original version, but it has less than half the fat.

—**DEBRA TORRES** LYNCHBURG, VA

PREP: 15 MIN. • **COOK:** 40 MIN.
MAKES: 8 SERVINGS

- 1 **large onion, chopped**
- 1 **tablespoon olive oil**
- 4 **garlic cloves, minced**
- 2 **cans (one 28 ounces, one 14.5 ounces) diced tomatoes**
- ¼ **cup vodka**
- 1 **package (12 ounces) whole wheat penne pasta**
- 2 **teaspoons prepared pesto**
- ¼ **teaspoon salt**
- ¼ **teaspoon crushed red pepper flakes**
- 2 **tablespoons all-purpose flour**
- ½ **cup heavy whipping cream**
- 1 **cup whole milk**
- ½ **cup shredded Parmesan cheese**

1. In a large saucepan, saute onion in oil until tender. Add garlic; cook 1 minute longer. Stir in tomatoes and vodka. Bring to a boil. Reduce heat; simmer, uncovered, for 30-35 minutes or until slightly thickened, stirring occasionally.
2. Meanwhile, cook penne according to package directions.
3. Stir the pesto, salt and pepper flakes into tomato mixture. In a small bowl, combine the flour and cream until smooth; stir into pan. Add milk. Bring to a boil; cook and stir for 2 minutes or until slightly thickened. Drain penne; serve with sauce. Sprinkle with cheese.
THE SKINNY *The makeover recipe replaces 1½ cups heavy cream with a mixture of cream and whole milk, thickened to the correct consistency with a little flour. This cut 76 calories and 38 mg cholesterol per serving.*
PER SERVING *⅔ cup pasta with ⅔ cup sauce and 1 tablespoon cheese equals 324 cal., 11 g fat (5 g sat. fat), 27 mg chol., 379 mg sodium, 44 g carb., 7 g fiber, 12 g pro. Diabetic Exchanges: 2 starch, 2 vegetable, 2 fat.*

Buffalo Chicken Meatballs

I serve these game-day appetizer meatballs with blue cheese or ranch dressing for dipping. If I make them for a meal, I skip the dressing and serve them with blue cheese polenta on the side. Yum! See photo on page 253.

—**AMBER MASSEY** ARGYLE, TX

PREP: 15 MIN. • **BAKE:** 20 MIN.
MAKES: 2 DOZEN

- ¾ **cup panko (Japanese) bread crumbs**
- ⅓ **cup plus ½ cup Louisiana-style hot sauce, divided**
- ¼ **cup chopped celery**
- 1 **large egg white**
- 1 **pound lean ground chicken**
  Reduced-fat blue cheese or ranch salad dressing, optional

1. Preheat oven to 400°. In a large bowl, combine bread crumbs, ⅓ cup hot sauce, celery and egg white. Add chicken; mix lightly but thoroughly.
2. Shape into twenty-four 1-in. balls. Place on a greased rack in a shallow baking pan. Bake 20-25 minutes or until cooked through.
3. Toss meatballs with remaining hot sauce. If desired, drizzle with salad dressing just before serving.
PER SERVING *1 meatball equals 35 cal., 1 g fat (trace sat. fat), 14 mg chol., 24 mg sodium, 2 g carb., trace fiber, 4 g pro.*

QUICK & EASY NEW ORLEANS SHRIMP

EAT SMART

Quick & Easy New Orleans Shrimp

I've simplified my mom's Shrimp Creole—she made it for us growing up. Now it's effortless comfort food I make for my own family.

—**CRYSTAL MILNE** URBANA, IL

PREP: 15 MIN. • **COOK:** 25 MIN.
MAKES: 4 SERVINGS

- 2 **tablespoons olive oil**
- 1 **small onion, chopped**
- 1 **celery rib, finely chopped**
- 1 **small green pepper, chopped**
- 2 **garlic cloves, minced**
- 1 **can (15 ounces) Italian tomato sauce**
- 1 **can (14½ ounces) no-salt-added diced tomatoes, undrained**
- ½ **cup water**
- ½ **teaspoon Worcestershire sauce**
- ⅛ **to ¼ teaspoon cayenne pepper**
- 1 **pound uncooked shrimp (31–40 per pound), peeled and deveined**
- 3 **cups hot cooked brown rice**

1. In a large skillet, heat oil over medium heat. Add onion, celery and pepper; cook and stir 5-7 minutes or until tender. Add garlic; cook 1 minute longer.

2. Stir in tomato sauce, diced tomatoes, water, Worcestershire sauce and cayenne; bring to a boil. Reduce heat; simmer, uncovered, 10-15 minutes or until slightly thickened, stirring occasionally. Add shrimp; cook 2-4 minutes or until shrimp turn pink. Serve with rice.

PER SERVING *1⅓ cups with ¾ cup cooked rice equals 371 cal., 10 g fat (2 g sat. fat), 138 mg chol., 720 mg sodium, 48 g carb., 6 g fiber, 24 g pro.*

EAT SMART **FAST FIX**

Chardonnay Pork Chops

I began perfecting these juicy chops when I moved to another state and missed my step-dad's best pork recipe. His dish inspired my version with wine sauce.

—**JOLEEN THOMPSON** FARMINGTON, MN

START TO FINISH: 25 MIN.
MAKES: 4 SERVINGS

- 4 **bone-in pork loin chops (6 ounces each)**
- ½ **teaspoon salt**
- ¼ **teaspoon pepper**
- 1 **cup seasoned bread crumbs**
- 1 **tablespoon olive oil**
- 3 **green onions, chopped**
- 2 **garlic cloves, minced**
- 1 **cup chardonnay or chicken broth**
- 2 **tablespoons lemon juice**
- 1 **teaspoon dried rosemary, crushed**

1. Sprinkle pork chops with salt and pepper. Place bread crumbs in a shallow bowl. Dip pork chops in bread crumbs to coat both sides; shake off excess. In a large skillet, heat oil over medium heat; cook chops 4-5 minutes on each side or until golden brown and thermometer reads 145°. Remove from pan and keep warm.

2. In same pan, add green onions and garlic; cook and stir 1-2 minutes or until tender. Add chardonnay, stirring to loosen browned bits from pan. Bring to a boil; cook 1-2 minutes or until liquid is reduced by half. Stir in lemon juice and rosemary. Serve pork chops with sauce.

PER SERVING *1 pork chop with 3 tablespoons sauce equals 270 cal., 11 g fat (3 g sat. fat), 74 mg chol., 509 mg sodium, 9 g carb., 1 g fiber, 28 g pro.* **Diabetic Exchanges:** *4 lean meat, ½ starch, ½ fat.*

CHARDONNAY PORK CHOPS

Cheesy Bean Dip

This reworked version of a go-to Mexican party dip has the same great taste as the original, but it uses lower-fat ingredients to keep it light.

—TASTE OF HOME TEST KITCHEN

START TO FINISH: 30 MIN.
MAKES: 4 CUPS

- 1½ cups (6 ounces) shredded reduced-fat Mexican cheese blend
- 1½ cups (6 ounces) shredded reduced-fat cheddar cheese
- 1 can (16 ounces) fat-free refried beans
- 1 can (10 ounces) diced tomatoes and green chilies
- 1 package (8 ounces) reduced-fat cream cheese, cubed
- ½ cup reduced-fat sour cream
- 1 tablespoon taco seasoning
  Tortilla chips and fresh vegetables

1. In a bowl, combine cheeses; set aside 1 cup for topping. Add beans, tomatoes, cream cheese, sour cream and taco seasoning to the remaining cheeses; stir until blended. Transfer mixture to a greased 2-qt. baking dish; sprinkle with reserved cheeses.

2. Bake, uncovered, at 350° for 20-25 minutes or until bubbly around the edges. Serve warm with chips and assorted fresh vegetables.

PER SERVING *2 tablespoons dip equals 61 cal., 3 g fat (2 g sat. fat), 10 mg chol., 177 mg sodium, 4 g carb., 1 g fiber, 5 g pro.* **Diabetic Exchanges:** *½ starch, ½ lean meat.*

Chicken & Sweet Potato Potpie

Chicken potpie definitely ranks in my Top 10 list of favorite comfort foods. To save time, I use ready-made phyllo dough and store-bought rotisserie chicken.

—JACYN SIEBERT SAN FRANCISCO, CA

PREP: 40 MIN. • **BAKE:** 10 MIN.
MAKES: 6 SERVINGS

- 2 teaspoons olive oil
- ½ pound sliced fresh mushrooms

CHICKEN & SWEET POTATO POTPIE

- 1 small onion, chopped
- 1 large sweet potato, cubed
- 1 cup chopped sweet red pepper
- ½ cup chopped celery
- 2 cups reduced-sodium chicken broth, divided
- ⅓ cup all-purpose flour
- ½ cup 2% milk
- 1 skinned rotisserie chicken, shredded
- 2 tablespoons sherry or reduced-sodium chicken broth
- ¾ teaspoon minced fresh rosemary
- ½ teaspoon salt
- ½ teaspoon dried thyme
- ¼ teaspoon pepper
- 5 sheets phyllo dough (14x9-in. size)
  Butter-flavored cooking spray

1. Preheat oven to 425°. In a skillet, heat oil over medium-high heat. Add mushrooms and onion; cook and stir until tender, 3-4 minutes. Stir in sweet potato, red pepper and celery; cook 5 minutes longer. Add ¼ cup broth.

Reduce heat; cook, covered, over medium-low heat until vegetables are tender, 6-8 minutes.

2. Sprinkle flour over vegetables; cook and stir 1 minute. Gradually add milk and remaining broth. Bring to a boil; cook and stir until thickened, about 1-2 minutes. Stir in chicken, sherry and seasonings. Transfer to an 11x7-in. baking dish coated with cooking spray. Bake, uncovered, until heated through, 10-15 minutes.

3. Meanwhile, stack all five sheets of phyllo dough. Roll up lengthwise; cut crosswise into ½-in.-wide strips. In a bowl, toss strips to separate; spritz with butter-flavored spray. Place on an ungreased baking sheet; spritz again. Bake until golden brown, 4-5 minutes. Arrange strips over filling.

PER SERVING *1 cup equals 329 cal., 10g fat (2g sat. fat), 75mg chol., 517mg sodium, 30g carb. (10g sugars, 3g fiber), 30g pro.* **Diabetic Exchanges:** *4 lean meat, 2 starch, ½ fat.*

Glazed Coconut-Banana Bread

Use up your too-ripe bananas with my healthier twist on banana bread. I lighten up this tropical loaf by using plain yogurt to replace the fat found in traditional versions. The potassium-rich bananas also pack a dose of magnesium, great for fighting off high blood pressure.

—**KATHERINE NELSON** CENTERVILLE, UT

PREP: 20 MIN. • **BAKE:** 50 MIN.
MAKES: 1 LOAF (16 SLICES)

- ¼ cup butter, softened
- 1 cup sugar
- 2 large eggs
- 1½ cups mashed ripe bananas (2 to 3 medium)
- ¼ cup reduced-fat plain yogurt
- 3 tablespoons unsweetened apple juice
- ½ teaspoon vanilla extract
- 2 cups all-purpose flour
- ¾ teaspoon baking soda
- ½ teaspoon salt
- ½ cup plus 1 tablespoon flaked coconut, divided
- ½ cup confectioners' sugar
- 1 tablespoon lime juice

1. Preheat oven to 350°. Grease and flour a 9x5-in. loaf pan. In a large bowl, beat butter and sugar until crumbly. Add eggs, one at a time, beating well after each addition. Beat in bananas, yogurt, apple juice and vanilla. In another bowl, whisk flour, baking soda and salt; stir into butter mixture. Fold in ½ cup coconut.

2. Transfer to prepared pan. Sprinkle with remaining coconut. Bake 50-60 minutes or until a toothpick inserted in center comes out clean. Cool in pan 10 minutes before removing to a wire rack to cool.

3. In a small bowl, mix confectioners' sugar and lime juice until smooth; spoon over warm bread.

PER SERVING *1 slice equals 193 cal., 5 g fat (3 g sat. fat), 34 mg chol., 174 mg sodium, 35 g carb., 1 g fiber, 3 g pro. Diabetic Exchanges: 2 starch, 1 fat.*

Great Grandma's Italian Meatballs

My great-grandmother started the Italian meatball tradition in our family. We use ground beef and turkey, and the flavor's so good, you won't miss the extra calories.

—**AUDREY COLANTINO** WINCHESTER, MA

PREP: 30 MIN. • **BAKE:** 20 MIN.
MAKES: 8 SERVINGS

- 2 teaspoons olive oil
- 1 medium onion, chopped
- 3 garlic cloves, minced
- ¾ cup seasoned bread crumbs
- ½ cup grated Parmesan cheese
- 2 large eggs, lightly beaten
- 1 teaspoon each dried basil, oregano and parsley flakes
- ¾ teaspoon salt
- 1 pound lean ground turkey
- 1 pound lean ground beef (90% lean)
  Hot cooked pasta and pasta sauce, optional

1. Preheat oven to 375°. In a small skillet, heat oil over medium-high heat. Add onion; cook and stir 3-4 minutes or until tender. Add garlic; cook 1 minute longer. Cool slightly.

2. In a large bowl, combine bread crumbs, cheese, eggs, seasonings and onion mixture. Add turkey and beef; mix lightly but thoroughly. Shape into 1½-in. balls.

3. Place meatballs on a rack coated with cooking spray in a 15x10x1-in. baking pan. Bake 18-22 minutes or until lightly browned and cooked through. If desired, serve with pasta and pasta sauce.

PER SERVING *(calculated without spaghetti and pasta sauce) equals 271 cal., 13 g fat (5 g sat. fat), 125 mg chol., 569 mg sodium, 10 g carb., 1 g fiber, 27 g pro. Diabetic Exchanges: 4 lean meat, 1 fat, ½ starch.*

GREAT GRANDMA'S ITALIAN MEATBALLS

4. Add broth to pan. In a small bowl, mix flour and milk until smooth; stir into sausage mixture. Return to a boil, stirring constantly; cook and stir 10-12 minutes or until thickened.

5. Split biscuits in half; serve warm with gravy.

THE SKINNY *Classic biscuits and gravy slim down with a few smart changes. Whole wheat biscuits boost fiber, spicy chicken sausage replaces pork and the gravy uses reduced-sodium broth and herb seasonings to cut down on salt.*

PER SERVING *1 biscuit with 1/3 cup gravy equals 308 cal., 10 g fat (5 g sat. fat), 48 mg chol., 854 mg sodium, 40 g carb., 3 g fiber, 15 g pro.* **Diabetic Exchanges:** *2 1/2 starch, 1 1/2 fat, 1 lean meat.*

EAT SMART **FAST FIX**

Crab Rangoon

Bite into these golden appetizers, and you'll find a creamy crab filling that rivals restaurant fare. Best of all, these delightful crowd-pleasers are baked and not fried.

—*TASTE OF HOME* **TEST KITCHEN**

START TO FINISH: 25 MIN.
MAKES: 14 APPETIZERS

- 3 ounces reduced-fat cream cheese
- 1/8 teaspoon garlic salt
- 1/8 teaspoon Worcestershire sauce
- 1/2 cup lump crabmeat, drained
- 1 green onion, chopped
- 14 wonton wrappers

1. In a small bowl, combine the cream cheese, garlic salt and Worcestershire sauce until smooth. Stir in the crab and green onion. Place 2 teaspoonfuls in the center of each wonton wrapper. Moisten the edges with water; bring corners to center over filling and press edges together to seal.

2. Place on a baking sheet coated with cooking spray. Lightly spray wontons with cooking spray. Bake at 425° for 8-10 minutes or until golden brown. Serve warm.

PER SERVING *2 appetizers equals 83 cal., 3 g fat (2 g sat. fat), 19 mg chol., 248 mg sodium, 10 g carb., trace fiber, 4 g pro.* **Diabetic Exchanges:** *1 starch, 1/2 fat.*

MAKEOVER BISCUITS & GRAVY

MAKEOVER	TYPICAL
308 Calories	**444** Calories
10g Fat	**26**g Fat
5g Saturated Fat	**14**g Saturated Fat

EAT SMART

Makeover Biscuits & Gravy

We lightened up our favorite biscuits and gravy recipe to curb our guilt for eating them the day after we went to a big pancake breakfast. It's a terrific homemade recipe to serve your brunch guests.

—**IAN CLIFFE** MILWAUKEE, WI

PREP: 25 MIN. • **COOK:** 20 MIN.
MAKES: 6 SERVINGS

- 1 1/3 cups all-purpose flour
- 2/3 cup whole wheat flour
- 2 teaspoons baking powder
- 1/2 teaspoon baking soda
- 1/4 teaspoon salt
- 3 tablespoons cold butter
- 1 cup buttermilk

GRAVY

- 1 teaspoon olive oil
- 1/2 pound bulk chicken sausage
- 1 medium onion, finely chopped
- 1 garlic clove, minced
- 1 teaspoon minced fresh thyme
- 1/8 to 1/4 teaspoon crushed red pepper flakes
- 1/8 teaspoon pepper
- 2 cups reduced-sodium chicken broth
- 2 tablespoons all-purpose flour
- 1/2 cup 2% milk

1. Preheat oven to 425°. In a large bowl, whisk flours, baking powder, baking soda and salt. Cut in butter until crumbly. Add buttermilk; stir just until moistened.

2. Turn dough onto a lightly floured surface; knead gently 8-10 times. Pat dough into a 7x5-in. rectangle (about 1 in. thick); cut into six pieces. Place 2 in. apart on a parchment paper-lined baking sheet. Bake 8-12 minutes or until golden brown.

3. Meanwhile, in a skillet, heat oil over medium heat. Add sausage and onion; cook 4-6 minutes or until the sausage is no longer pink and onion is tender, breaking up sausage into crumbles. Add garlic, thyme, pepper flakes and pepper; cook 30 seconds longer.

Cookout Caramel S'mores

These classic treats make a great finish to an informal meal. And toasting the marshmallows extends our after-dinner time together, giving us something fun to do as a family.

—**MARTHA HASEMAN** HINCKLEY, IL

START TO FINISH: 10 MIN.
MAKES: 4 SERVINGS

- 8 **large marshmallows**
- 4 **whole reduced-fat graham crackers, halved**
- 2 **teaspoons fat-free chocolate syrup**
- 2 **teaspoons fat-free caramel ice cream topping**

Using a long-handled fork, toast the marshmallows 6 in. from medium heat until golden brown, turning occasionally. Place two marshmallows on each of four graham cracker halves. Drizzle with the chocolate syrup and caramel ice cream topping. Top with remaining crackers.

THE SKINNY *The original s'more used full-fat graham crackers and caramel, as well as half of a chocolate bar per serving. Using lighter ingredients cuts down on both fat and saturated fat.*

PER SERVING *1 s'more equals 87 cal., 1 g fat (1 g sat. fat), 1 mg chol., 82 mg sodium, 20 g carb., 1 g fiber, 1 g pro. Diabetic Exchange: 1 starch.*

COOKOUT CARAMEL S'MORES

TOMATO-POACHED HALIBUT

Tomato-Poached Halibut

EAT SMART **FAST FIX**

My halibut with a burst of lemon comes together in one pan and stays super moist. Try it with polenta, angel hair pasta or crusty bread.

—**DANNA ROGERS** WESTPORT, CT

START TO FINISH: 30 MIN.
MAKES: 4 SERVINGS

- 1 **tablespoon olive oil**
- 2 **poblano peppers, finely chopped**
- 1 **small onion, finely chopped**
- 1 **can (14½ ounces) fire-roasted diced tomatoes, undrained**
- 1 **can (14½ ounces) no-salt-added diced tomatoes, undrained**
- ¼ **cup chopped pitted green olives**
- 3 **garlic cloves, minced**
- ¼ **teaspoon pepper**
- ⅛ **teaspoon salt**
- 4 **halibut fillets (4 ounces each)**
- ⅓ **cup chopped fresh cilantro**
- 4 **lemon wedges**
  Crusty whole grain bread, optional

1. In a large nonstick skillet, heat oil over medium-high heat. Add poblano peppers and onion; cook and stir 4-6 minutes or until tender.

2. Stir in the tomatoes, olives, garlic, pepper and salt. Bring to a boil. Adjust heat to maintain a gentle simmer. Add the fillets. Cook, covered, 8-10 minutes or until fish just begins to flake easily with a fork. Sprinkle with chopped cilantro. Serve with lemon wedges and, if desired, bread.

THE SKINNY *If you're on a reduced-sodium diet, you know that every little bit adds up quickly. Subbing in one can of no-salt-added diced tomatoes in this recipe saves 160 mg per serving.*

PER SERVING *1 fillet with 1 cup sauce (calculated without bread) equals 224 cal., 7 g fat (1 g sat. fat), 56 mg chol., 651 mg sodium, 17 g carb., 4 g fiber, 24 g pro. Diabetic Exchanges: 3 lean meat, 1 starch, ½ fat.*

DID YOU KNOW?

Poaching is a cooking technique used for delicate foods, such as fish fillets. The proper temperature for poaching is 160° to 180°, which is lower than simmering.

Spicy Coconut Shrimp with Quinoa

Help yourself to a plateful—generous servings of this dish are low in calories and big on protein. Expecting company? Just toss together an easy salad to serve alongside.

—**KERI WHITNEY** CASTRO VALLEY, CA

PREP: 20 MIN. • **COOK:** 20 MIN.
MAKES: 4 SERVINGS

- 1 cup quinoa, rinsed
- 2 cups water
- ¼ teaspoon salt

SHRIMP

- 1 teaspoon olive oil
- 1 medium onion, chopped
- 1 tablespoon minced fresh gingerroot
- ½ teaspoon curry powder
- ½ teaspoon ground cumin
- ¼ teaspoon salt
- ¼ teaspoon cayenne pepper
- 1 pound uncooked shrimp (26–30 per pound), peeled and deveined
- 2 cups fresh snow peas (about 7 ounces), trimmed
- 3 tablespoons light coconut milk
- 1 tablespoon orange juice
- ¼ cup flaked coconut, toasted
- ¼ cup minced fresh cilantro

1. In a saucepan, combine quinoa, water and salt; bring to a boil. Reduce heat; simmer, covered, 12-15 minutes or until liquid is absorbed. Remove from heat; fluff with a fork.
2. Meanwhile, in a large nonstick skillet, heat oil over medium heat. Add onion; cook and stir 4-6 minutes or until tender. Stir in ginger, curry powder, cumin, salt and cayenne; cook 1 minute longer.
3. Add shrimp and snow peas to skillet; cook and stir 3-4 minutes or until shrimp turn pink and snow peas are crisp-tender. Stir in coconut milk and orange juice; heat through. Serve with quinoa; top each serving with coconut and cilantro.
NOTE *To toast coconut, bake in a shallow pan in a 350° oven for 5-10 minutes or cook in a skillet*

over low heat until golden brown, stirring occasionally.
PER SERVING *1 cup shrimp mixture with ¾ cup quinoa equals 330 cal., 8 g fat (3 g sat. fat), 138 mg chol., 451 mg sodium, 37 g carb., 5 g fiber, 26 g pro.* **Diabetic Exchanges:** *3 lean meat, 2 starch, 1 vegetable, ½ fat.*

Apricot-Rosemary Pork Medallions

I had a pork tenderloin in my fridge, but I didn't want to wait for it to roast in the oven. I tried this quick stovetop method, and my family loved it!

—**MILDRED LYNN CARUSO** BRIGHTON, TN

PREP: 10 MIN. • **COOK:** 30 MIN.
MAKES: 8 SERVINGS

- 2 pork tenderloins (1 pound each)
- ½ cup seasoned bread crumbs
- 2 tablespoons olive oil
- 6 cups fresh broccoli florets
- ⅔ cup apricot preserves
- ¼ cup white wine or chicken broth
- 2 teaspoons minced fresh rosemary or ½ teaspoon dried rosemary, crushed
- ½ teaspoon salt
- ⅛ teaspoon pepper
- 5⅓ cups hot cooked brown rice

1. Cut each tenderloin crosswise into eight 1-in. slices. Place bread crumbs in a shallow bowl. Dip the pork slices in crumbs, patting to help the coating adhere. In a large nonstick skillet, heat oil over medium heat. Add the pork in batches; cook 3-4 minutes on each side or until a thermometer reads 145°.
2. Meanwhile, in a large saucepan, place steamer basket over 1 in. of water. Place broccoli in basket, and bring water to a boil. Reduce heat to maintain a simmer; steam, covered, 4-6 minutes or until tender.
3. In a small saucepan, mix preserves, wine, rosemary, salt and pepper. Cook and stir over medium-low heat 3-5 minutes or until preserves are melted. Serve with pork, broccoli and rice.
PER SERVING *404 cal., 9 g fat (2 g sat. fat), 64 mg chol., 321 mg sodium, 53 g carb., 4 g fiber, 28 g pro.*

APRICOT-ROSEMARY PORK MEDALLIONS

Hearty Garden Spaghetti

My husband and I wanted a pleasing dish that didn't leave a ton of leftovers. My spaghetti with beef and fresh veggies is the perfect size for a family of four.

—WANDA QUIST LOVELAND, CO

PREP: 15 MIN. • **COOK:** 30 MIN.
MAKES: 4 SERVINGS

- 1 pound lean ground beef (90% lean)
- 1 small onion, finely chopped
- 1 medium sweet red pepper, finely chopped
- 1 medium zucchini, finely chopped
- ½ pound sliced fresh mushrooms
- 1 can (8 ounces) tomato sauce
- 2 teaspoons Italian seasoning
- ½ teaspoon salt
- ¼ teaspoon pepper
- 8 ounces uncooked multigrain spaghetti
  Grated Parmesan cheese, optional

1. In a Dutch oven coated with cooking spray, cook beef, onion and red pepper over medium-high heat 5-7 minutes or until beef is no longer pink, breaking up beef into crumbles; drain.

2. Add zucchini and mushrooms; cook 3-5 minutes longer or until tender. Stir in tomato sauce, Italian seasoning, salt and pepper; bring to a boil. Reduce heat; simmer, covered, 15 minutes to allow flavors to blend. Meanwhile, cook spaghetti according to package directions.

3. Serve spaghetti with sauce and, if desired, cheese.

PER SERVING *1¼ cups sauce with 1 cup spaghetti (calculated without cheese) equals 432 cal., 11 g fat (4 g sat. fat), 71 mg chol., 649 mg sodium, 48 g carb., 7 g fiber, 36 g pro.* *Diabetic Exchanges: 3 lean meat, 2½ starch, 2 vegetable.*

Makeover Reuben Melt

This twist on a classic Reuben keeps the corned beef and uses a sauce made with Swiss (and plenty of thousand-island flavor). Fresh slaw on top replaces the sauerkraut.

—JENNI SHARP MILWAUKEE, WI

START TO FINISH: 25 MIN.
MAKES: 4 SERVINGS

- 2 tablespoons white vinegar
- 1 tablespoon olive oil
- ½ teaspoon caraway seeds
- ⅛ teaspoon salt
  Dash pepper
- 2 cups finely shredded cabbage

CHEESE SAUCE

- 1 tablespoon all-purpose flour
- ¾ cup cold fat-free milk
- ½ cup shredded baby Swiss cheese
- 2 teaspoons sweet pickle relish
- 2 teaspoons ketchup
- ⅛ teaspoon sweet paprika

ASSEMBLY

- 4 slices marble rye bread
- 2 teaspoons olive oil
- 10 ounces sliced deli corned beef

1. Preheat broiler. In a bowl, whisk vinegar, oil, caraway seeds, salt and pepper. Add cabbage; toss to coat.

2. In a saucepan, whisk flour and milk until smooth. Bring to a boil, stirring constantly; cook and stir 1-2 minutes or until thickened. Stir in cheese, relish, ketchup and paprika until cheese is melted. Keep warm.

3. Meanwhile, place bread slices on a baking sheet. Brush both sides with oil. Broil 4-6 in. from heat 45-60 seconds on each side or until golden brown. Layer corned beef over bread slices. Broil 1-2 minutes longer or until meat is heated through. Top with cheese sauce and slaw.

PER SERVING *1 open-faced sandwich equals 293 cal., 14 g fat (5 g sat. fat), 53 mg chol., 1,172 mg sodium, 24 g carb., 3 g fiber, 20 g pro.*

MAKEOVER REUBEN MELT

MAKEOVER	TYPICAL
293 Calories	650 Calories
14g Fat	40g Fat
1,172mg Sodium	2,300mg Sodium

BAKED BUFFALO CHICKEN

Grecian Pasta & Chicken Skillet

We love a homemade meal at the end of the day. But as for the prep involved? Not so much. My Greek-inspired pasta is full of lemon and herb flavors and is a breeze to make.

—**ROXANNE CHAN** ALBANY, CA

PREP: 30 MIN. • **COOK:** 10 MIN.
MAKES: 4 SERVINGS

- 1 can (14½ ounces) reduced-sodium chicken broth
- 1 can (14½ ounces) no-salt-added diced tomatoes, undrained
- ¾ pound boneless skinless chicken breasts, cut into 1-inch pieces
- ½ cup white wine or water
- 1 garlic clove, minced
- ½ teaspoon dried oregano
- 4 ounces multigrain thin spaghetti
- 1 jar (7½ ounces) marinated quartered artichoke hearts, drained and coarsely chopped
- 2 cups fresh baby spinach
- ¼ cup roasted sweet red pepper strips
- ¼ cup sliced ripe olives
- 1 green onion, finely chopped
- 2 tablespoons minced fresh parsley
- ½ teaspoon grated lemon peel
- 2 tablespoons lemon juice
- 1 tablespoon olive oil
- ½ teaspoon pepper
   Crumbled reduced-fat feta cheese, optional

1. In a large skillet, combine the first six ingredients; add spaghetti. Bring to a boil. Cook 5-7 minutes or until chicken is no longer pink and the spaghetti is tender.
2. Stir in artichoke hearts, spinach, red pepper, olives, green onion, parsley, lemon peel, lemon juice, oil and pepper. Cook and stir 2-3 minutes or until spinach is wilted. If desired, sprinkle with cheese.

PER SERVING *1½ cups equals 373 cal., 15 g fat (3 g sat. fat), 47 mg chol., 658 mg sodium, 30 g carb., 4 g fiber, 25 g pro.* **Diabetic Exchanges:** *2 starch, 2 lean meat, 2 fat, 1 vegetable.*

Baked Buffalo Chicken

I double the recipe for this tangy chicken because it disappears so fast. Cut any leftover chicken into cubes or slices, and add it to salads or sandwiches.

—**BETH ZIMMERMAN** WILLINGBORO, NJ

PREP: 20 MIN. + MARINATING
BAKE: 25 MIN. • **MAKES:** 4 SERVINGS

- ¾ cup Buffalo wing sauce, divided
- 4 boneless skinless chicken breast halves (6 ounces each)
- ¾ cup all-purpose flour
- ¾ teaspoon dried tarragon
- ½ teaspoon pepper
- 1¼ cups panko (Japanese) bread crumbs

1. Pour ⅓ cup wing sauce into a shallow dish. Add chicken breasts and turn to coat. Let stand 15 minutes or refrigerate, covered, up to 24 hours.
2. Preheat oven to 400°. Drain chicken, discarding marinade. In a shallow bowl, mix flour, tarragon and pepper. Place bread crumbs and remaining wing sauce in separate shallow bowls. Dip chicken in flour mixture to coat all sides; shake off excess. Dip in wing sauce, then in bread crumbs, patting to help coating adhere.
3. Place the coated chicken on a rack in a 15x10x1-in. baking pan. Bake for 25-30 minutes or until a thermometer reads 165°.

PER SERVING *1 chicken breast half equals 277 cal., 5 g fat (1 g sat. fat), 94 mg chol., 811 mg sodium, 18 g carb., 1 g fiber, 37 g pro.* **Diabetic Exchanges:** *5 lean meat, 1 starch.*

GRECIAN PASTA & CHICKEN SKILLET

**JOE COLAMONICO'S
WHITE SEAFOOD LASAGNA**
PAGE 283

Table Traditions

Take a peek inside the **warm and welcoming** kitchens of these *Taste of Home* readers. Discover their **favorite meals** for Easter, Christmas and special **family dinners** in between.

LORRAINE CALAND'S HONEY-LEMON ASPARAGUS
PAGE 279

ALLY PHILLIPS' BUTTERMILK BLUEBERRY SCOOKIES *PAGE 276*

NANCY HEISHMAN'S TURKEY CURRY WITH RICE
PAGE 280

Easter Keepers

Celebrate the happiest Sunday of the year with a tasty glazed ham, plus sweets for your little lambs. South Carolina reader Ally Phillips shares the recipes that bring spring to her family.

RECIPES & STORY BY **ALLY PHILLIPS** MURRELLS INLET, SC

Easter Sunday always means a huge spread and lots of food-love followed by the traditional egg hunt. Even the big "kids" grab a basket and search for the golden egg, which always contains a surprise (OK, cash) inside. My Easter tables are a buffet of internationally inspired dishes for all to try, along with the classic foods that family and friends expect when they sit down, give thanks and break bread in my kitchen.

Before starting my food blog, *allyskitchen.com*, and publishing my cookbook, I was an educational therapist. Ultimately, however, my passion for food and cooking won out.

All of my recipes reflect my love for eating close to the earth and bringing global spices to my table. I love to create a dining experience for my family, but because these dishes use simple ingredients, anyone can prepare them. When I make them for our holidays and get-togethers, I always have my grandchildren underfoot in the kitchen. Forget the toys—they want pots, pans and wooden spoons!

EAT SMART **FAST FIX ▸**

Honey Kale Currant & Almond Salad

START TO FINISH: 10 MIN. • **MAKES:** 4 SERVINGS

- 4 **cups thinly sliced fresh kale**
- ¼ **cup slivered almonds**
- ¼ **cup dried currants**
- 2 **tablespoons grated Asiago cheese**
- 1 **tablespoon balsamic vinegar**
- 1 **tablespoon olive oil**
- 1 **tablespoon honey mustard**
- 1½ **teaspoons honey**
- ¾ **teaspoon coarsely ground pepper**
- ½ **teaspoon sea salt**

**HONEY KALE CURRANT &
ALMOND SALAD**

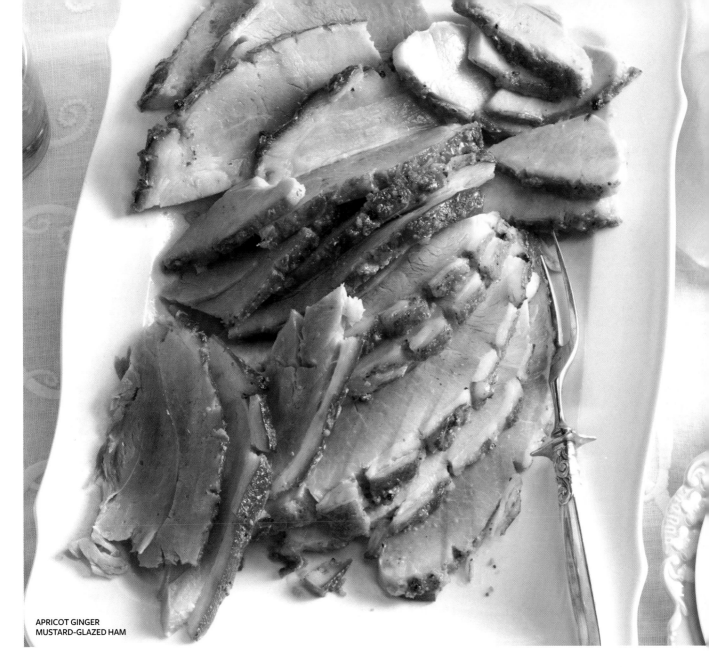

**APRICOT GINGER
MUSTARD-GLAZED HAM**

Place kale, almonds and currants in a large bowl. In a small bowl, whisk remaining ingredients until blended. Drizzle over salad; toss to coat.

PER SERVING *1 cup equals 135 cal., 8 g fat (1 g sat. fat), 3 mg chol., 287 mg sodium, 15 g carb., 2 g fiber, 3 g pro. Diabetic Exchanges: 1½ fat, 1 vegetable, ½ starch.*

Apricot Ginger Mustard-Glazed Ham

PREP: 15 MIN. • **BAKE:** 2 HOURS • **MAKES:** 16 SERVINGS

- 1 **fully cooked bone-in ham (7 to 9 pounds)**
- ½ **cup apricot halves, drained**
- ½ **cup stone-ground mustard**
- ⅓ **cup packed brown sugar**
- 2 **tablespoons grated fresh gingerroot**
- 1 **tablespoon whole peppercorns**
- ½ **teaspoon sea salt**
- ½ **teaspoon coarsely ground pepper**

1. Preheat oven to 325°. Place ham on a rack in a shallow roasting pan. Using a sharp knife, score surface of ham with ¼-in.-deep cuts in a diamond pattern. Cover and bake for 1¾-2¼ hours or until a thermometer reads 130°.

2. Meanwhile, place the remaining ingredients in a food processor; process until blended. Remove ham from oven. Increase oven setting to 425°. Spread the apricot mixture over the ham.

3. Bake ham, uncovered, 15-20 minutes longer or until a thermometer reads 140°. If desired, increase the oven setting to broil; broil 2-4 minutes or until golden brown.

PER SERVING *4 ounces cooked ham equals 201 cal., 6 g fat (2 g sat. fat), 87 mg chol., 1,258 mg sodium, 8 g carb., trace fiber, 30 g pro.*

BUTTERMILK BLUEBERRY
SCOOKIES

FAST FIX ▶
Buttermilk Blueberry Scookies

START TO FINISH: 25 MIN. • **MAKES:** 1 DOZEN

- 2 **cups all-purpose flour**
- ½ **cup plus 1 tablespoon sugar, divided**
- 2 **teaspoons baking powder**
- 1 **teaspoon baking soda**
- ½ **cup cold butter, cubed**
- ½ **cup buttermilk**
- 1 **large egg, lightly beaten**
- 1 **cup fresh or frozen blueberries, thawed**

1. Preheat oven to 375°. In a large bowl, whisk flour, ½ cup sugar, baking powder and baking soda. Cut in butter until mixture resembles coarse crumbs. In another bowl, whisk buttermilk and egg until blended; stir into crumb mixture just until moistened.

2. Drop the dough by scant ¼ cupfuls 2 in. apart onto a parchment paper-lined baking sheet. Form a ½-in.-deep indentation in the center of each with the back of a spoon coated with cooking spray. Gently press blueberries into indentations; sprinkle with remaining sugar.

3. Bake 11-14 minutes or until golden brown. Serve warm.

PER SERVING *1 scookie equals 197 cal., 8 g fat (5 g sat. fat), 36 mg chol., 258 mg sodium, 28 g carb., 1 g fiber, 3 g pro.*

Roasted Tater Rounds with Green Onions & Tarragon

PREP: 25 MIN. • **BROIL:** 10 MIN. • **MAKES:** 8 SERVINGS

- 4 **pounds potatoes (about 8 medium), sliced ¼ inch thick**
  Cooking spray
- 2 **teaspoons sea salt**
- 1 **teaspoon coarsely ground pepper**
- 6 **green onions, thinly sliced (about ¾ cup)**
- 3 **tablespoons minced fresh parsley**
- 2 **tablespoons minced fresh tarragon**
  Olive oil, optional

1. Preheat broiler. Place potatoes in a large microwave-safe bowl; spritz with cooking spray and toss to coat. Microwave, covered, on high 10-12 minutes or until potatoes are almost tender, stirring halfway through cooking.

2. Spread potatoes into greased 15x10x1-in. baking pans. Spritz with additional cooking spray; sprinkle with salt and pepper.

3. Broil 4-6 in. from heat 10-12 minutes or until golden brown, stirring halfway through cooking. In a small bowl, mix green onions, parsley and tarragon. Sprinkle over the potatoes; toss to coat. If desired, drizzle with olive oil.

PER SERVING *¾ cup equals 185 cal., 1 g fat (trace sat. fat), 0 chol., 497 mg sodium, 41 g carb., 5 g fiber, 5 g pro.*

ROASTED TATER ROUNDS WITH GREEN ONIONS & TARRAGON

Come Home To Classics

Richly seasoned roast pork, plus bright spring veggies and a luscious dessert—an Ontario reader brings back the recipes that remind her of the good old days.

RECIPES & STORY BY **LORRAINE CALAND** SHUNIAH, ON

I've been cooking since I was 7 years old. My parents went duck hunting each year and it was my job to make a meal for their return. My dad especially loved when I prepared pork—roasted, then sliced nice and thick. And he lived to be 90! I miss him so much, and cooking his favorite recipes can make him feel close and dear to me.

I've made Sunday dinners like this for my husband, kids, nine grandchildren and 14 great-grandchildren for years, and I've submitted recipes to *Taste of Home* since forever (1,962 submitted, 66 published).

I cherish the favorites, but I like to mix up our menus—keeping them guessing is the order of the day in our home! Several years ago, when we'd just moved, we saw women on the roadside harvesting something. After quizzing our new neighbors, I found out it was wild asparagus. This started our lasting love of asparagus, and I now try it in all sorts of dishes.

My guy, Wally, adores raspberries in pancakes, loaves and my Raspberry Rumble cake. (Other berries work, but guess who insists on raspberries!) Wally fills up on my cooking and somehow loses weight. I can simply look at a recipe and gain, but I'll never skimp on good home cooking.

EAT SMART
Thyme & Basil Roast Pork

PREP: 30 MIN. • **BAKE:** 1 HOUR + STANDING • **MAKES:** 8 SERVINGS

- 1 tablespoon all-purpose flour
- 2 teaspoons dried basil
- 2 teaspoons dried thyme
- 2 teaspoons ground cinnamon
- 1½ teaspoons salt
- ½ teaspoon pepper
- 1 boneless pork loin roast (3 to 4 pounds)
- 2 tablespoons canola oil
- 1 medium apple, cut into wedges
- 1 medium onion, cut into wedges
- 1 medium lemon, cut into wedges
- 1 fresh rosemary sprig

1. Preheat oven to 325°. In a small bowl, mix flour, basil, thyme, cinnamon, salt and pepper; rub over pork.

2. In a large skillet, heat oil over medium-high heat. Brown roast on all sides. Place the roast in a shallow roasting pan, fat side up. Arrange apple and onion around roast. Squeeze lemon juice from one wedge over pork; add lemon wedges to pan. Place rosemary over pork.

3. Roast 1–1½ hours or until a thermometer reads 145°. Remove roast, onion and apple to a serving platter; tent with foil. Let stand 15 minutes before slicing.

PER SERVING *4 ounces cooked pork equals 266 cal., 11 g fat (3 g sat. fat), 85 mg chol., 493 mg sodium, 6 g carb., 1 g fiber, 33 g pro.* **Diabetic Exchanges:** *4 lean meat, 1 fat, ½ starch.*

THYME & BASIL ROAST PORK

RASPBERRY RUMBLE

Honey-Lemon Asparagus

START TO FINISH: 15 MIN. • **MAKES:** 8 SERVINGS

- 2 **pounds fresh asparagus, trimmed**
- ¼ **cup honey**
- 2 **tablespoons butter**
- 2 **tablespoons lemon juice**
- 1 **teaspoon sea salt**
- 1 **teaspoon balsamic vinegar**
- 1 **teaspoon Worcestershire sauce**

1. In a large saucepan, bring 8 cups water to a boil. Add the asparagus in batches; cook, uncovered, 1-2 minutes or just until crisp-tender. Drain and pat dry.

2. In a small saucepan, combine the remaining ingredients. Bring to a boil. Reduce heat; simmer, uncovered, 2 minutes or until slightly thickened.

3. Transfer asparagus to a large bowl; drizzle with glaze and toss gently to coat.

PER SERVING *73 cal., 3 g fat (2 g sat. fat), 8 mg chol., 276 mg sodium, 12 g carb., 1 g fiber, 2 g pro.* **Diabetic Exchanges:** *1 vegetable, ½ starch, ½ fat.*

HONEY-LEMON
ASPARAGUS

Raspberry Rumble

PREP: 40 MIN. • **BAKE:** 25 MIN. + COOLING • **MAKES:** 12 SERVINGS

- 2 **cups fresh raspberries**
- ¼ **cup butter, softened**
- ¾ **cup sugar**
- 2 **large eggs**
- 2¼ **cups all-purpose flour**
- 2 **teaspoons baking powder**
- 1 **teaspoon salt**
- ¾ **cup 2% milk**

TOPPING
- 3 **large egg whites**
- 1 **cup sugar**
- ⅛ **teaspoon cream of tartar**
- ¼ **to ½ cup boiling water, optional**
- ¼ **teaspoon almond extract**
  Sliced almonds

1. Preheat oven to 350°. Place raspberries on a baking sheet; freeze until firm.

2. In a large bowl, cream butter and sugar until light and fluffy. Beat in eggs. In another bowl, whisk flour, baking powder and salt; add to the creamed mixture alternately with milk, beating well after each addition. Fold in the frozen raspberries.

3. Spread into a greased 13x9-in. baking pan. Bake for 25-30 minutes or until a toothpick inserted in center comes out clean. Cool completely in pan on a wire rack.

4. For topping, place egg whites in a small bowl; let stand at room temperature 30 minutes. Combine the egg whites, sugar and cream of tartar in the top of a double boiler or a metal bowl over simmering water. Beat on low speed until a thermometer reads 160°, about 5 minutes. Transfer to a large bowl; beat on high until stiff glossy peaks form, about 5 minutes. If desired, gradually beat in enough boiling water until mixture reaches desired consistency; beat in extract. Spread over cake; sprinkle with sliced almonds.

PER SERVING *(calculated without sliced almonds) equals 266 cal., 5 g fat (3 g sat. fat), 42 mg chol., 323 mg sodium, 51 g carb., 2 g fiber, 5 g pro.*

Creative Classics

This Las Vegas great-grandmother knows **big family meals aren't just for Thanksgiving Day.** Her party-pleasing specialties include turkey with a wallop of curry flavor and apple crisp spiked with rum.

RECIPES & STORY BY **NANCY HEISHMAN** LAS VEGAS, NV

Now that I'm 70 and retired from the medical marketing industry, I have lots of time for trying out new recipes on my five grown children, six grandchildren and great-grandchild. I've lived in Las Vegas for 38 years—before that, California's Bay Area and Mexico, where I had my first two children.

I like entering cooking contests—been published a dozen times—so I'm a real food lover who's always experimenting with flavors. Because we're all good cooks in my family, we enjoy lots of potluck meals together. My favorites—Mexican food and Indian curries—are fantastic with leftover Thanksgiving turkey. I like my curries with cilantro and coconut milk but not too much heat. I'm also known for the chutneys I make.

My colorful ribbon salad is a cool, crunchy, tangy side dish. I frequently whip up uncommon desserts with sherry or rum. And I dabble with different toppings, such as the gingersnaps I substituted in the apple crisp recipe I got from my mom, Joann Campbell. She's 94.

GINGERSNAP RUM APPLE CRISP

Gingersnap Rum Apple Crisp

PREP: 25 MIN. • **BAKE:** 35 MIN. • **MAKES:** 8 SERVINGS

- ¾ cup packed brown sugar
- 3 tablespoons all-purpose flour
- 2¼ teaspoons ground cinnamon
- 1¼ teaspoons ground allspice
- 1 teaspoon salt
- ¼ teaspoon ground ginger
- 6 cups thinly sliced peeled tart apples (about 6 medium)
- 6 caramels
- ⅓ cup rum or orange juice

TOPPING
- ¾ cup crushed gingersnap cookies (about 15 cookies)
- ¾ cup packed brown sugar
- ½ cup all-purpose flour
- ½ cup cold butter, cubed
  Vanilla ice cream

1. Preheat oven to 375°. In a large bowl, mix the first six ingredients. Add apples; toss to coat. In a small saucepan, combine caramels and rum. Cook and stir over medium-low heat until caramels are melted. Pour over the apple mixture; toss to coat. Transfer to a greased 8-in. square baking dish.

2. For topping, in a small bowl, mix crushed cookies, brown sugar and flour; cut in butter until crumbly. Sprinkle over filling. Bake 35-40 minutes or until apples are tender. Cover loosely with foil if top browns too quickly. Serve warm with vanilla ice cream.

PER SERVING *1 piece (calculated without ice cream) equals 430 cal., 14 g fat (8 g sat. fat), 31 mg chol., 483 mg sodium, 76 g carb., 2 g fiber, 3 g pro.*

EAT SMART **FAST FIX**
Turkey Curry with Rice

START TO FINISH: 30 MIN. • **MAKES:** 6 SERVINGS

- 1⅓ cups chicken broth
- 2 tablespoons curry powder
- 2 tablespoons minced fresh cilantro
- 3 garlic cloves, minced
- ¾ teaspoon salt
- ½ teaspoon ground cardamom
- ½ teaspoon pepper
- 3 medium carrots, thinly sliced

RIBBON SALAD WITH
ORANGE VINAIGRETTE

TURKEY CURRY
WITH RICE

1 medium onion, finely chopped
1 package (16 ounces) frozen cauliflower, thawed
3 cups chopped cooked turkey
½ cup mango chutney
2 teaspoons all-purpose flour
1 cup coconut milk
4½ cups hot cooked rice

4 green onions, finely chopped
½ cup chopped walnuts
½ teaspoon salt
½ teaspoon pepper
½ cup golden raisins, optional

VINAIGRETTE
¼ cup olive oil
4 teaspoons white wine vinegar
1 tablespoon finely chopped green onion
2 teaspoons honey
¼ teaspoon salt
¼ teaspoon pepper

1. In a large saucepan, mix the first seven ingredients. Add carrots and onion; bring to a boil. Reduce heat and simmer, covered, for 3-5 minutes or until carrots are crisp-tender. Add cauliflower; cook, covered, 4-6 minutes longer or until vegetables are tender.

2. Stir in turkey and chutney; heat through. In a small bowl, mix flour and coconut milk until smooth; stir into turkey mixture. Bring to a boil, stirring constantly; cook and stir 1-2 minutes or until slightly thickened. Serve with rice and, if desired, additional chutney.

PER SERVING *1 cup turkey mixture with ¾ cup rice equals 363 cal., 9 g fat (7 g sat. fat), 1 mg chol., 787 mg sodium, 64 g carb., 5 g fiber, 7 g pro.*

EAT SMART **FAST FIX**
Ribbon Salad with Orange Vinaigrette

START TO FINISH: 30 MIN. • **MAKES:** 8 SERVINGS

1 medium zucchini
1 medium cucumber
1 medium carrot
3 medium oranges
3 cups fresh baby spinach

1. Using a vegetable peeler, shave zucchini, cucumber and carrot lengthwise into very thin strips.

2. Finely grate enough peel from the oranges to measure 2 tablespoons. Cut one orange crosswise in half; squeeze juice from orange to measure ½ cup. Reserve peel and juice for vinaigrette. Cut a thin slice from the top and bottom of the remaining oranges; stand oranges upright on a cutting board. Cut off peels and outer membranes. Cut along the membrane of each segment to remove fruit.

3. In a large bowl, combine spinach, orange sections, green onions, walnuts, salt and pepper and, if desired, raisins. Add the vegetable ribbons and gently toss to combine. Combine vinaigrette ingredients. Add reserved orange peel and juice; whisk until blended. Drizzle half of vinaigrette over salad; toss to coat. Serve with remaining vinaigrette.

PER SERVING *1½ cups equals 162 cal., 12 g fat (1 g sat. fat), 0 chol., 240 mg sodium, 14 g carb., 2 g fiber, 3 g pro.* **Diabetic Exchanges:** *2 fat, 1 vegetable, ½ starch.*

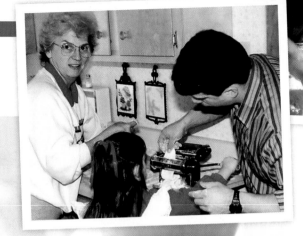

TABLE TRADITIONS

An Italian Classic

Seafood lasagna often appears at this South Carolina **grandpa's holiday dinners.**
Everyone gathers after church, and **the whole *famiglia* helps in the kitchen.**

RECIPES &STORY BY **JOE COLAMONICO** NORTH CHARLESTON, SC

M y Christmas Eve seafood lasagna recipe came from my maternal grandmother, Maria DiMarzio, who hailed from Bari, Italy. My extended family all love it, so it's often on the table for Sunday dinner celebrations, prepared with the super-fresh seafood available in my coastal town. And the family always shares this dish for the Feast of the Seven Fishes, the traditional Italian Christmas Eve dinner.

Family members gather here after church and change into comfy clothes that they don't mind cooking in. (When a bunch of Italians get together, the food will fly.) My two daughters bring their children. Jacob, Joey and Sidnie help out in the kitchen, just as I helped my grandma, stirring in ingredients and serving at the table.

This special dinner starts early, around 4 o'clock. We begin with my Italian dinner rolls: yeast dough spread with garlic butter, then rolled up and sliced like cinnamon rolls. We tear off pieces to dunk in marinara. Then lasagna and salad are on. Dessert's simple: ice cream with fruit and chocolate sauce.

We have a full house and celebrate with as many family members as possible—that's the Italian way!

(5)INGREDIENTS FAST FIX
Insalata Caprese

START TO FINISH: 25 MIN. • **MAKES:** 8 SERVINGS

- 2½ **pounds plum tomatoes (about 10), cut into 1-inch pieces**
- 1 **carton (8 ounces) fresh mozzarella cheese pearls**
- ½ **cup pitted ripe olives**
- 3 **tablespoons olive oil**
- ¼ **cup thinly sliced fresh basil**
- 2 **teaspoons minced fresh oregano**
- ½ **teaspoon salt**
- ¼ **teaspoon pepper**
  Balsamic vinegar, optional

In a large bowl, mix tomatoes, cheese pearls and olives. Drizzle with oil. Sprinkle with basil, oregano, salt and pepper; toss to coat. Let stand for 10 minutes before serving. If desired, drizzle with vinegar.

PER SERVING *¾ cup equals 160 cal., 12 g fat (5 g sat. fat), 22 mg chol., 257 mg sodium, 7 g carb., 2 g fiber, 6 g pro.*

WHITE SEAFOOD LASAGNA

White Seafood Lasagna

PREP: 1 HOUR • **BAKE:** 40 MIN. + STANDING • **MAKES:** 12 SERVINGS

- 9 uncooked lasagna noodles
- 1 tablespoon butter
- 1 pound uncooked shrimp (31-40 per pound), peeled and deveined
- 1 pound bay scallops
- 5 garlic cloves, minced
- ¼ cup white wine
- 1 tablespoon lemon juice
- 1 pound fresh crabmeat

INSALATA CAPRESE

CHEESE SAUCE
- ¼ cup butter, cubed
- ¼ cup all-purpose flour
- 3 cups 2% milk
- 1 cup (4 ounces) shredded part-skim mozzarella cheese
- ½ cup grated Parmesan cheese
- ½ teaspoon salt
- ¼ teaspoon pepper
  Dash ground nutmeg

RICOTTA MIXTURE
- 1 carton (15 ounces) part-skim ricotta cheese
- 1 package (10 ounces) frozen chopped spinach, thawed and squeezed dry
- 1 cup (4 ounces) shredded part-skim mozzarella cheese
- ½ cup grated Parmesan cheese
- ½ cup seasoned bread crumbs
- 1 large egg, lightly beaten

TOPPING
- 1 cup (4 ounces) shredded part-skim mozzarella cheese
- ¼ cup grated Parmesan cheese
  Minced fresh parsley

1. Preheat oven to 350°. Cook lasagna noodles according to package directions; drain.

2. Meanwhile, in a large skillet, heat butter over medium heat. Add shrimp and scallops in batches; cook 2-4 minutes or until shrimp turn pink and scallops are firm and opaque. Remove from pan.

3. Add garlic to same pan; cook 1 minute longer. Add wine and lemon juice, stirring to loosen browned bits from pan. Bring to a boil; cook 1-2 minutes or until liquid is reduced by half. Add crab; heat through. Stir in shrimp and scallops.

4. For cheese sauce, melt butter over medium heat in a large saucepan. Stir in flour until smooth; gradually whisk in milk. Bring to a boil, stirring constantly; cook and stir 1-2 minutes or until thickened. Remove from heat; stir in the remaining cheese sauce ingredients. In a large bowl, combine the ricotta mixture ingredients; stir in 1 cup of cheese sauce.

5. Spread ½ cup cheese sauce into a greased 13x9-in. baking dish. Layer with three noodles, half of the ricotta mixture, half of the seafood mixture and ⅔ cup cheese sauce. Repeat layers. Top with remaining noodles and cheese sauce. Sprinkle with remaining mozzarella and Parmesan cheeses.

6. Bake, uncovered, 40-50 minutes or until bubbly and top is golden brown. Let stand for 10 minutes before serving. Sprinkle with parsley.

PER SERVING *1 piece equals 448 cal., 19 g fat (11 g sat. fat), 158 mg chol., 957 mg sodium, 29 g carb., 2 g fiber, 39 g pro.*

GRANDMA NARDI'S ITALIAN EASTER BREAD FROM PAT MERKOVICH *PAGE 289*

Cooking School

Looking to up your game with the **best apple pie,** applause-winning **roast turkey** and **adorable holiday rolls?** Make dishes that dazzle with **how-to's and tips** from the pros at *Taste of Home*.

NICHOLAS IVERSON'S THE BEST APPLE PIE
PAGE 299

SHANNON ROUM'S CLASSIC CANDY CANE BUTTER COOKIES *PAGE 301*

BETHANY VAN JACOBSON'S ROASTED SAGE TURKEY WITH VEGETABLE GRAVY *PAGE 296*

Beautiful Breads

Every good cook needs at least one **homemade yeast bread** recipe. Follow these simple steps to bake up **gorgeous golden brown loaves and rolls** for the holidays and every day.

HOW TO MAKE YEAST DOUGH

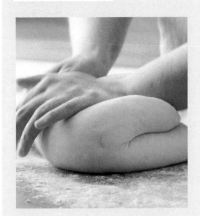

1. Fold top of dough toward you. With your palms, push dough with a rolling motion away from you. Turn dough a quarter turn; repeat folding, kneading and turning until dough is smooth and elastic. Add flour to surface as needed to prevent sticking during rising.

2. Press two fingers ½ in. into the dough. If the dents remain, the dough has doubled in size.

BASIC HOMEMADE BREAD

⑤INGREDIENTS

Basic Homemade Bread

I enjoy the aroma of fresh homemade bread in my kitchen. Here's a simple yeast version that bakes up golden brown.
—**SANDRA ANDERSON** NEW YORK, NY

PREP: 20 MIN. + RISING
BAKE: 30 MIN. + COOLING
MAKES: 2 LOAVES (16 SLICES EACH)

- 1 **package (¼ ounce) active dry yeast**
- 2¼ **cups warm water (110° to 115°)**
- 3 **tablespoons sugar**
- 1 **tablespoon salt**
- 2 **tablespoons canola oil**
- 6¼ to 6¾ **cups all-purpose flour**

1. In a large bowl, dissolve yeast in warm water. Add the sugar, salt, oil and 3 cups flour. Beat until smooth.

Stir in enough remaining flour, ½ cup at a time, to form a soft dough.

2. Turn dough onto a floured surface; knead until smooth and elastic, about 8-10 minutes. Place in a greased bowl, turning once to grease the top. Cover and let rise in a warm place until doubled, about 1½ hours.

3. Punch dough down. Turn onto a lightly floured surface; divide dough in half. Shape each into a loaf. Place in two greased 9x5-in. loaf pans. Cover and let rise until doubled, about 30-45 minutes.

4. Bake at 375° for 30-35 minutes or until golden brown and bread sounds hollow when tapped. Remove from pans to wire racks to cool.

PER SERVING *1 slice equals 102 cal., 1 g fat (trace sat. fat), 0 chol., 222 mg sodium, 20 g carb., 1 g fiber, 3 g pro.*

3. Place in greased pans. Cover with a towel and let rise in a warm (80°-85°), draft-free area until dough has doubled.

Dove Dinner Rolls

Fluffy dinner rolls shaped like doves are a sweet nod to the holidays. They dash away faster than Santa himself.

—**FRANCES WIRTZ** WEST ALLIS, WI

PREP: 50 MIN. + RISING • **BAKE:** 10 MIN.
MAKES: 2 DOZEN

- 2 **cups whole wheat pastry flour**
- ½ **cup sugar**
- 3 **packages (¼ ounce each) active dry yeast**
- 2 **teaspoons salt**
- 1 **cup water**
- 1 **cup 2% milk**
- ½ **cup butter, cubed**
- 1 **large egg**
- 4 **to 4½ cups bread flour**

ASSEMBLY

- 48 **dried currants**
- 24 **slivered almonds**
- 1 **large egg**
- 2 **tablespoons 2% milk**

1. In a large bowl, mix pastry flour, sugar, yeast and salt. In a small saucepan, heat water, milk and butter to 120°-130°. Add to dry ingredients; beat on medium speed 1 minute. Add egg; beat on high 2 minutes. Stir in enough bread flour to form a soft dough (dough will be sticky).

2. Turn dough onto a floured surface; knead until smooth and elastic, about 6-8 minutes. Place in a greased bowl, turning once to grease the top. Cover with plastic wrap and let rise in a warm place until doubled, about 45 minutes.

3. Punch down dough. Let stand, covered, 15 minutes. Turn onto a lightly floured surface; divide and shape into 24 balls. Roll each into a 10-in. rope; tie into a loose knot. Bring one end up and tuck into center of roll to form head. Flatten opposite end; with a sharp knife, cut four slits to form five tail feathers. Press two currants into head for eyes and one

almond for beak. Place 2 in. apart on greased baking sheets.

4. Cover with kitchen towels; let rise in a warm place until doubled, about 30 minutes. Preheat oven to 400°.

5. In a small bowl, whisk egg and milk; brush over rolls. Bake 10-12 minutes or until golden brown. Remove from pans to wire racks; serve warm.

PER SERVING *1 roll equals 177 cal., 5 g fat (3 g sat. fat), 27 mg chol., 239 mg sodium, 28 g carb., 2 g fiber, 5 g pro.*

DOVE DINNER ROLLS

SHAPING DINNER ROLLS

Let the dough rise, then roll. Keep your birds plump and pretty by making sure each dough rope is no longer than 10 in.

After tying the dough in a loose knot, use the shorter end to form each dove's head.

Coat the blade of a small knife with nonstick cooking spray to help you cut crisp, clean tail feathers.

GRANDMA NARDI'S
ITALIAN EASTER BREAD

Grandma Nardi's Italian Easter Bread

My Grandma Nardi's bread with dyed Easter eggs represents family and tradition. I fondly remember how she taught me the recipe when I was a little girl.

—**PAT MERKOVICH** SOUTH MILWAUKEE, WI

PREP: 35 MIN. + RISING
BAKE: 30 MIN. + COOLING
MAKES: 1 LOAF (16 SLICES)

3 large eggs
Assorted food coloring

BREAD
⅔ cup warm whole milk (70° to 80°)
2 large eggs
2 tablespoons butter, melted
2 tablespoons sugar
1½ teaspoons salt
3 cups bread flour
1 package (¼ ounce) quick-rise yeast
1 tablespoon canola oil

EGG WASH
1 large egg
1 tablespoon water
1 tablespoon sesame seeds or poppy seeds

1. Place three eggs in a single layer in a small saucepan; add enough cold water to cover by 1 in. Cover and quickly bring to a boil. Remove from heat. Let stand 15 minutes.

2. Rinse eggs in cold water and place in ice water until completely cooled. Drain; dye hard-cooked eggs with food coloring, following package directions. Let stand until completely dry.

3. In bread machine pan, place the first seven bread ingredients in order suggested by manufacturer. Select dough setting. Check dough after 5 minutes of mixing; add 1-2 tablespoons additional milk or flour if needed.

4. When cycle is completed, turn dough onto a lightly floured surface. Punch down dough; divide into thirds. Roll each into a 15-in. rope. Place ropes on a greased baking sheet and braid. Shape into a ring. Pinch ends to seal. Lightly coat dyed eggs with oil; arrange on braid, tucking them carefully between ropes. For egg wash, whisk egg with water. Brush over dough; sprinkle with sesame seeds.

5. Cover with a kitchen towel; let rise in a warm place until almost doubled, about 30 minutes. Preheat oven to 350°.

6. Bake 30-35 minutes or until golden brown. Remove from pan to a wire rack to cool. Refrigerate leftovers.
PER SERVING *1 slice equals 157 cal., 5 g fat (2 g sat. fat), 75 mg chol., 264 mg sodium, 21 g carb., 1 g fiber, 6 g pro.*

TO PREPARE DOUGH BY HAND

To prepare dough by hand In a large bowl, mix sugar, yeast, salt and 1 cup flour. In a small saucepan, heat milk and butter to 120°-130°. Add to dry ingredients; beat on medium speed 2 minutes. Add eggs; beat on high 2 minutes. Stir in enough remaining flour to form a soft dough (dough will be sticky). Turn the dough onto a floured surface; knead until smooth and elastic, about 6-8 minutes. Place in a greased bowl, turning once to grease the top. Cover with plastic wrap and let rest 1 hour. Shape and bake as directed.

SHAPING EASTER BREAD

Place ropes almost touching on a greased baking sheet. Loosely braid them, then press ends to seal.

Shape dough into a ring, pinching the ends to seal. Disguise the area with an Easter egg. Decorate as desired with additional eggs.

Making Meringue

Don't be afraid to make **meringue.** We're here to help. This fancy take on the **classic campfire recipe** is worth the effort. It'll **melt in your mouth.**

Chocolate S'mores Tart

I created this tart for my kids, who love having s'mores on the fire pit. It's truly indulgent. We simply can't get enough of the billowy marshmallow topping.

—DINA CROWELL FREDERICKSBURG, VA

PREP: 55 MIN. + CHILLING
MAKES: 16 SERVINGS

- 1½ cups graham cracker crumbs
- ¼ cup sugar
- ⅓ cup butter, melted

FILLING
- 10 ounces bittersweet chocolate, chopped
- ¼ cup butter, cubed
- 1½ cups heavy whipping cream

TOPPING
- 5 large egg whites
- 1 cup sugar
- ¼ teaspoon cream of tartar

1. In a small bowl, mix cracker crumbs and sugar; stir in butter. Press onto bottom and ½ in. up sides of an ungreased 9-in. fluted tart pan with removable bottom. Refrigerate 30 minutes.
2. Place the chocolate and butter in a large bowl. In a small saucepan, bring cream just to a boil. Pour over chocolate and butter; let stand for 5 minutes. Stir with a whisk until smooth. Pour into prepared tart shell. Refrigerate 1 hour or until set. Place egg whites in a large bowl; let stand at room temperature 30 minutes.

3. In top of a double boiler or a metal bowl over simmering water, combine egg whites, sugar and cream of tartar. Beat on low speed 1 minute. Continue beating on low until a thermometer reads 160°, about 5 minutes. Transfer to a large bowl; beat on high until stiff glossy peaks form and the mixture is slightly cooled, about 5 minutes.
4. Spread the meringue over tart. If desired, heat meringue with a kitchen torch or broil 2 in. from heat until meringue is lightly browned, about 30-45 seconds. Refrigerate leftovers.
PER SERVING 1 slice equals 332 cal., 24 g fat (13 g sat. fat), 49 mg chol., 122 mg sodium, 33 g carb., 2 g fiber, 4 g pro.

CREATIVE CRUMB CRUSTS

You likely have everything you need in your pantry to put a clever twist on a standard 9-in. crumb crust.

SALTINE
Preheat oven to 350°. Mix 2 cups crushed saltine crackers and ¼ cup sugar; stir in ½ cup melted butter. Press onto bottom and up the sides of a 9-in. pie plate. Refrigerate for 20 minutes. Bake 15-18 minutes or until lightly browned. Cool on a wire rack.

PRETZEL
Preheat oven to 350°. Mix 2 cups finely crushed pretzels and ¼ cup sugar; stir in ¾ cup melted butter. Press onto bottom and up the sides of a 9-in. pie plate. Bake for 8-12 minutes or until lightly browned. Cool on a wire rack.

ANIMAL CRACKER
Preheat oven to 325°. Mix 2 cups finely crushed animal crackers and 2 Tbsp. sugar; stir in ¼ cup melted butter. Press onto bottom and up the sides of a 9-in. pie plate. Bake 13-15 minutes or until browned. Cool on a wire rack.

CAP'N CRUNCH
Preheat oven to 350°. Mix 2 cups finely crushed Cap'n Crunch cereal and ½ cup melted butter. Press onto bottom and up the sides of a 9-in. pie plate. Bake 8-12 minutes or until lightly browned. Cool on a wire rack.

HOW TO TEST PEAKS

To create soft or stiff peaks, beat egg whites in a clean bowl with an electric mixer on medium speed until they are thick and white.

To test for soft peaks, lift the beaters from the whites—the egg-white peaks should curl down from the beaters as shown above.

For stiff peaks, continue beating egg whites after they have reached the soft-peak stage until the volume increases and thickens.

To test for stiff peaks, lift the beaters from the whites—peaks should stand straight out from beaters as shown in photo above. If you tilt the bowl, the whites should not slide around.

CHOCOLATE S'MORES TART

Simple Salmon

This seafood preparation is like your little black dress. **Easy, classic and perfect** all by itself. But you can **glam it up** when the mood strikes. Jeanne Ambrose, executive editor of *Taste of Home*'s sister publication *Country Woman,* shows you how.

Oven-Roasted Salmon

When I'm starving after work, I want a fast meal with no-fail technique. Roasted salmon is uber-tender and has a delicate sweetness. It's also an easy wowza for company.

—**JEANNE AMBROSE** MILWAUKEE, WI

START TO FINISH: 20 MIN. • **MAKES:** 4 SERVINGS

- **1 center-cut salmon fillet (1½ pounds)**
- **1 tablespoon olive oil**
- **½ teaspoon salt**
- **¼ teaspoon pepper**

1. Place a large oven-safe skillet in a cold oven. Preheat oven to 450°. Meanwhile, brush salmon with oil and sprinkle with salt and pepper.

2. Carefully remove skillet from oven. Place fish, skin side down, in skillet. Return to oven; bake uncovered, 14-18 minutes or until salmon flakes easily and a thermometer reads 125°. Cut salmon into four equal portions.

PER SERVING *1 fillet equals 295 cal., 19 g fat (4 g sat. fat), 85 mg chol., 380 mg sodium, trace carb., trace fiber, 29 g pro.* **Diabetic Exchanges:** *4 lean meat, ½ fat.*

JEANNE'S TOP TIPS

START WITH A SIZZLE

A superhot skillet holds the key to a quick-cooking, mellow salmon. Some people swear by cast iron, but I've even used a high-sided cookie sheet. (Shh. Don't tell the Test Kitchen cooks. They love cast iron!) The high heat magically crisps the skin and cooks the salmon very quickly.

20 MINUTES TO DONE

It's so easy to overcook seafood. That's why you should keep an instant-read thermometer on hand. When it hits 125°, the salmon is done. We mean it. Or you can double-check by using a fork to make sure that the thickest part of the fish is opaque inside.

WHITE STUFF?

You might notice a white substance appear when you cook salmon. Fear not. It's simply a harmless protein that coagulates as the fish cooks (kind of like an egg white). Scrape it off if it bothers you.

WHOMP IT UP

This weeknight-reliable salmon is perfect with just salt and pepper. But it's easily fancied up with flavor. Add a slather of lemony herbs, a maple glaze or melted dill butter after it's cooked and get ready for the "wows."

FOR GREMOLATA

In a small bowl, mix ¼ cup minced fresh parsley, 2 tablespoons olive oil, 1 tablespoon lemon juice, 1 minced garlic clove, 1 teaspoon grated lemon peel, ½ teaspoon salt and ¼ teaspoon pepper.

FOR MAPLE SOY GLAZE

In a small bowl, mix ¼ cup maple syrup, 2 tablespoons soy sauce, 1 minced green onion, ½ teaspoon grated fresh ginger and ¼ teaspoon red pepper flakes.

FOR DILL AND CAPER BUTTER

In a small bowl, mix ¼ cup softened butter, 1 tablespoon minced shallot, 1 tablespoon minced fresh dill, 1 teaspoon Dijon mustard and 1 teaspoon chopped capers.

Potato Salad

Staffer Ellie Martin Cliffe brings her mom's **famous potluck side** to the Test Kitchen to prove it's all that, with a **dash of paprika.**

Mom's Super Stupendous Potato Salad

In college, my best friend and I debated whose mom made the best potato salad. Turns out they were almost identical! Even though I've since tweaked our recipe, it still takes me home again.

—**ELLIE CLIFFE** *TASTE OF HOME* SENIOR EDITOR

PREP: 20 MIN. • **COOK:** 15 MIN. + CHILLING
MAKES: 12 SERVINGS

- 1 garlic clove, peeled
- 3 pounds small red potatoes, quartered
- 2 tablespoons cider vinegar, divided
- 1½ teaspoons salt, divided
- 6 hard-cooked large eggs, divided
- 1 cup mayonnaise
- ½ cup sour cream
- 1 tablespoon Dijon mustard
- ½ teaspoon paprika
- ¼ teaspoon pepper
- 1 medium sweet onion, finely chopped
- 2 celery ribs, finely chopped
- 2 tablespoons minced fresh parsley

1. Skewer garlic with a toothpick (to make it easy to find after cooking). Place potatoes, 1 tablespoon vinegar, 1 teaspoon salt and skewered garlic in a Dutch oven; add water to cover. Bring to a boil. Reduce heat; simmer until tender, 10-12 minutes. Drain potatoes, reserving garlic; remove skewer and crush garlic.
2. Meanwhile, chop five eggs. Whisk together mayonnaise, sour cream, mustard, paprika, pepper, garlic and remaining vinegar and salt. Stir in potatoes, chopped eggs, onion and celery. Refrigerate 4 hours or until cold.
3. Just before serving, slice remaining egg. Top salad with egg; sprinkle with parsley and, if desired, additional paprika.

PER SERVING ¾ *cup equals 281 cal., 19 g fat (4 g sat. fat), 107 mg chol., 472 mg sodium, 20 g carb., 2 g fiber, 6 g pro.*

MOM'S SUPER STUPENDOUS POTATO SALAD

ELLIE'S INSIDE SCOOP

CHOOSE RED POTATOES over russets—the waxy flesh has a better texture, and the skins add earthy flavor and that pretty color.

ADD VINEGAR TO THE WATER before cooking to set the flesh of the potatoes so they won't fall apart when you stir everything together.

POP THE GARLIC INTO THE COOKING WATER to mellow it and infuse the potatoes with its savory goodness at the same time.

TOSS WITH DRESSING while the potatoes are still warm so they'll better absorb the creamy, tangy amazingness.

Use a grid-style cooling rack to "chop" your hard-cooked eggs. It's faster (and less slippery). Set the rack on top of the bowl and smoosh the peeled egg through. Done.

TATER TOSS-UP

You say mayo, they say Miracle Whip. Let's call the whole thing amazing. Our Facebook fans share the twists on potato salad that make it a summer superstar.

1 I use the standard ingredients plus a few veggies like **cucumber** and **celery**...but the real standout is a cubed **apple!** You don't see it but you get this lovely, refreshing crunch!
—Sue Vail,
St. Catharines, ON

2 My secret ingredient is a pinch of **curry powder** added to a mayonnaise base. Everyone loves it!
—Cheryl Boots,
Corunna, MI

3 I make a bacon-ranch version that's to die for. Boil red potatoes (no need to peel) and add **hard-cooked eggs, celery, cooked bacon, cheddar cheese, ranch dressing** and **pepper** to taste. Add a little more bacon on top—so good.
—Katie Lapare,
Tucson, AZ

4 I use red potatoes, cooked with skins on, and add a drained jar of **marinated artichoke hearts,** a small jar of **green olives** and thinly sliced **red onion.** I use a zesty **Italian dressing with lime,** starting with a little and adding until all the ingredients are nicely covered.
—Jane Kirkham,
Grants Pass, OR

5 I mix in some minced **habanero.** We like things spicy around here!
—Christianna Madden,
Big Bear, CA

6 I make a simple potato salad but use **honey mustard** instead of regular mustard. Wonderfully tasty.
—Bo McCollom,
Decatur, AL

7 Miracle Whip, plenty of **eggs,** plus **pickle relish, mustard** and slightly cooked **green peas.** And sometimes I stir in a bit of **shredded carrots.** It's always eaten up.
—Lelia Maguire Oster,
La Salle, CO

8 Unpeeled red potatoes, **hard-cooked eggs, celery, green onions, sweet pickle relish** and my favorite addition: **sliced radishes.** A little pickle relish juice in the dressing thins it out a bit.
—Leoda Johnston Barr,
Lincoln City, OR

9 To make it extra creamy, we use mayo and **ranch dressing.** All the credit goes to my husband; everyone requests his potato salad.
—Kathy Luka, Chicago, IL

10 My mother always added **tomatoes** to her potato salad, so I do the same.
—Laura Prince, Weaver, AL

Top Turkey

This is it! The **juiciest, crispiest, most golden bird** Thanksgiving has ever seen. Our turkey pro—who tested and tested again—shares her secrets.

Roasted Sage Turkey with Vegetable Gravy

There's no place like home-style when roasting the big bird. Instead of s age stuffing with turkey, stuff this bird with fresh sage and sprigs of thyme.

—BETHANY VAN JACOBSON

TASTE OF HOME LEAD PREP COOK

PREP: 30 MIN. + CHILLING
BAKE: 2 HOURS 10 MIN. + STANDING
MAKES: 16 SERVINGS (3½ CUPS GRAVY)

- 1 **turkey (14 to 16 pounds)**
- 1 **tablespoon kosher salt**
- 1 **teaspoon ground sage**
- ½ **teaspoon garlic powder**
- 1 **large onion, chopped**
- 3 **celery ribs, chopped**
- 3 **medium carrots, chopped**
- 1¼ **cups water, divided**
- 3 **tablespoons canola oil**
- ½ **teaspoon freshly ground pepper**
- ¾ **cup white wine**
- 3 **fresh sage sprigs**
- 4 **fresh thyme sprigs**

GRAVY
- 1 **to 1½ cups reduced-sodium chicken broth or homemade chicken stock**
- ¼ **cup all-purpose flour**
- ¼ **teaspoon minced fresh sage**
- ¼ **teaspoon freshly ground pepper**

1. Remove giblets and neck from turkey. Reserve the turkey neck; refrigerate, covered, overnight. Place turkey in a 15x10-in. baking pan, breast side up. Secure skin to underside of neck cavity with toothpicks. Mix salt, sage and garlic powder. Tuck wings under turkey; tie drumsticks together. Pat turkey dry. Rub outside of turkey with salt mixture. Refrigerate turkey, loosely covered, overnight.

2. Preheat oven to 475°. Place onion, celery, carrots and reserved neck in bottom of a broiler pan; add ½ cup water. Place broiler pan rack over top; transfer turkey to rack. Rub outside of turkey with oil; sprinkle with pepper. Pour wine and remaining water into turkey cavity; add sage and thyme sprigs.

3. Place turkey in oven, legs facing toward back of oven. Roast, uncovered, 40 minutes.

4. Reduce oven setting to 350°. Cover breast tightly with a double thickness of foil. Roast 1½-2 hours longer or until a thermometer inserted in thickest part of thigh reads 170°-175°. (Thermometer should not touch bone or fat.)

5. Remove turkey from oven. Let stand, uncovered, 20 minutes before carving. Using a turkey baster, remove liquid from turkey cavity to a large measuring cup. Line a strainer or colander with cheesecloth; place over measuring cup. With a slotted spoon, remove vegetables from bottom of broiler pan, reserving 1¼ cups. Discard turkey neck. Strain cooking liquid into measuring cup. Skim fat, reserving ¼ cup fat. Add enough broth to the cooking liquid to measure 2 cups.

6. In a large saucepan, mix flour and reserved fat until smooth; gradually whisk in broth mixture. Bring to a boil over medium-high heat, stirring constantly; cook and stir 1-2 minutes or until thickened. Add half of the reserved vegetables. Puree gravy using an immersion blender; or, cool gravy

ROASTED SAGE TURKEY WITH VEGETABLE GRAVY

slightly and puree in a blender. Stir in sage, pepper and remaining vegetables; heat through. Serve with turkey.

PER SERVING *9 ounces of cooked turkey with about ¼ cup gravy equals 514 cal., 24 g fat (6 g sat. fat), 215 mg chol., 562 mg sodium, 4 g carb., 1 g fiber, 64 g pro.*

◖ ROASTING TIMELINE ▭

COVER WITH FOIL
after 40 min.
Carefully cover the breast only with the foil shield. (See page 297, Tip 8, for make-ahead details.) Remember to turn the oven down to 350°.

TEMP IT
after 2 hours, 10 min.
Insert your thermometer in the thickest part of the thigh (without touching the bone). The goal temp is 170°-175°. If it's not there, keep roasting.

LET IT REST
for 20 min.
This keeps the juices in the bird instead of on the cutting board. No need to tent the turkey, which would steam the crispy skin. (Use this time to make gravy!)

BUY IT When choosing a frozen turkey, size matters. A typical 14-pound bird serves 16 people. Add a pound or two if you're looking forward to leftovers.

THAW IT Every 4 pounds of frozen turkey needs 24 hours of thawing time. So for a 14-pound bird, move the turkey to the fridge from the freezer five days before the big feast.

RUB IT The day before Thanksgiving, don't forget to pull the giblets from the turkey (check both the neck area and the back area). Save the neck—it's the key to making some seriously good gravy. Then rub the salt mixture over the outside of the turkey, cover it and send it back to the fridge.

PREP IT It's the big day! Preheat the oven, give the turkey one last rub and load the broiler pan with veggies and

stock ingredients. Don't wing it! Step 2 of the recipe lays the groundwork for a picture-perfect bird.

10 SECRETS TO THE MOST FLAVORFUL TURKEY... EVER

Taste of Home's Bethany Van Jacobson makes it easy for you to roast Thanksgiving's star attraction. Just know you're going to be asked to make this bird next year and, well, ever after.

1. Place fresh herbs, wine and water inside the turkey cavity to create a flavorful broth that you'll add to your gravy later.

2. Use toothpicks to secure skin to the inside of the bird near the legs (see top photo). This makes the turkey look extra pretty when it's done.

3. Rub the skin with oil instead of butter for a crispier skin and an allover golden brown glow.

4. Use a broiler pan instead of a roasting pan. The turkey sides and thighs will be better exposed to the oven's heat so the bird cooks more evenly.

5. Add vegetables and turkey neck to the roasting pan. They stretch the drippings and act as a natural thickener for gravy (see middle photo).

6. Roast at a high temperature when you first put the bird in the oven to speed up the cooking time and make the legs and thighs crispy.

7. Slide the turkey into the oven legs first. Oven temps are often warmer near the back, so the thighs get that higher heat they need while the breast cooks in the lower heat by the door.

8. Shield the breast with foil to prevent overbrowning and to keep the meat tender (see bottom photo). *Make-ahead tip:* Before you even unwrap the bird, create a form-fitting shield by taking a double layer of foil and shaping it over the breast. Stash the foil until roasting day.

9. Try not to peek inside the oven while the turkey's roasting (except of course for those important steps like adding the foil shield and temping the bird). Opening the door cools the oven, adding extra cooking time.

10. Save the turkey drippings to make a fat/flour mixture called a roux. It makes the gravy extra silky and adds tons of rich flavor.

The Best Apple Pie Ever

Add a few new moves to your **pie-making skills.** *Taste of Home* Lead Test Cook Nicholas Iverson leads the way to a tasty **apple filling** packed inside a **buttery crust** that no fork can resist.

THE BEST APPLE PIE

The Best Apple Pie

Boost your apple pie with a buttery crust, pre-cooked apples and an incredible filling with cider, cinnamon and lemon juice.

—NICHOLAS IVERSON
TASTE OF HOME LEAD TEST COOK

PREP: 40 MIN. + COOLING
BAKE: 1 HOUR + COOLING
MAKES: 10 SERVINGS

- 2½ cups all-purpose flour
- 2 tablespoons sugar
- 1 teaspoon salt
- 1¼ cups cold unsalted butter, cubed
- ⅓ cup cold water

FILLING

- 4 tablespoons unsalted butter
- 5 pounds medium Honeycrisp apples, peeled, sliced ¼ in. thick
- ½ cup sugar
- ¼ cup packed dark brown sugar
- ½ teaspoon salt
- ½ teaspoon ground cinnamon
- ¼ teaspoon ground allspice
- ¼ teaspoon grated lemon peel
- ½ cup apple cider
- 1 tablespoon lemon juice
- 1 teaspoon vanilla extract
- 1 large egg yolk
- 1 tablespoon heavy whipping cream
  Coarse sugar

1. Pulse flour, sugar and salt in a food processor until blended. Add butter; pulse until butter is the size of peas. While processing, add just enough ice water to form moist crumbs. Divide dough in half. Shape each into a disk; wrap in plastic wrap. Refrigerate 30 minutes or overnight.

2. Meanwhile, melt butter in a Dutch oven over medium heat. Add apples and next six ingredients; stir to combine. Cook, covered, stirring occasionally, until apples soften and release their juices, 10-12 minutes. With a slotted spoon, transfer apple slices to a 15x10-in. baking pan; spread into a single layer. Add cider to remaining liquid in Dutch oven and bring to a boil; cook until juices reduce to ½ cup, 10-12 minutes. Remove from heat; add lemon juice and vanilla extract. Pour over apple slices; cool completely. (Filling can be made 24 hours in advance and refrigerated.)

3. Preheat oven to 425°. Adjust oven rack to lowest position; place foil on rack to catch any spills. On a lightly floured surface, roll half of dough to a ⅛-in.-thick circle; transfer to a deep-dish 9-in. pie plate. Trim pastry to within ½ in. of rim. Add filling. Roll remaining dough to a ⅛-in.-thick circle; place over filling. Trim, seal and flute edge. Cut slits in top. Whisk together egg yolk and cream; brush top of pie. Sprinkle with coarse sugar. Chill 15 minutes.

4. Bake 20 minutes. Reduce oven setting to 350°. Bake until crust is golden brown and filling bubbly, 40-50 minutes longer. Cool pie on a wire rack.

PER SERVING *1 slice equals 557 cal., 30 g fat (18 g sat. fat), 94 mg chol., 363 mg sodium, 73 g carb. (43 g sugars, 5 g fiber), 4 g pro.*

NICK'S TRICKS

THICKEN YOUR FILLING with cooking juices from the apples, plus sugar and cider. You get a sweet, gooey sauce that's a lot tastier than a flour or cornstarch filling.

COOL YOUR APPLES to room temperature after precooking. This helps prevent steam from collecting under the top pastry, which will turn into an air pocket when your pie bakes.

BE AS PATIENT as you can—cool the finished pie completely. It helps the filling set and ensures that each slice is just as juicy as the next.

BRAIDED TOP CRUST

For a braided top crust, roll dough into a 12x10-in. rectangle; cut into fifteen ½-in.-wide strips lengthwise. Working three pieces at a time, braid strips. Arrange over filling; trim edges as needed to fit. Flute bottom pastry edge around filling.

Cookies with a Twist

O come, all ye bakers! Our food stylist shows you how to shape this classic dough into **a buttery batch of candy canes.**

(5) INGREDIENTS
Classic Candy Cane Butter Cookies

To make cookies that look like candy canes, we color half the dough in classic red and twist away. They're fun to hang on the side of a coffee mug, or devour all on their own.

—SHANNON ROUM
TASTE OF HOME FOOD STYLIST

PREP: 45 MIN. + CHILLING
BAKE: 10 MIN./BATCH
MAKES: 3 DOZEN

- 1 **cup butter, softened**
- ⅔ **cup sugar**
- ¼ **teaspoon salt**
- 1 **large egg yolk**
- 2 **teaspoons vanilla extract**
- 2¼ **cups all-purpose flour**
    Red paste food coloring

1. In a large bowl, cream butter, sugar and salt until light and fluffy. Beat in egg yolk and vanilla; gradually beat in flour. Divide dough in half; mix food coloring into one half. Roll each dough into a 6-in. square. Wrap each in plastic wrap; refrigerate at least 1 hour or overnight.

2. Preheat oven to 350°. Cut each dough into 36 squares. Work with a quarter of the dough at a time; keep remaining dough refrigerated. Roll one piece plain dough into a 6-in. rope; roll one piece red dough into a 6-in. rope. Place ropes side by side. Lift left rope over the right; repeat to form a twist. Repeat with remaining dough. Place twists 1 in. apart on parchment paper-lined baking sheets, curving top of each twist to form hook of cane.

3. Bake 7-9 minutes or until set. Cool on pans 3 minutes. Remove to wire racks to cool.

PER SERVING *1 cookie equals 90 cal., 5 g fat (3 g sat. fat), 19 mg chol., 57 mg sodium, 10 g carb., trace fiber, 1 g pro.*

GIVE IT A TWIRL

A roll here, a flip there, and a pretty little curve to finish it up—our food stylist's simple method is easy to master at home.

Roll both plain and red dough into 6-in. squares on a cutting board covered in parchment paper; chill. Then cut each square into six rows in one direction, then six rows in the other to get 36 even squares.

Soften a dough square slightly in your hands till just pliable. Roll dough into a 6-in. rope. Repeat. No worries if your ropes aren't 6 inches on the dot. (Once they're baked, they're gonna get eaten!)

Place a red rope and a plain rope side by side on parchment paper. Gently lift the strand on the left, cross it over the other and lay it back down. Repeat until you've formed a twist.

Transfer each dough twist to a parchment paper-lined cookie sheet. Create the hook of the candy cane as you set down the twist.

Substitutions & Equivalents

EQUIVALENT MEASURES

3 teaspoons	=	1 tablespoon	16 tablespoons	=	1 cup
4 tablespoons	=	1/4 cup	2 cups	=	1 pint
5-1/3 tablespoons	=	1/3 cup	4 cups	=	1 quart
8 tablespoons	=	1/2 cup	4 quarts	=	1 gallon

FOOD EQUIVALENTS

GRAINS

Macaroni	1 cup (3-1/2 ounces) uncooked	=	2-1/2 cups cooked
Noodles, Medium	3 cups (4 ounces) uncooked	=	4 cups cooked
Popcorn	1/3 to 1/2 cup unpopped	=	8 cups popped
Rice, Long Grain	1 cup uncooked	=	3 cups cooked
Rice, Quick-Cooking	1 cup uncooked	=	2 cups cooked
Spaghetti	8 ounces uncooked	=	4 cups cooked

CRUMBS

Bread	1 slice	=	3/4 cup soft crumbs, 1/4 cup fine dry crumbs
Graham Crackers	7 squares	=	1/2 cup finely crushed
Buttery Round Crackers	12 crackers	=	1/2 cup finely crushed
Saltine Crackers	14 crackers	=	1/2 cup finely crushed

FRUITS

Bananas	1 medium	=	1/3 cup mashed
Lemons	1 medium	=	3 tablespoons juice, 2 teaspoons grated peel
Limes	1 medium	=	2 tablespoons juice, 1-1/2 teaspoons grated peel
Oranges	1 medium	=	1/4 to 1/3 cup juice, 4 teaspoons grated peel

VEGETABLES

Cabbage	1 head	=	5 cups shredded	Green Pepper	1 large	=	1 cup chopped
Carrots	1 pound	=	3 cups shredded	Mushrooms	1/2 pound	=	3 cups sliced
Celery	1 rib	=	1/2 cup chopped	Onions	1 medium	=	1/2 cup chopped
Corn	1 ear fresh	=	2/3 cup kernels	Potatoes	3 medium	=	2 cups cubed

NUTS

Almonds	1 pound	=	3 cups chopped	Pecan Halves	1 pound	=	4-1/2 cups chopped
Ground Nuts	3-3/4 ounces	=	1 cup	Walnuts	1 pound	=	3-3/4 cups chopped

EASY SUBSTITUTIONS

When you need...		Use...
Baking Powder	1 teaspoon	1/2 teaspoon cream of tartar + 1/4 teaspoon baking soda
Buttermilk	1 cup	1 tablespoon lemon juice or vinegar + enough milk to measure 1 cup (let stand 5 minutes before using)
Cornstarch	1 tablespoon	2 tablespoons all-purpose flour
Honey	1 cup	1-1/4 cups sugar + 1/4 cup water
Half-and-Half Cream	1 cup	1 tablespoon melted butter + enough whole milk to measure 1 cup
Onion	1 small, chopped (1/3 cup)	1 teaspoon onion powder or 1 tablespoon dried minced onion
Tomato Juice	1 cup	1/2 cup tomato sauce + 1/2 cup water
Tomato Sauce	2 cups	3/4 cup tomato paste + 1 cup water
Unsweetened Chocolate	1 square (1 ounce)	3 tablespoons baking cocoa + 1 tablespoon shortening or oil
Whole Milk	1 cup	1/2 cup evaporated milk + 1/2 cup water

Cooking Terms

Here's a quick reference for some of the cooking terms used in *Taste of Home* recipes:

BASTE To moisten food with melted butter, pan drippings, marinades or other liquid to add more flavor and juiciness.

BEAT To combine ingredients with a rapid movement using a fork, spoon, wire whisk or electric mixer.

BLEND To combine ingredients until *just* mixed.

BOIL To heat liquids until bubbles form that cannot be "stirred down." In the case of water, the temperature will reach 212°.

BONE To remove all meat from the bone before cooking.

CREAM To beat ingredients together to a smooth consistency, usually in the case of butter and sugar for baking.

DASH A small amount of seasoning, less than 1/8 teaspoon. If using a shaker, a dash would comprise a quick flip of the container.

DREDGE To coat foods with flour or other dry ingredients. Most often done with pot roasts and stew meat before browning.

FOLD To incorporate several ingredients by careful and gentle turning with a spatula. Used generally with beaten egg whites or whipped cream when mixing into the rest of the ingredients to keep the batter light.

JULIENNE To cut foods into long thin strips much like matchsticks. Used most often for salads and stir-fry dishes.

MARINATE To tenderize and/or flavor foods, usually meat or raw vegetables, by placing in a liquid mixture of oil, vinegar, wine, lime or lemon juice, herbs and spices.

MINCE To cut into very fine pieces. Used often for garlic or fresh herbs.

PARBOIL To cook partially, usually used in the case of chicken, sausages and vegetables.

PARTIALLY SET Describes the consistency of gelatin after it has been chilled for a short amount of time. Mixture should resemble the consistency of egg whites.

PUREE To process foods to a smooth mixture. Can be prepared in an electric blender, food processor, food mill or sieve.

SAUTE To fry quickly in a small amount of fat, stirring almost constantly. Most often done with onions, mushrooms and other chopped vegetables.

SCORE To cut slits partway through the outer surface of foods. Often used with ham or flank steak.

STIR-FRY To cook meats and/or vegetables with a constant stirring motion in a small amount of oil in a wok or skillet over high heat.

General Index

This handy index lists every recipe by food category, major ingredient and/or cooking method, so you can easily locate recipes that suit your needs.

✓Indicates an EAT SMART recipe

RECIPE INDEXES

Alphabetical Index

This convenient index lists every recipe in alphabetical order, so you can easily find your favorite dishes.

✓Indicates an EAT SMART recipe